The Kennedy Persuasion

The Kennedy Persuasion

THE POLITICS OF STYLE SINCE JFK

Paul R. Henggeler

CHICAGO
Ivan R. Dee
1995

Library of Congress Cataloging-in-Publication Data:
Henggeler, Paul R.
    The Kennedy persuasion : The politics of style since JFK
/ Paul R. Henggeler.
        p.   cm.
    Includes bibliographical references and index.
    ISBN 1-56663-078-9
    1. Kennedy, John F. (John Fitzgerald), 1917–1963—Influence.
2. United States—Politics and government—1945–1989.   3. United States—Politics and government—1989–   4. Presidents—United States—History—20th century.   5. Presidential candidates—United States—History—20th century.   I. Title.
E842.1.H46   1995
973.922—dc20   94-42712

For Pam

Contents

Acknowledgments

DURING MY RESEARCH AND WRITING, I carried with me the lessons and examples of three teachers: Frank Burdick, Lawrence Friedman, and Bernard Sternsher. Whatever modest talent I may have as a historian I owe to their wisdom and encouragement.

I am especially grateful to my colleagues in the Department of History and Philosophy at the University of Texas–Pan American. Rodolfo Rocha and Hubert Miller helped greatly by accommodating my scheduling, arranging funding, and approving my heavy telephone usage. Janice McDowell and Eva Gomez patiently waded through my neglected paperwork. I am extremely appreciative of the University of Texas–Pan American for providing an all-important Faculty Research Grant. The Department of History at Bowling Green State University also absorbed travel expenses during the initial stages of research. Northeastern University provided housing accommodations during my work in Boston. Research was also generously supported by a Gerald R. Ford Foundation grant administered by the good people at the Ford Library.

This book benefited greatly from the contributions of those subjects who agreed to be interviewed. Gary Hart, Michael Dukakis, George McGovern, Gerald Ford, Eugene McCarthy, and Geraldine Ferraro each offered thoughtful recollections about the influence of John Kennedy on their lives and careers. In written response, President Bill Clinton offered observations on the influence of JFK on his presidency. Fred Brown, Carl Hilliard, and Jules Witcover provided unique perspectives owing to their vast experience as political reporters. Harry McPherson, Hal Haddon, Kathryn Bushkin, Stephen Smith, Thomas Caplan, Thomas Campbell, Mauria Jackson Aspell, Joe Newman, and David Leopoulis helped fill important political and biographical gaps.

Numerous archivists and administrators assisted my research. Heather Beckel, secretary to George Stephanopoulos at the White House, helped greatly in obtaining answers to my questions for the president. Susan Naulty of the Richard Nixon Library and Birthplace demonstrated a refreshing commitment to securing materials necessary to tell the whole story. William McNitt and David Horrocks of the Gerald Ford Library were exceedingly conscientious and thorough. Claudia Anderson of the Lyndon Johnson Library made an extra effort to update my earlier research on President

Johnson. Byron Parham and Bob Blackwell of the Nixon Presidential Materials Project, and Susan Dewberry and Paul Wormser of the Pacific Southwest Branch of the National Archives were knowledgeable and courteous. Ceri Escodi, Keith Shuler, and James Yancey of the Jimmy Carter Library showed that archivists can be both professional and pleasant. Ruben Coronado from Interlibrary Loan at UTPA and Hays Traylor retrieved books and data that eluded me. Jennifer Atwood assisted in the thankless job of proofreading and indexing.

Others helped in less conspicuous ways. Tom Southern and Ann Bernhard provided annual relief from the grind of research and writing. Marian Smith was typically generous during my research in Washington. David Vassberg often lent a sympathetic ear and encouragement. Ken Buckman, Te Norman, and Michael Weaver understood my professional needs and unprofessional moods. A special thanks to Roger Hall and Ray Elbin for providing antithesis and counterpoint.

I am extremely grateful once again for the friendship and expertise of Alicia Browne. She devoted inordinate time and effort to reviewing early drafts of the manuscript. Her editing and critiques fostered clarity and often prevented me from embarrassing myself. Likewise, this work would have suffered greatly without the exceptional editorial guidance of Ivan Dee. With a mixture of patience and prodding, he brought much needed focus and cohesion to this study.

Three women contributed in ways that are difficult to fathom and express. When I was five years old, my mother sat me in front of the television set to watch John Kennedy thank his supporters for helping to elect him president. It was my first and most perplexing history lesson. I extend deep appreciation to Walling Mariea for guiding me through the attic. Finally, there would be no book without Pam Kromer. While reading numerous drafts, she spotted nuances and offered insights that added greatly to my understanding of the Kennedy image. As vital as her editorial contributions were, however, it was her selflessness, encouragement, and laughter that truly sustained me and made this book possible. The pages that follow are more than a culmination of research and writing; they reflect a journey she and I took together.

                                                                        P. R. H.

Edinburg, Texas
January 1995

John F. Kennedy

I want to be a stream of water falling—
Water falling from high in the mountains, water
That dissolves everything,
And is never drunk, falling from ledge to ledge, from glass to
    glass.
I want the air around me to be invisible, resilient,
Able to flow past rocks.
I will carry the boulders with me to the valley.
Then ascending I will fall through space again:
Glittering in the sun, like the crystal in sideboards,
Goblets of the old life, before it was ruined by the Church.
And when I ascend the third time, I will fall forever,
Missing the earth entirely.

From "Three Presidents" by Robert Bly

The Kennedy Persuasion

Introduction

THE TEXAS SCHOOL BOOK DEPOSITORY, once a warehouse for books, today houses our imagination. In February 1989 the room from which Lee Harvey Oswald killed President Kennedy was converted into a museum, "The Sixth Floor: John F. Kennedy and the Memory of a Nation." The exhibits, tasteful but sentimental, recall through photographs, text, and video displays John Kennedy's presidency and the events surrounding his assassination. About 350,000 paying customers visit the museum each year. Near the exit, guests are invited to record their impressions in three oversized notebooks. It is here, just yards from where Oswald stashed his rifle, that memories mingle with dreams. Within these pages Kennedy is remembered with profound affection and praised as a president whose death denied the nation its proper, more noble destiny. "This nation would be a better place to live if JFK had not been killed," writes one person. "Oh, that he could have lived on," writes another wistfully. Some people write directly to the president: "Dear John F. Kennedy. We truly miss you presents [sic] here. God bless you and keep you safe." Young people, too, are persuaded by the memorabilia. "I wish I could have knewn [sic] you!" one child writes. "I wish Kennedy didn't die," writes another. Steeped in nostalgia, their enchantment with Kennedy is derived purely from fantasy.[1]

Death, particularly the unexpected death of someone young, may play tricks on the memories and imagination of surviving loved ones. The haze surrounding the pain and loss may sometimes obscure unpleasant memories, or romanticize them. Remembrances about good experiences may become inflated, making the past seem better than it was. As survivors get on with their lives, some honor the dead not only through memorials but sometimes by their actions. They may vicariously fulfill the goals of the departed. Sometimes that task can be inspiring; other times it may prove daunting, locking survivors in the past. America's response to the death of John Kennedy, a

3

young president beloved by millions, suggests that the individual response to death can translate into a communal one.

In the summer before his death, polls reflected John Kennedy's declining approval among the electorate, and there was considerable speculation that he would not be reelected in 1964. Kennedy's distinct charm and "charisma" had been instrumental in his rise to power, but his lack of substantive achievements seemed to be catching up with him. Critics charged that the president had failed to live up to expectations. How is the Kennedy presidency like a rocking chair? one popular joke went. There's movement, but you don't get anywhere. After his assassination, however, and in the years since, public opinion polls have consistently indicated that the American people have a higher regard for John Kennedy than any president in United States history. Despite questions surrounding his character, and despite the unsavory reputations of some surviving Kennedys, a Gallup poll in 1991 suggested that Americans ranked JFK with Lincoln as the two greatest presidents ever. Another poll on the thirtieth anniversary of his death indicated that 78 percent of the American people approved retrospectively of Kennedy's presidency.[2]

America has experienced considerable turmoil since John Kennedy's death. It suffered other acts of political violence, lost a war, saw a president resign in disgrace, witnessed racial strife, struggled to keep pace with a changing global economy, and grew cynical toward its leaders. When experiencing hardships, many Americans have expressed nostalgia for the Kennedy years and their imagined hope and promise. The subsequent war, violence, poverty, and self-doubt are sometimes attributed to the disenchantment that followed his assassination. Although Kennedy continues to have his detractors, anniversaries of his assassination inspire editorials and television programs reaffirming the need for the optimism and confidence associated with his brief presidency. In this context, the Kennedy years are exalted as a Golden Age, a time of higher spirit and idealism. The present is rendered illegitimate, lost in the belief that life would be better if only John Kennedy had lived. The future is delusional, consumed in the fantasy that the nation may resume its proper course only with the return of the rightful heir to the throne. John Kennedy's death colored the progression of time and events.[3]

Our nation's leaders have not been immune to these feelings associated with loss and remembrance. Nor were they oblivious to the political implications of the Kennedy "mystique." Since Jacqueline Kennedy lit the eternal flame at her husband's grave in Arlington, the words, memories, and aura of JFK have been woven into each presidency and presidential campaign. Appreciating its political appeal, Democrats and Republicans, liberals and conservatives have laid claim to the Kennedy mantle. The popular photograph of young Bill Clinton shaking hands with John Kennedy, or Lloyd Bentsen's reproach of Dan Quayle, "You're no Jack Kennedy," were memorable instances of the "mystique's" political usage. Beyond these obvious flashpoints, the Kennedy image has been an indelible presence in presidential politics. Some presidents and national candidates have been inspired by his memory. Others have been haunted. Often they have adjusted their public image and political strategies to accommodate either lessons learned from the Kennedys or public longing for a return of Camelot. When used sparingly and within the context of more relevant themes, the Kennedy image might enhance a political figure's stature or provide historical context for a larger vision. When evoked too obviously or inappropriately, it might severely impair his identity. Periodically, presidents and candidates have been willing and unwilling participants in this thirty-year death march. By choice and by circumstance, cynically and sincerely, consciously and unconsciously, our leaders have assumed the role of "keeper of the flame."

Despite hundreds of books about the Kennedy family that have told us about JFK's sexual escapades, his manipulation of the news media, and his policies and programs, we are less clear about what he left behind. What was John Kennedy's legacy? How did he and his legend influence his successors and those who have pursued the presidency? Political reporters have addressed these questions in only cursory fashion. In an underrated work, *JFK: History of an Image* (1988), Thomas Brown showed how the Kennedy myth reflected the needs and temperament of the American people. But no one has examined White House memoranda or spoken with national candidates about the precise influence of John Kennedy's memory. This book seeks to fill this void, to see how the Kennedy image has been sustained in our political culture and to consider the implications of that influence.[4]

How a president or candidate responds to or uses the Kennedy image depends on several factors. First, a politician's personality and early career provide initial clues. Some people are predisposed either to feel hostile toward the Kennedys or to aggrandize them. Some are more studied observers, possessing a confidence that enables them to confront the "mystique" with greater detachment. Other political figures are encumbered by a void within themselves or their own public image, encouraging them to rely on the Kennedy legend as a crutch. How a politician responds to the Kennedys and their image tells us much about who they are and how they lead. Their reaction betrays their confidences and insecurities, their vision and their pettiness, their fantasies and their fears. In some cases their relationship with the myth helps to clarify the totality of their career.

A second factor is the nature of the politician's relationship with the Kennedys. Those who knew John and Robert Kennedy responded more cynically to the Kennedy legend than those who knew *of* them. Some contemporaries had fond memories of the Kennedys, others were embittered by political defeat at their hands. The generation of politicians who followed Kennedy was moved more by the legend than the man. Consequently their references to Kennedy were often sentimental and nostalgic, readily feeding the imagination of the voters.

A third factor that determines the usage of the Kennedy image rests with the legend's status at any given moment. Presidents and candidates did not react to the Kennedys, living or dead, solely from personal motives. They were moved by genuine political conditions and demands, as well as public pressures. Because of the proximity of the Kennedy assassination to their own presidencies, Lyndon Johnson and Richard Nixon were more mindful of the Kennedy legacy than their successors. The Vietnam War, Watergate, and the Iran hostage crisis eclipsed the Kennedy years as historic reference points. The revisionism and counterrevisionism surrounding JFK's reputation, and the trials and tribulations of surviving Kennedys, made for an evolving and controversial political symbol, one that both inspired the political process and invited ridicule, depending upon the prevailing atmosphere. Ultimately the Kennedy image transcended politics. In the 1960s it was readily identifiable with the liberal wing of the Democratic party. By the 1980s, however, Ronald Reagan, a conservative Republican, invoked John Kennedy without any seeming contradiction.

Finally, the political viability of Robert or Edward Kennedy played a role in the use of the Kennedy legend. The presence of another Kennedy with presidential aspirations hindered an incumbent's ability to claim rights to the Kennedy mantle. Presidents Johnson, Nixon, and Carter were cautious of heralding a myth that might ultimately benefit a potential opponent. Moreover, Robert and Edward wreaked havoc on the decision-making processes of those incumbents who saw the brothers as the embodiment of the Kennedy myth. After Edward

Kennedy's failed campaign in 1980, President Reagan and leading Democratic contenders could more readily recall the Kennedy myth without feeling hostage to the senator's ambitions.

The appropriation of presidential myths and symbols is, to be sure, long-standing. Barry Schwartz's *George Washington: The Making of an American Symbol* (1987) detailed the iconography of the "the Washington cult" and showed how politicians once antagonistic toward the first president helped elevate him to the status of myth following his death. Merrill D. Peterson's *The Jefferson Image in the American Mind* (1962) traced the uses and abuses of Thomas Jefferson's ideas and doctrines by successive generations of politicians who exploited them for political gain. John William Ward's *Andrew Jackson: Symbol for an Age* (1955) discussed the process by which the general public made Jackson a symbol of popular values, attributing to him qualities which they admired. Peterson's *Lincoln in American Memory* (1994) analyzed Lincoln's place in American thought and imagination, noting how his changing image ultimately made him accessible to diverse groups. And William Leuchtenburg's *In the Shadow of FDR* (1985) defined the personal and philosophical influence of Franklin Roosevelt and the New Deal on succeeding presidents from Truman through Reagan.[5]

Collectively such works show that presidents have long borrowed the images, ideas, and rhetoric of their predecessors. John Adams felt compelled to eulogize George Washington in ways that he found privately troublesome. Andrew Jackson was touted during his campaigns as both the "second Jefferson" and the "second Washington." Theodore Roosevelt tried to deny the Republican party the Lincoln legacy during his independent bid for the presidency in 1912. Franklin Roosevelt honored Thomas Jefferson even as he created a vast bureaucracy in contrast to Jeffersonian ideals. Ronald Reagan embraced FDR as he articulated a decidedly anti–New Deal philosophy and worked to dismantle its surviving programs.[6]

Since 1963 no presidential symbol has played a more visible role in national politics than the "mystique" surrounding the unfulfilled presidency of John F. Kennedy. The Kennedy myth does not decide the outcome of each contest, but it does appear and reappear— sometimes distracting the electorate, other times boosting a president or a candidate, however temporarily.

This book traces the politics of the Kennedy myth and its consequences for the American presidency. It is not a history of the presidency but a case study of one historical image and how it influenced the politics of the moment. Not every major political figure since JFK receives equal treatment. The influence of Kennedy on Lyndon Johnson and Richard Nixon was far greater than on George Bush, who receives only cursory treatment. Nor is this study concerned to a great extent with how the Kennedys exploited their own myth. That story has been told. Of more relevance here is how the Kennedy image affected those presidents and candidates who were *not* Kennedys but who grappled with the Kennedy image after November 22, 1963.[7]

My research involved the examination of primary materials at the Kennedy, Johnson, Nixon, Ford, and Carter presidential libraries, as well as the Nixon Presidential Materials Project at the National Archives in Washington, D.C., and the Pacific Southwest Branch of the National Archives in California. Some political figures generously cooperated with this project. Gerald Ford, Gary Hart, Michael Dukakis, George McGovern, Eugene McCarthy, and Geraldine Ferraro were interviewed for this book. So too were numerous aides, reporters, associates, and friends. And President Bill Clinton corresponded with the author.

The function of the Kennedy myth enables us to see how the American presidency has evolved. Initially there was considerable substance to the Kennedy legacy. Lyndon Johnson invoked Kennedy to promote important reform at home and to justify America's commitment to combating communism overseas. Gradually, however, more superficial remnants of the Kennedy legacy eclipsed whatever substance and ideas John Kennedy had brought to the presidency. By the 1970s and 1980s it was seldom Kennedy's ideology or programs that politicians drew upon; like the public, they were mindful of Kennedy's style, or more precisely, his manner—his wardrobe and hairstyle, his toothy smile, his walk and hand gestures, his slogans. The rise of John Kennedy altered the stylistic standards by which succeeding presidents sometimes measured greatness, and by which they were measured. After Kennedy, leaders were increasingly conscious of the need to be good-looking, stylish, someone with whom the public felt intimate and comfortable—part ski-instructor and part talk-show host. Candidates promoted their athleticism, youthfulness, and energy. Shirt-sleeves were rolled up, ties were loosened, hair was tousled. The goal was to emote the elusive Kennedy "charisma," an indefinable essence that entailed conflicting qualities of intelligence and courage, detachment and charm, glamour and a common touch, toughness and compassion, humor and seriousness, self-depreciation and confidence. Presidents and candidates parroted pithy phrases designed to recapture the optimism, idealism, and hope engendered by a man who by now was more fantasy than fact. Kennedy's ideas were reduced to meaningless phrases—to get the country moving again, to lead a new generation of Americans, to pass the torch. JFK seemed to become a source less of inspiration than of impersonation.

The Kennedy legend has thus distracted presidents and candidates, compelling behavior and decisions that have often been debilitating. It has contributed to the unraveling of three presidencies and has played a role in the outcome of every presidential election since 1964. Unlike the Jefferson and Roosevelt myths, John Kennedy's legacy is tied less to philosophy than emotion and style, encouraging an inattention to substance that continues to haunt our government today. When used disingenuously for political consumption, it has contributed to the derivativeness of presidential leadership. It has frustrated incumbents who have competed against romanticized memories of a glorified past. Despite these misuses, the Kennedy legend has also inspired an entire generation of politicians to pursue public service and try to make a better world. In our exaggerated fondness for John Kennedy, we have been drawn to politicians who remind us of his qualities and who promise his return. In turn, they know this, resent it, and use it. As "keepers of the flame," they harbor our memories and feed our fantasies. Together we remain trapped on "The Sixth Floor."

1

Lyndon Johnson:
The Interloper

OF ALL THE PRESIDENTS and national candidates who grappled with the Kennedy myth, none faced a more daunting task than Lyndon Johnson. Substantively he inherited from John Kennedy an ambiguous program, stalled legislation, and an unresolved conflict in Southeast Asia. Politically he confronted a potentially antagonistic wing of the Democratic party headed by his nemesis Robert Kennedy. In terms of personal image, JFK's emerging martyrdom and fresh memories of his wit, charm, and grace diminished the Texan by comparison. Dealing with the Kennedy legacy, Johnson was forced to reconcile both its substance and image, two elements that were not always distinguishable. With each honor that Johnson paid to John Kennedy's memory, he darkened the shadow over his own mortal presidency. He shared credit with JFK for his achievements but had to accept sole responsibility for his failures. He pursued a war that was not of his initiative, and then was attacked by the "heir apparent" who used his brother's myth for his own ambitions. In later years, time and distance would muffle many of John Kennedy's footsteps. But they were never clearer than when Johnson became president.

The relationship between Johnson and the Kennedys has been popularly portrayed as a dark Macbethian feud. From Barbara Garson's 1967 theatrical parody *MacBird* to Oliver Stone's 1991 film *JFK*, Johnson has been cast as an interloper, a representative of the forces of evil responsible for John Kennedy's murder and the prevention of Robert Kennedy's rightful ascension to the throne. No one appreciated the air of illegitimacy better than Johnson, who just days after John Kennedy's assassination asked FBI director J. Edgar Hoover whether anyone had shot at *him* during the motorcade. It was as if he wished

Oswald had. A stray shot into his limousine would have made him a victim rather than a benefactor whose inheritance invited relentless suspicion and contempt.[1]

From the beginning of his relationship with John Kennedy, Johnson was predisposed to conflict with a man so different in temperament and background, yet so similar in ambition. Born in the Hill Country of Texas, Johnson grew up in a land of dirt roads and bare feet. His mother, Rebekah, was cultured and well educated. She tried to live vicariously through her son, attempting to enlighten him with violin and dance lessons. From his father, Sam, Lyndon learned about politics, fascinated by his father's tales as a member of the state legislature and accompanying him on campaigns. As he matured, Johnson emerged the quintessential wheeler-dealer. He dominated every institution of which he was a part, whether it was campus politics at Southwest Texas State Teachers College or the Little Congress when he served as a congressional secretary. Before John Kennedy was elected to Congress, Johnson had already served ten years in the House of Representatives from Texas's Tenth District. A glad-hander and power broker, he became the youngest majority leader in the Senate's history in 1955.[2]

During the 1950s Johnson and Kennedy each eyed the presidency but advanced themselves through wholly different means. Johnson built his reputation through the accumulation of power and a notable record of achievement. He served on powerful and prestigious committees, and he coopted his colleagues by controlling the allotment of office space, the scheduling of legislation, and the appointment of committee assignments. In contrast, Kennedy was more a celebrity than a man of substantive accomplishments. He first gained national recognition as a writer and war hero. He was bored with legislative duties and impatient with the traditional avenues to power. In Congress he showed little inclination for the daily grind of legislation, cloakroom politics, and covert power plays. Instead he advanced himself in the national spotlight through elaborate public relations efforts that had long been part of the Kennedy apparatus. He cultivated friendly relations with journalists, honed his television skills, and won the Pulitzer prize for a book he did not write.[3]

Like most young senators of his day, Kennedy depended on Johnson for his Senate stature. Kennedy often requested appointment to more prestigious committees; Johnson politely turned him down, citing correctly that he lacked the required seniority. Still, they remained friendly. When the Democratic nominee, Adlai Stevenson, opened the vice-presidential selection to the delegates at the 1956 Democratic National Convention, Johnson announced on the second ballot that "Texas proudly casts its vote for the fighting sailor who wears the scars of battle." Kennedy did not win, but he gained important national media attention and was tagged as the Democrats' new "knight in shining armor." Afterward, Johnson drew closer to Kennedy, and in January 1957 Kennedy won his long-awaited seat on the Senate Foreign Relations Committee—an important milestone toward enhancing his image as a foreign-policy expert.[4]

By the summer of 1958, as presidential politics gained attention, Johnson grew anxious about this new rising political star. Privately he envied Kennedy's glamour, wealth, elite education, and "playboy" life-style. Johnson's Silver Star, bestowed under questionable wartime circumstances, was no match for Kennedy's widely publicized PT-109 heroics. Kennedy also stood to benefit from recent changes in the party structure that had diminished the role of party regulars. By 1960 the nomination process required the constant courtship of delegates and appearances before state conventions, local organizations, and Democratic dinners. With this in mind, Kennedy had worked aggressively since the 1956 election. He fulfilled speaking engagements in every state, appeared on dozens of national television programs, and fine-tuned his campaign themes and style. Johnson, on the other hand, refused to campaign openly for the presidency until one week before the convention. He expressed frequent doubts about the prospect of running for president in 1960, knowing he would face unique stylistic problems in a contest against Kennedy.[5]

Johnson decided instead on a covert campaign, hoping that the nomination would eventually be bestowed upon him after the other contenders had bloodied one another in the primaries. With this in mind he stalled Kennedy's legislative efforts in the Senate. Embarking on a modest campaign swing through the Midwest, he promoted himself as a mature, experienced leader. He further worked to discredit Kennedy as an absentee senator, purposely forcing roll-call votes and quorum calls to emphasize Kennedy's lax regard for his duties. It was during this time that Johnson and Robert Kennedy began to fall out. Robert Kennedy and other Senate staff members of similarly elite backgrounds mocked Johnson as a representative of the older Southern senators and old-school pols who dominated the Senate at the time. "I have this mental image of Bobby walking around in back of the chamber with that hunched over, rather tentative look, the look of a dog more than a person," Johnson aide Harry McPherson recalled. "It was kind of a panting dog looking for a quarry, and the kind of jumping back when some big fat Southern or Midwestern senator suddenly blocked his way." As Johnson came to recognize that his real foe for the nomination would be John Kennedy, and that Robert was the man determined to win his brother the presidency, tensions between them escalated.[6]

Johnson received a constant flow of advice from his staff on John Kennedy's progress during the primaries. "It is *possible—perhaps even probable*—that Senator Kennedy will stop himself," George Reedy told LBJ. He believed that each victory for Kennedy would inspire closer scrutiny of his qualifications and thereby diminish his appeal among party regulars and voters. Johnson might win the nomination provided that he continued to demonstrate effective leadership of Congress. After Kennedy won the crucial West Virginia primary, Reedy sensed that with the religious issue behind him, Kennedy's superficiality would warrant greater attention. "Is the Presidency a toy that a wealthy man can buy as a birthday or Christmas present to his son?" Reedy asked. "He has absolutely nothing that wasn't bought and paid for all the way from his education and medical care to his seat in the United States Senate." Reedy thought Kennedy was a good, competent senator. "But does anyone who knows Jack Kennedy take seriously his slogan 'A Time for Greatness'?" He further questioned Kennedy's toughness against Khrushchev and whether he had the necessary maturity to confront the nation's problems. "The White House cannot be wrapped up in a Bonwit Teller box," Reedy concluded, "enshrouded with blue ribbon and served up to a wealthy man's son along with breakfast in bed."[7]

In sync with Reedy, Johnson told a reporter after the West Virginia primary, "I think now they will start looking to see who's qualified and nobody has ever examined Kennedy from that standpoint. . . . It's kinda like who's the home run hitter." Johnson seldom attacked Kennedy on issues. Rather, he projected himself as a man of experience while emphasizing Kennedy's meager accomplishments. Speaking with colleagues and reporters, he referred to Kennedy as "the boy" and as a "little scrawny fellow with rickets." He accused Kennedy of ingratitude and credited himself with guiding Kennedy's career, giving him the best committee assignments when his "daddy" called up and begged on behalf of his "little boy." Meanwhile, Johnson's longtime aide, Walter Jenkins, actively collected disparaging data on Kennedy, including information about Ambassador Joseph

Kennedy's "pro-Nazi" past. On the day Johnson announced his candidacy, Jenkins learned that Kennedy had deceived the public about his poor health and was currently being treated for Addison's disease, an adrenal deficiency which is often fatal if not controlled.[8]

Eight days before the balloting was to begin, Johnson declared his candidacy. "Jack was out kissing babies while I was passing bills," he told reporters. "I think you're rewarded for what you do, what you produce and not for kissing babies. I'll believe this until I'm proven wrong." Privately he hoped to win the nomination by undercutting Kennedy's front-runner status and convincing Adlai Stevenson to declare his candidacy. Stevenson would draw support from Kennedy and prevent him from winning on the first ballot. Rather than nominate the two-time loser Stevenson, delegates would turn to the man of experience as a compromise candidate. When that strategy failed, Johnson found one last opportunity to block Kennedy's nomination. He granted Kennedy's request to meet with the Texas delegates and further suggested that they appear together in an informal debate. Priding himself as a skilled debater, Johnson thought Kennedy would fold in a direct confrontation. His adviser, Horace Busby, urged him to be conscious of stylistic matters. "Above all, be happy and confident," he wrote. "Showing your mood is the single most important aspect of the show—especially since it will be on television. A little puckishness is good—plus, some shows of what is expected of you: *masterful needling*." Busby suggested he appear as an "at ease old pro . . . with something up your sleeve." If Johnson could project the proper mood and shake Kennedy, the "pro-Johnson rumors" could lead to his nomination. "This is a very good thing you are doing," Busby assured LBJ.[9]

But Kennedy embarrassed Johnson, who appeared mean-spirited and sarcastic, gesturing broadly like a country preacher. He accused Kennedy of being an absentee senator while presenting himself as the voice of responsibility and accomplishments. In response Kennedy tossed off three minutes of one-liners, leaving the audience laughing. "My God," John Roche reflected, "Jack made mincemeat of him." Johnson later expressed puzzlement at Kennedy's appeal, wondering how this "young whippersnapper" who "never said a word of importance in the Senate and never did a thing" had managed to win the nomination. "His growing hold on the American people was simply a mystery to me," he recalled. Kennedy had overwhelmed Johnson's record of achievements with his pleasing personality and image. He transcended Johnson's leadership strengths, using the tools of elocution and grace that Rebekah had tried to instill in her son. When Kennedy finally won the nomination, friends sensed that Johnson was relieved it was over. But his struggle with the Kennedy image was just beginning.[10]

II Before the nominating convention, John Kennedy had considered Johnson as a potential running mate. Johnson had considerable political stature, would give regional balance to the ticket, and represented a state with a large number of electoral votes. But Kennedy assumed that Johnson would not be interested in sacrificing his powerful position as majority leader for the anonymity of the vice-presidency. Nevertheless, not wishing to offend the sensitive Johnson, he decided to give him the right of first refusal. Viewing the vice-presidency as a viable stepping-stone to the ultimate prize, Johnson surprised him by accepting. The selection process involved a series of secret meetings, bluffs, and conciliatory phone calls that eventually left Johnson hurt and angry. At the moment Johnson resolved to accept the nomination, John and Robert conspired to remove him, but not at the expense of irreparably damaging their relationship. John sent Robert to bluff Johnson by warning him of mounting opposition from labor leaders and liberals. Johnson was shaken by the request but stood firm, insisting he would fight for the nomination. To avoid a rift, Robert acquiesced. Johnson was on the ticket—hurt, anxious, and blaming the "little shitass" Robert Kennedy for causing all the confusion.[11]

Years later, after Johnson became president, he was still trying to figure out what happened at the Los Angeles convention, asking reporters and friends how they recalled the selection process. He wanted desperately to believe he was truly John's choice, and he consistently placed the best spin on the information he collected. This revisionism was partly designed to reduce the sense of illegitimacy he felt after assuming the presidency. If John Kennedy did not genuinely want him as his vice-president, Johnson would be viewed as a usurper. So he reconstructed events to make clear that John had wanted him and that Robert had acted independently. In the process, Johnson came to perceive the two brothers in distinctly opposite terms. Toward John he felt a measure of affection, believing the two men had entered into a sincere alliance. But Robert evoked feelings of rejection. For the next eight years Johnson remained wary, convinced that the younger brother was determined to complete the task he had started in Los Angeles.[12]

Entering into a partnership with John Kennedy, Johnson remained puzzled by his new mentor's success. "There was something in John Kennedy himself," he recalled, "some sort of dignity that people just liked when they saw it, for without this his incredible rise to power simply makes no sense at all." He pondered the reasons why he had been rejected in favor of a colleague with so little experience and accomplishment. "Tell me," he asked a friend, "just what is it that people like so much about Jack Kennedy?" The question spoke of the rejection he felt. "What Johnson was asking in that innocent question," Rowland Evans and Robert Novak observed, ". . . was really this: why do they love Jack, but not me?" In the past he had often emulated the attributes of those above him to strengthen him for the future. If Johnson could deduce why the public had greater affection for John than himself, he could remodel his persona to suit new political conditions which seemed to escape him. But the qualities that John Kennedy embodied were not to be found in Johnson. Youth, charm, grace, Ivy League background, a pleasing personality—these were characteristics alien to him. Indeed, they were qualities that Rebekah had yearned for in her son but that he was never able to give her. Joining the New Frontier, Johnson was heading into personally troublesome territory.[13]

The differences between the Johnson and Kennedy images were plainly evident during the campaign. Apart from Kennedy, Johnson sought to portray himself as a "true man of the people." Nixon too, Reedy wrote Johnson, tried to project himself in such a fashion, "but his performance still lacks a certain note of sincerity." Johnson was also advised to minimize his appearances with JFK because their age differences made Kennedy seem immature and inexperienced. "The contrast between you and Kennedy, in my opinion, is always poor," James Rowe wrote Johnson. "When you get together, Kennedy looks like your son." Rowe confided that Kennedy's closest advisers thought the visual contrast hurt Kennedy's image. "Since you are not going to be elected if Kennedy is not, we all think these joint appearances should be kept to a minimum." Johnson agreed.[14]

Ultimately Johnson helped Kennedy carry Texas, Louisiana, and the Carolinas, states crucial to Kennedy's slim margin of victory. But the new vice-president was unenthusiastic when victory came: he knew he was not suited for the office. He had thrived on activity, power, and "wheeling and dealing." In the early weeks of the administration, he failed to finagle measures to maintain his old Senate power. When he composed an executive order designed to give him significant authority within the administration, the new president gracefully ignored the request. Johnson was eventually appointed to the chairmanships of the President's Committee on Equal Employment Opportunity and the National Aeronautics and Space Council. He attended staff and cabinet meetings when Kennedy staff members remembered to inform him. But beyond surface appearances, he was out of the loop. Privately some Kennedy aides smugly mocked his lack of refinement. He tried to fit in stylistically, holding elaborate parties at his new home in Washington. He changed his eating habits to reflect the tastes of the New Frontiersmen. He insisted that his aides eat salads garnished with only three shrimp, as Secretary of Defense Robert McNamara ate his. Having read that the president enjoyed eating soup, he stocked the vice-presidential plane with canned soups despite his personal distaste for them.[15]

Johnson remained loyal and never spoke disparagingly of the president. He felt neglected and useless as vice-president, yet he consistently praised Kennedy for his kind and generous treatment. "Where you lead," he once wrote, "I will follow." The expressed devotion did not bring him closer to Kennedy. He remained aloof. He slept too much, ate too much, smoked too much, and grew suspicious. He hated the vice-presidency—and Kennedy knew it.[16]

Nowhere did Johnson's depression and frustration express themselves more completely than in his relationship with Robert Kennedy. The attorney general had considerable disdain for Johnson, once describing him as "mean, bitter, vicious—an animal in many ways." Johnson was convinced that the "runt" was determined to replace him as the heir presumptive to the Kennedy presidency. Those closest to Johnson thought he became obsessed if not paranoid over the issue. Robert, he said, was conducting secret daily press briefings on the investigation of LBJ's former protégé, Bobby Baker, to embarrass the president and eventually "dump" him from the 1964 ticket. His fears stemmed more from his insecurities than from reality. Despite misgivings about Johnson, his capacity to draw needed electoral votes from the South was vitally important to Kennedy's reelection. Still, while John Kennedy was well aware of Johnson's sensitivities and insecurities, he never directly assured him that his place in the New Frontier was secure. Indeed, by 1963 Kennedy's patience was wearing thin. "I don't know what to do with Lyndon," he told Arthur Krock. "I've got to keep him happy somehow. My big job is to keep Lyndon happy."[17]

Johnson's "splitting" of John and Robert was near completion. He firmly believed that he and John had formed a lasting partnership, and he reminded reporters and the public that the "last thing President Kennedy said to me" in Dallas was his desire to keep the winning ticket together. "President Kennedy worked so hard at making a place for me, always saying nice things, gave me dignity and standing," he told a reporter in 1968. "But in the back room they were quoting Bobby, saying I was going to be taken off the ticket." After November 22, 1963, the "good" Kennedy was gone, and Johnson continued to go forward together with his spirit. But the surviving "bad" Kennedy would also claim rights to his brother's memory.[18]

III Johnson's first year as president was trying on several levels. In addition to the expected anxieties of succeeding a murdered president, he had to make hard choices about the growing military conflict in Southeast Asia. Civil rights protests compelled more active response from the federal government. And Johnson had to be mindful of his own political future, with less than nine months before the Democratic National Convention. The most immediate crisis, of course, pertained to the assassination of John Kennedy, a popular president whose style had captivated millions of Americans. As an accidental president, Johnson had to be mindful of paying proper respect to the emerging Kennedy legend. "I can't sit still," Johnson said to House Speaker John McCormack the day after the assassination. "I met with the cabinet this afternoon. We've got the budget to resolve next week, but I don't want the family to feel that I am having any lack of respect. So, I have a very delicate wire to walk there." He walked it brilliantly.[19]

Johnson first comforted the grieving widow. Jacqueline Kennedy was a powerful symbol of the past and fundamental to Johnson's image of continuity. During his vice-presidency she seemed to understand his discomfort in the administration and tried to reassure him. She once asked him to speak at a reception for the French minister of cultural affairs: "It is so vital that the most important and the most eloquent person—you—be there." In the weeks following the assassination, Johnson worked conscientiously to soften Jacqueline's grief and to pull her closer to his administration. He sent word that she should take all the time she desired in leaving the White House and forwarded tender notes of sympathy. He sent letters to her children, praising their father as "a great man" and "a wise and devoted man." He worked with the widow to build a lasting tribute to her husband's memory, personally calling the governor of Florida to fulfill her request to rename Cape Canaveral and the space center in his honor. And he gave a personal contribution to the establishment of the Kennedy Presidential Library. When she left the White House two weeks after the assassination, she left a note: "Goodbye Mr. President and thank you for everything. Jackie."[20]

Always the consummate politician, Johnson understood Jacqueline's value in smoothing his transition to power. He was photographed with her aboard Air Force One while he took the oath of office. He considered appointing her ambassador to France or Mexico, or making her special adviser on the arts. But he was sensitive to stories suggesting that he was trying to use Jacqueline for his own purposes. He was particularly upset when he thought a reporter planned to disclose details of a conversation he had had with the former First Lady. Speaking with Frances Lewine, the reporter in question, the president explained, "I don't want to get hurt, honey. . . . I just don't want to be carrying on my private conversations in public and have her think I'm using her or something."[21]

It was difficult to determine where Johnson's compassion for Jacqueline ended and his own self-interest began. During Johnson's 1964 campaign, aides considered her endorsement. "Mrs. Kennedy's support and expression of her knowledge of the faith and confidence that JFK held for Mr. Johnson can be our home run ball even if the going doesn't get rough," one aide advised. Johnson made a surprise but well-publicized visit to her Manhattan apartment, but he never fully received Jacqueline's blessing. He repeatedly sent her and her children gifts and cards for their birthdays. He frequently invited her to the White House to attend state dinners and ceremonies. Although Jacqueline knew that Johnson was hurt by her repeated rejections, she made little effort to associate herself with him. Returning to those familiar surroundings, she explained, would be too painful. Johnson eventually grew quietly bitter about her failure to recipro-cate his kindness, knowing that her rebuffs affirmed his image as an interloper.[22]

Johnson's greater problem in the Kennedy family was Robert, now its head and the recipient of much displaced affection for John. Johnson's authority over Kennedy was limited by Robert's emerging embodiment of his brother's legend. "I do not want to get into a fight with the family," Johnson told a cabinet member. "The aura of Kennedy is important to us all." If he fired Robert or pressured him to resign as attorney general, the Kennedy forces might regroup before the August convention and challenge him for the nomination. Just two weeks after the assassination Johnson was already fending off rumors of a movement among some Northern party leaders to make Robert Kennedy the party's presidential nominee.[23]

In the immediate aftermath of the assassination, tensions between Johnson and Robert Kennedy escalated. Clark Clifford, who served as an intermediary between the two men, reported to Johnson that Robert agreed to stay on as attorney general. "We really had it out," Clifford told Johnson. "It's a relationship that I think is exceedingly important. And it's one we ought to look out to get." A week later, Johnson asked Kennedy's brother-in-law Stephen Smith to "tell me what to do about Bobby." "If you were down in Texas trying to shoot a deer you might need a little knowledge from us," Johnson told Smith. "But we need some of these things, particularly the backing of the family."[24]

Johnson tried to be civil with Kennedy, attempting to clarify misunderstandings and writing him personal letters that evoked John's memory. "Your brother would have been very proud of the strength you have shown," he wrote Kennedy on New Year's Day 1964. "As the New Year begins, I resolve to do my best to fulfill his trust in me. I will need your counsel and support." Robert rebuffed Johnson's efforts at reconciliation. He stayed on with the administration despite his obvious displeasure. But as Johnson honored John Kennedy and worked to maintain his link to Robert, he was slowly becoming wedged between two Kennedys—one a reminder of a glorified past, the other promising the fulfillment of a mythical future.[25]

Johnson's appeal to the Kennedy family also extended to the Kennedy staff and cabinet. He worked diligently to persuade prominent Kennedy aides to remain with his administration. They too were important to the image of continuity. "I needed that White House staff," Johnson recalled for Doris Kearns. "Without them I would have lost my link to John Kennedy, and without that I would have had absolutely no chance of gaining the support of the media or the Easterners or the intellectuals. And without that support I would have had absolutely no chance of governing the country." Throughout his first few weeks as president he pleaded with and cajoled the New Frontiersmen to remain for the sake of fulfilling John Kennedy's intentions. "I need you a lot more than he did," Johnson typically told Lawrence O'Brien. "I don't expect you to love me as much as you did him, but I expect you will after you've been around a while." In general, Kennedy aides were divided between "loyalists" and "realists." "The loyalists," recalled Arthur Schlesinger, Kennedy's special assistant, "were those who were there because of their association with Kennedy and who had other things to do, as I did. The realists were those who loved Kennedy but loved power, the opportunity to do things, more." Although Schlesinger's definition was rather arbitrary, in a highly generalized fashion the "loyalist-realist" split distinguished the staff's reaction to Johnson.[26]

Among the more high-profile "loyalists" were Schlesinger, Theodore Sorensen, and Pierre Salinger, his wordsmiths and tacticians. They were men drawn to Kennedy personally. Harvard scholar Arthur Schlesinger bolstered Kennedy's intellectual image and served as resident historian. As Kennedy's chief speechwriter, Sorensen provided Kennedy with some of his most memorable rhetoric and wrote *Profiles in Courage*, the book for which JFK won the Pulitzer prize. Salinger served as Kennedy's press secretary and acted as an effective buffer between the president and the press. In the immediate aftermath of the assassination, Johnson persuaded them to remain, but their tenure was trying. Salinger, for example, found himself drinking a quart of scotch a day. By the spring of 1964 all had resigned from the administration, and by 1966 they had written separate best-selling books about the Kennedy years. Their works served as an early trilogy in John Kennedy's elevation to myth, helping, as McGeorge Bundy acknowledged, to "color reality with legend."[27]

Johnson's inability to maintain close links with the loyalists had long-term implications. He alienated those who later popularized a myth that shadowed his presidency. Of more immediate importance, he lost aides exceptionally skilled at public relations. Achieving a working relationship with them might have been impossible given their depressed emotional state and Johnson's domineering personality. But if Kennedy aides had been willing to adjust their skills to Johnson's personality, and if Johnson had been more receptive to outside advice, his public image might have suffered less than it did. As it was, he never developed an effective public relations team and had to contend with unfavorable comparisons with a glorified past.

Johnson's relations with the Kennedy realists were founded largely on substantive goals. Cabinet members and policy advisers such as Lawrence O'Brien, Walter Heller, McGeorge Bundy, Robert Mc-

Namara, and Dean Rusk each had considerable affection for Kennedy, but they also had an overriding commitment to government service. They were determined to pursue John Kennedy's unfinished agenda, a goal of which Johnson often spoke as a means of enticing them to remain with the administration. Domestic policy realists such as O'Brien and Heller had considerable success in securing Johnson's legislative goals. The foreign policy realists were less fortunate. Johnson had little foreign policy experience of his own and therefore placed excessive faith in the advice of Kennedy's "best and brightest," the men who had guided the nation through a series of crises from Berlin to Cuba.[28]

The most important decisions in which the foreign-policy realists participated during the transition year concerned Vietnam. John Kennedy's interest in Vietnam had dated to 1951 when he first traveled there as a congressman. In the Senate in 1953 he spoke out against the French involvement in Vietnam, but he also declared that the United States had a responsibility to keep the nation free from Communist subversion from the North. He became a member of American Friends of Vietnam, a group lobbying on behalf of Ngo Dinh Diem. In April 1954, shortly after Diem became prime minister, Kennedy gave a major speech in which he opposed any negotiated settlement that would allow Communist participation in the government of Vietnam. By the end of 1961 Kennedy had a clear partnership with President Diem, providing his nation with massive aid and ultimately sixteen thousand American "advisers." Kennedy, having been humiliated at the Bay of Pigs and bullied by Khrushchev at their Vienna summit, pushed for American involvement, determined to avoid the appearance of retreat.[29]

In October and November 1963 Kennedy more fully committed the United States when he acquiesced to a military coup removing the unpopular Diem. Johnson had opposed the idea during an August meeting. At the same time, however, Johnson did not think the United States should withdraw. The coup deepened United States involvement and commitment. Much has been written about Kennedy's supposed plans to withdraw from Vietnam, but such considerations were based on South Vietnam's ability to deal effectively with the Communist threat. Although Kennedy's ultimate designs in Vietnam remain cloudy, his actual intentions were less relevant than the way Johnson construed them. LBJ had every reason to believe that Kennedy was committed to South Vietnam and intended to hold the line there against Communist aggression.[30]

Like Kennedy, Johnson took an improvisational approach to Vietnam. About one week after the assassination he worked actively to replace Henry Cabot Lodge as ambassador to South Vietnam. In terms of the larger picture, he remained open-minded. "We've got to either get in or get out or get off," he told a confidant. Soliciting Senator William Fulbright's opinion, Johnson listened while the chairman of the Foreign Relations Committee reminded the new president that Kennedy's efforts in Laos showed that "there are some things you just can't do anything about." In general, however, Johnson, Kennedy, and most of the key advisers were prisoners of their assumptions. They held firm to a cold war mind-set, overlearned the lessons of World War II, accepted military assurances, and were strongly guided by personal and political fears of appearing weak.[31]

As the war unraveled Johnson's presidency, he became increasingly frustrated with those realists who had been closest to the Kennedys, interpreting their shifts in opinion about the war as indications of their loyalty. When Defense Secretary McNamara expressed doubts about America's involvement, Johnson interpreted his change of heart as a mark of his affection for the Kennedys. McNamara left the Defense Department in November 1967. Johnson was similarly suspicious of National Security Adviser McGeorge Bundy, who never felt he gained Johnson's trust and resigned in the spring of 1966. Secretary of State Dean Rusk, on the other hand, remained with the Johnson administration until the end. Unlike McNamara, Bundy, and other realists, Rusk had never developed a close relationship with the Kennedys and was committed to the war.[32]

The Vietnam War ultimately became "Lyndon Johnson's War," a tragic failure both in policy and image. In later years the Kennedy loyalists alleged that, had JFK lived, he would not have escalated American involvement in Vietnam. In response, Johnson insisted correctly that he had always acted on the advice of Kennedy aides and was following the intentions of his predecessor. He quoted JFK and utilized surviving realists to set the public record straight. But his arguments were no match for the writings of the loyalists, who dedicated themselves to fueling fantasies that things would have been better had John Kennedy lived. Defeated on two fronts, Lyndon Johnson lost those Kennedy aides who were skilled at manipulating public opinion while he retained those whose advice contributed to a policy disaster.[33]

Johnson's domestic legislative record during the transition year was more successful in projecting continuity. Kennedy's policies were in keeping with LBJ's own philosophy of an activist federal government. By moving Kennedy's pending legislation, Johnson would appeal to Kennedy liberals who questioned his commitment to social reform. The day after the assassination he spoke with numerous members of Congress, making immediate efforts to break various committees out of deadlock particularly on issues related to the budget, tax reform, and civil rights. He appreciated the value of Kennedy's rising martyrdom in terms of moving legislation, telling Senator George Smathers, "We've got to keep this Kennedy aura around us through the election." The task of achieving passage of Kennedy's legislation was perfectly suited to Johnson's skills. Relying on his unmatched legislative experience and drawing on public sympathy for the martyred president, he maneuvered Congress out of its deadlock.[34]

Johnson was sensitive about appearing overassertive. Preparing for his first address before Congress, he discussed with Horace Busby the difficulty of conveying both independence and continuity. "I don't believe I want to say that the old program is *my* program," Johnson said. "I don't want them to every time they want to see what Johnson's program is, go look and see what Kennedy did." Busby, however, advised Johnson of the need to explicitly note that he was pursuing Kennedy's agenda. "You mean," Johnson asked, "if we don't say it they might not think we are carrying on?" In his first nationally televised speech to a joint session of Congress five days after the assassination, he committed himself to Kennedy's unfinished agenda, pledging "Let us continue." That night he explained to a friend, "I tried so hard to pay just tribute and still let the country know that I had some thoughts of my own." Johnson keenly knew the risk of conveying the image of a caretaker rather than a leader. He determined to create his own legislative agenda, embarking on a twofold strategy that at once drew him nearer to and away from the Kennedy legend.[35]

Among Johnson's first initiatives was to secure passage of Kennedy's civil rights bill. Johnson's own record on civil rights was inconsistent, leaving many Democratic liberals justifiably skeptical of his commitment. During the Kennedy administration Johnson had been critical of the timing of Kennedy's proposed civil rights bill, believing that White House legislative aides were not adequately prepared to deal with Congress. The bill's primary purpose was to prohibit discrimination in places of public accommodation—a goal repugnant to many white Southerners. By the time of the assassination, the bill was stalled in the Rules Committee.[36]

Determined to demonstrate his concern for civil rights and sensitive to the image that he was racist, Johnson worked diligently to strengthen the Kennedy bill and to secure its passage. Speaking with *Washington Post* publisher Katherine Graham, Johnson compared Kennedy to baseball legend Mickey Mantle, lamenting, "If *he* couldn't [get the bill passed], how do you expect some plug-ugly from Johnson City to come in and do it pretty quick?" Hoping it might be passed before Christmas, he became increasingly frustrated by congressional delay tactics. "What they're trying to do," Johnson told John McCormack, referring to Republicans and conservative Southern Democrats, "is try to get as far away from the memory of this man as they can. And I think let a lot of this stuff die so we won't have much record."[37]

Johnson consulted, cajoled, bargained, and pressured. He spent hours conferring with senators or their wives, using flattery, offering pork-barrel projects, and appealing to their morality. After much maneuvering and debate, the Senate passed the bill in early July. "We could have beaten Kennedy on civil rights," Richard Russell told a former Kennedy aide, "but we can't Lyndon." During the signing ceremony, Johnson recalled John Kennedy's memory while largely ignoring Robert, who attended but had played little role in securing its passage. In 1965 and in 1968 Johnson pushed two more civil rights bills through Congress, marking the most impressive accomplishments of his presidency and moving far beyond the expectations and intentions of the New Frontier.[38]

Try as he might, however, Johnson could not escape the Kennedy shadow. President Kennedy's reputation among blacks had improved markedly after the summer of 1963 when he declared his moral commitment to civil rights and met with organizers of the March on Washington. A Harris poll indicated that blacks ranked him behind only Martin Luther King and the NAACP in having most advanced the cause of equal rights. In early 1964 black writers described Kennedy as the second Lincoln. The emotional bond was reinforced by Robert Kennedy's assertion that, had John lived, the civil rights bill would have been passed anyway. Some people later argued that if Kennedy were still president, blacks would not have felt the discontent that culminated in violence during the later Johnson years. Although the premise was questionable, it fixed John Kennedy's image as a moral leader of a movement and underscored Lyndon Johnson's role as a mere political operator.[39]

Johnson's second immediate priority was to secure passage of

Kennedy's tax reform bill while trimming the proposed federal budget to under $100 billion. In addition to privately conferring with congressional leaders, Johnson asserted his demand for passage of a tax cut during his first two major addresses. Each time he evoked the memory of John Kennedy. He eventually pared the budget to appease Congress and echoed Kennedy's campaign pledge "to keep this country moving." His budgeting gesture, rhetoric, and personal persuasion moved the Tax Revenue Act out of the Finance Committee where it had been stalled. Johnson signed the law on television in February, invoking Kennedy's name, and then drove to Georgetown where he publicly presented Jacqueline Kennedy with the ceremonial pens.[40]

While working to pass Kennedy's pending legislation, Johnson determined to construct his own legislative legacy by drawing upon undeveloped programs to which the Kennedy team had given only passing consideration. From his first day as president, Johnson advisers and former Kennedy aides alike had urged him to formulate his own legislation before the next election. Johnson instructed Walter Heller to develop an imaginative poverty program. "You go on and get me a good solid program. . . . Let's have something good for this State of the Union so that [John Kenneth] Galbraith won't be giving us hell saying Johnson's not forward-looking enough." Gradually the War on Poverty was developed and declared during LBJ's State of the Union Address in January 1964. The program generated enthusiasm among the Johnson staff. "Up to this point," Jack Valenti wrote Johnson, "you have been carrying on Kennedy's programs—NOW, it's your show."[41]

Johnson advanced the Economic Opportunity Act, naming Sargent Shriver, the late president's brother-in-law, to direct the War on Poverty program. Shriver was director of the Peace Corps and friendly with one of Johnson's closest aides, Bill Moyers. He also concurred that the War on Poverty needed to be waged on a grand scale with quick victories. Shriver developed a comprehensive legislative package, including job training, work relief, remedial and adult education, rural assistance, and a domestic version of the Peace Corps. As he had done with the civil rights and tax bills, Johnson drew on his years of experience with Congress, lobbying senators and congressmen. The Economic Opportunity bill passed in Congress just one week before the Democratic convention. "I never saw anybody work with Congress like that," Lawrence O'Brien commented. "The man's a genius."[42]

In trying to emerge from the Kennedy shadow, however, Johnson had chosen an ambiguous issue. The War on Poverty included a number of programs which were either developed by Kennedy men within the Johnson administration or reflected items on Kennedy's long-term agenda. Robert Kennedy and his allies eventually cast aspersions on Johnson and claimed the poverty issue for their own. Former members of the Kennedy staff said publicly that the eradication of poverty was their fallen leader's last request. While there was some truth to their assertion, there was little validity to the notion that John Kennedy planned an antipoverty program on the scale that Johnson envisioned. Johnson took the rudimentary, small-scale plans developed by Kennedy's people and vastly increased their funding and size, pushing for a large, well-publicized program that would offer concrete results before the fall election.[43]

The emerging Kennedy myth placed Johnson's legislative success in a bind. LBJ had frequently invoked John Kennedy's memory as a means of generating public support for his legislation and to pressure Congress to do the right thing. "I tried to pick up where President Kennedy had left off," he typically told one audience. "I tried to carry forward a program for all of you that he had dreamed for you." After the 1964 election he continued to promote himself as the executor of his predecessor's will, hoping to inspire more legislation. "How much I know he must enjoy this very moment," Johnson told an audience of young adults at the dedication of a Job Corps center. "President Kennedy is watching all of you. He would be mighty proud of you." He referred to Kennedy's heavenly presence and approval on a number of other occasions, but in doing so he unwittingly positioned himself in Kennedy's shadow. He heightened John Kennedy's reputation as a man of inspiration and idealism while reinforcing his own image as a mere politician. The contrast was painfully clear when he went on a poverty tour of Appalachia. He remembered speaking to a poor family about his future intentions for them as president. "But then as I walked toward the door," he recalled, "I noticed two pictures on the shabby wall. One was Jesus Christ on the cross; the other was John Kennedy. I felt as if I'd been slapped in the face."[44]

Johnson grew resentful of John Kennedy receiving credit for the War on Poverty, despite having promoted the theme himself. He frequently demanded that his aides find evidence of how he, not JFK, was its true creator. He repeatedly asked for box-score comparisons of his legislative record against Kennedy's. The competitiveness underscored Johnson's frustration with the Kennedy myth. Privately he turned hostile. "Kennedy," he remarked, "couldn't get the Ten Commandments past Congress." "They say Jack Kennedy had style," he noted during a meeting with senators, "but I'm the one who's got the bills passed." His comments illustrated his fundamental misunderstanding of the changing nature of politics. He had tried to surpass Kennedy in terms of substance when presidential popularity was increasingly turning into a matter of public image. Substantive comparisons might prove him superior by his own criteria, but in terms of gaining public affection, achievements perhaps mattered less than personality and style.[45]

IV In the summer of 1964 a Harris survey showed the public overwhelmingly impressed with Johnson's legislative skills and achievements. In contrast to John Kennedy, he was rated thirty-three points higher in "getting Congress to act" and eleven points higher in "handling race problems." While respected as a president, however, Johnson was not loved as a person. His leadership style brought with it an undertone of disappointment. Where Kennedy had offered lofty expressions of purpose and goals, Johnson was a wheeler-dealer who could be corny, mean, and evasive. Critics charged that he was motivated more by self-interest than idealism. Although Johnson had his defenders, much of the public and press felt vaguely uncomfortable with the change in style. "To admit [Johnson's skills]," Tom Wicker wrote, "is to admit that we need politicians and politics, we need manipulation, we do have ambitions and interests and weaknesses and beliefs that ensnarl or release us—we are not golden but human."[46]

Aware of the growing importance of image, White House aides devoted considerable attention to remodeling the president during the transition year of 1964. The effort involved a number of layers; among them was a curious effort to imbue Johnson with John Kennedy's attributes—such was the initial advice offered by adviser Horace Busby. In mid-January 1964 he brought to the president's attention comparative surveys on the popular images of John Kennedy and Lyndon Johnson. Measured against Kennedy, Johnson's most unfavorable quality was that he appeared "too much of a politician." Busby wanted to emphasize Johnson's "warm and friendly personality," which he believed could offset his "political" image. The problem, however, was how to publicize Johnson's "folksy" attributes without appearing contrived, thus compounding the political image his advisers wanted to minimize. Busby reminded Johnson that "personality is the main force of identification between the public and the Presidency." Johnson needed to "convey a stable, steady, somewhat remote and reflective personal image so that people can individually feel close to the President." Kennedy, Eisenhower, and Roosevelt, he noted, were personally popular because they were viewed as "above run-of-the-mill politicians." "A concerted program should be developed and implemented in the very near future to create the seedbed for this type of image to flourish about President Johnson." Johnson had to project an image that disguised what he was—an astute bargainer, a brilliant manipulator of the political system.

Busby contrasted Kennedy to Johnson to determine an effective image-management strategy. Kennedy had been "fartherest" above Johnson in four personality categories: (1) "speaking his own mind," (2) "having strong convictions," (3) "being progressive and forward looking," and (4) "being serious and thoughtful." The four categories, central to Kennedy's appeal, had been "weak points" for Johnson. Busby credited Johnson for thus far developing his "progressive" image, but the other categories "require more subtle handling and more concentrated effort than the situation has permitted until now." He advised that Johnson's positive traits "be carefully exploited, cultivated, and added to by deliberate image activities." Busby's analysis reflected an ambivalence that burdened the administration. On the one hand he sought to depart from Kennedy's image by promoting Johnson's natural "folksy" attributes. This entailed an emphasis on his Western heritage as well as an effort to identify him with the general population rather than East Coast urbanites. On the other hand Busby advised Johnson to emulate characteristics reminiscent of Kennedy.[47]

Given Johnson's propensity to make himself the center of attention, it was inevitable that he would brand his unique personality onto the White House. Images of barbecues, beagles, and horseback riding quickly replaced rocking chairs, sailboats, and elegant balls. In the spring Busby warned Johnson that his "common man" image was susceptible to Republican attacks that it was "shallow and superficial." Nevertheless, he and other Johnson aides urged the president to strengthen his populist image because it endeared him to the "average man." That spring Johnson embarked on a series of tours across the Northeast and through the poverty pockets of the Appalachian region. He toured small towns, donned his Texas hat, and thickened his accent. The trips not only promoted his antipoverty programs but distinguished him from Kennedy.[48]

The departure from the Kennedy past at once prompted criticism from the news media. A popular refrain heard in Washington that spring typified the reaction: "From Kennedy to Johnson—from culture to corn." Aides defended Johnson, disparaging news media elitism for its demand that he try to be something he was not. Still, Johnson seemed determined at times to draw unnecessary attention to his unique manners. He took a handful of reporters on a tour of his ranch, driving eighty-five miles an hour while drinking a beer and narrowly avoiding a head-on collision. Johnson believed that the excessive attention paid by the media to such incidents reflected cultural prejudices and violated rules of hospitality that reporters would have respected if they had been covering Kennedy. At issue was a sense of unfairness. Both Kennedy and Johnson had strong regional accents. But the former's was considered cultured while the latter's was regarded as ignorant. In an age when the most popular television show was "The Beverly Hillbillies," Johnson's "outlandish" behavior confirmed expectations. Like the television character Jed Clampett, he was portrayed by the press as a man suddenly thrust into a situation for which he lacked proper refinement.[49]

To some degree Johnson's capacity to "sell" himself was hampered by a media environment outside his control. Polls showed that reporters were better educated, increasingly liberal, and predominantly from northeastern areas of the country—qualities that Johnson felt prejudiced them against his Southern heritage and made them partial toward Kennedy. Indeed, many journalists were openly disappointed with Johnson's rise to power, lamenting publicly the lost excitement, wit, grace, and glamour of the Kennedy years. What's more, Johnson's physical appearance, background, and temperament were poorly suited to television. His mannerisms were too overbearing, his accent too strong, his appearance too homely, particularly when matched against Kennedy. His years of political stumping prepared him inadequately for such a "cool," intimate medium. And knowing that he followed Kennedy's television legacy only heightened Johnson's aversion.[50]

Johnson could not have been expected to appreciate the larger trends at work, so he directed his frustrations onto his predecessor. He fluctuated between wanting to prove he had as much appeal as John Kennedy and dismissing charisma as "a lot of crap." Sometimes he avoided television. Other times he devoted inordinate attention to presenting himself in an appealing fashion. When his attempts fell short he tried to "beat" Kennedy by holding more press conferences and answering more questions. He was convinced that John Kennedy's media managers were responsible for the late president's "success," and he insisted that his own people do the same for him.[51]

Faced with negative comparisons with Kennedy, Johnson and his advisers decided to blend his image with more "acceptable" Kennedy-esque images. Among the images that Johnson's aides sought to create was that of an intellectual. Johnson, of course, possessed superior intellect, evident in his brilliant handling of legislation and capacity to manipulate people. His problem was not intelligence but image. By the 1960s the intellectual image emphasized the pursuit of "existential" excellence through words, ideals, and philosophy. It was an image personified by Kennedy, and Johnson could not match it. Still, his aides tried to create an environment that conveyed consistency with the late president. Busby suggested that Johnson portray himself as above the political fray by associating with the academic and cultural communities, which he characterized as "an important segment still withholding judgment." He recommended that Johnson court artists and intellectuals like conductor Erich Leinsdorf and writer John Steinbeck. He was advised to maintain close links to Kennedy's special assistant Arthur Schlesinger, and to cultivate Princeton historian Eric Goldman, who appealed to "anti-Schlesinger" intellectuals outside the East. Busby further recommended that Johnson sponsor a White House Conference on the Arts and that he and Lady Bird be photographed reading books to dispel the "widespread false impression that [the] President is not a 'reader.'" Aides further advised Johnson to appear on television with intellectuals, to hire academicians such as John Roche, and to speak at the ground-breaking ceremony at the Kennedy Library so he could address "the rich, the well-born and the intellectuals." Johnson acted on most of these suggestions.[52]

In addition to presenting a more "thoughtful" exterior, Johnson emulated other aspects of the Kennedy image. Among the personal traits popularly associated with the late president were youth, athletic prowess, family values, and a reputation as a trend-setter—all of which made him appear less political. Accordingly, Busby recommended that Johnson be photographed with his family or bowling with his daughters to demonstrate the "graceful, in-motion Presidential form." Johnson was further advised to be photographed wearing a cap to create "a style-setting story" and to counter the press emphasis on his ten- and five-gallon hats. Busby recommended that Johnson be photographed in a youthful, intellectual setting reminiscent of the Kennedy era by inviting, as Kennedy had, the American Foreign Field Service to the White House.[53]

In the summer of 1965 the White House made a deliberate attempt to imitate Kennedy as a trend-setter. GQ, a men's fashion magazine, requested that President Johnson appear on the cover of its March 1966 issue wearing Western-style clothing. Bill Moyers forwarded the proposal to the president, noting the successful impact that Kennedy's appearance on the March 1962 cover had as a "fashion setter" for the two-button suit. "Presumably," Moyers wrote, "the appearance of the President would create similar publicity." In March 1966 Johnson was pictured on GQ's cover. Rather than wearing Texas apparel, however, he was photographed standing on the front porch of his ranch house wearing a dark, two-button suit similar to the one worn by Kennedy.[54]

This effort to match Johnson with elements of Kennedy's image revealed a fundamental misunderstanding of image projection. Photographing Johnson in an Ivy League suit on his ranch was contrived and comical. The suggestion for photographs of him in "graceful, in-motion Presidential form" were clearly outside his bounds. On a cosmetic level, Johnson competed against a figure who conveyed similar images with less effort and more skill. Johnson overate, frequently drank alcohol, smoked cigarettes, and had little patience for athletic recreation. Although he was vain about his appearance, he also prided himself on his earthiness. He thought nothing of lifting his shirt in front of photographers to display the scar from his gall bladder operation. Such insensitivity hindered his ability to compete against Kennedy and underscored the differences between them. More significantly, he could neither emulate Kennedy nor be himself without being criticized from one segment of the news media or another. When he imitated Kennedy he seemed forced and artificial, but when he revealed his more authentic qualities he inspired lament for a bygone era.

V The presidential campaign of 1964 fused Johnson's concerns for personal image, continuity of policy, and "family" matters. It also presented a unique opportunity both to exploit John Kennedy's memory and to assert his own independence. LBJ set about the difficult task of promoting himself as a legitimate extension of the Kennedy legacy while removing Robert Kennedy from his political realm. The attorney general did not make the solution easy for him. Those who hoped for a Kennedy restoration looked toward Johnson to choose the attorney general as his running mate. In the spring of 1964 Kennedy implied publicly that Johnson had somehow mismanaged his brother's legacy and was particularly lacking in idealism. He made clear his intention to pick up the fallen torch and dropped hints that he would be willing to serve as vice-president.[55]

Politically Johnson had sound reasons not to bring Kennedy on the ticket. Polls showed that Kennedy's presence would alienate a significant percentage of Southern Democrats. Once the Republicans nominated Barry Goldwater in July, his extremism virtually assured Johnson a victory in November, whoever his running mate. Personally Johnson was irritated by Kennedy's presumptuousness. After John was killed, Johnson later told Doris Kearns, "I became the custodian of his will. I became President. But none of this seemed to register with Bobby Kennedy, who acted like he was the custodian of the Kennedy dream, some kind of rightful heir to the throne." Johnson knew that if Kennedy were on the ticket, "I'd never know if I could be elected on my own." The explanation alluded both to Johnson's desire for independence and the assertion that he, not Robert, was the proper heir.[56]

Determined to put an end to mounting rumors, Johnson arranged for a White House "summit" between himself and Kennedy. Before the meeting Clark Clifford prepared for the president a memorandum detailing five points Johnson wished to convey to Kennedy about his role in the upcoming campaign. The first point noted the president's desire to "win a victory as clear and sweeping as possible, in vindication of the Administration of President Kennedy and President Johnson." A Johnson victory was "the most important service he can give to the memory of the man who put him on the ticket." The second point noted the need to choose someone in distinct regional contrast to William Miller, the New York congressman and the Republican party's vice-presidential nominee. The third point noted that Goldwater's nomination and the need to appeal to the South eliminated Kennedy as a potential nominee. But Johnson still wanted Kennedy's help for three reasons: to "sustain the full effectiveness of the original Kennedy/Johnson partnership;" to appeal to Catholics and young people; and to utilize his "unequaled talent for the management of the campaign." The fourth point argued that the "best possible means" of achieving these goals was for Kennedy "to be the campaign chairman." The final point noted that, after the election, Johnson would like Kennedy to "accept a most senior post in the new Administration." Cloaking his rejection of Robert in terms of political expediency and pragmatism, Johnson implied that Kennedy's presence on the 1964 ticket might hinder the achievement of his brother's goals.[57]

Although Johnson later told Clifford that he "literally read" his prepared memo to Robert Kennedy, he actually drew on a separate three-and-a-half page statement which diluted many of Clifford's points. The prepared statement was intended to be the "official" record of the meeting. Absent from the text was Johnson's request that Kennedy manage his campaign. So too was the offer of a senior post in the administration. Sometime between the preparation of the memorandum and the writing of the text, Johnson had become unwilling officially to acknowledge his need for Kennedy. Johnson wanted Kennedy's help, but he did not want anyone to know it. To lessen the public impact of his decision, he told reporters the following day that it was "inadvisable" for cabinet-level officials to be considered as vice-presidential nominees; their important duties should not be distracted by politics. The smokescreen fooled few. Pundits correctly interpreted the maneuver as an elaborate scheme to "dump Bobby" without offending the Kennedy myth.[58]

Johnson next worried that the attorney general's mere appearance at the Democratic National Convention and the planned tribute there to John Kennedy might overshadow his own triumph. While Johnson intended to tap into the emotional power of his relationship with John Kennedy, he wanted the convention to be a celebration of himself. White House special assistant Douglass Cater feared that the film tribute to President Kennedy might upstage Johnson. He was particularly disturbed by a soundtrack of "tear-jerker" music from the Broadway show *Camelot*. The theme song was "highly schmaltzy," he warned, and would likely leave the delegates weeping. "I have a vague unrest about engaging in such an emotional bender just before the Johnson acceptance speech." To remedy the problem, Cater advised that Johnson himself consider giving the tribute to John Kennedy, a suggestion that alarmed James Rowe. "If the President appears for the memorial before accepting the nomination," he warned, "it will make his speech 'one hell of an anti-climax.'" Johnson and his staff made additional scheduling adjustments to create a sufficient lull between the Kennedy tribute and Johnson's speech.[59]

The Democratic National Convention paid various tributes to John Kennedy though memorials and memorabilia exhibits. A wellspring of emotion erupted when Robert Kennedy made his appearance in the hall at Atlantic City. As a living symbol of the late president, he was greeted with a sixteen-minute ovation. His carefully crafted speech recalled his brother's commitment to the underprivileged and cited JFK's skills during the Cuban missile crisis and in formulating the Test Ban Treaty. The undertone of his speech made clear that Robert would do his best to fulfill John's dreams. Robert originally intended to say that John "would feel his life was worthwhile" if Lyndon Johnson received support. Instead he toned down his enthusiasm by simply asking the delegates to transfer their commitment and energy from John Kennedy to the new Democratic ticket. Following the speech, delegates were shown the twenty-minute film *A Thousand Days*. The resulting outpouring of emotion caused some people to acknowledge Johnson's astuteness in rescheduling the tribute after the selection of the vice-presidential nominee.[60]

According to Johnson's diary, he took a nap during the tribute. Shortly afterward he entered the convention hall and sat restlessly as he watched the succeeding ceremonies and reviewed his acceptance speech—an address now upstaged by John Kennedy's memory. Invoking Kennedy's name six times, he asked the nation not to rest "until we have written into the law of the land all the suggestions that made up the John Fitzgerald Kennedy program. And then let us continue to supplement that program with the kinds of laws that he would have us write." As he strained to assert his independence, he found himself looking backward.[61]

As the fall campaign evolved in 1964, Johnson's desire to identify himself with the Kennedy image intensified and entailed new strategies. He persistently invoked John Kennedy's name and at times mimicked his rhetorical style. He promised to "get the country moving again," quoted historical figures, and used inverted sentences typical of Kennedy. Johnson's early speeches were so similar in style to Kennedy's that they prompted one adviser to complain openly. "Too often, there is a Kennedy or pseudo-Kennedy tone in prepared remarks," W. J. Jorden warned. Johnson, he noted, was giving "an erroneous picture" of himself and his leadership style.[62]

By the last week of September a more "authentic" Johnson emerged and generated considerable enthusiasm from the crowds. Unfortunately Johnson was informed that he still lacked the personal affection accorded the late president. Busby sent him the results of a

Gallup poll indicating that voters viewed him as experienced and qualified, but he was rated lowest on the very character traits his image-management efforts had sought to improve: "Attractive Personality" and "Intellectual." Although voters respected his performance, they had not warmed to Johnson personally. The president soon drifted into melancholy, contending that the enthusiasm of the crowds was inspired more by negative feelings toward Goldwater than positive feelings toward himself.[63]

From late September until the November 3 election, Johnson moved away from Kennedy's rhetorical style, but he invoked Kennedy's name in approximately seventy separate speeches. To contrast himself with Goldwater's image as a reckless reactionary, Johnson drew on Kennedy's memory to remind voters of the need for rational behavior during a nuclear age. Goldwater had made the mistake of suggesting that Kennedy had used the Cuban missile crisis for political purposes. Johnson aides jumped at the opportunity to exploit the error, believing it "could easily become one of the two or three most important single developments in the whole campaign." Clifford reminded Johnson of his obligation "to the memory of President Kennedy." Now Johnson repeatedly recalled the Cuban missile crisis, praising Kennedy's "cool," "caution," "the steel in his spine," "wisdom," and "care." "It adds no luster to a man's statesmanship," he told one audience, "and it is no tribute to a man's character, to refuse to give John Fitzgerald Kennedy the credit that he is justly entitled to when he is not here to claim it for himself." Such tributes did more than elevate Kennedy's stature; they reinforced Johnson's role as the "keeper of the flame" —and the proper successor.[64]

In addition to identifying himself with Kennedy through rhetorical references, Johnson used other campaign devices as well. In October Busby suggested that Johnson make a public appearance at Kennedy's grave. "Goldwater will be on night TV with personal attack," he noted. "News clips of the President in a dignified, solemn role would be effective contrast." Johnson did not pay his respects at Arlington that fall. But he did participate in a publicity event that recalled the assassination: he was pictured sitting in the limousine in which Kennedy was murdered. The 1961 black Lincoln Continental had been rebuilt and made "bullet proof" during the summer of 1964. Johnson's understanding of the car's symbolic importance was later evident when the White House announced that the president planned to travel to Dallas, where he would ride in the same car during a motorcade virtually duplicating Kennedy's fateful route. Indeed, John

Connally intended to ride with Johnson, and together they would pass beneath the Texas School Book Depository. The White House canceled the planned visit after rumors of assassination plots against Johnson surfaced and dramatic world events necessitated abrupt changes in campaign scheduling.[65]

As part of Johnson's effort further to associate himself with John Kennedy, he reopened relations with Robert. About a week before the convention, Kennedy had announced his impending resignation as attorney general in order to run for the Senate from New York. The two candidates appeared together before large crowds in New York state. Kennedy praised Johnson for his contributions to the Kennedy administration, calling him "already one of the greatest Presidents in the United States." Johnson praised Kennedy's "compassion" and asked voters to elect Kennedy to ensure that "we win President Kennedy's programs and my program." On election night Johnson carried New York by two million votes; Robert Kennedy won by 600,000 votes. Johnson had the satisfaction of knowing that his coattails had opened power to a Kennedy. But as each embarked on his own path, their relationship would be severely complicated by competing ambitions.[66]

Despite extensive efforts at image management, Lyndon Johnson failed to alter his image substantially in 1964. Consistent with earlier polls, fall surveys indicated that the American people respected the Johnson presidency, but they disliked Johnson. According to the Survey Research Center of the University of Michigan, his most detrimental quality continued to be the perception that he was "too much a 'politician.'" Voters thought he lacked integrity and ethical standards. In terms of his positive qualities Johnson benefited significantly from his identification with the Kennedy legacy. His two most attractive attributes were his experience and his record. Ranking third in terms of voter appeal was his willingness to continue Kennedy's policies. Johnson acknowledged JFK during his election-night victory speech in Austin. After thanking his supporters, he read extensively from the speech John Kennedy did not make upon his trip to Dallas. As he had done throughout the campaign and his first year in office, he sought strength from his predecessor, but he was troubled by the process. "And now we look ahead," he concluded. "For those who look backward to the past will surely lose their future."[67]

2

Johnson as His Own Man

WITH HIS LANDSLIDE VICTORY in 1964, Lyndon Johnson achieved the mandate he had sought since assuming the presidency. Determined to achieve a lasting, independent legacy, he embarked on the creation of the Great Society, the massive legislative program intended to eliminate poverty and racial injustice. At the same time he quietly escalated America's involvement in Vietnam, trying to postpone painful choices between "guns and butter." His many achievements and failures during this period resulted from a myriad of forces, raising issues beyond the scope of our concerns. In terms of the Kennedy image, however, an important transition occurred: Johnson's focus shifted from John Kennedy toward his brother Robert. The forces that once strengthened him now intimidated him.

After the election Johnson determined to distance himself from the Kennedy past. On the first anniversary of the Kennedy assassination, he spoke graciously of the late president and paid tribute during a ground-breaking ceremony for the John F. Kennedy Center for the Performing Arts. His sense of obligation, however, was limited. He rejected the suggestion that he present a five-minute television tribute. He avoided appearances with the Kennedy family. And he physically removed himself from the occasion by traveling to his Texas ranch. Still, he carefully considered his activities, agreeing with advisers that it would be in poor taste if he went hunting on the day of the anniversary.[1]

Johnson determined that his January 1965 inauguration would celebrate him, not John Kennedy. The parade and festivities had a distinct Western flair, but the deviation from the Kennedy past was not easily achieved. Horace Busby recommended that the theme for the inauguration be the 175th anniversary of the presidency because it would "eliminate adverse comments or unwelcome pressure for associating the late President Kennedy with your inauguration." As if to bid farewell to the past, Johnson visited John Kennedy's grave the day before January's State of the Union Address. The next day Johnson, who just one year earlier had proclaimed, "Let us continue," failed to mention Kennedy once in his speech. Nor did he mention him in his Inaugural Address two weeks later.[2]

As the year progressed Johnson did not entirely abandon his link with the Kennedy myth. Seeking support for a variety of legislation involving health care for the aged, education, and space exploration, he recalled John Kennedy's earlier commitments and sometimes shared credit with him when Congress passed various acts. On occasion he reminded legislators that John Kennedy was judging their decisions from heaven. But his own acts of independence, combined with the passage of time, made John Kennedy's "presence" less formidable. The president vigorously pursued his legislative agenda and took great pride in bills that separated the Great Society from the New Frontier, publicizing them with elaborate signing ceremonies. Meanwhile, he obliquely denigrated the Kennedy presidency, telling historian William Leuchtenburg that "no man knew less about Congress than John Kennedy." Leuchtenburg was "startled" by Johnson's "animus against JFK."[3]

Assessing the president's public image after the 1964 election, Busby was pleased that the contest had resolved whether Johnson could get elected in his own right. He now thought the news media and public would focus less on Johnson's personality than on "what he stands for." Consequently he called for a "a wrenching change in our attitude toward, approach to and relations with the media world." Busby thought he and others had miscalculated the president's image during the transition year. When addressing the "news media or intellectual community or 'Kennedy people,'" they had "grown accustomed to thinking and talking in terms of the man, rather than ideas, agenda, actions of the future." He recommended a change in this frame of reference, believing that the news media were more interested now in Johnson's policies and thinking. He warned that reporters would return to personality-oriented topics unless the staff "are able to talk about programs rather than personnel problems or similar non-substantive material." Johnson needed to learn from John Kennedy, Busby noted. Kennedy's success in image-management stemmed from having people around him who promoted his plans and ideas. "But, by contrast, the edginess, evasiveness and simple 'in the dark' ignorance of persons in this Administration works against any successful image program." Busby recommended that Johnson allow his own people greater access to the media. "So long as our thrust focuses on the 'man,' the negative [reporting] will continue—on the 'man'—and will prove irritating. Conversely, stories about programs of the Great Society will generally portray the President favorably."[4]

Busby's memorandum underscored the ambivalence within the administration regarding the Kennedy "mystique." Aides sought to move away from the Kennedy image but found themselves drawn to his media strategies. They were inspired by the very past from which they wanted to disassociate the president. This sense of entrapment reached deep into the thinking of the White House staff as advisers appropriated Kennedy's media techniques in order to improve Johnson's image. Aides such as Douglass Cater and Jack Valenti wanted Johnson to duplicate Kennedy-style press conferences by holding them in the State Department auditorium and conducting them as frequently as Kennedy had. Johnson refused. Likewise he resisted repeated advice that he appear as Kennedy had in a televised discussion between the president and three network correspondents.[5]

Despite Busby's advice to focus on substance, aides continued to emphasize impressionistic matters. The president was inundated with favorable reviews of his television appearances, and he received a constant flow of theatrical suggestions. Once he was even urged to point his finger as Kennedy had done when responding to reporters' questions. By the end of 1965 Johnson was employing television more extensively than any previous president. But his manner of using the medium differed from his predecessor's. Kennedy had used it to convey a personal style of leadership. Johnson used television to communicate the activity of his presidency. Of his thirty-seven live television appearances during the first nine months of 1965, only ten were press conferences. Thirteen of his appearances were special reports on foreign and domestic matters, and thirteen were formal addresses. He also opened bill-signing ceremonies to live television. To some degree Johnson's television image reflected reality—he was a doer who wished to publicize his achievements. But in thrusting himself into the limelight each time a bill was passed, Johnson generated criticism that he was using the occasions more to promote himself than to call attention to the nation's needs.[6]

The emerging Johnson staff, meanwhile, faced their own competition with the Kennedy past. Measured against the flamboyant reputation of the New Frontiersmen, the Johnson team suffered. In a memorandum, McPherson thought the problem with their image rested less with the reality of the situation than with the Kennedy myth. "There was a mystique about the Kennedy staff," he wrote, "that it was a free-swinging, free-spirited collection of brilliant and independent intellects; each man became a personality, and oh what a good time they had running the government." The Johnson staff, however, had the reputation as "docile calves hustling around at the will of a singular bull." "It wasn't true about the Kennedy staff, and it's not true about us, but it is a myth that dies hard." McPherson and other Johnson staff members regularly complained that their "humorless" and "frightened" image was "directly related to the image of the Kennedy staff—young, vibrant, lighthearted, Finding Government Fun." Johnson's aides resented their sycophant image, especially in light of the obvious loyalty of former Kennedy aides.[7]

The White House staff was fighting a losing battle. The president's own dominating and abrasive personality reflected negatively upon the people who surrounded him. Had the problem confronting Johnson's staff been all a matter of public image, aides would have faced a relatively minor distraction. Unfortunately the "mystique" also warped the composition of the president's staff. Directing his energy toward protecting himself from Robert Kennedy, Johnson removed aides whom he believed to be tainted by the senator. He rebuffed Harry McPherson's plea to keep Kennedy aides to better advance the substance of his administration. "It is possible, in my opinion, for people to work hard for you, maintain confidences, and still find the Kennedys (including Bobby) attractive and adventurous," McPherson wrote. "An obsession with Bobby and with the relationship of your best people to him may, I believe, distort policy and offend the very men you need to attract." Publicly Johnson told reporters that he hired people regardless of their relationship with the Kennedys. Clearly, however, loyalty eclipsed talent in Johnson's personnel changes.[8]

Johnson's concern for loyalty related to larger problems confronting his presidency as well as to Robert Kennedy's assumed ambitions. In retrospect Johnson offered Doris Kearns a litany of self-serving reasons why liberals began to oppose his administration in 1965: "Because I wasn't John F. Kennedy. Because I wasn't friends with all their friends. Because I was keeping the throne from Bobby Kennedy. Because the Great Society was accomplishing more than the New Frontier." He felt "sabotaged" by a handful of unnamed intellectuals in the news media who manipulated public opinion against the war. "Then Bobby began taking it up as his cause and with Martin Luther King on his payroll he went around stirring up the Negroes and telling them that if they came out into the streets they'd get more." Seemingly undone by some diabolical conspiracy, Johnson maintained that Communists controlled the news media, manipulated liberal members of Congress, and poisoned the opinions of his own staff.[9]

Kearns interpreted Johnson's ramblings as a reflection of his growing psychological instability. While the precise nature of Johnson's fears remains open to question, there is little doubt that his growing anxiety prompted disconcerting behavior. In this context Robert Kennedy played a pivotal role in the evolving tragedy of Johnson's presidency; he was a common thread that bound Johnson's "enemies" —the quintessential Eastern, elitist, intellectual liberal, and the favorite of the news media. As the "heir apparent," he symbolized hope to those who yearned for the restoration of the Kennedy presidency.

Robert Kennedy's potential threat to the Johnson presidency was in fact difficult to gauge. On the one hand he was the living link to the Kennedy myth. He openly associated himself with his brother's memory, and his celebrity status was worrisome in an age when "success" seemed increasingly measured by style as much as substance. On the other hand, a significant segment of the public suspected his ambitions, believing he unfairly capitalized on his name. In terms of political and legislative accomplishments there was little comparison between Johnson and Kennedy. "What makes Johnson's fascination with Bobby all the more peculiar," McPherson recalled in 1994, "is that it was coming from someone who was President of the United States and a former Majority Leader who had these huge achievements to his credit, yet who was obsessed with the hatred and contempt that this 'little prick' felt for him." He compared the two politicians to "Big Daddy" and a "feisty terrier," and correctly noted, "Bobby Kennedy is a pigmy compared to Lyndon Johnson in political significance to the nation." McPherson was mystified by Johnson's inability to see the contest from this vantage point. He attributed it to Johnson's low self-confidence and the criticism that he was not as appealing as John Kennedy. "It was very much a continuing barrier for Johnson being able to see who he was and who Bobby Kennedy was. Kennedy had that kind of hold on him."[10]

As early as June 1965 McPherson warned Johnson that Kennedy intended to undermine his presidency. "Bobby was a mean little shit," he later recalled. "Quite mean. He was a vicious fellow. He had real hatred." While urging the president not to become obsessed with Kennedy, McPherson predicted that he would use the Senate as "a platform in his search for power" and cultivate liberal senators, journalists, intellectuals, and the like. He further warned that Robert would reconstruct himself in his brother's image. Through a liberal voting record and "adventurous speeches," Kennedy would endear himself to those who came to view him as "a voice of reason and enlightenment." John Kennedy had done the same thing, McPherson wrote Johnson. But Robert's courtship of liberals would be more strained because he lacked John's "attractiveness."[11]

Scholars, aides, and political observers have long debated this cynical view of Robert Kennedy. Valid or not, Johnson and his aides believed it. Acting upon these assumptions, they worked to counter Kennedy's growing political influence and closely monitored his criticisms of Johnson. The tension between them revealed itself most noticeably in 1965 as the president embarked on his own foreign policy initiatives. The most ominous issue separating Johnson and Kennedy was Southeast Asia. In February Johnson ordered air attacks against North Vietnam, and by July he committed 125,000 American combat troops to the war. His willingness to deploy extensive military force contrasted with John Kennedy's propensity for low-scale counter-insurgency.[12]

As Johnson faced increased criticism that summer, Kennedy aligned himself with his liberal power base. By July he began to quote his brother extensively, implying that Johnson had abandoned John's foreign-policy goals. But he did not break with the administration. His cautiousness underscored the dilemma he faced in using the war to his political advantage. Not only was there little evidence from his brother's presidency to challenge Johnson's policies, but he also had to be wary of offending former New Frontiersmen who were advising Johnson to escalate the war. Severe criticism would also alienate him from the voters at large, who, in the summer of 1965, overwhelmingly approved of Johnson's handling of the war.[13]

To ward off potential criticism, Johnson and his advisers collected public statements of Truman, Eisenhower, and John Kennedy to show that the president was consistent with the intentions of his predecessors. Throughout a half-dozen press conferences in 1965, Johnson argued that his policy in Vietnam was in part a fulfillment of John Kennedy's commitment. Preparing the president's March address at Johns Hopkins University, Bundy included John Kennedy references "designed to give us protection and encouragement with some of the 'liberals' who are falsely telling each other that your policy is different than his." For the time being Johnson could plausibly portray the war as an extension of his predecessor's will.[14]

During the year academicians, writers, editors, and government officials in growing numbers had spoken out against Johnson's foreign policies, comparing them poorly with his predecessor's heralded skills at crisis management. Irritated by their criticisms, Johnson stopped issuing the Medal of Freedom, an award initiated by John Kennedy and intended to recognize citizens who had contributed to the nation's intellectual and cultural well-being. Speaking with reporters, he boasted about polls comparing him favorably to both John and Robert Kennedy. His delight in doing so prompted McPherson to warn him that the practice was "unwise." "It is valuable and encouraging information," he wrote, "but in my opinion it should not be delivered by you."[15]

Johnson's anxiety over Kennedy's influence extended to his concern for the "Georgetown crowd," a loose collection of government employees, academicians, publishers, columnists, and newspaper writers who socialized together in Washington. Among their binding characteristics, and the most troublesome to Johnson, was their affection for the Kennedys. During social occasions, McPherson recalled, they mocked Johnson as a "rube" and "vulgarian." Johnson was convinced that this social environment eventually translated into negative interpretations of his foreign policies. By 1965 he directed his anger against political columnists and editors, believing, according to McPherson, that "their devotion to John Kennedy's memory made them incapable . . . [of] fairness to him." Johnson soon developed an obsession toward the press which aides and reporters had never before fully observed in him. He was convinced that reporters were working as spies for Kennedy and that they intended to search out embarrassing secrets. "He let it get to him," McPherson recalled. "He nursed a grudge. He nursed the bitterness that came from being regarded with scorn."[16]

Ironically, as Johnson became more aggressive toward the press, he inspired numerous articles that compared his press relations unfavorably with those of the late president. Johnson became defensive. He refuted the assertion that he was less accessible than John Kennedy by delineating every contact he had had with reporters since becoming president. He tried to convince the press that he treated reporters as Kennedy had. He frequently asked for tabulations comparing the number of press conferences each had given, requesting that his aides disseminate the findings and "ask for justice only." The problem, he wanted to believe, rested with the press's prejudice against him, not in his treatment of reporters.[17]

For the moment Johnson's continued legislative success and foreign policy adventures remained popular, partially obscuring a personal image that grew more and more unappealing. A *Time* magazine interview with a cross section of citizens found consistent praise for Johnson's expertise. "He's not a glamour boy like Kennedy," an auto worker said, "and I think he has more on the ball." "Listen, the common man identifies with Lyndon," a salesman added, "and this is a big change from the smart jet-set image of the Kennedys." "The difference between the two men," a reader wrote, "is the difference between form and substance." But Johnson's aggressive behavior in 1965 also emphasized an unflattering personal image. Many Americans viewed him as insincere, "a crook and a liar," and "a power-oriented egoist." "In this case," one person told *Time*, "we have to sacrifice love for accomplishment." As long as his achievements continued to impress a sufficient number of the public, Johnson could meet the challenges of a more charismatic rival.[18]

II From the fall of 1965 through December 1966, as Lyndon Johnson entered his third year in office, the Vietnam War beleaguered his administration. As "hawks" and "doves" expressed dissatisfaction with the president's middle-course strategy, his approval rating fell by more than twenty percentage points between June 1965 and September 1966. Seizing upon Johnson's failures, Robert Kennedy became more outspoken against the administration, sometimes to the point of carelessness. During Senate Foreign Relations Committee hearings on Vietnam in February, he tried to exploit Johnson's vagueness about conditions for negotiations by implying that one condition for a settlement might be the acceptance of "a compromise government" involving the National Liberation Front. Administration officials responded on political talk shows, dismissing the proposal as one that would inevitably lead to Communist domination of Vietnam. At the National Freedom Award ceremony, Johnson quoted at length from John Kennedy's Inaugural Address, pledging America's commitment to "pay any price, bear any burden, meet any hardship, support any friend, oppose any foe to assure the survival and success of liberty." Robert attended the function and was visibly uncomfortable with the innuendo. "Perhaps a [telephone] call [to me] would not have taken any more time than for someone to look up the quote of President Kennedy to use against my position," Kennedy wrote Bundy after he too had quoted JFK.[19]

While Kennedy cultivated Johnson's dissenters within the Democratic party, the news media, and academia, Johnson received disquieting updates about his rival's influence upon opinion-makers. Aides and supporters forwarded articles to the president noting how the Georgetown social circle continued to benefit Kennedy, encouraging the notion that Johnson was a pretender to the throne. British journalist Peregrine Worsthorne had witnessed the Georgetown crowd firsthand. "The impression, of course, is that if only John F. Kennedy was still alive . . . then all would be well," he wrote. "The Washington pundits love to dilate how brilliantly 'Bobby' has put this idea across." To counter Robert's efforts and image, some aides urged Johnson to cultivate reporters in the Kennedy manner. "Let's start working to soften up the Kennedy columnist set," Liz Carpenter, Lady Bird's secretary, wrote—"subvert them from 'buying' everything Bobby does." She suggested inviting some members of the "jet set" to the next White House social event, "even though they are personally obnoxious." After receiving the memo, Johnson wrote a curious response: "Tear this up and flush it down the toilet."[20]

The president avoided openly challenging the senator, hoping to maintain a fragile Democratic consensus on the war. He was congenial toward Kennedy in public and blamed the press for exaggerating their difficulties. He occasionally lashed out against his opponents in a generalized fashion, but he avoided mentioning any names. He continued to quote the late president when publicly defending his policies. By drawing on John Kennedy's memory, Johnson implied that Robert was outside the mainstream and (unlike John) was "soft" on communism. But Johnson was at a distinct disadvantage in trying to use President Kennedy for his own purposes. Logic dictated that, as a Kennedy himself, Robert, not Johnson, best understood John's intentions. He was the true spokesperson for the myth—an image that was difficult, if not impossible, to challenge. Furthermore, it was becoming implausible to identify Johnson's Vietnam policies with John Kennedy's: the war in 1966 hardly resembled the conflict that Johnson had inherited in 1963. Perhaps sensing the distinctions, Johnson did not quote JFK as much as he might have or planned, seldom drawing on the extensive lists of quotes available to him.[21]

By 1966 Robert Kennedy began more fully to identify himself with his brother's memory. He often recalled John Kennedy during his speeches and seemed deliberately to mirror his brother's gestures. The shift away from the "ruthless Bobby" image was orchestrated by Frederick Dutton, who reminded Kennedy of the need to appear less political than Johnson. "Your pacesetters are not Lyndon Johnson, Hubert Humphrey, Chuck Percy and other aspirants for the Presidency but, quite frankly, Ghandi, John F. Kennedy, Pitt the Younger, Alexander the Great, Pope John and others," he wrote Kennedy. He advised Robert to "avoid appearing the politician," exude his "existential" qualities, and exhibit "qualities of the spirit" in direct contrast to Johnson and more in keeping with the memory of his brother. As Robert embraced his brother's idealism and image and received the attention and praise of John's former supporters, he encouraged followers to transfer their affections from his late brother onto himself, thus widening the gap between Johnson and JFK.[22]

Throughout 1966 Johnson slowly relinquished his claim to the Kennedy myth. He rejected a request that he appear in a memorial film on John Kennedy. Unlike in previous years, he made no formal recognition of John Kennedy's birthday. Staff members began openly to express hostility to the media attention devoted to John Kennedy's memory. Aides deliberated about conducting a public signing ceremony for the John F. Kennedy Library Bill. Some argued that it presented Johnson with an opportunity "to identify with President Kennedy and force the Senator [Robert Kennedy] onto neutral ground." Larry O'Brien opposed Johnson's attendance because "the bill is so unimportant that this will appear to be an obvious attempt at trying to drive a wedge into the Kennedy camp." Johnson decided against the idea.[23]

Johnson continued to mention John Kennedy during his speeches, but he less frequently praised our "beloved late President." Indeed, by the summer he seemed less willing to mention John Kennedy by name, usually referring to "the previous administration." Where he had earlier contrasted the "Kennedy-Johnson administrations" to Eisenhower's, he now began to compare "this" administration with "the previous one" or with a particular time during the Kennedy years. Assessing Johnson's relations with Kennedy, *Newsweek* reported that just as Robert Kennedy was moving farther from the Johnson administration, Johnson was seeking "to disassociate himself from the late John F. Kennedy."[24]

Johnson's deemphasis of the Kennedy myth had mixed implications. On the one hand, Robert may have inhibited Johnson from attacking him, for the president could not be critical of the senator without implicitly attacking John. "It's impossible to separate the living Kennedys from the Kennedy legend," a Johnson aide lamented. "I think President Kennedy will be regarded for many years as the Pericles of a Golden Age. He wasn't Pericles and the age wasn't golden, but that doesn't matter—it's caught hold." The more Robert promoted himself as John's avatar (and the more he posed a serious threat to Johnson's presidency), the less Johnson seemed inclined to counterattack. Furthermore, by exalting John Kennedy, the president would indirectly enhance a myth that was ultimately more beneficial to Robert than to himself. On the other hand, Johnson was liberated from the past. If, in Johnson's mind, John Kennedy became less significant or mystical, Robert became more mortal and frail. And with John's mythic being pressing him less, Johnson could more easily assail his brother.[25]

Throughout the summer of 1966, Johnson's presidency rapidly deteriorated. Rampant inflation hampered domestic programs, civil rights violence erupted in cities across the nation, and the Vietnam War continued to drain the economic resources and executive attention necessary to achieve the Great Society that Johnson once envisioned. By August Robert Kennedy inspired a wave of enthusiasm for the "restoration" of John Kennedy's unfinished presidency. For the first time a Gallup poll showed voters favoring him over Johnson as the 1968 Democratic nominee. Memories of the Kennedy administration assumed greater significance. "With the passage of time," pollster Lou Harris reported, "the President seems to be haunted more rather than less by the image of his predecessor." John Kennedy's "memory seems to stand at his elbow—posing to many a contrast of calm elegance with crudity and corn." More important, Johnson was losing hold of the one element that had traditionally brought him approval— his achievements. The fraction of people who had praised him as one who "gets things done" had declined by one-third in two years; three times as many people now defined him as a political opportunist. Cover stories were devoted to "The Bobby Phenomenon." By the end of 1966 Hugh Sidey reported that the president seemed to be "drifting on an island of time between Kennedys."[26]

Johnson's struggle with the Kennedy image assumed new dimensions with the serial publication of William Manchester's *Death of a President*. Manchester had earlier been authorized by the Kennedy family to write an "official" account of the assassination. His depiction of Johnson was so harsh that some Kennedy aides worried they would be accused of character assassination. The manuscript began with Johnson pressuring Kennedy to shoot a deer while at his Texas ranch after the 1960 convention. Arthur Schlesinger implored Manchester to edit the book because "the unconscious argument of the book is that Johnson killed Kennedy." In December 1966 Jacqueline Kennedy announced a lawsuit to stop its publication. The suit, however, pertained only to the personal material that she had revealed to the author.[27]

Johnson was deeply troubled by the negative images advanced by Manchester. In early December he told Nicholas Katzenbach, the undersecretary of state and a friend of the Kennedy family, that Manchester's account was "full of forty-six mean, vicious errors" that was "going to rock us when it comes out." "All of it makes Bobby look just like a great hero and makes me look like a son-of-a-bitch," Johnson said angrily. He helped coordinate efforts with his friend, Supreme Court Justice Abe Fortas, to gather relevant information for the purpose of challenging the account. The Manchester book, he believed, was just one in a series of ten works under Kennedy's direction intended to discredit him. He was convinced that Manchester and Theodore White were "agents of people who want to destroy me."[28]

Johnson was particularly frustrated that he could not compete against the Kennedys' public relations machinery. "They are going to write history as they want it written, and as they can *buy* it written," he told Moyers. Johnson added that he was content for now to know in his heart what transpired after the assassination. "I don't want to debate with them," he told Moyers. "I don't think the President of this country at this time ought to. I think it's just unthinkable that my whole morning would not be spent on the Vietnam [War] or anything else, but be spent on this kind of stuff." Still, he was particularly upset with the subtext that he had somehow contributed to Kennedy's death. Johnson insisted that Kennedy was thrilled to shoot the deer. He "hoorayed one right on the fender of the car" and then insisted on shooting another. "Nobody forced this man to do a damn thing," he added. "He wouldn't be competent to be president. I think that it's the greatest desecration to his memory that an impotent vice president could force this strong man to do a God-damn thing."[29]

To his credit, Johnson maintained public composure. "I'll never make a critical word of any Kennedy at any time," he told Katzenbach. "I'm just not going to do it. I'm not going to say it. I'm dodging. I'm taking these damn books and these things." Less than a week after her suit was filed, Johnson sent a Christmas card to Jacqueline: "Some of these accounts attribute your concern to passages in the book which are critical or defamatory of us. If this is so, I want you to know while we deeply appreciate your characteristic kindness and sensitivity, we hope you will not subject yourself to any discomfort or distress on our account." Johnson assured her that he had learned to live with slander and that "your own tranquility is important to both of us, and we would not want you to endure any unpleasantness on our account." On December 21 the Kennedys abruptly settled their suit out of court. Sixteen hundred words were excised from the Manchester book, none of which pertained to Johnson.[30]

Johnson was ultimately satisfied that the Kennedys bore the brunt of the bad publicity. He expressed pleasure with a Harris poll that showed the Manchester affair had dimmed the noble aura from which the Kennedys had benefited. "God! [The Harris poll] murdered Bobby and Jackie both," Johnson told Katzenbach in late January 1967. "It just murders them on this thing." One in three people thought less of Jacqueline Kennedy because of the Manchester book. And 20 percent of those people polled now thought less of Robert. The Harris poll further indicated that Kennedy trailed Johnson in presidential trial heats. Although the precise reasons for the juxtaposition rested with a variety of broad political concerns, part of Kennedy's decline in the polls, according to Harris, could be traced directly to the Manchester affair.[31]

Although Johnson's own political status remained tenuous, the Kennedys now appeared manipulative and mean-spirited—characteristics that were antithetical to the Kennedy myth and more reminiscent of Johnson. Robert Kennedy suffered further negative publicity when it was disclosed, with Johnson's encouragement, that as attorney general he had approved the wiretapping of telephones and the illegal use of listening devices by the FBI. In the past Johnson had refrained from challenging his rival because he feared alienating Kennedy supporters or indirectly insulting John Kennedy's memory. But Robert Kennedy had transformed the conflict into a highly personal and public battle, and he had tarnished the Kennedy image in the process. With the semblance of political and personal courtesies now undone, and with Robert behaving less like his mythical brother, Johnson could more freely challenge him with less fear of repercussion.[32]

On February 6, 1967, the public deference between Johnson and Kennedy shattered. Traveling to Europe in January, Kennedy participated in a discussion with a North Vietnamese representative and an embassy expert on Vietnam. Reports soon printed in *Newsweek* described a supposed peace overture from the North Vietnamese. Johnson was convinced that Kennedy had leaked the story. For weeks the United States had been toughening its negotiating position toward Vietnam; now Johnson suspected that Kennedy was forcing the president's hand in negotiations just as the tougher policy was taking effect. Or, Johnson speculated, Kennedy might be encouraging hopes of peace in order to spread dissension if talks broke down. Operating through Katzenbach, Johnson demanded to know the nature of Kennedy's excursion. A late-afternoon meeting was arranged between the senator and the president.[33]

Accounts of the February 6 meeting indicate that it "ended in a complete rupture." "I'll destroy you and everyone of your dove friends in six months," Johnson vowed to Kennedy at one point. "You'll be dead politically in six months." He accused Kennedy of prolonging the war, decreeing, "The blood of American boys will be on your hands." "I never want to hear your views on Viet Nam again," Johnson told him. "I never want to see you again." Katzenbach and Walter Rostow tried to restore order and limit the damage. After some prodding, Kennedy eventually met with reporters in the White House lobby to deny he had brought home any "peace feelers." Afterward, both sides tried to cover the rift with attempts at humor. But insiders knew that their relationship would never be the same. It "was the final break between Bobby and LBJ," a Kennedy aide recalled. "If there had been any chance for reconciliation between the two men, there was certainly no chance after that."[34]

III On March 2 Kennedy officially broke with Johnson on Vietnam. Speaking on the Senate floor, he disarmed critics by confessing that he too, as a member of the Kennedy administration, had been partly responsible for the escalation of the war. Still, he stressed the need to reevaluate our policy in light of "the horror." He offered a three-point peace proposal, including a bombing halt, negotiations, and the creation of an international military presence in Vietnam. Privately Johnson felt victimized by the Kennedy myth. "Bobby wouldn't be talking that way if Jack Kennedy were still president," he confided to a reporter. "I kept faith with Jack Kennedy on Vietnam." Johnson was advised to play down his hostility. "The sympathy backlash grows larger when the President seems to be unfairly attacked, and when he doesn't hit back," Jack Valenti wrote Johnson. "Prime example of this: the Manchester book. You never talked about it or referred to it and that turned out to be the best decision made in a long time." Johnson checked his anger during his next press conference, and was later informed that his tempered response was "nothing short of genius and did more than anything to halt the onward rush of LBJ vs. RFK writings in the press."[35]

Johnson soon revealed more authentic feelings for Kennedy during a speech before the Democratic National Committee. Without mentioning Kennedy by name, he accused critics of selfish political motives based on "a temporary lust for popularity." He also read a letter written to a grieving sister of a soldier killed in Vietnam: "Your brother was in South Vietnam because the threat to the Vietnamese people is, in the long run, a threat to the free world community." The letter, Johnson announced, had been written four years before by President John F. Kennedy. The implication was clear: Johnson was a more legitimate servant of the Kennedy legacy than Robert.[36]

Anticipating a presidential challenge from Kennedy, Johnson's advisers sought to prevent Robert from exploiting the Kennedy image. Kennedy had recently participated in highly publicized tours of poverty-stricken areas, advancing the image of compassion to deny Johnson the constituency that the president had tried to call his own. "The fact that [Kennedy] looks bored and probably doesn't give a damn about what he is seeing, is beside the point," McPherson wrote Johnson. "To the concerned voter, certainly to the young, he is 'out among us.'" Johnson therefore needed to "get out more among the people" and to tour poor areas to publicize his new legislation and to generate funding for existing programs. Likewise, he was urged to revive his own link with the Kennedy image by cultivating Kennedy supporters who had become disillusioned with the senator. Johnson's attempts to reach out to young intellectuals, however, were quickly criticized for their transparency. The White House received a political cartoon of Johnson trying on a toupee fashioned like a Kennedy hairstyle. The president soon vetoed a proposal to establish a Special Assistant for Youth Affairs. "The creation of a new post with a lot of fanfare," an aide argued, "would appear to the press as being an overly as well as overtly calculated attempt to counter Senator Kennedy's appeals to youth." Johnson remained caught in the paradox of the Kennedy "mystique." By presenting himself as an intellectual or youth-oriented president, he elevated the prestige of those images that were related more to the Kennedys than to himself. He ran the risk of suffering by comparison, especially when such efforts appeared alien to his own character.[37]

In late May 1967 this dilemma was illustrated by an event that brought Lyndon Johnson and Robert Kennedy together with John Kennedy's memory. On John Kennedy's birthday, Johnson was scheduled to speak at the christening of an aircraft carrier named in the late president's honor. Benjamin Wattenberg characterized the occasion as *"the most dramatic single appearance you will make all year."* He agonized over the event's political implications, noting that it was both "a great opportunity and a great hazard." There was inherent drama in having the nation's attention focused on Johnson, but there were risks concerning how much the president should praise his predecessor. Wattenberg anticipated "problems" if Johnson focused solely on "the legacy of John F. Kennedy." If he noted that Kennedy was "a man of *peace*, and that he brought a *new* style of politics to America—you are, by indirection, almost saying what your critics say, that you are a man of *war* and *old* style politics." Because of "the absurd way the press has dealt with Johnson vs. Kennedy," he would be vulnerable to unfair comparisons. "On the other hand, if you don't talk about 'the legacy of JFK'—the question arises, why not?, how ungracious, etc." Meanwhile, Robert Kennedy's presence made it inappropriate to talk blatantly about Vietnam. Wattenberg therefore enclosed an outline which fulfilled the goals of a "good" speech: "broad in scope, for world consumption, considerate of the Kennedys, and paying authentic homage to the memory of JFK." "Outline is a good speech," Johnson wrote on the memorandum, but he requested a more "euphonious" tone.[38]

The speech ultimately offered subtle analogies between Johnson's policy in Vietnam and John Kennedy's commitment to protect freedom around the world. Johnson reminded the audience that JFK "saw the failure of appeasement." The aircraft carrier named in his honor represented America's determination to serve "as a beacon to the oppressed and to the enslaved." In the past, Johnson said, our nation's "conflicts with aggressors" had "always required not only strength but patience." No president understood these necessities better than Kennedy. Johnson quoted Kennedy: "It is the fate of this generation . . . to live with a struggle we did not start, in a world we did not make." Implicitly, Johnson suggested that it was his fate to preside over a war that was not his initiative. The subtext of the speech, however, was so subtle that the press generally failed to note the innuendo. By all accounts the president was universally praised for his gracious appearance. Rose Kennedy thanked him "for all you have done to perpetuate [John's] memory."[39]

In the early summer of 1967 Johnson appeared politically stable. Although polls were extremely sensitive to political conditions and suggested only temporary moods, they indicated that Johnson might salvage his presidency provided he could quickly end the war. By mid- and late July, however, race riots erupted in Newark and Detroit, leaving scores dead. Johnson's approval rating fell to 39 percent, the lowest presidential approval rating since the last year of the Truman administration. Between June and September a Harris poll indicated that one of five Americans had reversed a once positive opinion of the president. Some of Johnson's most loyal supporters in Congress began to desert him, and Kennedy supporters began organizing a "Dump Johnson" movement. In November Johnson was painfully informed that polls showed a continuation of a year-long trend: "RFK benefits when LBJ declines."[40]

As public support for the war plummeted that fall and Robert Kennedy took new aim at the president, the prospect of invoking the late president was reconsidered. Earlier in the year John Roche had been frustrated by Kennedy aides "inventing quotes—mostly on Vietnam—by John Kennedy" to criticize Johnson's escalation of the war. Johnson secured transcripts of John Kennedy's two network interviews from September 1963, when he articulated the "domino theory" and vowed to defend South Vietnam. A Johnson aide was hopeful that some of the statements could be effective in "bringing back into the fold some of the doves in the Democratic Party." Nine days later National Security Adviser Walt Rostow sent Johnson a forty-one-page text containing a compilation of John Kennedy's statements on Vietnam. "I don't believe any objective person can read this record without knowing that President Kennedy would have seen this through whatever the cost," Rostow wrote.[41]

Hesitantly, Johnson reminded audiences of John Kennedy's commitment to interventionism. But he recalled his predecessor's avowals on Vietnam only periodically and continued to mix his references with quotes from other presidents. Often he rejected suggestions that he lace his speeches with relevant Kennedy quotes. Similar to his earlier reluctance to link his policy with Kennedy's, Johnson likely understood the incredulousness of the analogy; the war was quite different from the one Kennedy had left behind. And by 1967 he may have further realized that no matter how much he invoked John Kennedy, Robert's opposition to the war and his own invocations were more powerful persuaders. His self-restraint was not easy. Johnson was privately embittered by the public's failure to acknowledge John Kennedy's role in Vietnam.[42]

In late November 1967 Senator Eugene McCarthy of Minnesota became the first Democrat openly to challenge Johnson for the nomination. Low on funding and limited in national appeal, McCarthy's candidacy was regarded by the news media and White House more as a symbol than a real threat. As a peace candidate, he demonstrated a division within the party that Johnson preferred to avoid. But Johnson was well ahead of McCarthy in the polls, and he and his advisers remained focused on Robert Kennedy. Roche was confident that Kennedy would not enter the race because he would create a division within the party that would undermine his presidential ambitions. "By 1976," Roche reasoned, "it would be a whole new ballgame—the *Camelot* records will be gathering dust in the attic— and a new generation of Democratic leaders would seek a non-controversial compromise candidate." Although Kennedy was "an arrogant little schmuck," he was sufficiently astute to "play it safe." Other aides feared Kennedy's hatred of Johnson might blind him to such political reason.[43]

Whatever hope Johnson sustained that he might weather this latest political crisis dissolved with the Tet offensive. On January 31, 1968, Viet Cong forces launched a concerted attack upon principal American strongholds in South Vietnam. The enemy's surprising strength shattered public support for the war. Approval of Johnson's handling of the war dropped from 40 percent to 26. As the party's only announced peace candidate, McCarthy stood to gain considerably from events. Kennedy, meanwhile, bitterly attacked the president for promoting "wishful thinking, false hopes, and sentimental dreams." The political reports remained ominous. "[Hugh] Sidey said that Kennedy has almost a mystique about his future," one White House memorandum read, "that he has it 'all inside him' that he has to [run for president]." Johnson generally remained silent, withdrawing into seclusion.[44]

A controversy soon arose which underscored Johnson's dilemma with the Kennedy "mystique." In February the president became alarmed by the publication of Evelyn Lincoln's *Kennedy and Johnson.* In her book Kennedy's secretary asserted that she had heard him say in late October 1963 that he intended to deny Johnson the vice-presidential nomination in 1964 and select North Carolina governor Terry Sanford. The accusation carried two implications. First, its timing was suspicious in light of Kennedy's anticipated candidacy. Second, it threatened Johnson's link to John Kennedy. Johnson ordered checks on factual matters related to Lincoln's account. Similar to his response to the Manchester book, he believed that Lincoln's book was just one in a series of planned anti-Johnson books designed to boost Robert's candidacy and separate Johnson from the Kennedy image.[45]

On March 12 Johnson "lost" the New Hampshire primary when Eugene McCarthy received 42.4 percent of the vote compared with Johnson's 49.5 percent. Few pundits expected McCarthy to receive so much support, consequently the media proclaimed him the "victor." Two days later Kennedy announced his candidacy, issuing his statement in the Senate caucus room, where his late brother had announced his candidacy eight years before. As in 1960, Johnson acted as the dutiful public servant with little time for the trivialities of a political campaign. McPherson criticized the strategy in a lengthy memorandum; it "will lead either to Kennedy's nomination or Nixon's election, or both." He recommended that Johnson move to the left on both foreign and domestic issues by deescalating the war and showing greater concern for urban violence, thus preventing Kennedy from appearing as the "responsible politician who cares." Other aides devised a scathing television campaign ridiculing Kennedy as "Senator Bugs Bunny playing Hamlet" and mocking him as a "bad boy." Forwarded articles assured Johnson, "Robert F. Kennedy is not John F. Kennedy. Bobby is not Jack." To minimize the "mystique," the White House staff looked to publicize the darker elements of Robert's image, including his attempts to censor books about his brother. "Can you imagine John F. Kennedy permitting people to ruffle his hair and manhandle him?" one aide asked. "Do people really want a President whom they can pinch, pull, squeeze and hug?" George Reedy suggested that "despite all of his assets (name, money, experience, ability to command headlines, close relationships with publicists, organization, etc.) it is still difficult to see Kennedy as President. He just doesn't look big enough. . . ." Other assessments, however, warned that Kennedy's television persona indicated that he had "acquired the mystical Kennedy magic."[46]

While some White House aides assessed Kennedy's appeal, others sought to lay claim to the "mystique." When Lawrence O'Brien toured Wisconsin he reminded audiences that Johnson was "John Kennedy's choice for Vice President and thus the true inheritor of the New Frontier." Other aides wanted to publicize Robert's earlier endorsements of Johnson. The president was further advised to appropriate certain Kennedy images for his own purposes. Douglass Cater looked to counteract Kennedy's "emotional" appeal through "a series of action images of the President at work." He suggested eighteen Kennedy-styled photo opportunities. Johnson himself intended to evoke the Kennedy myth when he traveled to Dallas in February for the first time since the assassination and passed within sight of the Texas School Book Depository.[47]

The advice that Johnson embody the "mystique" was poorly considered. In 1968 it would have been folly to present himself as John Kennedy's surrogate. Vietnam was a policy disaster while poverty and urban violence persisted at home. To try to link mortal failures to a myth would have drawn attention to Johnson's limitations and fallibility. Moreover, Robert and his "Kennedy magic" designated him as John's proper surrogate. Vulnerable to attack, Johnson confronted a Kennedy bolstered by myth and motivated by seeming hatred. Even if he survived Robert's challenge, he would likely face Nixon in the fall—the man who had lost to John Kennedy by only 119,000 votes. In late March Johnson lamented to a friend Kennedy's expert organization and media skills. "However, I can't do anything about it," he explained. "I've got too much to do here. . . . If they want Bobby Kennedy, that's what they'll get; and they may wind up with Nixon in the end." On March 31, 1968, Johnson concluded a policy address on Vietnam by stating that he would neither seek nor accept the nomination of his party for a second term. He would instead concentrate on seeking a peaceful solution to the war. Asked during a short press conference that followed if Kennedy's entrance had contributed to the timing of the announcement, he acknowledged that "it added to the general situation [of disunity] I talked about that existed in the country."[48]

Years later Johnson told Doris Kearns that "the final straw" to his decision was Kennedy's announcement of "his intention to reclaim the throne in the memory of his brother." Scholars, journalists, and White House aides have debated the source of Johnson's resignation. Some saw it as a shrewd political move. Some cited his poor health. Others thought it was a move to undermine Kennedy by appearing above the battle. Clearly, however, the prospect of facing Kennedy was a factor that concerned not only Johnson but Nixon and Humphrey as well. When Johnson informed Humphrey that he intended to withdraw, the vice-president appeared visibly shaken. "There's no way I can beat the Kennedys," Humphrey commented softly. He knew he would be running not only against Robert but "the Kennedys"—an enigmatic force composed of Robert, John, Edward, the widow, the New Frontiersmen, the media, the magic, the legacy, the "mystique." Like Johnson, Humphrey had once been humiliated by the Kennedys, losing to John during the crucial 1960 West Virginia primary. What had immediately distressed the vice-president was the thought of battling John's avatar.[49]

Not all of Robert Kennedy's opponents were so intimidated. Eugene McCarthy had known John Kennedy since their days together in Congress in the 1950s and shared a generally amiable relationship. In the years after the Kennedy assassination, McCarthy was decidedly unimpressed with the emerging Camelot myth. "I knew Jack," he recalled in 1994. "I had known him and his politics a long time. And the idea of the 'mystique' was a little hard for me to identify with." Whatever magic John Kennedy possessed, McCarthy noted, he did not believe it was transferable to Robert in 1968. He therefore devoted only cursory attention to it in the primaries. Of greater concern to McCarthy was Kennedy's capacity to personalize the campaign and to divide the antiwar faction. Like Johnson, McCarthy viewed Kennedy as an ambitious opportunist who was motivated by an overriding hostility toward the president. "Kennedy wasn't against the war," he argued. "He was against the way it was being run. He was really not an anti-war candidate. He was an anti-Johnson candidate, or anti-administration, or pro-power." With Kennedy's entrance, McCarthy knew the campaign was "going to be corrupted or perverted or changed."[50]

Dealing with the mythical dimensions of Kennedy's campaign, McCarthy viewed John and Robert as separate entities. Robert, he noted, "was a different kind of person" from John. His image as a compassionate, existential politician was bogus. "When Teddy said he had to carry on for his brother Jack, you kind of believed it. When Bobby said it, you had to believe he was quite willing to carry on for himself." Moreover, McCarthy believed that *he* was more readily identifiable with the Kennedy image than Robert. In 1968 McCarthy puzzled advisers with an offhand comment: "It's narrowed down to Bobby and me," he said. "So far he's run with the ghost of his brother. Now we're going to make him run against it. It's purely Greek: he either has to kill him or be killed by him. We'll make him run against Jack... And I'm Jack." McCarthy confirmed the quote in 1994, explaining that Kennedy was forced to run against his brother's reputation, his war, his cabinet, and his vice-president. McCarthy recognized that he had the support of committed young people and was a more credible intellectual and idealist. "I was closer to Jack in terms of basic background and issues and age than Bobby was," he recalled. "Bobby was running against Jack."[51]

During the campaign, McCarthy tried to exploit this connection by praising John Kennedy's efforts on behalf of the Nuclear Test Ban Treaty, the Alliance for Progress, and the Peace Corps. At the same time he called for leadership "independent from the mistakes of the past," and he blamed Robert Kennedy for participating in the formation of policies which led to "disastrous adventures." McCarthy rejected the argument that he held Robert accountable for the failures of the Kennedy administration while projecting himself as heir to select nobler elements of the New Frontier. "The aura may have helped [Kennedy] win," he reasoned, "but challenging it wouldn't have helped us any." McCarthy determined not to focus on the Kennedy image but to steer the campaign toward the issue of the war. "We probably should have exploited [the mystique] more, but it wasn't the issue we were really interested in." Indeed, it was precisely the issue of the war, McCarthy believed, that earned him the victory over Robert Kennedy in the Oregon primary, the first electoral defeat the Kennedys had ever suffered. And nothing diminished the Kennedy aura more neatly than defeat.[52]

Twenty-five years later McCarthy expressed less hostility over the fact that Kennedy had entered the race than over the type of campaign Kennedy ran. "He didn't take the chance on the mystique" sustaining his popularity among minorities, McCarthy noted. Kennedy implied that McCarthy was a racist and attacked him for his willingness to negotiate with the Communists in Vietnam. Kennedy was not intent on making a case against the war, McCarthy concluded. "It was to win." And like Johnson, McCarthy was exasperated by Kennedy's self-promotion through his family, the aura, and slick public relations, all of which distracted the electorate from the issues confronting America. After Kennedy's death, McCarthy rolled his eyes over the hagiography that followed. "He was still lying about me the Sunday before he was killed," he observed.[53]

Johnson and Kennedy, meanwhile, met for the last time in the cabinet room on April 3. After talking about the political situation, Johnson waxed nostalgic. He reflected on the 1960 Democratic convention and his decision to accept the vice-presidential nomination as a means of helping John carry the South. He noted how John had always treated him well. He then elaborated on the bond he felt toward him. As vice-president he had entered into a "partnership" with President Kennedy, a partnership that continued into his own presidency. Indeed, it had blossomed into a deep sense of "duty to look after the family and the members of the firm, which they had formed together." Attempting to reach out and belong, Johnson said he had "never thought of his Administration as just the Johnson Administration, but as a continuation of the Kennedy-Johnson Administration. It was carrying on a family matter." He assured Kennedy that he had tried his best to carry on his brother's policies and programs. He added that "as President Kennedy looked down at him every day from then until now, he would agree that he had kept the faith."[54]

Johnson's reference to "a family matter" carried important connotations. He spoke not only of his wish to reattach himself to the "mystique" but of his resolve in coming to terms with John and Robert Kennedy. In defeat he may have been able to reconcile his feelings toward the Kennedys. Having previously perceived the two brothers as two polarities, Johnson, by bowing out, had now linked them directly. John and Robert were bonded into a single entity of which Johnson was a vital component, for he served as an interlude between two Kennedy presidencies. John and Robert were neither "good" nor "bad"; they were "family." As a member of the "family," Johnson could neither lose to the Kennedys nor beat them because he was among them.

Johnson, of course, was much too shrewd a politician not to have appreciated the meeting's larger implications. By withdrawing from the race he was forced to acknowledge a direct line from John to Robert—a line of which he was never truly a part. His claim for inclusion reflected a desperate search for approval as he sought to convince himself and others that he was an extension of a more glorious past. His claim to family membership was transparent. Part of him had always been contemptuous of the Kennedys. But with an eye toward history, Johnson finagled the "mystique," hoping to restore his name. Indeed, he included the verbatim notes of the meeting in the text of his memoir.[55]

In the two months that followed, Johnson continued to monitor Robert's political activities and to orchestrate the nomination of Hubert Humphrey. His political interest in Kennedy became moot on June 5 when the senator was shot in Los Angeles shortly after winning the California primary. By all accounts, Johnson was greatly agitated by the news. When Kennedy died, Johnson addressed the nation, calling the occasion "a time of tragedy and loss." He helped the Kennedy family in making the necessary funeral arrangements. Privately, however, he felt cheated. Having struggled for five years under illusions of what the future might hold based on a glorified sense of the past, he knew that Robert's presidency would have finally revealed the "mystique" for what it was. "It would have been hard on me to watch Bobby march to 'Hail to the Chief,' " Johnson recalled, "but I almost wish he had become President so the country could finally see a flesh-and-blood Kennedy grappling with the daily work of the Presidency and all the inevitable disappointments, instead of their story book image of great heroes who, because they were dead, could make anything anyone wanted happen."[56]

Robert Kennedy's death complicated Johnson's struggle with the Kennedy "mystique." Now two martyred Kennedys would haunt the administration through its final days. As in 1963, Johnson heard oblique accusations that he was somehow responsible for Robert's death. Why, it was asked, had he not assigned Secret Service protection to the senator earlier? Letters to the White House demanded that he resign and relinquish the presidency to Edward Kennedy. Robert's death seemed to refortify the "mystique." Indeed, at the 1968 Democratic National Convention, Johnson grew fearful that Edward Kennedy intended to stampede the convention just as he feared Robert's presence in Atlantic City in 1964. When George McGovern declared his candidacy as a stand-in for Robert, Johnson was convinced that the South Dakota senator was a stalking horse for Edward. He frantically accelerated his involvement in the convention to assure Humphrey the nomination. As he had done at the 1964 convention during the JFK tribute, Johnson arranged to reschedule a film tribute to RFK until after the nominee had been chosen. Privately he remained hopeful that the delegates, if deadlocked, might even draft him as the nominee.[57]

Except for his obligatory comments following Robert's death, Johnson did not mention the senator in his remaining public remarks. In his memoir he reflected little on his rival's passing, noting, "I was glad that my last meeting with Bobby Kennedy had been friendly." John, however, became his refuge. Throughout the remainder of his presidency, Johnson spoke fondly of JFK during his various speeches on foreign and domestic matters. "When President Kennedy and I came into office in 1961, the choice that we faced together was quite clear," Johnson told an audience while campaigning for Humphrey. They could choose either to close their eyes to the nation's problems, "or we could get this country moving toward meeting those needs. I think everyone in this room knows the choice we made. And for all the Gallup polls and all the pundits in the world, I would not take back that choice we made." On the fifth anniversary of John's assassination, Johnson spoke nostalgically about his predecessor. And in his final State of the Union Address, he recognized the great influences on his presidency, including "my pleasant and close association with the beloved John F. Kennedy."[58]

But Johnson's ambivalence continued. In October 1968 he was pleased to learn of Jacqueline Kennedy's controversial marriage to Aristotle Onassis. "That'll sure take its toll on the Kennedy myth," he remarked privately. In retirement on the LBJ Ranch, he began to drop broad hints that JFK was involved in assassination attempts against Castro, and that Castro might have responded in kind. He scorned the press's kind treatment of Edward Kennedy following the Chappaquiddick accident. "You know, if I'd killed a girl like he did," he said privately, "they'd have wanted to send me to the electric chair." In public, however, Johnson worked to reidentify himself with the Kennedy legacy. During his retirement, until his death in January 1973, he repeatedly wrote and tried to persuade biographers and journalists that he had always viewed himself as a surrogate for John Kennedy.[59]

The tragedies of Lyndon Johnson were many. From the standpoint of the Kennedy myth, his most unfortunate fate was to survive. "The only difference between the Kennedy assassination and mine," he told reporters in the spring of 1968, "is that I am alive and it has been more torturous." Unlike John of the mythic past and Robert of the mythic future, Johnson was condemned to the present, wedged between two illusions and forced to deal with harsh realities. Retreating to fantasy, he sought his own place in the Kennedys' "story book image of heroes." Better to reside in Camelot than reality, for myths had won the power, approval, and love that had eluded him.[60]

The story of Lyndon Johnson and the Kennedys was not a morality play. It was the tale of one man whose political and personal insecurities prevented him from effectively contending with new symbols and myths. Ultimately, of course, it was the war that destroyed Johnson's presidency. He understood correctly that all the manipulation of his public image could not make body bags disappear. But at a more subtle level, Johnson's demise and Robert Kennedy's corresponding ascension illustrated an important transition in American politics. As a wheeler-dealer obscured by the Camelot myth, Johnson was eclipsed by stylistic demands that he never fully understood. He was among the last of a breed of leaders who held to the notion that popularity and public affection came from proficiency and accomplishments. Hoping to be measured by his achievements, he was haunted by the appeal of his more charismatic predecessor and the growing popularity of a similarly attractive "heir apparent." Robert Kennedy had little else going for him except a name and a myth. His rise in presidential politics and his utter disruption of the Johnson White House showed plainly how the Kennedy image could obscure a president's success and seize upon his failures. In losing to John Kennedy in 1960 and in "losing" to Robert Kennedy in 1968, Johnson never did figure out how to deal with a media environment that rewarded charm, telegenic appeal, and a pleasing personality. In this sense, Lyndon Johnson was neither "good" nor "bad"; he was an old-style politician who confronted a set of circumstances for which he was tragically unprepared.

3

Richard Nixon:
The Anti-Kennedy

IN SOME WAYS Richard Nixon's struggle with the Kennedy myth was a cruel replication of Lyndon Johnson's conflict. Like Johnson, he felt deflated less by Kennedy himself than by his reputation for glamour, wit, and style. After Robert Kennedy's murder in June 1968, Nixon too was viewed as a usurper. Had John or Robert lived, the argument went, Nixon would never have become president. Fearful of being defeated by the "mystique" in 1972, Nixon turned his attention to the new "heir apparent," Edward Kennedy. While Nixon's obsession with the Kennedy image was reminiscent of his predecessor, his struggle was given to greater extremes. His resentment ran deeper than Johnson's, owing to his defeat by John Kennedy in 1960. Indeed, he seemed vexed by the Kennedy myth before it had even fully evolved into myth. Paradoxically, Nixon emulated Kennedy's attributes even more deliberately than Johnson had. And unlike Johnson, he determined to destroy the reputation of the man whose image he envied.

Nixon brought to the presidency a powerful ambivalence toward the Kennedy image. Former White House correspondent Dan Rather once related a story to illustrate the extent to which Nixon was haunted by the Kennedys. Nixon had been irritated by photographs of the Kennedys frolicking by the ocean. Over the years, *Life* and *Look* magazines had often graced their covers with sentimental pictures of John Kennedy sailing off Hyannis Port or of Bobby Kennedy running along the shore. H. R. Haldeman, Nixon's chief of staff in the White House, was similarly cynical about the images, but he appreciated the emotional power of a solitary figure against the vastness of the sea. He determined that Nixon too should benefit

66   THE KENNEDY PERSUASION

from such an image. After all, Nixon had served in the navy like Jack Kennedy, and he had homes on the ocean at San Clemente and Key Biscayne. After weeks of planning, photographers and reporters were gathered on an oceanfront bluff overlooking Nixon's estate at San Clemente, California. On cue, Nixon appeared walking alone by the water. Reporters and photographers grew momentarily still until the scene turned sadly comical. "Good Christ," a reporter interjected, "he's wearing *shoes*."[1]

The scene seemed vaguely reminiscent of Lyndon Johnson's decision to appear, like Kennedy, on the cover of GQ, only to be pictured on the porch of his ranch wearing a Kennedy-style dark blue suit. Like Johnson's attempt to be a trend-setter, Nixon's walk by the water showed the capacity of the Kennedy "mystique" to confuse the pretender's self-image. Miscasting himself, Nixon too failed to see that the image of a romantic, sunswept president was incompatible with who he was. The reasons for this strange re-creation, as well as Nixon's ambivalence for the Kennedy image in general, can be traced in large measure to the 1960 campaign, a contest determined more by the candidates' contrast in public styles than differences on issues.

In some ways Nixon was predisposed to resent Kennedy. He was raised in a working-class family, reminded by his father that things would not come easily to him. "You boys have got to get out and scratch," Frank Nixon told him and his brothers. "You're not gonna get anywhere on your good looks." In high school he lost his bid to become class president to an opponent whom he later dismissed as an "athlete and personality boy." Economic and family hardships prevented him from competing for Yale and Harvard scholarships. After attending Whittier College, he went to Duke Law School but was rejected by New York City law firms following his graduation. Years before Nixon faced Kennedy in 1960, he had been involved in bitter political battles against people of similarly privileged backgrounds, including Jerry Voorhis, Alger Hiss, and Helen Gahagan Douglas, all of whom were wealthy, well-educated, New Deal Democrats. Yet part of Nixon secretly admired the Kennedy personality type and yearned to be part of their world. As early as 1946 the *Los Angeles Times* noted that Kennedy "was the Nixon that Nixon longed to be."[2]

After the war both Nixon and Kennedy began their political careers by running for Congress in their respective districts in California and Massachusetts. They were as far apart in upbringing and manner as they were geographically. Meeting Kennedy in 1947, Nixon remembered him as "a good-looking, good-humored" freshman colleague.

"Kennedy and I were too different in background, outlook, and temperament to become close friends," he later wrote, "but we were thrown together throughout our early careers and we never had less than an amicable relationship." Nixon viewed himself as Kennedy's generational peer. Both had come of age in the 1930s, fought in the navy during World War II, and entered politics in 1946. Nixon joined Kennedy on the Education and Labor Committee in January 1947. In determining seniority for the committee, each man drew the shortest straws of their respective political parties, and, according to Nixon, they sat at opposite ends of the committee table "like a pair of unmatched bookends."[3]

Similar to the contrast between Lyndon Johnson and John Kennedy, there were obvious disparities between Nixon and Kennedy in terms of wealth, gregariousness, and physical appeal. Unlike Kennedy, Nixon was hardworking, obedient, quiet, diligent, a loner, and a planner—the embodiment of the self-made man, working his way through college and law school, striving for success within each institution. In Congress, Nixon was ambitious and focused. He had a far more distinguished congressional record than Kennedy, who, *Time* noted in 1960, was often absent from his Senate duties and spent his time "in pursuit of pretty girls and higher elective office." Nixon was only four years older than Kennedy, but he looked much older, dressed less stylishly, had an older wife and older children, and had aligned himself with the grandfatherly Eisenhower. Their political styles, the methods they used to advance their careers, and their personalities made these two former navy men seem as different as Captain Queeg and Mr. Roberts.[4]

In an appearance that foreshadowed Nixon's struggle with the Kennedy image in 1960, the two men debated in McKeesport, Pennsylvania, in the spring of 1947. The topic was the legislation that would become the Taft-Hartley Act. Spectators remembered Nixon as tense and argumentative while Kennedy seemed "free and easy... smooth and genteel," less willing to battle than to charm. Photographs of the two congressmen published in the *McKeesport Daily News* showed Nixon wearing a floral tie with a disheveled collar. His face betrayed a five-o'clock shadow, his mouth was crooked, and his eyes were shifted to his left. Kennedy, dressed in a solid dark tie with a button-down shirt, peered into the camera with a large youthful smile, a tanned face, and slicked-back hair. Returning together by train to Washington, D.C., the two men discussed the threat of communism, a more agreeable topic than labor policy.

They drew straws for the lower berth, "and—this time—I won," Nixon recalled.[5]

During the 1950s Nixon and Kennedy had an outwardly cordial relationship. They exchanged pleasantries and good wishes over personal and political occasions in their lives. Indeed, Kennedy helped Nixon's 1950 Senate campaign against Douglas, contributing a $1,000 check from his father. Despite conflicting political ambitions, Nixon spoke well of his rival, describing him as "attractive—and formidable." In 1959 he playfully sent Kennedy an article which noted that they worked across the hall from each other in the Old Senate Office Building. "To my friend and neighbor Jack Kennedy," Nixon wrote, "with best wishes for almost everything."[6]

By the 1960 campaign the two candidates had developed personal images that contrasted sharply. In the fall of 1957 Kennedy's personal pollster, Lou Harris, had completed a survey contrasting Kennedy's image with Nixon's. Those people polled perceived Kennedy as "young, enterprising, spunky." They thought he was adequately experienced, intelligent, a family man, honest, sincere, good-looking, and a convincing speaker who "makes you feel something when he speaks." In contrast, many people felt uncomfortable with Nixon. Voters found him untrustworthy, "slippery," "not entirely honest," an "opportunist," "too malleable," and "a reactionary." Nixon also suffered from an Eisenhower "mystique"; his leadership skills did not generate similar confidence. Kennedy, meanwhile, compared favorably with Eisenhower, projecting an image of vigor and freshness.[7]

Still, many commentators in 1960 argued that the two likely nominees offered voters no real choice. Their positions on major issues were predictable. Each man prided himself as a cold warrior, and in the domestic realm Kennedy was generally viewed as a new-style moderate Democrat who was likely to appeal to conservatives and liberals alike. Eric Sevareid and other pundits saw Nixon and Kennedy as largely two sides of the same coin, appraising them as "tidy, button-down men" and "completely packaged products" who "represent the apotheosis of the Organization Man." Kennedy was irked by such comparisons, and he determined to separate himself from Nixon. Speaking with historian Arthur Schlesinger, Jr., he noted contemptuously that Nixon had "no taste." With Kennedy's encouragement, Schlesinger subsequently wrote a brief book, *Kennedy or Nixon: Does It Make Any Difference?* Two-thirds of it was devoted to separating the two men by personality and style.[8]

The 1960 campaign tested Nixon not only politically but personally.

He had reason to feel threatened by Kennedy. Kennedy's political skills, his youthful, charismatic image, elite upbringing, and wealth were qualities and characteristics that had troubled and antagonized Nixon in the past. Most politicians, including Lyndon Johnson, were reluctant to compete against a Pulitzer prize–winning author, a millionaire who had transformed himself into a magazine cover boy.

II As part of a four-year effort to soften his combative image, Nixon had planned a "high-road" campaign in 1960. During the 1956 presidential campaign he had been warned by his pollster, Claude Robinson, that he was popularly perceived as a "hatchet man." Nixon was advised at the time to present himself as a "high level statesman" by being "charitable" toward his opponents. He soon subdued his criticism of Democratic nominee Adlai Stevenson, prompting the news media to note the emergence of a "New Nixon." Three years later Robinson reiterated his contention that, based on private polls, Nixon would be effective in the upcoming presidential campaign if he projected the image of an experienced, tough-minded, dignified statesman. The high-road posturing was expected to draw attention to Kennedy's image of immaturity and inexperience.[9]

During the Democratic primaries, Nixon closely monitored Kennedy's press coverage and was particularly concerned about his ability to use the press as a conduit to self-promotion. He discovered that the lead story citing his "upset" victory over Kennedy in the Indiana primary had been edited and toned down. "Herb," Nixon wrote to his press secretary, Herbert Klein, "Kennedy's press man must really have power to sell this!" His concern was more fully realized during the Democratic National Convention in July. In his acceptance speech Kennedy poked fun at his opponent. "Mr. Nixon may feel it is his turn now, after the New Deal and the Fair Deal," Kennedy told the delegates, "—but before he deals, someone had better cut the cards." The allusion to Nixon's dishonesty struck a sharp nerve. Nixon immediately wrote two memos to Robert Finch, his campaign director, complaining that the comment was "below the belt." "One of the most flagrant examples of the double standard in reporting and commentary in political campaigns has been the reaction to Kennedy's attacks against me in his acceptance speech," Nixon wrote Finch. "The only way to whip this thing is to develop a massive program of letters to the editor, letters to the three networks, to the radio and television commentators, objecting to Kennedy's direct charge that his opponent was 'crooked' and the failure of the commentators and/or editorial writers to attack more vigorously." Under Nixon's direction, his campaign embarked on a bogus letter-writing campaign to generate support for his candidacy and to intimidate the press by having his staff forge letters defending him. Like Johnson, Nixon feared being outmaneuvered by Kennedy's public relations machinery. "The purpose of this exercise," he explained, "is to begin early in the campaign to force the columnists and editorial writers to follow a single standard and not a double standard as far as campaign tactics are concerned."[10]

The covert letter-writing campaign allowed Nixon to express his combativeness while appearing above the battle. He wished to supplement these counterattacks by persuading friendly Republicans to defend him. "This must be done for two reasons," Nixon explained; "1) because it will take some of the gloss off of Kennedy as the knight in shining armor; and 2) because it lays the groundwork for a reply by me at an appropriate time." Nixon wanted both to tarnish Kennedy's aura and to create conditions that would make it acceptable for him to attack Kennedy later. He frequently demanded updates on the letter-writing campaign, reminding his staff of its centrality. "I know of nothing in the propaganda area that is more important than this, and I want some of our best people put on it."[11]

During his own acceptance speech two weeks later, Nixon's first instinct was to respond aggressively to Kennedy. Handwritten outlines of Nixon's address cited his desire to make "a few cracks, barbs at the opposition." Instead he wrote a harsh, contemptuous refutation. "This election must not be decided on the basis of who spends the most money, who has the most glamour, who had the slickest organization, who had the best P.R. experts," Nixon wrote. "It must be decided by the facts." He accused Kennedy of relying on "phoney passion," ghostwritten speeches, and of using "words sailing over the heads of people." In response to Kennedy's suggestion to "cut the cards," Nixon wanted to draw attention to JFK's below-the-belt insult, so he wrote, "I don't think [Kennedy] would cheat at cards." He argued broadly that Kennedy was too young and inexperienced to deal effectively with important world issues. The campaign, he promised, would "separate the men from the boys." "I have expressed my respect," Nixon wrote, failing to appreciate the irony. "The fact he has not returned that respect does not mean I shall answer in kind." Sensitive to his combative image, he seemed torn between wanting to strike forcefully and to appear dignified. "I will not tonight or in the future reply in kind to any personal attacks he may make against me," Nixon's second draft noted. "Personalities are one thing. The great issues are [another.]"[12]

These early drafts of Nixon's acceptance speech were a blueprint of his anxieties, echoing the same frustration that Johnson expressed about Kennedy's image before the Democratic convention. Nixon's stated hope that the election would be determined by "facts" suggested a private fear that intangible elements of personal style and public relations might indeed overshadow him. No match for Kennedy at a stylistic level, he hoped to defeat his opponent with facts, not flash; with issues, not personalities. Nixon wanted voters to believe as much as he did that Kennedy's passion and lofty rhetoric was cynical and insincere. As the acceptance speech went through revisions, the most insulting comments were struck. That Nixon edited his attacks showed a sound sense of restraint. But that he wrote them at all showed the extent of his frustration and fears.[13]

After his speech Nixon was angered that he was not as well received by the press as Kennedy. "This week I want concentration on the obvious unobjectivity and unfairness of most of the papers—New York Times, Washington Post are good examples, for failing to contrast Kennedy's personal attack on me in his acceptance speech with my 'high road' handling of him," Nixon wrote Finch. "We simply have to do a better job of hammering home the line that they have already started on the low road." He singled out the writings of specific reporters and ordered letters to the editors "talking about the great impact on the television audience of my acceptance speech and noting in passing the failure of these papers to take notice of this fact and to give credit for it in their editorial columns." "We must constantly hammer home the idea that they are being biased on Kennedy's side in their coverage of the news as well as in their editorial comments," Nixon concluded. "This is one of the most effective ways to needle them into coming around our way."[14]

Nixon's pollster repeatedly assured him that the image of experience and maturity would ultimately win him the election. "You are better qualified for the job," Robinson assured, "—more mature, more experienced, more sure in your grasp of the problem, and of tougher fiber in facing the Russians—than Jack." He continued to urge Nixon to project "a quiet, sure-footed confidence in the outcome, and fortify that quality of inner strength that is necessary for great leadership." Shortly after receiving Robinson's assessment, Nixon ordered Finch to find someone to speak highly of him, comparing him favorably to Kennedy as being "best in a crisis." On the stump he emphasized Kennedy's immaturity and inexperience. Although both men entered national politics at the same time, Nixon boasted that his own congressional record and his seven and a half years of extensive travel abroad as vice-president made him the substantively proven candidate, especially in matters of foreign policy. "The White House," he told audiences, "should not be a training school for Presidents." He repeatedly characterized Kennedy as "naive," "dangerously irresponsible," "rash," and "impulsive." Kennedy "shoots from the hip," "makes mistakes in the clutch," and "shows a very dangerous immaturity in world affairs." While willing to question Kennedy's leadership, Nixon walked a fine line, sensitive to his "hatchet man" image. In early September he was alarmed by a newspaper report alleging that he had said Kennedy was "soft" on communism. Nixon asked his speechwriter "to watch carefully for this kind of word in the future."[15]

While maintaining a "high road" posture, Nixon and his aides informally gathered information about Kennedy's infidelity, poor health, and shady family history. John Ehrlichman told Finch that the senator was "often on the make for Daisy Palmer, wife of sports announcer Bud Palmer, when the latter is working out of town." Finch received a dubious photograph of Kennedy allegedly leaving a girl friend's house at 1 a.m. He also collected information on Kennedy's affliction with Addison's disease. One anonymous memo suggested that an operative raise publicly Joseph Kennedy's alleged anti-Semitic, pro-Nazi past. "Jack Kennedy is very sensitive also about his excessive spending, Joe McCarthy, nepotism, and his integrity. If these are properly highlighted, he will be tempted to explode and lose his composure—and therein lies victory." In 1990 Nixon admitted he had had damaging personal material on Kennedy, but he contended it would have been "counter productive" to have used it because "the media would not have played an aggressive role" in exposing Kennedy's personal flaws.[16]

As part of an effort to weaken Kennedy's appeal, Nixon courted interest groups similar to those Kennedy sought. In July Nixon wanted to attract key leaders in business, editors, and "other influential groups." "I say this because Kennedy has been making an all-out appeal to such groups, both individually and collectively," he wrote. He wanted a Scholars for Nixon organized by August, "before Kennedy is able to work on them." "He has done a very effective job in winning over the Stevenson eggheads, in getting back the Negroes, the farmers and other groups that swore they were going to be against him before he began his operations." Four days later he asked staff "to get out some counter-propaganda regarding our organization, emphasizing not only its quality, but the accent on youth, brains, etc." He further wanted to "run a little competitive exercise with JFK" by inviting people associated with education, civil rights, youth, and science to speak with him. "I think the necessity of setting up a separate woman's organization of real potency has become even more acute in view of Kennedy's nomination than before," Nixon wrote. Such memos revealed an ambivalence that Johnson had also experienced. Although Nixon disparaged Kennedy's emphasis on style, he sought to embody some of the qualities that made his opponent so attractive. The subtext of his effort suggested a troubled candidate, one who mirrored images not because he felt they reflected his personality but because they won popularity and political strength for Kennedy.[17]

Nixon's memos revealed an embittered, combative candidate who was particularly frustrated by an inability to crack Kennedy's façade. If he seemed angry and petty, his behavior perhaps stemmed from a fear of having a lifetime of hard work and achievement overshadowed by Kennedy's style. He was convinced that Kennedy was hustling the public, using a biased news media and an elaborate public relations network to project an appealing but false image. To some degree he was correct. Most objective observers of the 1960 campaign agreed in retrospect that many reporters were successfully charmed or disarmed by Kennedy. And Kennedy himself was clearly not all that he professed to be. But Nixon staff members concurred that much of the campaign's problems with the press rested with the candidate himself.[18]

Nixon was understandably frustrated in competing against Kennedy's image. Personal assets that once benefited him paled in comparison. He seldom recalled his military service, perhaps knowing it was no match for Kennedy's PT-109 heroics. He proudly paraded his wife, Pat, before crowds. But Pat Nixon was to Jacqueline Kennedy what June Cleaver was to Elizabeth Taylor. Reporters respected Pat for her hard work on her husband's behalf and her simple tastes and manner. But she was not as glamourous or as youthfully sensual as Jacqueline. In addition to Jacqueline's physical attractiveness, press reports about her pregnancy highlighted her maternalism, emphasizing her femininity at an entirely different level: as John Kennedy sought to give life to the American spirit, Jacqueline symbolized the gift of life to a young American family.[19]

Nixon's speeches were longer and more leisurely than Kennedy's but were criticized for their obvious intent to make him seem warm and likable. While Kennedy joked with hecklers, Nixon threatened them. The utter seriousness with which Nixon took himself made him vulnerable to satirists, to reporters—and to Kennedy, who ridiculed Nixon's past triumphs with the skill of a stand-up comedian. While Nixon was often greeted enthusiastically by crowds, reporters noted that in his personal appeal he was no match for Kennedy, who fought off teenage girls clamoring to touch him, and was described as possessing a combination of Eisenhower's charismatic appeal and the "Roosevelt aura." Although both men had high expectations for America in the areas of education, race relations, poverty, and combating communism, Kennedy sounded a more optimistic theme as he beckoned the country to "get moving again." Nixon's response was to criticize Kennedy as "the modern Pied Piper who will pipe the troubles out of the land." He later acknowledged that Kennedy's "approach was simpler and more dramatic." "Nixon's theme is essentially the same," an aide complained to Finch, "but he cannot use it as such because Kennedy has preempted it."[20]

Other aides discouraged Nixon from trying to duplicate Kennedy's lofty calls to greatness. Kennedy's emphasis on "moving ahead" and the "New Frontier," Robinson wrote, was "the kind of talk one expects from a college senior in an oratorical contest." Nixon, however, was enticed by the passion and commitment that Kennedy generated. He sometimes adopted Kennedy's themes, adding his own middle-class slant. In mid-October he instructed his speechwriters to note in their texts that the "Kennedy economic policies are not adequate to conquer the new frontiers which lie before us. It is the individual and the pioneer spirit that we always used to conquer frontiers of the past." Nixon later adjusted his rhetoric and, according to biographer Stephen Ambrose, "sometimes sounded more like Kennedy than Kennedy." A year later, when Nixon organized his memoir on the 1960 campaign, his researcher, Charles Lichenstein, urged him to dispute the popular notion that he had emulated Kennedy's campaign themes. Lichenstein suggested that Nixon subtly include in his manuscript his earlier use of " 'New Frontier' themes many long years before John Kennedy climbed aboard." Kennedy copied Nixon, the argument went; Nixon did not copy Kennedy.[21]

Competing against the Kennedy image, the televised debates proved to be Nixon's greatest embarrassment and most valuable lesson in image management. Months before the first debate, aides assured him that he would appear more presidential and experienced than Kennedy. "It has uniformly been your experience that people who are critical of you go away greatly impressed once they have had an opportunity to hear you," Robinson wrote. "It is physically impossible to make this personal impression except via television." A month later he reassured Nixon, "You are going to come out on top because you know your stuff and you look and act more like a President than Kennedy." Nixon should concentrate on the issues, pressure Kennedy for specifics, and play "the role of the complete realist." "Viewers should come away from this first debate thinking that Kennedy is vague, starry-eyed, not firm in his grasp of the subject matter, too young and inexperienced for the job."[22]

Nixon prepared for the debates with his usual intensity. He made sure to reserve a full day of preparation before the debate. He studied the facts and planned his rhetorical strategy by reviewing questions and answers compiled on hundreds of index cards. His staff amassed documents to deduce Kennedy's strategy and to preempt his attacks. Meanwhile, he resisted theatrical advice. In late August he rejected the advice of Bill and Ted Rogers to use a sun lamp in order to minimize his pasty complexion. Focusing on substance, Nixon lost the first debate before it started. He appeared at the Chicago television studios physically exhausted, underweight, and wearing a light grey, ill-fitting suit that blended into the scenic backdrop. Stepping into the studio lights beforehand, he looked pale but confident, relaxing on the set by joking with reporters. When Kennedy entered several minutes later, Nixon was struck by his physical appearance. "I had never seen him look more fit," he recalled. Photographers flocked to Kennedy, leaving Nixon momentarily alone. The candidates then met center stage and shook hands for photographers. "I remarked on his deep tan," Nixon recalled, "and he jokingly replied that he had gotten it from riding in open cars while touring sunny California." Nixon's demeanor changed dramatically. He smiled sheepishly next to Kennedy, as if he had entered a classroom to take an exam only to realize he had studied the wrong chapters.[23]

Afterward, Nixon correctly sensed that he had outscored Kennedy on the issues. But he also had an uneasy feeling about his stage presence. Len Hall, a Nixon adviser, soon forwarded a study on audience reaction. Before the telecast, 42 percent of the viewers thought Nixon expressed himself well. Afterward, only 10 percent felt the same. The percentage who believed Kennedy was articulate rose from 28 to 60 percent. Before the debate, 21 percent thought Nixon had a "magnetic personality." The figure dropped to 7 percent, while Kennedy's numbers in the same category rose seventeen points to 59 percent. "I recognized the basic mistake I had made," Nixon wrote. "I had concentrated too much on substance and not enough on appearance."[24]

In terms of his personal image, Nixon did well in the debates that followed, making the necessary adjustments to his physical appearance. Drawing on his resourcefulness and savvy, he tried to recoup his losses. After the first debate he pulled even with Kennedy in terms of image projection, a remarkable feat considering his opponent's telegenic skills. In the end, however, Nixon believed that "Kennedy had gained more from the debates than I." The news media generally agreed, calling Nixon's decision to debate Kennedy among his worst tactical mistakes. Robinson's polls showed that after the first debate the percentage of Nixon supporters fell in the East and "trended downward slightly thereafter." Nixon avoided blaming himself and instead lashed out against the theatrical demands of television politics. He later demeaned the medium for inspiring "a greater premium on showmanship than on statesmanship." He called for greater fairness in "makeup, lighting, and other technical factors, to see that the candidates are on even terms." "In essence, what ought to be decisive in selecting a President is what is in a man's head rather than the type of beard he may have on his face." His critique was an implicit indictment of Kennedy's expertise. But his contempt for image management was founded more on jealousy and frustration than high-mindedness. In later years Kennedy became a media standard against whom Nixon measured himself.[25]

At a deeper level Nixon's apprehension with the debates and with image management in general perhaps derived from acute self-consciousness. He was distressed not about *how* to present himself but about *what* to present. "I knew that what was most important was that I must be myself," Nixon recalled after the first debate. ". . . I went into the second debate determined to do my best to convey three basic impressions to the television audience—knowledge in depth of the subjects discussed, *sincerity*, and confidence." [emphasis mine.] Nixon's intention was sound; he did not seek to be something he was not. But sincerity is a quality that one shares with an audience, not projects. Nixon seemed to think he could appear sincere by faking it. He failed to understand that the intent of showing sincerity was itself an act of *in*sincerity.[26]

Nixon's struggle with sincerity was revealing because it went to the issue of what was real. Kennedy's accusation that Nixon was "crooked" was especially goading because it came from a candidate whom Nixon believed used "phoney passion" and "baked-on" makeup as a means of appealing to voters. *Kennedy* was the one who advanced himself through glamour, ghostwriters, excessive expenditures, empty promises, public relations, and slick organizations. Yet the public found *him* passionate and committed while Nixon was the candidate about whom people wondered aloud, "Would you buy a used car from this man?" For Nixon the refrain was more than a long-standing joke. It was an indication of the uneasiness that many people felt toward him, and that he may have felt about himself.[27]

To the degree that a politician's telegenic appeal relied upon acting, Nixon's desire to project appealing qualities was not misconceived. Nixon and Kennedy were both actors and pitchmen. Kennedy had a gift for turning on the charm, engaging in witty conversation, and behaving as if he was enthralled by people whom he disliked or found boring. But he usually understood that he was playing a part. In contrast, Nixon lacked a sense of irony. Struggling internally perhaps with who he was, the task of projecting himself outwardly was taxing. Nothing that Nixon could ever learn in image management could bring him to Kennedy's level. The problem was not with his makeup, script, or five-o'clock shadow. Nor was the problem his intelligence, debating skills, or what was in his head. The problem was him.[28]

The behavior and thinking that Nixon showed toward Kennedy during the 1960 campaign persisted throughout his career. Like Johnson, he fixated less on Kennedy than on his image. His opponent's appeal embittered him as if it was a negative reflection on himself. In later years he accelerated his efforts to expose the Kennedy façade. But the line between resentment and envy was not always clear, for Nixon too continued sometimes to emulate the man who had humiliated him. Overshadowed by new stylistic demands, he tried to project a pleasing personality, sincerity, compassion, youth, energy, and idealism. He learned from Kennedy.

III Nixon lost the 1960 election by the narrowest popular margin in history. "Of the five presidential campaigns in which I was a direct participant," he wrote in 1978, "none affected me more personally." He had worked hard and brilliantly, matching his skills against a charismatic candidate and capturing nearly half the votes. For Nixon the campaign was marked not only by "unusual intensity" but by valuable, bitter lessons about image management. "The way the Kennedys played politics and the way the media let them get away with it left me angry and frustrated," he wrote. Their campaign, he charged, was "led by the most ruthless group of political operators ever mobilized for a presidential campaign."[29]

Less than a month after Kennedy was sworn in, Nixon proclaimed himself "the leader of the party." For the next three years he relentlessly criticized the administration. The Bay of Pigs fiasco in April 1961 seemingly gave Nixon a ready-made issue with which to criticize Kennedy on themes he had emphasized during the campaign— Kennedy's immaturity and inexperience in foreign affairs. Despite Kennedy's disastrous foreign policy, however, his approval rating rose to 82 percent, in part because of his skillful handling of the crisis through television and the printed press. After receiving a letter encouraging him to attack Kennedy on the issue, Nixon jotted a thought: "Public relations superb—obsessed with it—But comes a time for action to match words."[30]

Nixon postponed immediate career decisions to concentrate on writing a book. Soon after the election he sounded out the idea with Kennedy, who told Nixon that all public figures should pursue writing "for the mental discipline and because it tends to elevate him in popular esteem to the respected status of 'an intellectual.'" Although critical of Kennedy's policies, Nixon respected his advice about projecting an image. Unknown to Kennedy, however, Nixon intended to use the book to undermine flattering portrayals of Kennedy in the popular literature on the 1960 campaign. Privately Nixon wrote that he planned to refute "some of the more glaring inaccuracies" of Theodore White's popular book, *The Making of the President 1960*. Nixon had not read the book, nor did he intend to. But he asked Herbert Klein and his research assistants to read it and outline a refutation. His chief researcher, Charles Lichenstein, summarized the book as a "contemptuous and scurrilous" attack. Nixon was portrayed as "an aloof, confused, self-pitying, scared political infighter." Indeed, the adjectives were so harsh Lichenstein felt compelled to note, "Don't blame me, I'm only quoting him." Lichenstein supported Nixon's view that "the best way to meet the argument that the Kennedy campaign was a modern masterpiece" was to create "a positive image of your own." "To see in it some Crusade-to-the-New-Frontier is absurd: and by your own dispassionate description and analysis, I think the point can be fairly made." Nixon's account should challenge the Kennedy image and appeal to those people whose loyalties remained with Nixon. "[White's] 'images' will fade and be forgotten," Lichenstein assured. "When *Six Crises* appears, therefore, it will have its own audience—ready, willing, and malleable."[31]

Preparing the manuscript, Nixon asked researchers to find and arrange evidence to support preconceived conclusions. He ordered material gathered to "knock down the rather silly conclusions" derived from an academic study and by writings from "pro-Kennedy columnists and writers" who argued that Kennedy was hurt by the religious issue. He wanted another study to prove how "the Kennedy partisans" in the news media "had blown [the first debate] up into a decisive victory." Researchers were told to collect quotes from the news media predicting a Kennedy landslide. "The more big names of people who were strongly pro-Kennedy who make predictions of this type that we can find, the better," he noted. "It will build up the story and also be a source of rather acute embarrassment to some of them." He was especially irked by criticism that he had pulled his punches against Kennedy. "Due to the books that have been written from the Kennedy angle the impression has been conveyed that our campaign was [a] creampuff, rather leisurely kind of operation," he wrote researchers. The reason for this misconception was because "the Kennedy people exaggerated shamelessly" the amount of time and effort they devoted. He requested that his staff find estimates for the extent of his own appearances at rallies, asking them to "make it good and high." He ordered a collection of Kennedy's "more flagrant promises" and "any silly statements he may have made" in order "to show the problem I was confronted with as a responsible candidate."[32]

Nixon's first book, *Six Crises*, was modeled after Dwight Eisenhower's *Six Decisions* and Kennedy's *Profiles in Courage*. A third of the book was devoted to the campaign—the only part that Nixon organized and wrote largely by himself. Its publication coincided with Nixon's political return. In October 1961 he announced his candidacy for governor of California. Pundits speculated that he might use the governorship as a stepping-stone to a presidential bid in 1964. Years later Nixon argued that he thought Kennedy was "unbeatable" in 1964. He decided to let another Republican candidate go "against Kennedy, his money, and his tactics."[33]

Nixon's chances for winning the governorship were seriously hurt by the unfolding of the Cuban missile crisis during the final weeks before the election. For two weeks the crisis knocked the California election off the front pages and generated massive popular support for the president and residual support for Governor Edmund Brown, who was summoned to Washington to consult with Kennedy. Nixon lost by an overwhelming majority. The morning after his defeat, he met with reporters and launched into a rambling, seventeen-minute condemnation of the news media. Laced among his more newsworthy comments, Nixon took several swipes at Kennedy. Yet even as he attacked the president, he praised him for "that good Irish fight of his" and unconsciously used Kennedy phraseology of "moving ahead again" and contending that "America has got to move."[34]

While most political observers, including Kennedy, were convinced that Nixon was irreparably harmed by the episode, less than four months later Nixon reentered public life when he appeared on the NBC television program, the "Tonight Show," hosted by Jack Paar. Implicitly Nixon borrowed a page from the Kennedy book on self-presentation, following producer Paul Keyes's advice to appear warm and likable. Nixon prepared for the appearance by dictating a six-page transcript of questions and answers that he hoped might be scripted into the interview. He wanted talk about his hobbies, his interest in sports, his dog Checkers, major world personalities, America's youth, music, and a poem that his daughter Julie wrote in order to convey "the light—warm side." He and Keyes polished several jokes, some of which poked fun at Kennedy. Keyes reminded Nixon that the program would give the American people a chance to reappraise him since the "last" press conference. Because of Kennedy's poor leadership, the average American viewer "wants to like you because he knows he needs you," Keyes wrote. Nixon therefore needed to show warmth and commitment. "For if you do," Keyes noted, "I am convinced the history of our times will be altered this night."[35]

In a remarkable performance, Nixon out-Kennedyed Kennedy, using the talk-show format to make jokes at Kennedy's expense while projecting uncharacteristic warmth. Paar asked Nixon if in 1964 Kennedy could be defeated. "Which one?" Nixon quipped. The audience laughed and applauded, unaware that both the question and answer had been prepared beforehand. Nixon then recalled how he and Kennedy had once been friends in Congress. "We were low men on the totem pole in the labor committee, and we remained low men until he ran for President," he joked. His self-depreciation brought further laughter and applause from the audience. "President Kennedy can be defeated in '64," Nixon said seriously. He characterized Kennedy's record as "brilliant from the standpoint of sales-manship, brilliant from the standpoint of public relations, but the product doesn't live up to the words. It doesn't live up to the ads." He concluded his appearance by playing an original composition on the piano.[36]

Back in the spotlight, Nixon prepared for future conversations with reporters by writing himself a memo, most of which centered on Kennedy's image. He mocked Kennedy's 1960 campaign promise "to get the country moving again" and his pledge of "courage and greatness." "Looking back," Nixon wrote, "I wonder if we have ever had more ridiculous slogans—that is all they were." He cited James Reston's criticism that Kennedy was running the government like a PT boat. "We all know, of course, what happened to the PT boat," Nixon wrote with a hint of envy. "Indeed, in case we don't know, 20th Century Fox has produced a movie about the matter." Activity should not be confused with accomplishment, Nixon wrote, "even if much vigah accompanies the motion." He thought Kennedy lacked "conviction," "priorities," and "an understanding of what is important." "We live in a tough world and can ill afford such dilettantism, even if it is carried off with 'elegance.' Because the harsh reality is that the real enemy is not confused & he never has been interested in style."[37]

Nixon steadily criticized Kennedy right up to the day before the assassination. Appearing in Dallas on November 21, 1963, he accused Kennedy of promising more than he could deliver. "His public relations are brilliant," Nixon added, "but his performance is poor." Commenting on recent speculation about his presidential ambitions in 1964, Nixon noted, "I find there is a correlation between Kennedy's failures and interest in me." He was particularly irritated by charges that he lacked sufficient courage to challenge Kennedy in 1964. "Some people write in a challenging fashion," he told *Time*. "What's wrong, they ask, are you afraid of Kennedy? No one knows better than I what a formidable candidate he is. I'm not afraid of him. Running against him next time will be running against all his money, the federal treasury and all kinds of public relations. Kennedy will shoot the works." Nixon expressed simultaneously his fearlessness and his fears.[38]

Nixon had just arrived in New York City from Dallas when he learned Kennedy had been shot. While some people who saw Nixon immediately afterward suspected that he might have felt some guilt over Kennedy's death, Nixon dismissed such conclusions. Likewise he rejected the observations of those close to him that if he had been elected president in 1960 he might have been assassinated instead. In his 1978 memoirs he recalled his last conversation with Kennedy in the summer of 1963. "There had been no love lost between Kennedy and me," Nixon acknowledged. ". . . But I admired his ambition and his competence, and I could feel the terrible impact this tragedy would have on his closely knit family. . . . I wished there was something that I could do to ease the Kennedys' grief."[39]

For Nixon, the door to the Oval Office was widened by Kennedy's death. *Newsweek* declared in December 1963 that he was "far from dead politically." He mulled over the possibility of running for the Republican nomination in 1964, but Lyndon Johnson's vast popularity discouraged him. In the aftermath of the assassination he concentrated on his law practice, determined to succeed in what he called "the fast track." He was admitted to the New York bar in December 1963 and joined a Wall Street law firm. He was at last accepted by the Eastern Establishment he had long resented. Kennedy was gone, but he left Nixon with a final ironic twist. For four years Nixon had chastised Kennedy as more style than substance, more image than reality. In death, Kennedy became the full embodiment of a "mystique" Nixon resented while Kennedy was alive. Transformed into a brief shining moment, Kennedy gained a stature he could never have achieved had he completed his presidency. In life, the Kennedy image had irritated Nixon. Now it would haunt him.[40]

IV Richard Nixon owed his political resurrection in 1968 to a variety of factors far beyond the realm of the Kennedy "mystique." He benefited from a vacuum of leadership in the Republican party after Goldwater's overwhelming defeat in 1964 and the ensuing division between conservative and moderate Republicans. George Romney and Nelson Rockefeller, Nixon's primary opponents in 1968, proved ineffective and indecisive. During the off-year elections in 1966, Nixon had strengthened his position as the leading Republican spokesperson. Meanwhile, increased public disillusionment over Vietnam made Nixon an attractive candidate to those who sought foreign-policy expertise. Nixon's themes of "Law and Order" and "Peace with Honor" appealed to suburban middle-class voters weary of civil rights violence and antiwar protests.[41]

Within this broad framework the Kennedy "mystique" wove its influence into the image and subtext of the 1968 campaign. For many voters, Nixon was the antithesis of John Kennedy in his philosophy, personality, and style. Yet the two former rivals were blended oddly together in the public imagination. "There was something glamourous about being a survivor of Camelot," campaign chronicler Garry Wills recalled, "even if one played the role, in it, of Mordred." Nixon and his aides were conscious of his unique connection to the "mystique." "Memory fuses great opponents," Nixon speechwriter William Safire explained, "and men who had little in common are two sides of a common coin."[42]

Like any astute politician, Nixon was mindful of the political value of speaking respectfully of Kennedy after the assassination. "It was mostly in terms of he was so young, and so full of life," Nixon told a reporter when asked to reflect on the Kennedy death. It was "a supreme tragedy," having a more "traumatic effect" on the nation than Lincoln's death. Kennedy was "a man in his youth, so idealistic, so spirited," and his passing represented the "end of an era that had just begun." "To some people he was a President, to some a friend, to some a young man," Nixon noted. "To me he was all that, and on top of that, a man of history struck down in a tragic panorama of history. It probably had a greater effect on me than on some closer to him. Their feeling was personal. I thought of his age, his potential. . . ." Nixon had once devoted considerable energy to demeaning Kennedy. By 1968 he sounded almost nostalgic for a golden age. In harkening back to the lost potential of the Kennedy years, he connected himself to the longings of many Americans.[43]

Nixon's link with the Kennedy past was underscored by a new public style modeled implicitly after his former rival. After his appearance with Jack Paar he had worked hard to project a warmer, more likable personality, a man who was willing to show his vulnerabilities. He wooed reporters, spoke candidly, and promised them a more thorough and helpful press operation. "He's more relaxed," Mike Wallace noted in March 1968. "He's more accessible. He's more fun." "It will never be a love affair like some newsmen had with Kennedy," Nixon explained, "but I would like to have the newsmen's respect, if not their affection." *Time* described Nixon as projecting a "new urbanity and self-effacing if slightly forced humor. . . . Like John Kennedy, Nixon refuses to kiss babies or wear funny hats on the campaign circuit."[44]

Privately Nixon's advisers encouraged him to project a more Kennedyesque image. Harry Treleaven urged the staff to promote the boss's intellectual ability, toughness, vigor, glamour, humor, compassion, and warmth. "[Speechwriter Pat] Buchanan wrote about RFK talking about the starving children in Recife," Treleaven noted in a memo. "That's what we have to inject. . . ." Nixon was particularly mindful of conveying a "youth movement" within his campaign by parading before reporters a new group of "young intellectuals"—new campaign staffers, whom reporter Timothy Crouse suspected were intended "to create the impression that he was building up his own New Frontier." Campaign literature promoted him as "the thinking man's choice," a candidate who possessed a "combination of seasoned experience and youthful vigor." The "Youth for Nixon" organization publicized Nixon as a man of "Experience, Courage, Integrity, Ability, and Action." "We need new leadership," Nixon told young adults. "We need new ideas. Leadership and ideas that come from your generation."[45]

Stylistically Nixon learned from Kennedy to ask for help from the voters as a means of uniting them in a common cause. He also used greater eloquence. "The lamps of enlightenment are lit by the spark of controversy;" "Our cause today is not a nation, but a planet—for never have the fates of all the people of the earth been so bound up together." "This country must move again," Nixon told an audience; "how long will it take the United States to move?" "One is hearing the echo of the phrases of John F. Kennedy in 1960," Theodore White wrote, "the rub-off deep somewhere in the memory of his defeated rival. . . . The mark of John F. Kennedy was seared into Richard M. Nixon in 1960; it continues to surface even now, as he runs for President in 1968." The words were less "seared" than premeditated. "His guys gave him some great word-pictures," Nixon told his speechwriters, referring to Kennedy. He asked that they do the same.[46]

Among other important lessons Nixon learned from Kennedy was the need to master television. Despite his aversion to the medium, it provided him with direct access to the public, allowing Nixon to project an image unfiltered by pesky reporters. "After the 1960 campaign," he explained to the press, "Jack Kennedy and I got together for a post mortem. We agreed that while people usually judge a candidate by the number of miles he covers and the number of hands he shakes, that kind of campaign is madness. With modern communication, it is also a waste of time." Kennedy was successful on television because he was at ease with himself and was willing to test his wit and charm in relatively spontaneous settings. Nixon and his advisers, however, created formats that assured unprecedented control. As Nixon traveled from city to city, advisers constructed

stage-managed question-and-answer shows. Precise and careful attention was devoted to audience composition and participation, makeup,
lighting, music, scripts, and staging. Nixon himself had become
highly conscious of shifting his eyes, perspiring, and appearing
physically comfortable. Like a salesman in an infomercial, he was
made attractive by fake audiences asking rigged questions about a
product they had already bought.[47]

Nixon did not draw as heavily or as obviously from his Kennedy
connection in 1968 as Lyndon Johnson had in 1964. His appropriation
of the "mystique" was subliminal, obscured by the campaign's broader
issues and concerns. Nevertheless, the "New, New Nixon" resurrected
himself in part because he incorporated and expanded upon strategies
and images reminiscent of Kennedy. He transformed a troubling
image into a public persona that convinced millions of people they
saw a changed man. He moved beyond the glum image of the 1950s,
adapting himself adequately to the new politics of the 1960s. The
Nixon of 1968 had no sex appeal and charisma at the level of
Kennedy. But he did seem more likable and slightly more hip.
"There certainly is a new Nixon," he commented. "I realize, too,
that as a man gets older he learns something. If I haven't learned
something I'm not worth anything in public life."[48]

Nixon's ability to project a Kennedyesque persona in 1968 was
limited. Like Johnson, he understood that Robert Kennedy was the
true inheritor of the legacy. "Bobby Kennedy is formidable because of
four factors," Nixon told a reporter in 1966. "(1) He's got money, (2)
he's got the Kennedy mystique, (3) he has an organization and (4) he
has a dramatic flair for public relations." Like Johnson, Nixon
anticipated that Kennedy would likely seek the Democratic nomination, creating mixed possibilities. On the one hand Kennedy would
further divide Democrats and soften Johnson for Republican attacks
in the fall should the president capture the nomination. On the other
hand, if Kennedy won the nomination, Nixon would again have to
run against Kennedy's wealth, organization, and image. Like Johnson,
Nixon understood that Robert not only inherited the forces that once
defeated him, but he had one additional advantage that John had
not—a "mystique."[49]

In the spring of 1968 Nixon said little about the divisions within
the Democratic party, deciding to concentrate on securing the
Republican nomination. "I don't want to get into the crossfire
between LBJ and Bobby—let them hit each other, not me," he told
Safire. The Nixon staff offered considerable brave talk about running

against Kennedy as vindication for the 1960 campaign. "But listening to Nixon," reporter Jules Witcover recalled, "one often had the feeling there was nothing he wanted less than to come up against the Kennedy clan again." According to Pat Buchanan, an atmosphere of fear spread among the older members of Nixon's staff who dreaded running against another Kennedy.[50]

Although Gallup polls generally showed Nixon running stronger against Kennedy than against Humphrey, intangible and unpredictable forces accompanied Robert's candidacy. "A reporter can't help contrasting [Nixon's appearances] with the arrival any place of Sen. Robert F. Kennedy of New York," the *Christian Science Monitor* reported. ". . . When he arrives, not just hands, but often bodies, are slammed together in frantic greeting." As a vocal peace candidate, Kennedy would pressure Nixon to be more precise in his position on the war. But more important than their specific differences on issues was the concern that Nixon would be overwhelmed by the Kennedy nostalgia. With Kennedy's entry into the race, Nixon "seemed himself more like Johnson," Witcover wrote, "—the operator, wheeler-dealer. Tricky Dick." There was considerable speculation that Republicans might choose to nominate Nelson Rockefeller, a more charismatic challenger.[51]

As he closed in on the nomination, Nixon became more aggressive. Witcover recalled that Nixon was intent on "painting [Kennedy] as a spoiled little rich kid who would commit any deed to get what he wanted." As he had done against John, Nixon drew attention to "Bobby's" youth, inexperience, and immaturity. At the same time he presented himself as the true instrument of change, describing Kennedy, McCarthy, and Humphrey as "three peas in a pod, prisoners of the policies of the past." Occasionally Nixon's comments were less heavy-handed. He used humor to deflate Robert just as John had mocked *him* in 1960. He predicted that Kennedy would win the Democratic nomination "by a hair—or two or whatever he can spare."[52]

On the night of the California primary, Nixon's daughter Julie called him at his Key Biscayne home to tell him that Kennedy had been shot. Nixon described Kennedy's death as "a ghastly tragedy." In the short term he benefited politically from Kennedy's death. Rockefeller's campaign stalled as a result of a campaign moratorium. With Kennedy gone, Nixon was not pressed for details of his proposed policies on the Vietnam War. The nomination of Humphrey became a certainty, providing Nixon with an easier target than he would have had against Kennedy. In the long term, however, the death of another Kennedy haunted Nixon, renewing questions of what might have been and heightening a sense that America was again robbed of its proper destiny. For much of the public, the future was embodied by Edward Kennedy. Nixon entered the presidency in 1969 behind the paths of two ghosts, a fortified myth, and a new rival. [53]

Nixon in the White House

RICHARD NIXON brought to his presidency an eight-year fixation with the Kennedy image. In the whole cloth of the Nixon presidency, the Kennedy legend was a mere thread. But by following the Kennedy strain, the suspicion, bitterness, and resentment that burdened Nixon can be uniquely appreciated. As president he emulated John Kennedy's image while denigrating his reputation. At the same time he turned his attention to Edward Kennedy, the man who embodied those attributes that had humiliated him in 1960 and who now threatened his reelection. When it became clear that Kennedy would not run for president, Nixon transferred his anxieties for the "mystique" onto the Democratic nominee, George McGovern, a former second-echelon New Frontiersman. "Kennedy," Nixon's speechwriter William Safire neatly summarized. "The name was a memory, a challenge, and danger to Nixon men: A reminder of the 1960 defeat, a constant criterion held unfairly to today's President by people who like to compare him with a myth, and a genuine threat to his reelection."[1]

In the White House, Nixon's feeling of competition with the Kennedy image was immediate. According to Herbert Klein, the president-elect "spent more time than he would admit studying" Kennedy's inauguration and ceremonies. His address had marked points of similarity with Kennedy's and was judged by Garry Wills a "hand-me-down speech from the New Frontier." During his first term Nixon occasionally cited Kennedy during his speeches. He was particularly drawn to Kennedy's cold war rhetoric, though his own policy of détente was a vast departure from the Kennedy-Johnson years. Sometimes he tried to distinguish his foreign policies from Kennedy's. When Democrats accused him of maintaining the status quo, he instructed H. R. Haldeman, "Here is where our people should be talking about our bold foreign policy initiatives never undertaken by JFK, et al." In general, however, Nixon found it useful to cite Kennedy as a means of bolstering support for his foreign policies and keeping liberal Democrats in check. Speaking before Congress in November 1969 he tried to shore up Democratic support for the war by recalling his early relationship with John Kennedy in the House of Representatives: "The record will show that John F. Kennedy and Richard Nixon—on those great issues . . . involving security of the nation, involving foreign policy—voted together." He linked his efforts to secure a nuclear treaty with the USSR with those initiated by Kennedy. Accused of failing to consult Congress during the U.S. invasion of Cambodia, Nixon defended himself by recalling Kennedy's neglect of Congress during the Cuban missile crisis. He avoided mentioning Kennedy when he thought it counterproductive. Planning his first trip to Berlin, he refused to cite Kennedy's famous appearance at the Berlin wall. "Kennedy got the Berliners all excited," Nixon explained, "then let them down."[2]

Of all the areas in which the "mystique" influenced Nixon, he was most drawn to Kennedy's ability to project a flattering personal image. Polls showing Kennedy as America's most popular president since Franklin Roosevelt confirmed Nixon's long-held belief that the late president owed his popularity to shrewd image management. "H[alde-man] Note! This shows the effectiveness of JFK's PR," he wrote. Nixon yearned for a favorable personal image reminiscent of Kennedy. Continuing his long-standing practice of charting his public image, he once wrote a lengthy memorandum detailing the "definitive image" he hoped to project. Many of the compiled qualities were derivative of Kennedy's public image: "courage," "openness," "effective handling of press conferences—TV," "warmth," "takes attacks by press, et al.," "compassionate," "intelligent," "optimistic," "honesty," "vitality," "youth," "enjoyment," "excitement," "glamour," and "concern for problems of the poor, youth, minorities, and [the] average person." "Mystique," Nixon told Haldeman, "is more important than content."[3]

Although Nixon devoted considerable energy to criticizing Kennedy's excessive attention to style, he now tried to emulate Kennedy's elegance and class. He changed the uniforms of the White House security force to regal outfits complete with plumes. He was frustrated when the news media failed to acknowledge that White House social events were as classy as those of the Kennedy years. Kennedy had successfully balanced his glamorous image with a more masculine aura of toughness. Likewise, White House aides looked to publicize Nixon's "cool decision-making" during the Jordan-Syria confrontation, recalling how Kennedy's handling of the Cuban missile crisis "made good reading and helped him enormously in terms of drawing attention to dealing with crises." Citing White House–sponsored documentaries after the Cuban missile crisis, Haldeman recommended similar promotion of Nixon's prowess following the Cambodian invasion. He urged his staff to champion Nixon's courage as the New Frontiersmen had promoted Kennedy's, arguing, "We have a much better case to sell." Kenneth Khachigian recommended that Nixon attend an NAACP convention, recalling Kennedy's appearance before the Houston Ministerial Association in 1960. Kennedy "got the press slobbering all over him for his 'courage.' In fact, this was a public relations coup for JFK. For the same reasons, I recommend RN going right into the lion's den."[4]

To convey Nixon's personal qualities, aides borrowed from Kennedy's strategy of having staff members speak highly of their president. When Nixon failed to achieve the level of Kennedy's success, he, like Johnson before him, measured his staff's salesmanship against the New Frontiersmen. "Why can't we get some of this kind of reaction out publicly?" he once asked John Ehrlichman. "The Kennedy's [sic] always did so." He was particularly impressed with the Kennedy staff's capacity to obscure the president's shortcomings. "What the Kennedy people did with the failures of Kennedy," Nixon told Haldeman, "we've got to do at least as well with the successes." As much as Nixon tried to impress a favorable personal image upon the public, he never successfully measured up to John Kennedy. "Jack Kennedy had only to stand up to project a charismatic image of 'class,'" Haldeman lamented.[5]

Like Lyndon Johnson, Nixon blamed his inability to project a positive image partly on the press's attraction to the Kennedys. When reporters failed to praise his first speech on Vietnam in May 1969, he complained to Haldeman, "If JFK had made the speech they would have all been ecstatic." In February 1971 Nixon was irritated when a Gallup poll of college students ranked him fourth after John Kennedy, Martin Luther King, and Robert Kennedy. "H[aldeman]," Nixon wrote. "Result of the liberal bias in teaching and media." When Nixon duplicated a television format created by JFK, "A Conversation with the President," Patrick Buchanan complained in an anonymous letter to the New York Times about Tom Wicker's column on the soft line of questioning Nixon received. Unlike Nixon's program, Buchanan wrote, Kennedy's was "cut and edited by White House aides solicitous for JFK's image." Buchanan charged that Wicker's criticism was politically inspired because he "preferred the Kennedy-Johnson directions."[6]

Nixon's feelings of persecution from the Kennedy press were especially noticeable when he met with reporters. He was annoyed that his jokes during a Gridiron dinner were not received in the fawning manner that Kennedy's had been. Criticism about his few press conferences prompted Nixon to order quantitative comparisons with the Kennedy years. He consoled himself by contending that he treated the press with greater authenticity than Kennedy had. His memoranda expressed pride that, unlike Kennedy, he never planted a question, did not recognize favorite reporters, and preferred answering tough questions. He wanted Haldeman to publicize that "in preparing for press conferences the answers are not prepared so much as facts. . . . Preparing all the answers . . . was the Kennedy way. It is not our way." To compensate for the press's lack of praise for Nixon, aides often congratulated him after his television appearances, sometimes assuring him that he had been just as effective as Kennedy. After one press conference, Charles Colson was impressed with Nixon's "short and crisp" answers, likening the style to Kennedy's: "I remember looking back at the old Kennedy film; one of the things that impressed me was not what he said but how he said it. A quick, sharp answer gives the impression of being very much in control and, especially on Vietnam question, it makes the President appear less defensive."[7]

Nixon's frustration with the Kennedy press was succinctly expressed when he received a clipping from the *Richmond News Leader*. Its editorial noted that, after Nixon's first year in office, most pundits had concluded he "has done a so-so job as President, and suggest that you cannot expect anything more than a mediocre president from a mediocre man. In many of the commentaries, one senses the writer's vague pining for the halcyon days of John Kennedy." The editorial confirmed what Nixon had suspected. "I agree that this [is] probably the general tone of the commentary & expected because of make up of press," Nixon wrote in the margins to Haldeman, "—but I hope you are following through with unprecedented letters to editor, columnists, & commentators taking up the cudgels for our side." He ordered a progress report on the letter writing campaign in two weeks. "To those who say it won't help, reply, 'Remember Agnew,'" Nixon wrote, recalling the success of the campaign of intimidation advanced by Vice-President Spiro Agnew's public attack against the so-called liberal news media.[8]

Nixon's implementation of a bogus letter-writing campaign was a strategy that dated at least to the 1960 campaign. It was just a minor volley in his extensive war against the news media that ultimately involved wiretapping reporters, auditing their tax returns, and a general policy of harassment. The letter-writing campaign was partly designed, too, to preempt the Kennedys' influence on the news media. Less than one month into his presidency, Nixon informed his aides that the letter campaign "gives us what Kennedy had in abundance—a constant representation of letters to editor columns and very proper influence on the television commentators." "As I have pointed out ad infinitum," he explained on another occasion, "[complaining to the press] was automatic reaction on the part of the Kennedy adherents and it should be an automatic reaction wherever we are concerned. . . ."[9]

Nixon's difficulties with the news media would have existed even if he had not followed in Kennedy's footsteps. The Kennedy element merely exacerbated a long-standing bitterness dating back to the Hiss case. When Robert Novak published an article noting press opposition to Nixon, the president circulated the piece among his advisers, believing it "really puts the frosting on the cake as far as the theory I have held to since the 1960 campaign." As part of his expressed strategy "to discredit the national media among their readers and viewers," Nixon targeted reporters whom he thought were friendly with the Kennedys. Nick Thimmesch, who usually supported Nixon, aroused suspicion for merely writing favorably about the Kennedy family's philanthropic efforts on behalf of mental retardation. "You don't suppose that [the Kennedys] have gotten to our friend Nick?" Colson asked Buchanan. "I have never seen him say a good thing about them before. This concerns me somewhat." On the other hand, Buchanan encouraged White House cooperation with Jeffrey Hart because he showed "the instinct for the jugular" when he wrote about the Kennedys. That both Nixon and Johnson found the so-called Kennedy press troublesome showed the "mystique's" capacity to transcend ideological and partisan lines. The real issue was not the monolithic nature of the "Kennedy press" but insecurities of the presidents.[10]

Like the Johnson advisers, some Nixon staff members grew frustrated about competing against the Kennedy image. While some aides advised Nixon to project Kennedyesque qualities, others sought to persuade him of the futility of such efforts, citing the bias of the press and the image's incompatibility with Nixon's personality. "Kennedy is the classic example [of generating support through his personal image and charisma]," Colson explained to Haldeman. "Despite a mediocre Administration, an undistinguished record in foreign affairs and a poor legislative tally he might well have been re-elected in 1964; if so it would probably have been largely due to the successful mystique he created (with the help of a friendly press)." In anticipation of Nixon's reelection, Colson thought it was "foolish and counter productive to try to build a Kennedy-type mystique—there isn't time, the press would never let us get away with it nor is it necessarily a very reliable source of political strength. A President doesn't have to be likeable, have a sense of humor or even love children. It is important only that his personal qualities engender confidence." Buchanan too advised the president to stop trying to match the Kennedy image. "I have never been convinced that Richard Nixon, Good Guy, is our long suit," he wrote, "to me we are simply not going to charm the American people; we are not going to win it on 'style' and we ought to forget playing ball in the Kennedys' court." It was a mistake to sell Nixon through his "personality" because "even the most attractive and energetic and charming personalities don't last very long." Ray Price warned that, while such candidates as Robert Kennedy could "persuade large numbers of voters they're the Messiah" and project "charisma—star quality, sex appeal, celebrity status," a "backlash" could result wherein the "same qualities that contribute to the intensity of their support also contribute to the intensity of their opposition." Indeed, Price wanted to encourage an anti-Kennedy image. He hoped to contrast the "beautiful people" image associated with Jacqueline Kennedy Onassis with Pat Nixon's more conventional image: "I suspect that a lot of people today, comparing the two, might suddenly come to realize how refreshing it is to have a working, gracious, involved, concerned and mature First Lady, rather than a frivolous pleasure-seeker from Camelot."[11]

White House staff seemed to have as much trouble defining Richard Nixon as Nixon himself did. After 1960 he had borrowed from Kennedy's images and strategies to remodel himself, to make himself more appealing to those who wanted their president to be pleasing. Once he was president, it proved difficult to sustain the effort, but his need to measure up to the Kennedy image persisted. Nixon thought John Kennedy was "more ruthless" than he was, but, as he told Haldeman, Kennedy "came through as the warm, human guy sponsoring the arts, loving his family, and all that kind of stuff." Wanting to be liked, not just respected, Nixon turned to the image of a man who was admired more than any other president. Whether these traits were authentic to his personality was probably of little concern to him, for he was convinced that Kennedy himself had manufactured a similarly false persona. But many of the qualities Nixon wished to project stretched credulity, as some aides rightly noted.[12]

If Nixon truly believed he was identifiable with the Kennedyesque qualities he wished to project, he was confused about who he was. Johnson had enough sense of himself to know when he wasn't being "real." He loathed having to appeal to intellectuals, or to pretend to be interested in art and literature. He may not have liked his shadowy traits, but he knew that manipulation, bluffing, and grandiosity were part of his being. Nixon's misconceptions pointed to a poor sense of self-identity and unrealistic expectations for image management. While most people identify with personalities, real or fictitious, Nixon seemed to feel the need to invent a personality to experience himself as president. An admirer of Abraham Lincoln, Theodore Roosevelt, and Woodrow Wilson, Nixon often invoked their memory or considered their qualities when faced with difficult decisions. But in conveying an appealing personal image and style, Nixon turned to Kennedy. Like Walter Mitty, he acted out the role of president based on an idealized concept of what a hip, contemporary president ought to be.[13]

Nixon's infatuation with the Kennedy image reaffirmed a new trend in the American presidency. He was learning what Johnson had: Kennedy's image was so salient and appealing as to alter the expectations of symbolic leadership. Effective governing required not only the ability to move legislation and make difficult decisions but the capacity to project sex appeal, wit, grace, class, charm, and glamour. In other words, it helped if our presidents reminded people of Kennedy, or at least appeared somewhat consistent with attributes that the public sorely missed since the passing of his presidency. Clearly the desire for likable leaders has its origins well before Kennedy, reflecting trends in mass communications since Theodore Roosevelt. The slogan "I Like Ike" was the most recent manifestation of this prerequisite before the Kennedy presidency. But if Kennedy had looked like William Howard Taft, with the personality of Herbert Hoover, his influence on the presidency might have been negligible.

He had left little else that interested Nixon save the Vietnam War. JFK's pleasing personality, his transformation through television into an intimate stranger beloved by millions of Americans—even those who rejected his programs—made for a legacy that was increasingly richer in style than in substance. "JFK did nothing but appeared great," Nixon told Haldeman. "LBJ did everything and appeared terrible." Nixon succinctly understood the transition for which Kennedy was responsible and the problems it bode for his own presidency.[14]

II Nixon chose numerous ways to compete against the Kennedy image. One was to aspire to Kennedy's qualities. Another was to lower Kennedy's esteem, to deflate the Kennedy myth by exposing its realities. Of course, by the 1970s Kennedy's historical reputation had undergone serious revision apart from Nixon's contributions. The public had grown uneasy about manipulations of public images, a trend reflected by the popular book *The Selling of the President* and the film *The Candidate*. Early critics had addressed the Kennedy family's extensive effort to protect John Kennedy's reputation. The Kennedys themselves encouraged scrutiny through incidents that cast doubt on their character, including Jacqueline Kennedy's marriage to Aristotle Onassis and Edward Kennedy's accident at Chappaquiddick. Questions of character soon were extended to John Kennedy's infidelity. In light of the civil rights violence of the 1960s and the failure of Vietnam, conservatives and New Left critics alike viewed Kennedy as a rather conventional politician, holding him accountable for America's existing failures. Critics accused him of encouraging a political style and cult of personality that facilitated the growth of an imperial presidency. The nature of the writings, historian Kent Beck wrote in 1974, "leaped from contemporary debate to favorable (but not uncritical remembrance) and fundamental revisionism in less than fifteen years."[15]

While diminished, the "mystique" surrounding John Kennedy was scarcely undone. Kennedy may have had his detractors, but there were still millions of believers. A 1973 Harris poll showed that he was regarded as the nation's most popular president by an overwhelming margin. Residual affection or hope was extended to Edward Kennedy, who was repeatedly shown to be the Democrats' most popular candidate in 1972. Within this ambivalent historical setting, Nixon too responded to the Kennedy myth in a mixed fashion. He showed public deference to John and Robert Kennedy's memory while privately fueling revisionism.[16]

Nixon was not compelled to publicly honor the Kennedys as Johnson was. On occasion, however, he was placed in the awkward position of having to acknowledge Kennedy memorials. Shortly after his inauguration it was learned that Johnson had deleted from the Pentagon's 1970 budget $431,000 worth of funding for the Arlington National Cemetery memorial to Robert F. Kennedy. Johnson had shifted the request to the presidential contingency fund, leaving Nixon to decide whether to appropriate money. Patrick Moynihan, a Kennedyite hired by the Nixon administration in deference to liberal Democrats, suggested the president get involved in this "delicate and pained matter." "I fear it sounds altogether too much like the thirty-sixth President I came to know," Moynihan wrote, implying that Johnson had intentionally burdened Nixon with the problem. Nixon secured the funding, then instructed, "We ought to get some credit in the press."[17]

About two years later Nixon deliberated over how best to respond to the opening of the John F. Kennedy Center for the Performing Arts in Washington. Charles Colson advised Nixon not to attend. "The first night should be turned over to the Kennedy's [sic]; that should be their performance," he wrote. But Colson was moved less by grace than image, for he anticipated that the Kennedys would be embarrassed by the debut of Leonard Bernstein's opening score, *Mass*. Colson called the piece "anti-establishment and anti-war," and he relished the contradiction between the music and the event. "This after all is the John F. Kennedy Center and it was during his Administration that the Vietnam War began," he wrote. "Let's let the Kennedys suffer the wrath of bad taste that may well be left from Bernstein's score." Wanting the Kennedys to "stew in their own juice," he pushed for minimal recognition. Should the press not criticize the Kennedys, Colson assured Nixon that "we can carefully though outside sources, engineer the kind of reaction we want." To avoid criticism that "we are snubbing the Center," he suggested that Nixon merely send "token" representatives. The White House offered Jacqueline Kennedy Onassis the presidential box for the opening, explaining that the president would not attend because he wanted the focus to be on the Kennedys.[18]

Some critics viewed Nixon's absence as transparent. "Did he, after all, think he could steal the show from all the glittery people bound to be there?" Garry Wills asked in an article that crossed Nixon's desk. "Or, if it was his intention to give Mrs. Onassis special honor, why not invite her to the presidential box with the President in it (on the face of it, a higher honor)?" Wills concluded that Nixon avoided the opening not because he feared upstaging the event but because he knew the event would upstage him. Nixon scoffed at the failure of the press to criticize the opening. Privately he considered the Kennedy Center "the greatest eyesore" in Washington. When critics praised its architectural design, he took it as further evidence that the press held anything associated with the Kennedys in excessive esteem. "H[alde-man]," he wrote. "Compare this orgasm over this utter architectural monstrosity with the nit picking of the poor LBJ Library!"[19]

Although Nixon was sometimes compelled to show deference to the Kennedys, on one occasion he initiated a generous gesture. In early February 1971 he and Pat arranged for Jacqueline Kennedy Onassis and her two children to come to the White House for dinner and to view the official White House portrait of John Kennedy before its unveiling. For years Lyndon Johnson had tried unsuccessfully to coax Kennedy's widow to come to the White House. When Pat Nixon wrote to Jacqueline to inquire about her wishes for the official ceremony surrounding her late husband's portrait, the former First Lady suggested a private viewing, and the Nixons quickly accepted.[20]

Nixon handled the occasion with considerable "class." The White House kept the visit secret, banning reporters or photographers. Afterward, Jacqueline and her children wrote letters of appreciation. "A day I always dreaded," she wrote, "turned out to be one of the most precious ones I have spent with my children." Nixon handwrote two touching return letters to Kennedy's children. To John, Jr., he expressed his hope that "your visit to the House where you lived as a very young boy left pleasant memories." Writing to Caroline, Nixon recalled their conversation about her interest in history and Caroline's disappointment with a teacher. "History is the best foundation for almost any profession," he wrote in a fatherly fashion, "but even more important you will find the really most fascinating reading as you grow older is in history and biography."[21]

Having Kennedy's wife and children in the White House must have been emotionally trying for Nixon as well as for Jacqueline. For him it was a reminder of a difficult period in his life, for he resented Kennedy and his emerging myth. Now he found himself entertaining his widow and children. Despite his own discomfort, he was generous and empathic. He served as a caretaker, allowing the survivors to experience an element of closure. Reflecting on John Kennedy's death, Nixon once wrote that he was reminded of his feelings after the death of his two brothers, and how he wished there was something he could have done to ease the grief of the closely knit Kennedy family. Jacqueline's visit not only afforded her and her children a sense of resolution, it also gave Nixon an opportunity to resolve his own feelings.

In some ways Jacqueline's visit was an intensely private occasion. Indeed, the content of the letters among Jacqueline, the children, and Nixon were not made public for some twenty years. But the occasion was not without political overtones. White House aides cautiously monitored public reaction. "Truly an outstanding move here in having Jackie in and just the initial reports look very good," Mort Allin reported to Haldeman. "One thing we might avoid—too much description by the WH of what a warm evening it was. That's been said now—should ride." He was concerned that "overkill" could prompt Kennedy loyalists to criticize the evening. Robert Odle agreed: "However, it might be pointed out quietly to friendly columnists that this is Mrs. Onassis' first visit since 1963 and that she refused LBJ's invitations. Is this the line to use?" Perhaps any president or his staff would have exploited the visit, but they nonetheless tainted an otherwise gracious gesture.[22]

Nixon too allowed his political self-interest to overwhelm his better nature. While writing touching letters to Kennedy's children, he also worked to disparage their father's memory. Sometimes his efforts were fleeting. Once, he sought to publicize a *Wall Street Journal* editorial, "Camelot Reappraised," citing New Left criticism of Kennedy's presidency. Nixon highlighted a paragraph that accused Kennedy of having "too much vigor and too little restraint, too much grace and too little earthiness, too much eloquence and too little thoughtfulness, too much idealism and too little realism, too much flexibility and too little patience, too much brilliance and too little common sense." "This good line for us," Nixon wrote. Indeed, it recapitulated much of what Nixon had said about Kennedy while he was alive. Sometimes Nixon specifically requested articles critical of Kennedy, including Henry Fairlie's lengthy critique, "Camelot Revisited: The Promises Led to Bloodshed and Despair." He highlighted sentences and paragraphs pertaining to the politics of expectation that Kennedy had created, his compromising social relationships with reporters, and the demeaning and dangerous public fascination for Kennedy's style. Later he read Fairlie's book *The Kennedy Promise* as well as other revisionist monographs on the Kennedy presidency. Not all the material critical of Kennedy got to Nixon. Buchanan tried to forward to the president an article that detailed "some astounding revelations" about Kennedy's extramarital activity, but Haldeman did not think it was worth Nixon's time.[23]

When counterrevisionists defended Kennedy's reputation, the White House responded in accordance with Nixon's instincts. Nixon staff members once created a letter to the editor of the New York Times critical of the accolades bestowed on the late president. An op-ed column by William V. Shannon had questioned the general "downgrading" of Kennedy's reputation by those who blamed him unjustly for the Vietnam War. The vast number of people who visited Kennedy's grave, Shannon wrote, were "wiser than his latter-day critics and their judgment will outlast today's disparagement." The White House drafted a letter to the editor critical of Shannon's column: "Because of JFK's indecision, incompetence and lack of resolve [during the Bay of Pigs], several thousand men lost their lives." Senator John Tower of Texas obliged the administration by signing his name to the letter. It was later published in the New York Times.[24]

The effort to diminish Kennedy's reputation often involved more sinister strategies. As Nixon initiated the controversial policy of expanding the Vietnam War into neighboring Cambodia, he, like Johnson, tried to offset liberal criticism by reminding the public of Kennedy's role in escalating the war. After former Kennedy aide Kenneth O'Donnell wrote that Kennedy intended to withdraw U.S. troops from Vietnam after winning the election in 1964, William Safire sought to turn the revelation against him. He recommended that someone outside the administration attack O'Donnell for "a misbegotten attempt to paint President Kennedy as a dove on Vietnam." "According to O'Donnell," Safire argued, tongue-in-cheek, "Kennedy was a weak and cynical President—a political coward. This is a falsification of history for political purposes and the worst kind of disloyalty from a trusted assistant."[25]

Among Nixon's more deceitful and elaborate assaults against Kennedy's memory was his attempt to link Kennedy unequivocally to the Diem assassination. The Nixon White House investigated the coup, seeking to prove the president's gut suspicion that Kennedy had advance knowledge. If proven, his complicity in the murder of a foreign leader (and a fellow Catholic) would seriously undermine the Kennedy legend and keep Democratic critics of the war off balance. Publicly Nixon often promoted the unproven charge that Kennedy was a coconspirator, and he argued the less disputed point that Diem's death led to U.S. involvement in Vietnam. Lacking hard evidence against Kennedy, White House operatives led by E. Howard Hunt interviewed participants in the coup and examined 240 State Department cables from April through November 1963. When they found no definitive proof, Colson advised Hunt to "improve" the existing cables, and Hunt subsequently pieced together a forged cable that implicated Kennedy. Colson then tried to sell the story to *Life* magazine, but its editors first wanted to see the cable. He abandoned the project, fearing that a direct examination of the document would reveal its inauthenticity.[26]

A further effort to diminish Kennedy's memory came in June 1971 when the *New York Times* began publishing excerpts from a secret Pentagon study of the Vietnam War, the so-called Pentagon Papers. The papers illustrated the deception surrounding the Gulf of Tonkin incident in 1964 and showed that contingency plans for U.S. entry into the war were developed while President Johnson was promising voters that American combat troops would not be sent to Vietnam. The papers further showed a continuity of planning for the war between the Kennedy and Johnson administrations. Nixon later explained that he wished to use the papers to develop "ammunition against anti-war critics, many of whom were the same men who, under Kennedy and Johnson, had led us into the Vietnam morass in the first place."[27]

Colson sent Haldeman a lengthy memo proposing that the White House help release documents to show how Nixon had changed course on the war in an honest fashion. "The Kennedy-Johnson papers give us a real opportunity in this regard in that it permits us to do things that will be in vivid, sharp public contrast with the whole Kennedy-Johnson affair," he wrote. He also wanted to "subtley [sic], but very effectively encourage and fuel the division within the Democratic ranks *without* getting caught. . . ." One strategy was to "plant and try to prove the thesis that Bobby Kennedy was behind the preparation of these papers because he planned to use them to overthrow Lyndon Johnson (I suspect that there may be more truth than fantasy to this)." Colson later enjoyed Dean Acheson's criticism of John Kennedy as uninformed, indecisive, and lacking in leadership skills. He forwarded Acheson's published criticisms ro Nixon, believing it "to be a most helpful follow up to the revelations of the Pentagon Papers." By March 1973 Nixon asked Haldeman if it was a good time "to surface the Pentagon Papers on Kennedy and Vietnam in a more vicious way. . . ."[28]

In another attempt to cast doubt on Kennedy's reputation, Nixon ordered operatives to find information related to the Bay of Pigs invasion. Early in his administration, Nixon made several requests to the CIA to secure relevant files on the affair. Convinced that the forwarded records were incomplete, he personally summoned CIA director Richard Helms and again requested the full files. But Nixon's motives were murky. Having been involved in the preliminary planning of the invasion, he had a personal stake in wanting to see the records. Perhaps he hoped to discover the extent to which Kennedy was briefed on the impending invasion during the 1960 campaign. He may simply have wanted additional information with which to discredit Kennedy. Hunt, who had been involved in the planning of the invasion while working for the CIA, once told Colson that the truth surrounding the Bay of Pigs invasion could destroy Kennedy.[29]

The time and effort that Nixon devoted to battering Kennedy's reputation suggested a distracted and embittered president. His assault on the Kennedy legend contained a measure of cynicism that went beyond Johnson's response. When Johnson blamed Kennedy for the war, he did so more to defend himself against Robert than to settle old scores. Nor did he and his aides manufacture evidence to rewrite history. Not until after his failed presidency did Johnson publicly insult John Kennedy's memory, but he did so in passing and never to the systematic extent that Nixon employed. Nixon's revisionism seemed driven by grudges deep within his political soul. He did not split the Kennedy's into "good" or "bad" forces as Johnson had. The Kennedys, dead and living, were his enemies on all fronts. Although he had the capacity to separate his personal feelings from his political interests, more often than not his reaction to the Kennedy myth revealed a president burdened by past resentments that were now extended to the myth's living embodiment.

III Emerging from two and a half months of seclusion after Robert Kennedy's death, Edward Kennedy announced in August 1968 that he intended to "pick up a fallen standard" of his brothers. The *New York Times* assessed the speech as having "erased any doubt about [Kennedy] being a future contender for national leadership." Almost immediately after assuming office in January 1969, Nixon feared that Kennedy and his cohorts in the news media and the Democratic party would undermine his presidency and prevent his reelection. Sensitive to how the war had destroyed Lyndon Johnson's presidency, Nixon determined not to be similarly undone. He took extreme measures to build popular support for his foreign policies, to minimize leaks, and to retaliate against his critics. Kennedy was the most obvious of all Nixon's "enemies." Like Johnson and his obsession for Robert, Nixon saw Edward as the leader of the news media, the antiwar movement, and all the liberal elements that threatened him. Unable to dent the Kennedy legend, Nixon sought to separate Edward from the mythic ideals of his brothers.[30]

By most reasonable standards Nixon's concern for Kennedy should have been alleviated by the events at Chappaquiddick on July 18, 1969. The next day the president met with his inner circle to outline their response. According to Haldeman's notes, the White House would claim publicly that its interest in the accident was *"completely non-personal."* Nixon determined to show no outward reaction. He concluded that Kennedy was "obviously" drunk, "let her drown," and "ran from accident." He rightly feared, however, that the "mystique" might overshadow Kennedy's accountability, and he determined "to be sure he doesn't get away with it." The White House intended to pressure the news media thoroughly to investigate the story. "Put yourself in position if we were involved," Haldeman wrote cryptically, "play hard—terms of the facts." Nixon wanted to "really get dope on the girl, parents, etc., what they [were] doing together." Aides intended to use the accident to illustrate a consistent "flaw in character." The sordidness of the scandal confirmed that the Kennedys were hypocrites who took the high moral road in their public selves while engaging privately in debauchery.[31]

White House operatives secretly pursued various unsavory measures to investigate Chappaquiddick and further embarrass Kennedy. Privately Nixon seemed divided in his response. Initially he told Haldeman that the scandal "marks the end of Teddy" and "killed him as a presidential candidate." As he had with other Kennedy family members burdened by personal hardship, however, Nixon empathized with Edward. Anticipating a question from reporters related to Chappaquiddick, Nixon wrote a reminder for himself: "Defeat doesn't finish a man—quit—does. A man is not finished when he's defeated. He's finished when he quits." During a White House ceremony in early August, he consoled Kennedy, speaking briefly with him in the Oval Office about the need to muster personal strength to get through his crisis. While Kennedy appreciated the gesture, he was amused to see an account of their brief meeting in the afternoon newspapers. To Nixon's pleasure, many of the reports forwarded to him confirmed that Kennedy's public image was damaged. John Crown speculated in the *Atlanta Journal* that if Kennedy were president during a nuclear attack he would likely become paralyzed by fear. "Devastating," Nixon wrote in the margin. Howard K. Smith of ABC News assessed the meaning of Chappaquiddick in terms of the "mystique," noting that "the heart of the concern over the accident is the fact that it is hard to meet the superhuman standard of a legend such as that which has grown up around the Kennedys." "A very accurate & honest report," Nixon wrote.[32]

Although Nixon received polls showing the damage to Kennedy from the scandal, he sensed that the public relations machinery that had obscured John Kennedy's failings would now serve Edward. When Senator Birch Bayh, referring to Chappaquiddick, told reporters that "young people are prone to forgive and forget," Nixon wrote in the margins, "The fix must be on." Later he wrote that he was aghast at Kennedy's poor public explanation and the "mystique's" capacity to defy expected political equations. "I could not help thinking that if anyone other than a Kennedy had been involved and had given such a patently unacceptable explanation, the media and the public would not have permitted him to survive in public life," Nixon wrote. He was not altogether wrong.[33]

Two months after Chappaquiddick, Nixon was convinced that Kennedy intended to distract the public from his own problems by criticizing the administration. He pursued various efforts to out-maneuver Kennedy's supposed public relations effort. On September 20, in his first major policy statement after Chappaquiddick, Kennedy accused Nixon of making only "token" withdrawals of American troops from Vietnam and of pursuing a policy that leads "to war, and war, and more war." Nixon highlighted the criticisms, asking in the margins, "May be [a] declaration of war?" "We must get out speeches & articles to answer this," he instructed. "Some of our leaders & some columnists. Give me a *battle plan*." In a follow-up memo Nixon thought Kennedy was making a "very clever" attempt to "divert attention" from Chappaquiddick. "It is absolutely essential

that we react insurmountably and powerfully to this blunt attack."
Among his suggestions Nixon ordered "a major mailing-out to editors
and columnists in Massachusetts."[34]

Following revelations of the My Lai massacre in Vietnam in late
1969, a news summary noted that Kennedy was awaiting the court
martials and would demand that a commission investigate South
Vietnamese civilian deaths. Nixon instructed Haldeman to "see that
our total P.R. capabilities are ready for this (particularly the right
Buchanan, Nofziger, Agnew, etc.). . . . He & his group should be hit
hard on running down the U.S." Despite Nixon's efforts, a February
news summary noted that Kennedy's "political stock has swung
sharply upward"; time was eroding memories of Chappaquiddick and
bringing renewed speculation about his presidential potential. High-
lighting the summary, Nixon wrote, "The wish is probably father to
the thought. But a major rebuilding job is going on. Our people
should do what they can to blunt it."[35]

Like Johnson's efforts to hold Robert Kennedy accountable for a
war initiated by John, Nixon was mindful of Edward's attempts to
distance himself from his brother's less attractive legacy. He instructed
his aides to publicize how "those who got us into the war are now
trying to sabotage Nixon's efforts to get us out." When Kennedy
contended that the president preferred violence over a peaceful
solution to the war, Nixon demanded his "charges be answered
immediately." He wanted a plan to have "our own spokesman" refute
Kennedy with appropriate media coverage. Acting on behalf of the
administration, Senator Robert Dole argued that given Edward's
connection with the Kennedy-Johnson administrations, he "should
never accuse anyone of having blood on his hands." "Good," Nixon
wrote beside the news summary.[36]

Nixon continued to view Kennedy as "the most formidable
Democratic nominee in 1972," aware of the "mystique's" capacity to
transcend reason. He knew polls could not gauge intangible elements
and he sometimes questioned their accuracy. Although he thought he
could defeat either Edmund Muskie or Hubert Humphrey, a campaign
against Kennedy "would be much more difficult to predict because it
would involve so many emotional elements." Determined to diminish
Kennedy's noble aura, the White House found ways to embarrass
him. In November Kennedy traveled to France to attend the funeral
of Charles de Gaulle. A British tabloid reported that he "danced until
dawn" with an Italian divorcée at a Paris nightclub the night before
the funeral. The tabloid published a photograph of Kennedy with a

thirty-five-year-old Italian princess, speculating that Americans feared its publication in the United States because it would have "catastrophic effects on Kennedy's career." Nixon asked in the margins, "Will it be?" Colson discussed the matter with Nixon and was able to convince the weekly tabloid *National Enquirer* to publish the photograph. "It stuck a knife into Kennedy." Haldeman recalled. "One hundred points on the Oval Office chart... The President loved the picture."[37]

Nixon continued to monitor Kennedy's capacity to embody the "mystique." In March he reviewed a news summary noting that Kennedy's appeal was now "very weak due to Chappaquiddick; unfavorable comparisons with his brothers; and resentment that the Kennedys feel they should have another President." On the second anniversary of Chappaquiddick, a Harris poll was brought to Nixon's attention showing that 51 percent of the public did not believe Kennedy was qualified to be president. By a margin of eleven percentage points, a plurality believed Kennedy "is not in the same league with his older brothers." Kennedy now suffered from a form of comparison that had plagued Johnson and Nixon.[38]

By the spring and summer of 1971 White House aides were divided in their estimations of Kennedy's viability. Some advisers hoped that Kennedy would win the nomination, believing him more vulnerable than moderate Democrats like Humphrey or Muskie. Convinced that Kennedy was *"running actively for the President,"* Buchanan listed his assets: "Charm, 'commitment,' affinity with the young, polish, Kennedy looks, mystique, the Myth, charisma along the campaign trail." On the other hand, Buchanan thought, he lacked intellectual depth and had a tendency "to react somewhat hotly to attack." In a repeat of the strategy Nixon planned against JFK in 1960, Buchanan advised that either Agnew or Dole "unleash a stinging attack" against Edward so "we could see how he reacts." Moreover, he wanted Edward "portrayed as too reckless, too immature, too irresponsible, at his age, to be President of the United States." Buchanan suggested identifying Kennedy with "the Left and the Radical Kids" to diminish his appeal among centrist Democrats. "The more he acts like Brother Bobby the better off we are;" Buchanan wrote, "the less he acts like brother John, the better off we are."[39]

Buchanan regarded Kennedy's capacity to evoke the "mystique" as both a blessing and a burden. "Socially, Kennedy is out of touch with the political mood," he wrote. "The Jet Set, Swinger, See-Through

Blouse cum Hot Pants crowd, the Chappaquiddick Hoe-down and Paris highjinks—the more publicity they all get, the better." Still, Kennedy would remind voters of a golden age. "Since EMK will be trafficking on the JFK myth," he wrote, "it would be well to document JFK's tough line on Defense, foreign policy, Vietnam, Europe, etc. over against EMK's positions—to provide conservative Democrats with some rationale for abandoning the little brother of their hero." Thus Buchanan adopted against Edward a strategy similar to the one Johnson had designed against Robert—to show the incumbent president as closer to John Kennedy's policies than his brother.[40]

By the fall of 1971, news reports about Kennedy's political moves flowed regularly across the president's desk. "You still hear some people asking if you would buy a car from somebody like Nixon," columnist Mike Royko wrote. "I wish that the same people, just once, would ask if you would ride in a car with Edward Kennedy." Nixon ordered Colson to circulate the column "broadly." When Kennedy toured the West and upper Midwest, evoking memories of his brother's campaigns, aides reconsidered whom they preferred as the Democratic nominee. Colson anticipated that Kennedy would win the nomination. But he felt confident that he would go "downhill" if Nixon could remain above the battle and "demonstrate by contrast [Kennedy's] immaturity against the President's leadership."[41]

Concerned that some Nixon aides were "actually looking forward to Kennedy as the Democratic nominee as 'easiest to beat,'" Safire devised "Kennedy's Victory Scenario." Kennedy, he warned, would likely invoke his brothers to obscure his failure at Chappaquiddick. "Teddy will constantly harp on the brother's fallen torch theme," he wrote. "Not subtly, either." The senator had recently told a reporter, "We Kennedys can't make plans." Such comments served as "a sledgehammer, strictly emotional, playing on the guilt feelings of many Americans, and because it is bad taste does not make it bad politics." Safire predicted that Kennedy would note how John and Robert "underwent a deep sea-change" during their careers. "Similarly, the story will go, Teddy went from the high-living, irresponsible boy pre-Chappaquiddick, to the 'man of the family' after being deeply sobered by that tragedy." Edward could be expected to "break his silence on Chappaquiddick" much in the manner that John Kennedy "faced up" to the Catholic issue during his appearance before the Houston Ministers Conference. Later "a public yearning for a Nixon-Kennedy rematch on television would be well-nigh irresistible."

"Ducking or delaying would only play up their 'courage' pitch, which would directly answer that loss of courage at the bridge." Emotional elements involving "national guilt" and "past assassinations" could cause late shifts in voter sentiment. The constant danger of a possible assassination attempt would further enhance Kennedy's image. "He will motorcade in Dallas," Safire predicted. "The 'old' Teddy ran away from trouble; the 'new' Teddy will not run away. He will prove his courage once and for all in Dallas, on the final weekend of the campaign."[42]

The lengthy and tortured memoranda from Nixon's staff about the Kennedy charisma, magic, passion, and charm sounded all too familiar. Change a name here and a date there, and one was back in the Johnson White House of 1968 or reading Nixon memos from the fall of 1960. If Nixon and his aides exaggerated Kennedy's potential, they were not alone. At the time few Democrats or political scribes thought Kennedy was as seriously handicapped by Chappaquiddick or by comparisons to his brothers as he eventually proved to be in 1980. Still, the strategies, deliberations, and meditations revealed confusion among Nixon and his men. They seemed entrapped by past images rather than liberated by new ones. Fighting ghosts, they responded more to the myth surrounding John and Robert than to the realities encumbering Edward. Brilliantly devious in terms of their other campaign operations, Nixon's political advisers could offer only warmed-over advice and tired strategies that had not worked in 1960 and, as Safire warned, might not work in 1972. Their expressed fears pointed to the resiliency of the "mystique." Despite the revisionist assessments of John Kennedy, and despite Chappaquiddick, many White House aides thought Edward embodied a legend that could negate the accomplishments of Nixon's first term. Ultimately, their fears went unrealized. For now, Kennedy was unwilling to take up the mantle. When another candidate did, the White House responded in kind.

IV While Edward Kennedy had prompted anxiety in the White House, the candidacy of George McGovern evoked a measure of joyful skepticism. Initially, Nixon's advisers gave the South Dakota senator little real chance of winning the nomination. Surely, they thought, Democrats would not nominate a man whose "radicalism" would alienate a large portion of white middle-class America. Nixon's strategists were less concerned with McGovern than with his Kennedy connection. His relative obscurity made them assume he was serving as a front for Edward, just as Johnson's advisers had regarded Eugene McCarthy as Robert's stalking-horse in 1968. Buchanan, for example, analyzed McGovern's chances strictly in terms of Edward Kennedy and his accompanying myth. McGovern's campaign was stalled, Buchanan reported in April 1971, because "he is appealing to voters who already have a popular, first-line, left-wing candidate in Edward Kennedy, a candidate who gives them near all the positions McGovern does—at the same time Kennedy offers the realistic hope of winning, with those positions—and returning Camelot as well."[43]

Contrary to such assumptions, McGovern was not a Kennedy sycophant willing to concede the nomination at Edward Kennedy's whim. But his campaign did signify an important transition in the political use of the Kennedy legend. He was the first presidential candidate outside the Kennedy family to advance himself at a national level by *credibly* embodying the idealism and spirit remembered in John and Robert Kennedy. When Johnson held his seance with the Kennedy legacy in 1964, critics treated his invocations as a manipulative effort to gain support from the Kennedy faction of the party. McGovern's sincerity in identifying himself with the Kennedy past was seldom questioned, except by Nixon and his advisers. He personified the best of what the public wanted to remember about John and Robert Kennedy while projecting the virtue lacking in Edward. He showed that a nominee could admire the Kennedys and project elements of the "mystique" without losing his own identity or feeling overshadowed by the myth he invoked.

McGovern gravitated naturally toward the Kennedy idealism. The son of a Methodist minister from South Dakota, he developed a deep sense of social compassion when, as a child, he watched New Deal programs help downtrodden farmers. He adhered to the "Social Gospel," a religious belief that a person's salvation depended upon service to others. Receiving his Ph.D. in history, he focused his studies on the struggle of labor unions. As he gradually entered into active politics, he supported idealistic and progressive candidates like Henry Wallace and Adlai Stevenson.[44]

After narrowly winning a seat in the House of Representatives from South Dakota's Fifth Congressional District in 1956, McGovern met John Kennedy for the first time during a dinner party in Washington, D.C. He knew that Kennedy was already considered presidential material, but he was unimpressed. "I didn't think he was as profound or as deep as some of the senators," he recalled in 1993. Turned off by Kennedy's conservativism, McGovern believed JFK lacked the record, experience, and knowledge to be president. McGovern was "startled" by Kennedy's sudden rise in national politics, but he did not resent his advancement.[45]

During McGovern's Senate campaign in 1960, he appeared with John Kennedy when the presidential nominee came to Sioux Falls. To McGovern's surprise, Kennedy gave a flat, uninspired speech on agriculture. "The first two or three times I heard him I couldn't really believe that he wasn't more impressive than that," he recalled. Eventually he grew to respect Kennedy's political skills and his handling of crowds. "But I had to be converted to Kennedy," he recalled. Indeed, it was Robert, not John, who initially engaged McGovern. Nixon carried South Dakota in a landslide in 1960, and the GOP bandwagon contributed to McGovern's defeat by a mere percentage point. Two days later the president-elect asked him to become director of the Food for Peace program. "Jack Kennedy literally rescued me from my political defeat," McGovern recalled. "I will treasure until the day I die the fact that he called me two days after the election. . . . I don't care what the motive was. The results on me were permanent. From that point on, my life was caught up with [the Kennedys]."[46]

During his two years with the administration, McGovern was disheartened by Kennedy's caution on domestic issues and his aggressive foreign policies in Vietnam and Cuba. The Bay of Pigs invasion particularly distressed McGovern. Thirty-two years later he confided that shortly before the invasion he had sent an anonymous letter to the *Washington Post* raising questions about America's involvement in Cuban affairs. "I didn't dare put my name on it," he recalled, signing instead his secretary's name. If McGovern suffered from youthful indiscretion, he nevertheless showed noteworthy independence.[47]

Although he sometimes disagreed with Kennedy's policies, Mc-Govern recalled that he admired Kennedy greatly. "I'm emphasizing the fact it took me a while [to appreciate Kennedy]," he qualified, "but there's no question that once I went to work for him, I was caught up in the excitement of the administration. It was a time of renewal and energy and optimism and self-confidence. And all those things were very infectious." When McGovern again pursued South Dakota's Senate seat in 1962, conservatives accused him of being a mere pawn of the Kennedys. McGovern did not hesitate to invoke the president. "I could not have escaped the Kennedy identification if I had wished to," he reasoned, "and I sensed that John Kennedy was now more popular in South Dakota than he had been in 1960." The president's charismatic appeal was stronger. "Is it really a handicap to South Dakota to have a Senator who is close to the President of the United States?" he asked audiences. Many voters might have thought so. McGovern won by only two hundred votes.[48]

Like many people who were fond of John Kennedy, McGovern liked to believe that things would have been better had Kennedy fulfilled his presidency. He speculated that Kennedy might have been an exception to traditional patterns of two-term presidents, that he would have enjoyed a more successful second term than first. With Kennedy winning by a wide margin against Goldwater in 1964, McGovern hypothesized, he would have had a mandate to pursue bolder initiatives, such as recognizing China and pursuing a more relaxed relationship with the Soviet Union. "It might very well be that once reelected, Kennedy had enough self-confidence and more self-esteem than either Johnson or Nixon did to find it easier to pull out of Vietnam." Kennedy's successors had "certain doubts about themselves" that Kennedy did not have, giving him the capacity to admit his mistakes. "But that's just pure speculation," McGovern conceded. "There's no hard evidence to that at all."[49]

For a Kennedy admirer, McGovern could be unusually critical. Ironically, many of his assessments, like those of New Left critics, were consistent with Nixon's. He was dismayed by Kennedy's aggression in Vietnam. He regarded the president's brinksmanship during the Cuban missile crisis as "the most appalling single thing in the Kennedy administration." He was disturbed by revelations about the administration's wiretaps against Martin Luther King. And he was distressed in the mid-1970s when he learned of the administration's sponsorship of assassination attempts against Castro. McGovern, however, never felt disillusioned with Kennedy. "I began with a certain amount of skepticism," he explained. "You can have great personal affection for a person, which I did for John Kennedy, and still speak critically as I have. I love that family. . . . But I look back on it and I see things that historically just don't measure up to what one would hope."[50]

In the spring of 1968 McGovern avoided openly endorsing Humphrey, McCarthy, or Robert Kennedy. But when introducing Kennedy at a rally in Sioux Falls, he offered unusually high praise, making clear his persuasion. Like millions of people, he was later frustrated and furious that "another Kennedy had been shot down just at the moment of his greatest triumph." But there were deeper emotions that haunted McGovern. Kennedy had told reporters that if McGovern rather than McCarthy had challenged Johnson, he would not have sought the nomination. "If I had entered the presidential race in late 1967," McGovern wondered, ". . . perhaps Robert Kennedy would still be alive." Asked specifically in 1993 if he was alluding to feelings of guilt, McGovern acknowledged, "There was some guilt." "I didn't brood on it," he added, "but it was just a disturbing thought that would recur from time to time." He soon found a practical and comforting solution.[51]

After Robert Kennedy's funeral, some key Kennedy aides approached McGovern, asking him to serve as a "replacement for Bobby" and to lead the Kennedy delegates at the Chicago convention. Upon receiving assurances that Edward would not run, McGovern announced his candidacy on August 10, a fortnight before the convention. He told supporters that, although he was standing in for Robert Kennedy, "I wear no claim to the Kennedy mantle, but I believe deeply in the twin goals for which Robert Kennedy gave his life—an end to the war in Vietnam and a passionate commitment to heal the divisions in our own society." McGovern was too modest and self-conscious to claim the Kennedy mantle outright. "I thought it was presumptuous for me to think that I could do that," he noted twenty-five years later. He knew he lacked the charisma, stature, and national appeal of the Kennedys. "I just didn't want to leave the impression that I thought I had been anointed to take Bobby's place," he recalled. "I'd have been glad if *others* thought that." McGovern wanted to distinguish between his commitment to Kennedy's goals and his claim to the "mystique." "The mantle includes the whole personal aura," he explained, "the personal charisma, the historical standing, the political power, the family—all of those things I felt might be reaching too far."[52]

McGovern recalled having "a good feeling" from his eighteen-day campaign. After the convention, pundits considered him a possible Democratic contender for 1972. More important, he felt at peace with himself. Asked whether he intended to assuage his guilt by standing in for Robert, McGovern initially rejected the psychological interpretation but quickly allowed, "If that was a factor, it must have been a subconscious factor. It may be that having been distressed about [Kennedy's death], that I saw [standing in for Robert] as a way to kind of redeem the situation in part. Just thinking about it, that *was* probably in the back of my mind."[53]

After the 1968 election McGovern considered running for president in 1972. He knew his chances were slim. While most observers viewed Edward Kennedy as the leading contender for the nomination, McGovern thought he might not run because of the traumas of the assassinations. He learned of Kennedy's accident at Chappaquiddick on his forty-seventh birthday. "That night," he wrote in his autobiography, "I sat for several hours... thinking alternately about Ted, about my own future," and about the moon landing that had also occurred that weekend. The past, the stars, and the future seemed to converge. "The next morning," he wrote, "when I awakened late with the sun streaming in my face, I experienced a vague feeling that I might well be the Democratic presidential nominee in 1972." McGovern remembered the scene vividly. "It just kind of dawned on me," he later noted. "Teddy's not going to be able to run with this thing. And who else is there?... I'm probably going to be the nominee in '72."[54]

McGovern increasingly felt his political destiny intertwined with the Kennedys. He saw in Kennedy qualities that he identified with himself—a self-depreciating sense of humor, a love of history and historical analogies, a capacity for restraint, and a distaste for hyperbole. After standing in for Robert, the sensation grew. "There's no question that there was a feeling of us being part of a common movement and a common effort," McGovern recalled. "I sensed it among my supporters, too, that a lot of them saw me as trying to pick up the Kennedy banner." Indeed, he recalled "a couple of dreams of the Kennedys... in which both of them figured in it." Now, with the occurrence of Chappaquiddick, McGovern had a vague sense of predestination. By 1972 his identity with the Kennedys went beyond ideology and idealism. The Kennedys, it seemed, were part of his essence, a connection that Nixon found troubling.[55]

V   Unwilling to believe that McGovern's candidacy was for real, and suspicious of his link to the Kennedys, Nixon continued to monitor Edward's popularity throughout the primaries and looked to blunt his appeal. He ordered the circulation of a *Detroit News* editorial that defended those who openly criticized Kennedy's character. He brought to Haldeman's attention a *Life* magazine article which "implores EMK to save us from the dull, irrelevant '72 debate and lead us to those glorious days pre-RFK's death." Such interest in Kennedy confirmed what columnist Nick Thimmesch observed in a piece that crossed Haldeman's desk: "The odd blend of people who think [Kennedy] will run are those who cling to the Kennedy legend and the frightened fold in the White House who appreciate it."[56]

When Kennedy appeared in public in the spring of 1972, he was met by huge and sometimes unruly crowds reminiscent of John's and Robert's presidential campaigns. The scenes prompted concern for Kennedy's safety. Nixon learned that Senator Mike Mansfield had publicly asked Treasury Secretary John Connally to reverse his stated position and to assign Kennedy Secret Service protection. "H[aldeman] note!" Nixon wrote, darkening the exclamation point several times. "Connally is simply following the law, isn't he?" In response, Buchanan offered advice mindful more of Nixon's image than of legalities or Kennedy's safety. "If something should happen to EMK without SS protection," he wrote the president, "the media would turn on us in an instant, for not providing protection of the last of the Kennedys." He suggested that Nixon find a rationale to offer Kennedy protection. The gesture "would do the President some good among a goodly number of people, and no harm." The following month, after deliberating further on the political implications, Nixon granted Secret Service protection to Kennedy.[57]

In mid-April, Pat Buchanan and Ken Khachigian informed John Mitchell and Haldeman that Muskie had been effectively neutralized as a potential candidate. The two aides wanted further instruction, listing in order the candidates they would most prefer as Nixon's opponent in the fall—McGovern, Humphrey, Muskie, and Kennedy. "A Democratic Party deeply divided, thirsting for unity and victory, would welcome a Kennedy," Buchanan and Khachigian reasoned. "For this reason, we do not believe our strategy should be to flush Kennedy out. As Kennedy is elevated, McGovern recedes—and We Want McGovern. . . . We should elevate and assist McGovern in every way conceivable." The White House should avoid appearing "apprehensive" about Kennedy because "that makes his candidacy more likely." Haldeman subsequently ordered G. Gordon Liddy, an operative for the Committee to Re-elect the President (CREEP), "to transfer whatever capability he had from Muskie to McGovern with particular interest in discovering what the connection between McGovern and Senator Kennedy was."[58]

As the Democratic convention approached, Nixon continued to worry that Kennedy's "residual appeal" might take the nomination away from McGovern, just as Johnson had similarly feared in 1964 that Robert would hijack his nomination. "Even McGovern's supporters, no matter how emotionally committed to their man, would rally around Kennedy," he reasoned. As far as McGovern was concerned, the prospect that Kennedy would suddenly storm the convention and capture the nomination was absurd. "I always thought it was ridiculous that anybody could assume that you'd run that hard, spend the best part of two years working for the nomination just to turn it over to somebody else," he noted. "It isn't the way American politics works." McGovern surmised that Nixon and his aides "just couldn't conceive of a guy from South Dakota actually seriously thinking he could be nominated." More likely, they believed Kennedy wanted the nomination and, given McGovern's affinity for the Kennedys, thought he would gladly hand the nomination to the true heir apparent. McGovern knew Nixon wanted to run against him. "They feared Teddy," he noted, "and rightly so."[59]

Believing that with the exception of Edward he was the legitimate heir to the Kennedy mantle, McGovern continued subtly to evoke the Kennedy myth. As early as February 1971 Nixon received reports that McGovern frequently "discussed the similarities in style which he has with JFK." Nixon learned that columnist Mary McGrory believed McGovern offered hope of a "second Camelot"; the government "might become rational and human again, as it was in JFK's day." Shortly before the convention, Nixon's photographer, Ollie Atkins, was disturbed by the cover of *Life* showing McGovern holding his grandson. This and the other pictures, Atkins wrote, "smack very much of the old-time John Kennedy stuff. I fear this is going to hurt us." Atkins wanted to "counteract this kind of photography" by depicting Nixon in a similar fashion.[60]

When McGovern won the nomination, he knew the Kennedy myth was among the more important factors for his success. "I think it helped," he recalled. "No doubt about it. I think it helped bring a lot of the best operators, the best organizers, and advance people and trained campaigners as well as rank and file supporters." McGovern had therefore decided well before the convention that if he won the nomination he would ask Edward Kennedy to join his ticket. Kennedy's own image, McGovern reasoned, might have been enhanced by accepting the vice-presidential nomination. "We actually developed a memo saying that it would be a good way for him to do penance," he recalled. "It would open the way for him to be a [presidential] candidate in the future. Chappaquiddick would be thrashed out in terms of his bid as a vice-presidential candidate. It would be easier to handle at that level. And I would defend him. I thought we could ride it through." The public might have found Kennedy more palatable in the number two spot, McGovern thought. If McGovern won the presidency, Kennedy would then serve four or eight years in a humbled, subservient position during which Chappaquiddick would fade from the public's memory.[61]

After McGovern won the presidential nomination, he approached Kennedy as planned, presenting him with his rationale. Kennedy slept on the offer, then called McGovern the next morning to decline. Given Kennedy's failure during the 1980 campaign, Mc-Govern conceded retrospectively that his pursuit of Kennedy might have been a misjudgment. Perhaps he let optimistic polls and his own emotions distort his perspective. When he later campaigned on Kennedy's behalf in 1980, McGovern recalled, "I was absolutely startled at the resistance to that candidacy." Even if he had convinced Kennedy to join the ticket in 1972, McGovern concluded, it would have made some difference, but "not enough for us to have won."[62]

During the convention McGovern and the Democrats recalled the Kennedy legend in what was by then becoming a ceremonial tradition. When portraits of former Democrats were displayed in the convention hall, Robert Kennedy's picture was placed among the gallery of past presidents. Edward Kennedy made an electrifying appearance, introducing McGovern to the delegates and impressing Nixon and his inner circle. "Kennedy looked very good," Nixon wrote in his diary, "although some thought he looked fat. He has a magnetic smile, a lot of style, and a brilliantly written speech." He dismissed those who played down Kennedy's presence. He perused a news summary in which a columnist concluded that McGovern's candidacy "definitely put aside the Kennedy myth." Nixon circled the assessment, writing boldly in the margin, "Nuts!"[63]

What followed Kennedy's refusal to accept the number two spot was a comedy of errors. Soon after Senator Thomas Eagleton of Missouri was chosen by the delegates as the vice-presidential nominee, it was learned that he had earlier suffered from a series of psychological problems that he concealed from McGovern. Hoping to rescue his now deeply troubled campaign, McGovern asked Kennedy to re-consider the vice-presidential spot. Kennedy again refused. After six other Democrats similarly turned him down, McGovern settled on Sargent Shriver, the husband of Eunice Kennedy and brother-in-law to Edward. His connection to the Kennedys, McGovern recalled, was a factor in his selection but not an overriding one. "I think Sarge was the seventh choice," he noted. "So that's how important getting a

Kennedy [on the ticket was]." McGovern added that "the Kennedys were not enthusiastic about that choice. So it wasn't that it would have gotten *them* more committed. It was the fact that in the eyes of the country, [Shriver] was part of the old Kennedy group, and I thought maybe that might be helpful." Nixon, meanwhile, tasted political blood, telling Haldeman, "Destroy" Shriver and "kill him." The McGovern-Shriver ticket, he said, was "a double-edged hoax."[64]

During the fall campaign Nixon kept tabs on Shriver's appeal, receiving updates about his frequent allusions to John Kennedy. Some summaries were alarming. Shriver was reportedly imbued with the "magic," "energy," and "inspiration" associated with the "real" Kennedys. A minor controversy arose in August when McGovern commented that Johnson had been unfairly blamed for the war, having inherited the conflict from John Kennedy. Colson instructed that McGovern's comment be publicized in order to drive a wedge between him and the Kennedy family. McGovern expected criticism for his assessment. "I'm sure it was out there from the Kennedy people," he noted, but none of the criticism ever reached him.[65]

Although McGovern occasionally cited John and Robert Kennedy during speeches, he did not evoke the Kennedy image nearly as heavily as Democratic nominees would in later years. His most blatant attempt came in September when Edward campaigned with McGovern for three days. Nixon received press reports noting that Kennedy asked voters to give McGovern the same support they had given John Kennedy in 1960. Through McGovern, Kennedy told crowds, Americans could build the society that John and Robert Kennedy envisioned. "Good reports on all networks of Kennedy's travels with McGovern," Buchanan reported to Haldeman, ". . . [press] wires focused on electricity, spark, or lift given the campaign by EMK." Publicly the White House asserted that McGovern was using the Kennedy myth as a "crutch." Aides forwarded to Nixon numerous political cartoons that showed that the "mystique" surrounding Edward stole attention away from McGovern. Nixon was irked by the flattering press given to Kennedy. Speaking with a reporter, he alluded to Kennedy's drinking and suggested that he did not have the necessary discipline to be president. He also told John Connally that it was "vitally important" that Kennedy "not pick up the pieces after this election."[66]

McGovern knew that his invocations of the Kennedy legacy might perpetuate a myth against which he could not compete. "But I decided on balance that we'd get more lift out of identification with the Kennedys than any negatives that would come when they began to compare the two of us," he recalled. The negative comparisons of charisma and telegenic appeal would have been made even if he had not invoked the Kennedys, he reasoned. Besides, he knew they were true. "I think I do have a certain amount of self-confidence and self-esteem," he explained. "Maybe it's easier to take that under the circumstances. I never felt demoralized by it." Nor did McGovern feel he ever sacrificed his own identity. "If you went too far," he noted, "that would have happened. . . . I never thought I went that far. I thought I always maintained certain individual personality and integrity."[67]

McGovern lost to Nixon by an overwhelming margin, and the Kennedy myth turned out to be no more than a minor factor. In 1993 McGovern reflected upon the meaning and evolution of the myth and its role in presidential politics. As a historian he thought the "mystique" partly explained the disparity between John Kennedy's lack of substantive achievements and his popularity among the people. The public was exceedingly drawn to Kennedy's "attractive personal characteristics," he explained. Kennedy was a "gallant, graceful, and eloquent figure," "a handsome, cool, and humorous man." Moreover, the assassination obscured the shortcomings of his presidency. Kennedy's personal appeal, combined with "the terrific emotionalism and the pathos and the passion of his death has a lot to do with escalating his image with the American people," he recalled. "I think that created a permanent mystique around Kennedy that was not there the day before the assassination."

In general, McGovern always felt "the Kennedys were exempt from some of the criteria used to judge other politicians." They defied political labels and were excused for waffling on issues "partly because of their emotional appeal." "When it came to the Kennedys, somehow there was this kind of forgiveness; personal factors became more important than convictions and ideology." Consequently, Kennedy's stylistic elements endured more than his ideas. "These are the things that people seem to emulate. Pretty superficial, isn't it?" he asked. "Well, it *is* superficial. There's no other way to look at it." In some ways McGovern found the "mystique" disturbing because "it means that [style] can be substituted in voters' minds for achievement or for rational thought and reason and all the things we think are important to civilization." Republicans could also use the "mystique" because "they're invoking an image rather than an ideology." Ironically, McGovern was victimized by the stylistic demands that Kennedy advanced. Although McGovern projected the idealism reminiscent of Kennedy, his low-key demeanor contrasted sharply with the charisma of the Kennedy image. The Kennedy myth was never transferred to him powerfully or effectively.

McGovern recognized that in later years a new generation of candidates saw themselves in the Kennedy tradition as he had in 1972. He was not entirely pleased with them. More often than not, he noted, they clung to an idealized perspective formed during the impressionable years of their youth. "I think there are times when people look back too much and spend too much energy longing for Camelot and longing for something that probably is not going to be again," McGovern lamented of this trend. "That was a unique circumstance, a unique President. It can be debilitating and can prevent us from facing the problems of our own time and in our own way." Unfortunately, McGovern's point was lost on Kennedy's apostles— and on Nixon.[68]

Nixon never reached McGovern's level of awareness about the "mystique." Self-absorbed, unable to reconcile bad memories of the 1960 campaign, and chronically insecure, he could not view the Kennedys beyond his own political interests. He too knew that public affection for the Kennedys outdistanced their achievements. But he took it personally, and his perspective of the Kennedys remained trapped in the past. Like Johnson, he had every right to feel unfairly measured against the Kennedys, especially in light of his achievements. He once highlighted a column by Mike Royko in which he argued that if "a President named Kennedy" had achieved what Nixon had in his first three years in office, "his followers would be singing songs from 'Camelot,' while the workmen began carving his handsome likeness into Mt. Rushmore." Like Johnson, Nixon could not accept comparisons as part of the essence of the Kennedy myth—that those who admired the Kennedys would always look at the living and wish for the dead. So he worked to dismantle the Kennedy image, failing to see that he was only punching a ghost.[69]

The anger, fears, and hatred that encumbered Nixon's regard of the Kennedys were part of larger flaws that ultimately led to his downfall. On June 16, 1972, five burglars financed by CREEP were caught in an elaborate scheme to wiretap the phones of the Democratic National Committee at the Watergate apartment complex in Washington. Nixon later justified the overzealousness of his campaign in 1972 by referring to the 1960 campaign. "I vowed I would never again enter an election at a disadvantage of being vulnerable to them—or anyone—on the level of political tactics," he wrote in his memoirs. As the scandal unfolded, Nixon suspected Edward Kennedy and his loyalists of leading the investigation, particularly with the appointment of Archibald Cox as special prosecutor. "I guess the Kennedy crowd is just laying in the bushes waiting to make their move," he told John Dean. To offset disclosures about illegalities in his administration, Nixon ordered his staff to launch "a concerted public relations campaign" that emphasized John Kennedy's use of wiretaps. "Make the subtle point that the highest number of taps was when Bobby Kennedy was Attorney General," Nixon instructed. He informed Ehrlichman of a critical book about the Kennedys that had a "fascinating page" about Robert Kennedy using FBI agents to rouse several reporters during the middle of the night to question them about their knowledge of a possible price increase by steel companies. "This kind of thing, of course, goes far beyond anything we have attempted in the national security area," Nixon told Ehrlichman.[70]

The Watergate scandal and Nixon's resignation created a national crisis of confidence in the presidency, politics, and government that persists today. To some degree the reputation of the Kennedys, both dead and living, suffered as a result of the cynicism surrounding Watergate. Disenchantment with government and politics encouraged a reevaluation of the assumed heroes of the past. On the tenth anniversary of the Kennedy assassination, and just a month after Nixon fired Cox, the *New York Times* interviewed college students, once Kennedy's most avid admirers, to assess how America's youth viewed his presidency. "His initial charisma disintegrates in light of his faults," one student said. Another was more pointed: "Kennedy is not a hero anymore." The scandal also amplified Edward Kennedy's character issue for those convinced that Nixon had been unfairly victimized by liberals in Congress and the news media. "Nobody Drowned at Watergate," read one popular bumper sticker. Many people asked what right Kennedy had to question the criminal behavior of the president. "In a sense," *Newsweek* observed, "Kennedy was almost as much a victim of Watergate as Richard Nixon himself."[71]

But if Watergate made people wary of heroes and myths, it also produced a paradox. In light of Nixon's failed presidency, some writers began to assert that the Kennedy years had been relatively trustworthy, idealistic, and enlightened. Arthur Schlesinger and Theodore Sorensen matched Kennedy's virtues against the criminal behavior of Nixon. Historians and journalists expressed renewed appreciation for Kennedy's intangible contributions—idealism, hope, confidence, and inspiration in the political process. Four months after Nixon resigned, the first television docudrama about the Kennedys was produced, creating an important historical foundation for millions of young people who had vague or no memories of the Kennedy presidency. "The Missiles of October" was a three-hour dramatization of John Kennedy's leadership during the Cuban missile crisis. *Variety* called it a "celebration of the Kennedys and how they ran the country." The program seemed to serve as a reprieve for the turmoil surrounding the failure of the Nixon presidency. Regardless of its glaring inaccuracies, the docudrama reflected an impulse to restore the public's lost faith in presidential power.[72]

At another level Watergate reinforced the mythic dimensions of JFK's murder. The exposure of Watergate's vast conspiracies prompted renewed interest in the supposed conspiracies behind the Kennedy assassination. After several years of dormancy, a new wave of conspiracy books and full-length films inundated the market. People who may have dismissed the idea of a murder conspiracy before Watergate gave great credence afterward, especially in light of new "factual" revelations. In 1975, for example, a congressional committee learned of CIA- and Mafia-sponsored assassination attempts against Castro. Because those involved in the Watergate burglary and cover-up had connections to anti-Castro organizations or had been involved in the Bay of Pigs invasion, some people imagined that Nixon himself was involved in the Kennedy assassination. His presence in Dallas the day before the murder was viewed by conspiracy "buffs" as evidence of his complicity. Such notions made Kennedy an even greater mythical figure than he already was, and highlighted Nixon's role as a villain. "Treason dramatically sets off the hero's loyalty and honesty;" Bruce Rosenberg observed in 1976, trying to understand the widespread acceptance of conspiracy theories, "treachery 'explains' the only way good men can meet a bitter end in a reasonably just world."[73]

Kennedy's reputation not only survived Watergate but profited from it. In later years those who sought to rehabilitate Nixon's reputation appreciated the value of reidentifying him with this resilient historical figure. One of the first exhibitions created for the Richard Nixon Library and Birthplace was entitled "RN and JFK: Friendly Rivals." It was scheduled to run for the first five months in 1992, but because of its popularity the closing date was extended to September. John Taylor, the library's director, emphasized the commonalities of the two men. The exhibit contained touching letters exchanged between Nixon and Jacqueline Kennedy. Its text reminded visitors that congressional opponents "treat one another with respect and courtesy and frequently even become friends. As the items that follow show, such was the case with Kennedy and Nixon." There was no mention of Nixon's criticism of Kennedy as president or his later effort to discredit JFK's historical reputation. When Richard Nixon was buried at his library in April 1994, no members of the Kennedy family attended. George McGovern did, however, and he expressed a sentiment that John Kennedy surely would have appreciated for its "class," if not for its own personal relevance. "My own career has been so intertwined with [Nixon's] that I really had the feeling that an old friend has left the scene," McGovern told reporters. "I made my peace with him years ago."[74]

Beginning in 1960 the Kennedys, like characters in a Greek tragedy, played leading roles in Nixon's defeat, resurrection, and self-destruction. A Kennedy would die, but another would take his place, haunting the protagonist as he advanced in power. In the end, Nixon's obsession with the Kennedys and their image, like his obsessions with the news media, Congress, Democrats, and the courts, proved self-defeating. Just as his demise showed the resiliency of the institutions he sought to circumvent, his effort to destroy the Kennedys strengthened the dynamics of their myth. In a final act of irony, Nixon contributed to a greater longing for what the Kennedys ideally represented.

The national desire for healing, renewal, and restoration became the respective themes of Gerald Ford, Jimmy Carter, and Ronald Reagan. Each sought to pick up the pieces from Nixon's presidency and redirect the nation on its proper course, one that had seemed somehow misguided since Dallas. The presidents that followed evoked the optimism, idealism, and hope associated with the Kennedy myth, remodeling it to enhance their own qualities rather than trying to destroy it.

Restoration: Gerald Ford and Jimmy Carter

IN 1976 BOTH Gerald Ford and Jimmy Carter promised voters restoration—to take America "back to the future" before Watergate, Vietnam, political assassinations, and urban riots to a time of higher promise and confidence. Both men used the Kennedy years as a point of reference for their notion of an ideal America. The contest between them, however, offered two paths to renewal, pitting substance against style, experience against hope. Ford had served in the House of Representatives for twenty-four years. A loyal organization man, he was a plodder, a man known for, if not intelligence, certainly diligence and integrity. When he became president in August 1974 he set out to heal the nation by example. In marked contrast, Carter had served just one term as governor of Georgia. Running on the themes of trust and character, he successfully portrayed himself as an outsider who promised to return compassion and honesty to the presidency. Not since William Jennings Bryan had a candidate spoken so openly about a guiding Christian faith and a love of humankind. As part of this motif, Carter embraced distinctly Kennedyesque themes. Many voters who had turned cynical toward politics projected onto him their desire for redemption, to pursue if not the panache of Camelot at least its idealistic intentions.

Elected thirteen years after the assassination of John Kennedy, Carter was the first presidential candidate to successfully associate himself with the Kennedy myth without having met, let alone known, John or Robert Kennedy. The accomplishment was impressive given the obvious contrast between the Kennedys and Carter, a rural Southerner, a shy introvert, and a stringent moralist. Although his centrist philosophy departed from the Kennedy-Johnson liberalism of the 1960s, he was attracted to John Kennedy's noble goals. Thus he identified with and projected the trust, hope, and idealism imagined in the Kennedy years. But the same high, moral standards that drew him to JFK also fueled Carter's hostility toward Edward Kennedy, the man who personified the "mystique's" darker realities. This ambivalence, which differed from Johnson's and Nixon's in its moral thrust, had mixed results. Carter both embodied the Kennedy image and felt intimidated by it. So supremely confident in most facets of his political career, he sometimes showed uncharacteristic confusion, if not cowardice, in his response to the Kennedy image.

Gerald Ford, on the other hand, was unique in that he was the first president since the assassination to be undaunted by Kennedy's memory. The role of the Kennedy myth in his career was markedly less dramatic than its influence on Johnson and Nixon. Ford had suffered no humiliating defeat at the hands of John Kennedy. Nor had his career come into direct conflict with the ambitions of either Robert or Edward Kennedy. By the time he became president, Watergate, not the Kennedy "mystique," was the dominant presidential legacy. And Ford's personality and public image were in such contrast to the Kennedys that the idea of him emulating their style would have seemed comical. He reacted to the Kennedys and their legacy much as he reacted to many forces in his life—as a studied observer. This detachment is worth brief examination. While it worked to his benefit vis-à-vis the Kennedy image, it pointed to a shortcoming in his leadership style, one that Carter exploited.

Ford's indifference toward the Kennedy image was related to his inner security and emotional cool. Friends, aides, and critics nearly unanimously describe him as friendly, honest, considerate, self-confident, and hard-working. Those who knew him write of his constancy rather than his temper tantrums, mood swings, or overt power plays. His Protestant ethic was derived from the values of his parents and his Grand Rapids, Michigan, hometown, a straitlaced churchgoing community of Dutch immigrants. An optimist, he had decided early in his life to find the good in people. During his congressional career he maintained the status quo and rarely challenged the Republican Establishment. Receiving the American Political Science Association's Distinguished Service Award in 1961, he was praised as "the Congressman's Congressman," who "symbolizes the hard working, competent legislator who eschews the more colorful publicity-seeking role in favor of a solid record of accomplishment in the real work of the House: committee work."[1]

Ford first met Kennedy in 1949 after he was elected to the House of Representatives from Michigan's Fifth Congressional District. Upon being sworn in in January, he was assigned an office across the hall from Kennedy on the third floor of the Old House Office Building. Over the next few years the two partisan opponents became friendly. "I grew to like him," Ford noted. "We had a lot in common. We became, I would say, good personal friends." They had both attended Ivy League schools. (Ford had graduated from Yale Law School after receiving a bachelor's degree from the University of Michigan.) They were both navy men who had served in the South Pacific during World War II. They were athletic and shared an interest in skiing, a hobby which, Ford remembered, sometimes brought them together on the New England slopes. Although they had little in common in their personalities, political styles, and philosophies, Ford's amiability and Kennedy's charm made him feel akin to Kennedy.[2]

Ford was well aware that his legislative diligence contrasted with Kennedy's flamboyant personal style. "Kennedy was hardworking on the subjects that he was interested in," he recalled. "In something that he was not interested in, he didn't give a damn." Kennedy "enjoyed the social life" of the capital more than his legislative duties, Ford remembered. "He was single. He was young. He was attractive." They did not socialize together "because our lives were totally different." He was aware of Kennedy's philandering through second- and thirdhand gossip, "but it really was none of my business and I paid no attention to it."[3]

Ford credited Kennedy's success in 1960 to his tough, insightful political skills, personal wealth, and, of course, his "attractiveness." "In the Nixon-Kennedy contest, no doubt in my mind, [there was a] significant contrast between Kennedy, a young, sort of gladiator [and] Nixon, a serious, able student and politician," he recalled. Like most people, Ford saw the first televised debate between Kennedy and Nixon as a turning point in the campaign. Substantively, he believed that there was "no question" that "Nixon was the better of the two." Kennedy "was bright, but he wasn't what you would call a scholar or an in-depth student of issues." "Appearance," he observed, "made a tremendous difference." Ford felt somewhat frustrated by Kennedy's success, but not to the same degree as Johnson or Nixon. "I'm realistic about the situation," he recalled. "Kennedy had that capability [of conveying charisma]. Nixon did not. I do not. I guess, subjectively, I envy and to some extent resent people like Kennedy. But that's not something that's going to keep me awake at night." Unlike Johnson or Nixon, he did not begrudge Kennedy his success despite a paucity of achievements. Like McGovern, Ford had enough self-awareness to recognize his ambivalence and not allow those feelings to distress him.[4]

When Kennedy entered the White House, Ford found himself subtly influenced by his more charismatic, if less diligent, former colleague. Thirty-two years after the 1960 election, he was asked what, if any, influence Kennedy had on his career. "I suspect, subjectively, as I got to know Jack Kennedy and got to like him, because I admired certain characteristics that he had and I wanted to emulate, it had an impact." It was not Kennedy's charm and style that moved Ford, though he admired both qualities. Instead Ford was struck by Kennedy's ambition. "There's no doubt that after three or four years in the House together, I was impressed with him," he explained. "And I could easily detect that he had great ambition. There was never any disguise of that." Despite conflicting goals, Kennedy motivated Ford. "I think his ambition also added to my own personal ambition."[5]

After the 1960 election Ford regularly chided Kennedy for his domestic policies and failure of nerve against the "Red Imperialists." "The New Frontier is like touch football," he said, poking fun at a popular Kennedy image. "It touches everything and tackles nothing." "Most people [today] with their euphoria about Kennedy tend to forget that his administration was beginning to have a downside," Ford explained. Americans today "look upon the personality and all of that charisma of Kennedy and think that he was going to be a sure winner in '64. In 1963 that was not a certainty."[6]

Ford recalled that he felt "devastated" when he learned that Kennedy had been assassinated. "I felt very sad that his career ended in this tragedy," he said quietly. But his sorrow did not blind him to the realities of the Kennedy years. He was later amused by Kennedy enthusiasts who tried to deflect JFK's responsibility for the war. He was most critical of Kennedy's legislative record. "Here he came in with all this glamour and all these wonderful accolades," Ford recalled, "but his accomplishments with the Congress were not significant." Kennedy's "overall achievements were not up to the expectations." "The truth is," Ford said adamantly, "Lyndon Johnson in a legislative way did twice as much as Jack Kennedy."[7]

With the emergence of the Kennedy hagiography, Ford became increasingly cynical about the Kennedy image. "[The Kennedy myth] wasn't something that just happened," he argued. "It was promoted." And the assassination, he added, "wiped out the failures of his administration substantively. It had a significant impact in continuing in perpetuity the Kennedy myth." He defined the "mystique" as "a very personal one related to [John Kennedy's] attractive personality which he articulates, and his appearance." But he was hesitant to label Kennedy's popular style as a positive legacy. "I'm just saying it's a fact," he laughed. "I'm not complimenting it as a political development." Younger politicians who cited Kennedy's inspirational appeal were lost in the image, Ford argued. "I saw it differently because I was there and they weren't," he noted. "They were neophytes, newcomers in the ballgame. I saw him from a very intimate, personal friendship to a partisan political opponent. And so many of these well-intentioned Democrats are totally unrealistic about what the facts were." Devotees of the Kennedy myth, Ford explained, were "never there in the nitty-gritty." "I don't condemn them," he added. "I just smile when they talk [about the Kennedy legacy]."[8]

Ford contended that as president he "never" felt Kennedy's footsteps behind him. "Most of the measurements I had were against Nixon," he rightly noted. Among the numerous issues related to his expressed desire to "heal the nation," Ford confronted growing public suspicion of a conspiracy in the Kennedy assassination, a particularly sensitive issue because Ford had served on the Warren Commission. During his presidency Ford authorized the creation of the Commission on CIA Activities within the United States and appointed Vice-President Nelson Rockefeller as its chair. Among the duties of the Rockefeller Commission was an investigation of John and Robert Kennedy's alleged attempts to use the CIA to assassinate Castro. While neither the Rockefeller Commission nor congressional committees found conclusive evidence linking John Kennedy to direct involvement in the assassination plans, the mere speculation and ensuing publicity tarnished the Kennedy image.[9]

The investigations had political implications for those in charge. William Casey, who soon became a member of Ford's Foreign Intelligence Advisory Board, wrote to the president, citing a *Washington Times* article suggesting that Senator Frank Church did not wish to appear as "the intrepid investigator who pointed the finger and cried assassin at the martyred John F. Kennedy and Robert F. Kennedy." The Rockefeller Commission had similar implications for Ford. Some critics accused him of participating in an effort to disgrace the Kennedy years in revenge for Nixon's disgrace, or of trying indirectly to undermine the potential presidential candidacy of Edward Kennedy. Seventeen years later Ford was perplexed when asked if he ever felt remotely involved in the Kennedy revisionism. "I'm surprised," he noted. "I never felt I was involved in it." He explained that he had created the Rockefeller Commission "to make an honest evaluation." Nevertheless, he acknowledged, "To an extent, [the revelations] punctured the Kennedy myth."[10]

As new information about the circumstances surrounding Kennedy's murder surfaced during the mid-1970s, Ford's previous work for and adamant defense of the Warren Commission brought persistent inquiries from reporters about whether he favored a new investigation. For Ford, the Kennedy assassination was a double-edged sword. If one accepted the Warren Commission's findings, Ford's participation reinforced his image as a "healer"; he had helped to bring Kennedy's murderer to "justice" and renewed America's faith in its institutions. Seen in this light, his service on the commission helped obscure the differences he had had with Kennedy and gave him a footnote in Camelot's epilogue. On the other hand, if one regarded the Warren Commission as part of an effort to conceal the truth of Kennedy's death, as the vast majority of Americans did in the mid-1970s, Ford might be seen as contributing to the divisiveness of the 1960s: he was an obstructor of justice who accelerated distrust of our institutions by covering up a conspiracy. Some cynics argued that Ford's career had benefited from Kennedy's death. He first gained national attention by participating on the Warren Commission; he profited from the assassination by coauthoring a book on Lee Harvey Oswald; and he had become president due to a constitutional amendment created as a result of the Kennedy assassination.[11]

Ford never felt that his service on the Warren Commission hurt his image. In 1992 he continued to take pride in the commission's work and support its findings. "Unfortunately," Ford noted, "the public isn't interested in the cold, hard facts." But his defense of the commission and his frustration with public rejection of its findings illustrated his failure to appreciate the emotional dynamics of the Kennedy myth. He was correct to defend the commission; the facts surrounding the assassination point overwhelmingly to the conclusion that Oswald was the lone assassin. But his emphasis on the "cold, hard facts" neglects the despondency that many Americans felt about Kennedy's murder. The belief in a conspiracy allowed many people to alleviate their own feelings of vulnerability; a man as great as

Kennedy could only be killed by an elaborate plot, not by chance happenings. Had Ford understood the emotional preconditions of those who needed to believe in a conspiracy, he might have been able to hold fast to his own beliefs while still sympathizing with the insecurity that many Americans felt after the tragedy.[12]

Of all the elements of the "mystique" that potentially affected Ford, he was least concerned about Edward Kennedy's political ambitions in 1976. Within the Ford White House there was no hint of the obsession with the Kennedys that had consumed both Johnson's and Nixon's attention. Wire-service updates on Edward Kennedy's political intentions were filed but not discussed at length. There were no tortured memos agonizing over Kennedy's capacity to appropriate his brother's image. Ford was casually kept up to date about presidential trial heats, many of which indicated that Kennedy would give him the greatest challenge. When questioned by reporters, however, he repeatedly maintained that he took Kennedy at his word and did not believe that the senator would run.[13]

Ford was more accepting of things he could not control, and he appreciated the limits of the Kennedy legend. He did not view Edward in the same league as John or Robert. "Teddy is a different character," he argued. "He doesn't have the charm of Jack. He doesn't have the intellectual brilliance of Bobby. He's a different Kennedy. He's a Kennedy in his own right. But he doesn't have the two outstanding characteristics of his two brothers." Ford credited Edward for his political skills in the Senate and thought he was "more able than either of his two brothers." "But he didn't have the mystique that either Bobby or Jack had," Ford noted pointedly. Consequently, he doubted that Kennedy could have won the Democratic nomination in 1976. "I would have had more apprehension about Hubert [Humphrey] than Ted Kennedy," he noted. Nor did he think Kennedy would have been as formidable as Jimmy Carter.[14]

Ford showed that in the 1970s a president could pursue the duties of office and not be obsessed with the Kennedy myth. Politically he appreciated Kennedy's charisma without experiencing the jealousy and resentment that Johnson and Nixon felt. He liked Kennedy personally and took no perverse pleasure in the negative disclosures about his personal and public life. He admired Kennedy's public relations skills but did not feel compelled to change his own persona as a result. Unlike Nixon, he was able to view Edward Kennedy in contemporary terms. His gyroscopic calm encouraged a healthy sense of detachment not witnessed in his two predecessors. But the same impassiveness caused him to depreciate visceral elements of leadership, to the detriment of his presidency.

II Unlike Ford, Jimmy Carter struck sharp emotional chords with the American people. Although viewed as an outsider in 1976, his vaguely Kennedyesque image offered voters a comforting layer of familiarity. Before his presidential career, Carter shared with John Kennedy the public image of idealism, confidence, optimism, and nobility of public service. As Kennedy had moved a new generation beyond the stagnation of the 1950s, Carter worked to move the South into a new era of progress and liberalism. Both were impatient with bureaucratic and legislative processes. Both were politically restless. Kennedy was forty-three when he ran for president; Carter was forty-one when he first sought the governorship. Neither could resist the challenge of unseating powerful incumbents, unintimidated by the odds against him.

Like John Kennedy, Carter was enormously ambitious. Growing up in Plains, Georgia, he learned from his father, Earl, about the importance of winning and gained a sense of perfectionism and an interest in politics. In entering the Naval Academy in 1943 he fulfilled a goal he had set for himself since he was five years old. In the early 1950s he joined the nuclear submarine program and was chosen by Admiral Hyman Rickover to serve as an engineering officer. After his father died he took over the family farm and peanut brokerage business, transforming both into financial successes. By the time Carter ran for president, he fused contradictions. He spoke of the need to reawaken America's sense of idealism, but he was oddly impassive. He was a Southerner who wanted to escape the South. He combined the agrarian rhetoric of the Old South with the business ethic of the New South. He was guided by a deep faith in God but could be cold-blooded in his political dealings. Consistent with these contradictions, Carter saw himself as both part of the Kennedy legacy and separate from it.[15]

Writing about his first campaign, Carter did not recall specifically what prompted him to pursue politics. When he ran for the Georgia State Senate in 1962 he was conscious of a desire to replicate his father's career. As a political role model, Harry Truman offered similar small-town roots and a willingness to take unpopular stands for the greater good. Hamilton Jordan, Carter's early campaign manager, understood another influence. "Ironically, John F. Kennedy was the President who first inspired Carter's interest in politics," he observed. The Carters were one of a minority of whites in that area of Georgia who supported Kennedy's campaign in 1960. "The Kennedy example of public service, running for office, caring and thinking that government could make a difference, was a strong early motivation with Jimmy Carter," Jordan noted. "I'm not sure he'd remember it that way now after Ted Kennedy. It was originally the case with him, as it was with me."[16]

Carter admired John Kennedy, but he was not transformed by him. He had already decided to commit himself to public service upon his father's death. He supported Kennedy in 1960 but gave no indication that he was personally enamored of him. He was almost forty years old when Kennedy was assassinated, an event from which Carter said he never fully recovered. But the impressionable years of his youth had passed. It was Truman, not Kennedy, for whom Carter developed an idealized perspective, one formed in his youth. He respected and cared deeply for Kennedy as president, but given his powerful self-image and his pride in his rural Southern heritage, he was not a devotee.

In his early campaigns in Georgia, Carter established patterns that he would repeat throughout his career and that foreshadowed his contest against Edward Kennedy in 1980. Driven by what he termed "a somewhat naive concept of public service," Carter campaigned hard for the state legislature in 1962, but he lost the Democratic primary. He was a victim, he wrote, of "a shrewd and incredibly powerful political boss, often benevolent, who considered the rural community his own and could not accept any encroachment on his domain." Having personally witnessed vast voter fraud, Carter worked tirelessly to prove corruption and had the election overturned in his favor. His victory was a triumph for the qualities he professed to embody—ambition, determination, honesty, decency, and morality.[17]

From the beginning of his career, Carter saw himself as a morally superior underdog fighting against entrenched political opponents and institutions. After four uneventful years in the Georgia Senate, he ran unsuccessfully for governor of Georgia in 1966. He was again motivated in part by a self-righteous disdain for Republican challenger Howard "Bo" Callaway. His new nemesis was self-assured, attractive, and came from an elite segment of Georgia society. Carter admitted that he had a "natural competitiveness" with Callaway that interfered with his political judgment. He finished third in the Democratic primary owing to poor campaign organization and little name recognition. Likewise, in his contest against Governor Carl Sanders four years later, Carter dismissed him as an outdated liberal, a wealthy establishment figure, and a pretty boy. He pledged to save voters from "Cuff Links Carl," a candidate who benefited from endorsements of all the major newspapers. Carter's victory reinforced his self-confidence and encouraged his role as an outsider who could triumph over the political establishment.[18]

The degree to which Carter was mindful of his emotive similarities with John Kennedy during his early career is not known. But as he moved into national politics, he consciously accentuated his Kennedy-esque features. In the mid-1960s many political observers in Georgia saw this young, smiling, thick-haired man as vaguely reminiscent of JFK. The parallel was not entirely welcomed. John and Robert Kennedy's regionalism, Catholicism, and commitment to desegregation had alienated many Southern Democrats. "I never wanted to capitalize on it," recalled Carter's media manager, Jerry Rafshoon. "I didn't think that it would exactly be a big selling point in Georgia.... I didn't go out of my way to try to do any Camelot camera angles. And no shots on the beach and no touch football.... I tried to avoid the smiling pictures."[19]

If Carter and his media advisers shied from stylistic comparisons, Georgia newspapers did not. As early as November 1965 the *Columbus Ledger-Examiner* published photographs that showed Carter playing touch football, "just like another public figure, the late President John F. Kennedy." When Carter announced his campaign for governor in 1966, the *Atlanta Constitution* found it worthy mentioning that Carter "does strongly resemble Jack Kennedy, even to emphasizing points with jabs of an open hand." That same month the newspaper paralleled Carter's "quick wit," smile, physique, and hairstyle with Kennedy's. Like Kennedy, Carter attracted idealistic young men and women to his campaign, as well as "swooning" teenage girls. And Carter's televised inauguration for governor in 1970 was described by the *Atlanta Constitution* as "Camelot Down South." The fear of comparisons to Kennedy was apparently unwarranted as long as newspapers stressed stylistic rather than philosophical similarities.[20]

By 1971 the national media too began touting Carter as a Southern-fried version of Kennedy. In May 1971 he was pictured on the cover of *Time* magazine as part of a feature on the new wave of progressive Southern leaders. Wanting to broaden Carter's appeal, *Time*'s editors instructed the illustrator to make him appear as much as possible like John Kennedy. The cover subsequently showed Carter looking like the fifth Kennedy brother, with a sweeping shock of hair and a toothy smile. In case the point was missed, the text observed that Carter looked "eerily like John Kennedy from certain angles." Although Carter was not enthusiastic about comparisons, he eventually found the resemblance beneficial. After he returned from a trip to Latin America in April 1972, he told reporters that one reason for the generous treatment he received there was because he looked like Kennedy, a man "worshipped by the Latin American people." Soon he began to encourage comparisons.[21]

Throughout 1972 Carter and a handful of advisers including Jordan, Rafshoon, and Peter Bourne began organizing a presidential bid for 1976. Carter and his advisers vaguely appreciated the growing fragmentation in the Democratic party and the benefits that such divisions held for a moderate Southern Democrat. Even before the Watergate scandal had played itself out, they sensed that voters were cynical of government and politics. And if the Democrats intended to recapture the White House in 1976, they needed to regain control of the South.[22]

As Carter shifted from state to national politics, he and his advisers considered not only the Kennedy image but the strategies John Kennedy had used to gain national attention. Carter recognized that Kennedy's failed bid for the vice-presidential nomination in 1956 had earned him important national recognition. At the 1972 Democratic convention he and his staff worked unsuccessfully to persuade the McGovern organization to name Carter to the ticket. During the convention Carter attracted national media attention when he nominated Henry "Scoop" Jackson for president. His speech, typically laudatory of Jackson's career, made frequent references to John Kennedy, linking both himself and Jackson to the Kennedy legend. He recalled how his mother Lillian had served in the Peace Corps during the mid-1960s. He mentioned that Kennedy's margin of victory in Georgia in 1960 was the largest majority in the nation. He identified Jackson with the accomplishments of the New Frontier, and noted that Jackson too was an underdog for the nomination. Kennedy showed faith in Jackson, Carter reminded the delegates, by making him the Democratic party chairman.[23]

Carter was sufficiently detached to appreciate the dynamics of the Kennedy myth. After receiving a bust of John Kennedy in February 1973, he wrote to the donor, "Kennedy still occupies a position representing youth, idealism, vigor, etc.—which he may or may not actually deserve. Politically, of course, the image is the reality."

Comparisons between Carter and Kennedy, played down in Georgia, were now encouraged as Carter became a national figure. By November 1972 both Rafshoon and Jordan wanted to promote Carter's "Kennedy smile" and project an image of him as a "heavyweight thinker." Jordan suggested that Carter write a book, study foreign affairs under Kennedy's former secretary of state, Dean Rusk, and cultivate the Kennedy press. He was further advised to open relations with Edward Kennedy and to meet with him to discuss the senator's presidential ambitions. Although Jordan sensed an "anti-Kennedy feeling" among voters, he still regarded Edward as the front-runner. He urged Carter to be realistic by positioning himself as Kennedy's running mate in 1976.[24]

Carter did not ingratiate himself with Edward Kennedy. The idea was an affront to his pride and idealized sense of self. His reluctance also betrayed a lasting ambivalence toward the Kennedy legend. Although John Kennedy inspired Carter, Edward was the living embodiment of those qualities that had antagonized and threatened him in the past. Like the Georgia politicians he had earlier challenged, Kennedy was wealthy, arrogant, shrewd, powerful, lacking in moral fortitude, protective of his domain, and a leader in the political establishment. Like Lyndon Johnson, Carter split the Kennedys into opposing forces. He admired the "good," nonthreatening John, heralding the ideals he embodied. But he had a visceral disdain for the "bad" Edward, holding him accountable for realities that threatened his ambitions.

Carter might have been justifiably intimidated by Kennedy as well. Fear was not a trait readily associated with Carter. Biographers, aides, and friends often stressed his enormous self-confidence. Carter himself spoke easily of his mistakes, shortcomings, and disappointments. Seldom did he admit to feeling fearful, especially when asked about competing against Kennedy. He often told reporters that he respected Kennedy's power and influence, but he usually followed such comments with the assertion that he was unafraid of Kennedy and even welcomed the chance to run against him. Reporters usually took his boasts at face value, evidence of his high self-esteem. Like Ford, Carter may have appreciated the diminished aura surrounding the Kennedys. But such bravado hinted of overcompensation. Despite his personal problems, Edward embodied a legend and dynasty that had threatened to overwhelm the last three Democratic conventions and had thrown such powerful personalities as Lyndon Johnson and Richard Nixon into flux. Truly self-assured politicians such as George

McGovern and Gerald Ford were mindful of Kennedy in logistical terms, but they never felt the need to boast publicly of their own confidence. Carter seldom responded to Kennedy passively.[25]

Although Carter minimized Kennedy in his political equation, his aides were more mindful. Preparing for Carter's presidential bid, Rafshoon assessed Carter's image in light of Watergate. While tragic for the nation, Rafshoon wrote Carter, Watergate benefited him and others "who view themselves as alternatives to [Edward] Kennedy." The scandal had confirmed "the worse suspicions of the average man about people in politics." Carter's lack of stature and outsider image was more a plus than a minus. The American people wanted "new, fresh leadership." Because Carter was "untainted by Watergate," he could free the Democratic party from the Kennedy and Wallace influences. Wallace was a stale reminder of the politics of the past. "Kennedy," Rafshoon reported, "has suffered greatly because of Watergate," a scandal that "accelerated a public discussion of Chappaquiddick and Kennedy's involvement." While the public might view Watergate as politics as usual, Chappaquiddick represented "the personal failure of a man who . . . put his political career ahead of the safety of a young girl [sic]." To neutralize both Kennedy and Wallace, Rafshoon advised Carter to "challenge Kennedy outside the South and Wallace in the South." He hoped that Carter could finish a strong second in New Hampshire behind Kennedy and finish a strong second to Wallace in a major Southern primary. Carter might then "appeal to both elements of the party," presenting himself as a compromise between the Kennedy and Wallace extremes.[26]

By the spring of 1974 Edward Kennedy had not made clear his intentions for 1976. In May he accepted an invitation to speak at a Law Day ceremony at the University of Georgia. As a visiting celebrity and a living link to the Kennedy myth, the senator attracted considerable attention. Carter, however, was outwardly unimpressed. Rather than woo Kennedy or act awed by him, he upstaged him. Kennedy spoke first before the gathered audience and, according to Rosalynn, Carter's wife, said everything that her husband intended to say. Relying on a handful of scribbled notes, Carter improvised for forty-five minutes, presenting what Hunter S. Thompson termed "a king hell bastard of a speech." The speech ran the gamut, addressing Watergate, the corruption in the justice system, and the mistreatment of poor criminals. He invoked Bob Dylan, Reinhold Niebuhr, Martin Luther King, and Thomas Jefferson. It was, Thompson wrote, "the voice of an angry agrarian populist, extremely precise in its judgments and laced with some of the most original, brilliant and occasionally bizarre political metaphors anybody in that room will ever be likely to hear."[27]

On September 23, 1974, Kennedy announced publicly that he would not seek the Democratic nomination, citing an overriding commitment to his family. Political analysts speculated that he was also haunted by the lingering specter of Chappaquiddick. Some reports indicated that he no longer attracted the Kennedy magic during his forays around the nation, partly because of his scandal and partly because of the embarrassing disclosures about John Kennedy during the early 1970s. Carter was reportedly disappointed by Kennedy's withdrawal. His competitive instinct was stifled, aides asserted. His professed disappointment may also have stemmed from losing the chance to place himself above the "mystique" by defeating it.[28]

Two days after Kennedy withdrew, Carter wrote to Kennedy expressing his regret over the "tragedies which have made it necessary for you to withdraw from consideration for the Presidency in 1976." "Let me say quite frankly," he added, "that as one who has considered becoming a candidate myself, I've always viewed you as a formidable opponent... and I certainly take no pleasure from your withdrawal." Polls had repeatedly showed that Kennedy was the most viable Democratic challenger for 1976. Had Kennedy decided to run, Carter, an unknown Southerner, would have had more than a little trouble gaining media recognition and raising money. Carter had planned to finish a strong second in New Hampshire, followed by strong showings in the Southern primaries. No one can know if such a strategy would have led to his nomination. As it was, however, Kennedy's withdrawal gave Carter a chance to *win* the New Hampshire primary, creating unexpected momentum.[29]

For Carter, Kennedy's withdrawal hastened the declaration of his candidacy in order to get ahead of the anticipated pack of new challengers. "It is time for us to reaffirm and to strengthen our ethical and spiritual and political briefs," he said, setting the tone for his campaign. Although much of the press did not take Carter's candidacy seriously, he astounded political observers one year later with upset victories in the Iowa caucuses and the New Hampshire primary. He had correctly sensed that voters would turn to an outsider who offered hope for restoring trust to government. Carter defeated Wallace in the Florida primary, bested Morris Udall in Wisconsin, and eliminated Henry Jackson in Pennsylvania. Although Jerry Brown upset Carter in Maryland, it was not enough to stop Carter's momentum.[30]

Kennedy was reportedly unenthusiastic about Carter's campaign. After Carter spoke to the Democratic platform committee, Kennedy commented publicly that the front-runner had "intentionally made his position on some issues indefinite and imprecise" in a "tactic" to win the nomination. Kennedy thus contributed to growing voter discomfort with Carter's "fuzziness" on the issues and increased speculation about nominating an alternative candidate. Carter could not let the criticism go. "I'm glad I don't have to depend on Kennedy or Humphrey or people like that to put me in office," he told David Nordan of the *Atlanta Journal.* He wondered aloud why Kennedy would make such a comment, and then added, "I don't have to kiss his ass." Carter claimed that he did not intend the comment for publication, but the manner in which he insulted Kennedy was consistent with a deliberateness shown in later years. His animosity toward Kennedy, aide Jody Powell noted, was encouraged by "the congenital disinclination of a south Georgia farmboy to kowtow to some Massachusetts pol who had inherited everything he had, from his political position to his bank account." The ghosts of Callaway and Sanders lingered.[31]

As Carter captured the nomination and moved into the fall campaign, he maintained an amicable distance from Kennedy. While members of the Kennedy family were present during the Democratic convention, they maintained a low profile. As a loyal party man, Kennedy campaigned with Carter for four days in an effort to win over the Catholic, ethnic, and suburban liberals. Unlike the rhetoric he had used when campaigning for McGovern four years earlier, Kennedy never explicitly identified Carter with the legacy of his brothers.[32]

Carter may have been uncomfortable with the "bad" Edward, but he understood the residual affection he drew from the memories of his brothers. Despite continued embarrassing disclosures about John Kennedy, he was still admired more than any president since Franklin Roosevelt. During the primaries, numerous Democrats had tried to "get right" with JFK. Jerry Brown, Morris Udall, Hubert Humphrey, and Birch Bayh each portrayed himself as a vague heir to the Kennedy legacy. The most blatant effort came from Sargent Shriver. "[John Kennedy's] legacy awaits the leader who can claim it," he told his supporters, with Eunice and Ethel Kennedy at his side. "I intend to claim that legacy not for myself alone but for the family who first brought it into being; the millions . . . for whom the memory of John Kennedy is an inspiration and a lifting of the heart." Other than his strained linkage to the Kennedys, Shriver had little going for him. His campaign suggested that he thought the "mystique" was so strong that a post-Kennedy politician needed nothing else to attract voters.[33]

With the exception of Shriver, Carter grasped the Kennedy torch tighter than any other Democratic contender. Throughout the primaries and fall campaign he subtly infused the Kennedy image with his rural and Southern motif. His advisers did not wish to undercut powerful and effective images that had earned him important recognition as an outsider. "We're not going to walk away from the farmer, working-man image," Rafshoon commented. "But we're going to broaden our exposure, stress leadership, and show him as a competent problem-solver." Carter advertisements now fully exploited Carter's Kennedy-like features, particularly his smile. Their efforts were sometimes too obvious. Powell received a report that voters in Florida were suspicious of Carter's rustic television commercials. "It's like they're trying to make him a Bobby Kennedy in an open-neck shirt," a viewer complained.[34]

In the early Northern primaries Carter tried to address concerns about his Southern heritage by reminding voters that Georgians had set aside their regional prejudices to vote for John Kennedy in 1960. Faced with his own religious problem as a born-again Christian, Carter frequently praised Georgia and other Protestant states for supporting Kennedy. And he made several attempts to duplicate in reverse Kennedy's appearance before a hostile audience of Houston ministers. He spoke of the need for religious tolerance at a Catholic Charities dinner, and when speaking before the Jewish Educational Institute, Carter affirmed, as Kennedy had, his expressed belief in the "absolute and total" separation of church and state.[35]

Nowhere did Carter encourage a Kennedy identity more deliberately than in his rhetoric. On the stump Carter expressed his goal to inspire the nation in the manner of Kennedy and Franklin Roosevelt, two presidents who brought the nation a new spirit of optimism, patriotism, and self-sacrifice. There was a need, he said, for leaders who might again say, "Ask not what your country can do for you. Ask what you can do for your country." To emphasize the point, he repeatedly recalled his mother's service in the Peace Corps and expressed the desire to renew a similar commitment to volunteerism in his administration. The country, he argued, needed a president like John Kennedy who cared about the people. Indeed, when he accepted the nomination, Carter said he did so "in the words of John F. Kennedy, with a full and grateful heart and with only one obligation: to devote every effort of body, mind, and spirit to lead our party back to victory and our nation back to greatness." Like Ford, Carter implied that he could be trusted to heal the deep spiritual wounds experienced by the nation since Dallas.[36]

During his speeches Carter reminded the public of the personal traits he shared with John Kennedy. Opening his formal campaign in Warm Springs, Georgia, he noted that he, like Kennedy, was regarded by the political establishment as an outsider who had to overcome questions concerning his youth, relative inexperience, and religious beliefs. The nation in 1976, he asserted, was much like America in 1960, burdened by a similar sense of drift. "As in those critical years," Carter said, "it is time to restore the faith of the American people in our own government, and to get the country moving again! This is a year for new ideas, and a new generation of leadership." He credited Kennedy for his moral authority on civil rights and for inspiring young people. He promised an administration that would build on the framework of the New Frontier and the Great Society. Throughout the final days of the campaign, he urged people to participate in the voting process, noting that if the turnout had been low in 1960, Richard Nixon, not John Kennedy, would have become president.[37]

As had been the case since the early 1970s, the news media accommodated the Carter-JFK connection. National newsweeklies showed Carter in Kennedyesque fashion, jogging on the beach or wading into crowds with his shirt-sleeves rolled up. In a scene reminiscent of John Kennedy and his daughter Caroline, he was pictured carrying his daughter Amy after she embraced him when he stepped off a plane. He was shown hobnobbing with Hollywood stars, sitting in a rocking chair, and lying on a couch with his shoes kicked off. One widely circulated advertisement promoting *Time* magazine's coverage of the campaign featured Carter in a rocking chair with one leg propped up, "looking for all the world like John F. Kennedy," one reporter noted.[38]

Reporters regularly cited Carter's physical likeness to Kennedy. Elizabeth Drew described the resemblance as "unnerving." "It is hard enough to judge these politicians on their own without the further confusion of irrelevant memories," she lamented, as if comparisons were somehow beyond her control. For the first time a national candidate unrelated to the Kennedys was widely perceived as looking like John Kennedy. By early 1976 rumors circulated that Carter's mother was once Joseph Kennedy's secretary and that Jimmy was really Joe's illegitimate son. Reporters debated among themselves whether Carter was more reminiscent of John or Robert Kennedy. Some likened Carter's small stature, soft-spokenness, intensity, reserve, and commitment to basic principles to Robert. Others thought that Carter's youth, freshness, "cool," emphasis on character, and appeal to centrist elements of the party were more reminiscent of John.[39]

By hyping Carter as Kennedyesque, reporters fed their own fantasies of restoration. Carter, meanwhile, encouraged comparisons, understanding that in politics "the image is the reality." There was, of course, as much separating Carter from John and Robert Kennedy as there was linking him. Carter was far less liberal, charming, gregarious, charismatic, telegenic, eloquent, experienced, and stylish. Temperamentally he had more in common with Woodrow Wilson than Robert Kennedy. Physically some thought he resembled Eleanor Roosevelt. His ability to project Kennedyesque traits spoke as much of the emotional needs of the public as it did about Carter's image-management skills. Carter's own vagueness, John Kennedy's elusive image, a gullible public, and an accommodating press allowed opposites to blend together; a rural Southerner of modest upbringing and moral impeccability could credibly invoke a man who in many fundamental ways embodied traits of the earlier Georgian opponents he loathed.

The Ford White House, meanwhile, was sensitive to Carter's appropriation of the Kennedy image. Campaign memoranda to Ford characterized Carter as "appealling" [sic], "smooth," "self-assured, confident, and resolute." He exuded "kindness" and "compassion." Carter was "a warm, likable individual." "He is tough and demanding, educated, and intelligent, diligent and forceful," Michael Duval wrote Ford in summarizing a survey on Carter's popular image. "In the sense that charisma means shadow, unsubstantial, and ephemeral, Carter has charisma. . . . Overwhelmingly, people perceive Carter's style." Aides were conscious of Carter's use of "Kennedy-like" rhetoric and maintained a speech file that tracked his references to Kennedy. "His main pitch," one analysis concluded, "is to imply that Ford is *not as good* a leader as Truman and Kennedy."[40]

To neutralize Carter's association with the Kennedy myth, Ford aides tried to exploit Carter's strained relationship with Edward Kennedy. Campaign advisers recommended that Ford briefly tour the Bedford-Stuyvesant project in Brooklyn, New York, an urban renewal program that had been sponsored by Robert Kennedy. "It may result in some pro-Ford comments from the Kennedy crowd," Duval explained. "This is a Kennedy project and they certainly have every motive to oppose Carter." Ford would be able to demonstrate his nonpartisan attraction to the project and, in contrast to Carter, appear more compassionate: "Carter has never been to Bedford-Stuyvesant, probably because he is: (1) fearful of further identification with blacks in the campaign; and (2) jealous of the Kennedy project."[41]

Carter's Kennedy connection was most emphatically addressed as Ford prepared for the first televised debate between the candidates. Ford was cautioned that Carter "will stress Kennedy-like themes of the moral light throughout the world. . . ." Carter tended to employ Kennedy's technique of appearing as "a formal thinker" who could talk in "concrete" terms. While Carter was "fuzzy" on the issues, he had been able to do "an end run, a la Kennedy, pushing his 'concrete' strategy all the way." Duval urged Ford to emphasize how Carter relied on "the same old crowd of foreign policy experts who staffed the State Department and the National Security Council during the Kennedy and Johnson administrations. These are the people who brought us Vietnam."[42]

Ford and his media advisers were particularly mindful of stylistic matters as they studied John Kennedy's success in the televised debates with Nixon. "The public will perceive the debates as a 'beauty contest,'" Bill Carruthers wrote, "and we must acknowledge that they, the public, have a short memory for substantive issues." After watching videotapes of the first Kennedy-Nixon debate, Ron Nessen deduced that "answers to [the] questions are not [the] key. Style and personality are [the] key!" James Baker suggested that Ford do as Kennedy did and take notes while the other candidate was speaking because it "leaves [the] impression RN's facts will be rebutted." Ford was warned about his reaction shots, appreciating how Nixon had shifted his eyes in contrast to Kennedy who wrote on a legal pad. Kennedy "clearly spoke to TV audience—not [to] RN or [to the] pannalist [sic] in [his] closing," Ford was informed. Not all the advisers were consumed by technique and style. "*Substance does matter,*" David Gergen wrote. "Yes, JFK won the first debate because he was more poised and confident than Nixon; but JFK would have lost that debate if his poise had not also been accompanied by very sharp, very well-honed arguments."[43]

After viewing the first Kennedy-Nixon debate, Ford responded like the political technician that he was, mindful of Kennedy's physical movements, eye contact, phraseology, rhetorical organization, and general demeanor. He knew he could not match Kennedy's sex appeal, and he wisely did not try to supplant his own image with Kennedy's. He stayed himself and tried to increase his prospect for victory by studying technical fundamentals. "I was hoping I might get some of his charisma which I obviously never achieved," Ford explained. "But [watching Kennedy] was instructional. And, yes, I think I learned what I *should* do. Whether I accomplished it or not is a further question."[44]

During the first debate Ford did not fully use the techniques he had observed, and he fell especially flat in his closing statement. Carter called for a government "sensitive to our people's needs." He accused Ford of lacking leadership and suffering from a "loss of vision." He praised the American people's "character, intelligence, idealism, sense of brotherhood," and "inner strength." Ford, meanwhile, began by noting the "very, very important decision" the public would soon be making; their vote would be based on either Carter's "promises or my performance." He did not address the confusion and pain of the American people. He did not speak of the need for renewed hope. Instead he argued an ideological line of less government and more individual freedom. "Crucial point," an adviser wrote Ford afterward, "Carter's closing speech—'look to the future'—hard to beat. One of the criticisms of the Nixon-Kennedy debate was that Kennedy spoke to the people while Nixon spoke to Kennedy. President Ford should talk about the future also." Ford had spoken of theory, not feelings; of facts, not promises; of concepts, not empathy. He was his usual restrained, diligent self, in excellent command of information but painfully uninspiring.[45]

Carter too had watched the first Kennedy-Nixon debate, and he appreciated the advantage he held over Ford in terms of public image. Private polls confirmed that he successfully projected vision and idealism reminiscent of Kennedy. Ford reminded voters of Eisenhower, Carter was informed, "a decent person projecting strength abroad, yet taciturn and unimaginative, conducting a dull Administration." While 2 percent of those polled equated Ford with Eisenhower, 10 percent "mentioned JFK in connection with Carter." "The Kennedy analogy is working better for Governor Carter than the Eisenhower analogy for President Ford," the report noted. Carter's greatest strength, compared to Ford, was his capacity to appear "more dynamic" and his "offering hope for those under economic stress." "A campaign to 'get this country moving again' would be effectively consistent with present images," the report advised.[46]

After each debate both Ford and Carter aides measured their candidate's success against the Kennedy legacy, seeking to duplicate the postdebate atmosphere that Kennedy had enjoyed. "One of the most startling political phenomena of the 1960 election was the perceptibly larger and more enthusiastic crowd which greeted Senator Kennedy after the first debate," Duval noted. He recommended "a very firm plan" for Ford to generate this type of enthusiasm. The attempt to do so, however, brought Ford closer to the Kennedy image than he intended or wanted. After the second debate a commercial was produced when Ford traveled to Dallas and rode in an open-top limousine before a wildly enthusiastic crowd. America had come full circle, with Ford as the "healer" returning triumphantly to the city where Kennedy had been murdered. In the five-minute commercial, entitled "Feeling Good About America," Ford was pictured flinching when a cherry bomb exploded while he was speaking at a rally at the University of Michigan. The next scene depicted Ford in the Dallas motorcade. "When a limousine can parade openly through the streets of Dallas, there's a change that's come over America," the announcer noted. "After a decade of tension, the people and their President are back together again." Ford advisers agreed that the commercial was effective but perhaps too emotional, too powerful. Among lesser concerns, the producer recalled, was that it might prompt viewers "to focus in on their memories of Jack Kennedy, with the result that they would find Carter more akin to those memories than Ford." The commercial aired only after references to the Kennedy assassination were deleted.[47]

In retrospect Ford was more amused than impressed by Carter's attempts to appropriate the "mystique." "Oh, I thought it was phony," he laughingly recalled, "because there's very little comparison [with] Jimmy Carter versus Kennedy. But I understood that. That's the way any Democrat at that time would like to be portrayed. Kennedy still had the euphoric reputation and Carter was trying to latch on to it. Understandable but not factual." Although Carter's use of the "mystique" may have been contrived, to dismiss it as "phony" and "not factual" was perhaps to underestimate the visceral qualities Carter shared with Kennedy. The key to Carter's link with the "mystique" was not that he was perceived as "another Kennedy" but that, as Kennedy did, he articulated idealism and vision.[48]

In general, Ford miscalculated the inspirational force of the Kennedy legend, downplaying it as mere "charisma," "personality," "appearance," or as a self-generated myth. To some degree his detachment was an asset. Unlike Lyndon Johnson, who had tried to be everything from an athlete to an intellectual, and unlike Richard Nixon, who dressed White House guards in plumes to prove he had "class," Ford neither embarrassed nor compromised himself by trying to duplicate the Kennedy image. If he seemed dull, it was to the benefit of a presidency that had seen two of Kennedy's successors overextend themselves.[49]

Still, Ford might have learned more essentials from Kennedy without trying explicitly to imitate him. To judge Kennedy solely from a sentimental viewpoint was to exaggerate his presidency as a golden age. To view Kennedy just in terms of facts was to underestimate his capacity to inspire. The Kennedy emphasis on style and personality could indeed be debilitating; but his idealism, his sense of hope and optimism were perceived as "real" for millions of Americans and especially valued in the aftermath of Watergate. Ford tried to heal through example, not message. Even here he fell short. Although he did much to restore confidence in government, his pardon of Richard Nixon diminished his image of honesty, inviting suspicion that a deal had been struck. Ford remained himself—an honest, diligent, "good" person who wanted to move the nation forward by putting Nixon in the past. But in terms of inspiration, being "himself" was never good enough. He generated neither unifying themes nor a clear vision. Had he been more sensitive to the emotional layers of leadership that Kennedy had tapped, he might have been able to counter Carter's appeal. The solution was not to ape Kennedy but to express empathy and to offer a vision of his own in response to what people so desperately sought through Carter. Such sensitivities may have been beyond his personal nature and political framework. Nevertheless, his failure fully to recognize Kennedy's inspirational legacy was symptomatic of his shortcomings as president.

For Jimmy Carter, the invocations of John Kennedy added a basic layer of idealism and gave historical context to his campaign themes. He owed his November victory in part to his pledge to make government "honest, decent, open, fair, and compassionate." From the primaries to the fall campaign, Carter moved from center to left as he pledged to recapture the spirit, idealism, and policies associated with the Democratic presidencies since Roosevelt, a tradition of which he had never really been a part. In the process, however, he created unrealistic expectations. Within the course of the next four years the contrast between Carter's promise and performance brought to mind Herbert Hoover, not John Kennedy. As he lost control of his presidency, he concentrated less on the idealized Kennedy than on the "bad" Kennedy who threatened his reelection. Like Lyndon Johnson, he failed to understand that the "good" and "bad" Kennedys were one and the same. As he fought the "bad" living Kennedy he was also confronting the idealized, yet intangible dead.[50]

6

Carter and the Challenge of Edward Kennedy

AS JIMMY CARTER prepared to take the oath of office in January 1977, the Kennedyesque motif that had contributed to his election was considered as part of his Inaugural Address. In preparing the speech, Patrick Caddell harkened back to the early 1960s. Since John Kennedy's assassination, he contended, the American people had become "psychologically damaged" by the resulting thirteen years of upheaval. As part of a healing process, Caddell advised Carter to call for a "reassumption of traditional idealism." The speech needed to balance the optimism of the early 1960s with the soberness of the 1970s. "The approach should be purposeful, somber and involve a rekindling of hope," Caddell wrote, alluding to Kennedyesque sloganism. "Faced with the alternatives of stagnation and an attempt to move forward again, there really is no alternative at all." Caddell construed a "new realism" in which Carter noted that there were "limits to what the government can do and that there are limits to material development and growth." New approaches must be candidly acknowledged, involving "less government efforts and more responsibility for individuals." The goal was to carve a conservative path compatible with the idealism associated with the Kennedy years.[1]

Other advisers similarly recalled Kennedy's inauguration as they developed a defining theme for the new administration. Rafshoon admired Kennedy's call for a New Frontier but observed that the "frontier extended from the moon to Vietnam." He suggested that Carter herald "a new spirit . . . a new commitment." Reminiscent of Robert Frost's appearance at Kennedy's inauguration, Carter was advised to ask a writer of his choice to present "an original piece of poetry." Composer Leonard Bernstein, a friend of the Kennedy family, was commissioned to compose an original score entitled "The New Spirit." John Kennedy's chief speechwriter, Theodore Sorensen, suggested several catch phrases for the address. Carter's speech offered themes and images unique to his style and personality. But in a tone partly derivative of the Kennedy years, he called for "a new beginning, a new dedication," "a new spirit," and "a fresh faith in the old dream."[2]

Settling into the White House, Carter made minor symbolic gestures to the Kennedy past, replacing the desk in the Oval Office with the one used by Kennedy. In general, though, he branded his own unique style on the presidency. The popular images identified with his presidency were distinctly informal, Southern, and genteel— replete with symbols of peanuts, sweaters, jogging, softball, and country music. Once elected he seldom referred to the Kennedy past, or offered tribute to any other president for that matter, including his favorite president, Harry Truman. Nor did his speechwriters move Carter beyond his normal rhetorical style, aware of his disdain of orators. Carter's moderate policies and programs, which accepted the limitations of the federal government and reduced government spending for social programs, scarcely evoked memories of liberal Democratic presidents. Only the Panama Canal Treaty and the Camp David Accords were innovative and important achievements that distinguished his presidency.[3]

Because of his rural, Southern persona, Carter was more concerned about fending off negative comparisons with Lyndon Johnson than being measured against the Kennedy legend. Carter was sometimes criticized, as Johnson was, by elite Washington opinion-makers for failing to measure up to the dignity associated with the Kennedy years. If he felt victimized, he did not show it. He seldom complained about the press in general. He expressed minor frustration in July 1979 when the *Washington Post* failed to mention the passage of the Trade Act. Carter sent a handwritten letter to executive editor Benjamin Bradlee pointing out the newspaper's neglect. "It was different in 1962," he reminded Bradlee, who had been a friend of John Kennedy's.[4]

Ironically Carter fell short the one time he purposely used a Kennedyesque strategy. After the failed rescue attempt during the Iran hostage crisis in April 1980, he ordered aides to research how John Kennedy had responded publicly to the Bay of Pigs fiasco. Like Kennedy, Carter stepped before the gathered press and television cameras and took responsibility for the disaster, using phraseology reminiscent of Kennedy's. The ploy did not ward off criticism, owing to different circumstances. Kennedy's failure in Cuba came early in his presidency, in the midst of a "honeymoon" period when most of the press treated him sympathetically. Carter's crisis came deep into a presidency that had already suffered serious setbacks. For many Americans and reporters, the twisted and burned helicopters in the Iranian desert confirmed Carter's failure of leadership.[5]

The Kennedy myth haunted Carter not through comparisons of image but through Edward Kennedy. Tensions between Carter and Kennedy were evident even before the inauguration. Carter and his inner circle remembered Johnson's difficulties with Robert Kennedy and expected that Edward too would challenge Carter if the president were vulnerable by reelection time. In an often cited political strategy paper written in December 1976, Caddell regarded liberal Democrats as "potential adversaries" to the forthcoming administration. They had been "openly hostile" toward Carter during the campaign because of his moderate proposals and "because of differences over style and approach." He advised Carter to "maintain good personal relationships" with Kennedy and other liberals "so as not to add personal fuel to what are otherwise unemotional disagreements."[6]

Carter had not ingratiated himself to Kennedy as a candidate, and he was less inclined to do so as president. Mindful, however, of Caddell's advice to maintain a semblance of courtesy with liberal Democrats, he pursued cordial relations. He routinely met and conferred with Kennedy on important legislative issues, and Kennedy was generally supportive of Carter's programs. Carter's handwritten letters to Kennedy offered generous comments: "Thank you for coming over today to give me your good advice." "Your friendship and confidence are very valuable to me." "I really appreciate your help." Such accommodations could not have come easily to Carter.[7]

When Carter paid tribute to Kennedy in public, his compliments were laced with innuendo. He offered faint praise of Kennedy during a ceremony before the Equal Employment Opportunity Commission in early 1978. "It would be inappropriate not to recognize the fact that Senator Ted Kennedy is here," Carter said on the occasion. "And I will assume that he represents his great brother, who was the foremost leader in the enhancement of civil rights in our country." The reference might have been a sincere recognition of the Kennedy legacy; but it also reminded Kennedy that he was of lesser stature than his brother and not a leader in the area of civil rights in his own right. After Kennedy gave a podium-thumping speech before the

Democratic mid-term conference in Memphis, exhorting the delegates to "sail against the wind," Carter again alluded to Kennedy's vicarious appeal. "I think it's accurate to say," he told reporters, "that Senator Kennedy represents a family within the Democratic Party which is revered because of his two brothers and the contribution of his family to our party. There is a special aura of appreciation to him that's personified because of the position of his family in our nation in our party." He quickly added that Kennedy was powerful and respected in his own right. Carter had a legitimate point, but he again insulted Kennedy by implying that he drew his strength from the reputation of his brothers.[8]

By the summer of 1978 many observers suggested that Kennedy might challenge Carter for the Democratic nomination in 1980. Carter responded to such rumors with a mixture of confidence and conciliation. "I don't fear any competition that I might get in 1980," he told reporters. He noted that during the 1976 primaries he had been "perfectly willing, even eager" to run against both Wallace and Kennedy. "He's a great person and a close friend of mind." Carter minimized their policy differences, implying that any competition he might face from Kennedy stemmed not from issues and personality differences but from the senator's political aspirations. "There are no philosophical differences between me & the Senator," he wrote to Benjamin Mays. "He's just an impatiently ambitious man."[9]

Like Johnson, Carter suspected that Kennedy's appeal rested less in his differences with the administration than with a legend that grew in proportion to Carter's troubles. Beginning in late 1978 his presidency rapidly deteriorated. The Shah of Iran was overthrown by revolution, and Carter was held responsible for not foreseeing events or preventing the collapse of his regime. Oil prices skyrocketed. Congress continued to resist his energy policies. Inflation rose to 14 percent. And a gasoline shortage gripped the nation by the summer of 1979. Carter needed desperately to show leadership lest he perpetuate the failures that had brought him to the White House to begin with.[10]

In late May, Caddell sent Carter a bleak summary of his political status based on the results of privately solicited trial heats. Carter led all his opponents in both political parties, except Kennedy, who held an overwhelming 53 to 22 percent advantage. Kennedy had strong appeal not only among liberal Democrats but with moderates and conservatives as well. More remarkably, Kennedy received a plurality of support in Carter's native South. Caddell explained that most people preferred Kennedy because he "would bring more forceful and accomplished leadership." Very few respondents were mindful of Chappaquiddick. And his identity with the Kennedy legend drew nearly as much appeal as his perceived leadership skills. "His brother still ranks as the second largest specific reason for backing him," Caddell reported. Thirteen percent of the respondents wanted Kennedy because he "follows [in his] brother's footsteps" and was "like his brother." Sadly, Carter's greatest source of appeal came from people who simply did not want Kennedy as president. His own leadership and qualities did not sustain him.[11]

Seeking to bolster Carter's image, Rafshoon reminded Carter in a memo that "style is everything." His ability to win reelection "does not depend so much on what you do between now and the election as how you do it." Rafshoon credited Kennedy, Jerry Brown, Ronald Reagan, and John Connally for their ability to "look like leaders." "They speak well. They're forceful. Their presence suggests that they might be able to *lead* the country out of the dreary morass of problems we're presently caught in." Rafshoon noted bluntly that Carter had "failed to provide leadership" on the issues involving Iran, inflation, and energy because "you don't *look* like you're providing leadership." Carter's "low-key, soft spoken, gentleness" had worked well against lingering memories of Nixon in 1976, but voters wanted more forcefulness in 1980. *"You're going to have to start looking, talking and acting more like a leader if you're to be successful—even if it's artificial."* Although Kennedy was wrong on issues, "people love it when he stands up and raises his voice and says that, goddamit, we're going to do something about this problem. . . . They don't even listen to what he's saying. Nor do they listen to what you say; they only know that you say it slower and softer than Kennedy." Rafshoon suggested that Carter affect a stronger "speaking style," dress in dark suits, and "fire some people." He anticipated that Carter would find his suggestions about image management "repugnant." But he reminded him that, although his moderate ideology was popular and he was correct on his positions, the public would choose their next president "based on very subtle perceptual factors." He urged Carter to put aside his pride to make the "relatively small, cosmetic steps necessary to convey the accurate impression of your leadership."[12]

The leadership issue was increasingly problematic for Carter, particularly in relation to Edward Kennedy who bested Carter in terms of substance *and* style. Unlike John and Robert Kennedy, Edward served with distinction in the Senate, sustained as much by his achievements as his name. While the Kennedy aura was certainly advantageous, it was secondary to his "forceful and accomplished leadership." Caddell and Rafshoon concurred that the public craved the type of leadership, real or imagined, that Kennedy embodied. Carter fell short on both levels. His resumé paled in comparison to Kennedy's, having served only one term as governor and now widely perceived as inadequate to the task of being president. Nor did he *look* like a leader. Indeed, he was perceived as so ineffective that voters, in turning to Kennedy, appeared willing to overlook issues of trust and character, the same qualities that had helped bring Carter to the White House in 1976.

Carter's subsequent efforts to project forcefulness were often self-defeating. At times he seemed bent on doing a bad Truman impersonation. During a White House dinner with several congressmen in June, the president was asked what he planned to do about a potential challenge from Kennedy. Carter told them he was confident he would win reelection. Then he unexpectedly added, "If Kennedy runs, I'll whip his ass." The guests excused the comment, pretending not to hear it. Carter repeated himself, intent on showing his resolve to the point of obviousness. Determined to publicize the president's fortitude, the White House clumsily leaked the quote to the press. It backfired. Religious leaders condemned Carter's lack of dignity. One reporter mocked him as "a certified public accountant trying to be one of the boys." Most thought he was hardly in a position to assert such confidence. "I always felt the White House would stand behind me," Kennedy quipped, "but I didn't realize how close they intended to be."[13]

Another effort to project dramatic and forceful leadership proved far more damaging. Carter had scheduled his fifth energy speech for July 5. Caddell, however, convinced Carter that the problem with the nation was much deeper than an energy problem. In April he detailed for Carter the pessimism that burdened the American people. The source of the nation's gloom, he argued, rested in numerous factors dating back to John Kennedy's assassination and since compounded by the murders of Robert Kennedy and Martin Luther King, the Vietnam War, and Watergate. He recommended that Carter confront this "crisis of confidence" through an address to the nation. Such a catharsis would be the first step toward renewal and allow Carter to guide the nation honestly and more effectively. The final page of Caddell's lengthy assessment concluded with an inspiring three-paragraph quote from Robert Kennedy, which Caddell noted, "offers a vision of the courage and purpose that confronts us."[14]

Most of Carter's inner circle disapproved of the proposed speech. Rafshoon warned Carter that an apocalyptic speech "will be counterproductive" and "could even be a disaster." The public did not want to hear Carter "talk" and "whine" about America's problems. "They want to perceive you beginning to *solve* the problems, *inspire* confidence by your actions, and *lead*. You inspire confidence by being *confident*. . . . The Caddell speech sends all the opposite signals." He warned that Carter's negative comments about the "malaise" in America and his "mea culpa" about his leadership would come back to haunt him during the campaign. "People are not turning to Kennedy or Connally because they are attuned to the crisis of confidence in the country," Rafshoon warned, "but are turning to them because they look like the solution to the crisis."[15]

On July 15 Carter appeared on national television and described for the nation "a crisis of confidence . . . that strikes at the very heart and soul and spirit of our national will." He partly blamed events since the Kennedy assassination. He partly blamed the people themselves for their materialism and "self-indulgence." He accepted some fault himself, but he deflected much responsibility onto Congress which was "twisted and pulled in every direction" by "hundreds of well-financed and powerful special interests." In the end he urged Americans to rebuild confidence by conquering the energy problem. Although public reaction to the speech was initially favorable, it quickly shifted after the president ordered the resignations of his entire cabinet. He had taken Rafshoon's advice to heart and then some. The overhaul of his cabinet distracted from the message of the speech, disrupted the stock market, and bewildered the public. Later, explaining his decision to run, Kennedy asserted that Carter's defeatist tone had provoked him. Regardless of the validity of Kennedy's claim, Carter's speech was in stark contrast to the optimism and confidence that the Kennedy brothers had articulated since 1960, and which Carter himself had echoed in 1976.[16]

Carter's popularity now plummeted to the point where his renomination by the party seemed unthinkable. Throughout August and September he was frequently forced to defuse questions about Kennedy's ambitions or to respond to the senator's latest barbs and criticisms. Perhaps he projected his own feelings when he accused the White House press corps of being "obsessed" with Senator Kennedy. Carter aides insisted that the president was eager to take on Kennedy and was unintimidated by the "mystique." Romantic notions of Camelot and big-spending liberalism, they told reporters, would ultimately be seen by voters as incompatible with the harsh realities of the 1980s. Carter was no Lyndon Johnson, they insisted. He would not flee from a Kennedy challenge.[17]

In September Carter arranged to meet with Kennedy to smoke out his intentions and to let it be known that he would not shy from a confrontation. When the conversation turned to politics, Jordan advised beforehand, Carter needed to ease into the discussion by paying homage to the past: "Acknowledge the contribution that his family and the Senator have made to life in our country. You might mention the work that you and your family did for Kennedy back in 1960." Wanting to minimize friction, Jordan suggested that Carter should note he did "not begrudge any person wanting to be President" and that he neither relished nor feared a Kennedy candidacy. Such assertions, of course, were bogus, for it was precisely his concern over Kennedy that prompted the meeting. Carter met alone with Kennedy for an hour that afternoon. The details of their conversation remain unknown, but each man had politely convinced the other that a battle was about to begin.[18]

As Kennedy came closer to announcing, Carter shifted tactics. He knew he was no match for Kennedy in conveying strength and style. But on the image of trust, which Carter had used so effectively in 1976, he was superior to Kennedy. In September he began equating leadership with character, subtly reminding voters of Chappaquiddick without ever uttering the word. Defending his record during a town meeting, he questioned Kennedy's leadership, noting that he had been in the Senate sixteen years and still had not produced a national health-care act. Asked how he defined leadership, Carter said he was anxious to test his brand against Kennedy's. "We've had some crises [requiring] a steady hand and a careful and deliberate decision," Carter noted during a town meeting in Queens, New York. "I don't think I panic in a crisis." Carter was widely criticized. Columnist Tom Wicker chastised the president, noting that if he intended to raise the issue of Chappaquiddick, he should do so openly and not through innuendo and backhanded references. Carter sent a letter to Kennedy assuring him that he was referring only to high moments of state. Intentional or not, he showed a willingness to attack Kennedy where he was most vulnerable. But in the process he invited suspicion of his own cowardice toward the Kennedy legend.[19]

Carter's "panic" remark was consistent with an aggressive reflex he often showed when pressed. Unlike Johnson, Carter rarely lashed out against his opponents in private. Nor did he draw up an enemies list like Nixon. Instead his frustration, if not his fear, was expressed through biting sarcasm. Jimmy Carter may have professed indifference toward the Kennedys, but his behavior pointed to the opposite conclusion. His left-handed compliments, vague insults and innuendos, and expressions of virility suggested intimidation and insecurity. His reaction to Edward Kennedy and the Kennedy image evoked elements of avoidance, denial, dishonesty, and manipulation, traits he publicly claimed were not part of his makeup.

A few weeks after the panic statement, Carter demeaned Kennedy during a Washington dinner held for five hundred loyal Carter Democrats. Press stories had earlier noted that Edward Kennedy had asked his eighty-nine-year-old mother, Rose, for her blessing to run for president. Addressing his own presidential intentions, Carter joked, "I asked my Mama. For those of you who are waiting with bated breath, she said okay." Widely criticized for poor taste and insensitivity, he was reminded of the need for caution when attacking a living Kennedy. Like Johnson, he had to navigate around the memory of John and Robert, even though Edward lacked the full affection bestowed upon his brothers.[20]

Shortly before the anniversary of John Kennedy's sixty-second birthday, Edward Kennedy invited Carter to speak at the dedication of the John F. Kennedy Library scheduled for October 20. The president's appearance would give the occasion added prestige. Carter responded with typical ambivalence, explaining in a letter to Kennedy that "it is difficult to say with certainty what my schedule will allow this far in advance." Carter would have preferred not to appear at the ceremony. The memories threatened to upstage him, and Carter had little inclination to contribute to an aura which, by 1979, was associated more with Edward than with himself. As Kennedy's presidential ambitions became clear, however, Carter had little choice. Similar to Johnson's predicament in May 1967, when he spoke at the christening of the USS *John F. Kennedy*, Carter too needed to show that he was not afraid to confront the Kennedy myth. The drama of the event compelled his presence, and, like Johnson, he was well aware of the opportunities and hazards of the occasion. In September Jordan's deputy, Landon Butler, assessed the dedication as "a pivotal event—we must make plans, now, to insure that this speech is among the best the President has ever given." As he did in his earlier Law Day speech, Carter now determined to upstage Edward Kennedy.[21]

Although Carter had seldom identified himself with John Kennedy since becoming president, he now intended to lay claim to the myth.

Three weeks before the dedication he devised a strategy to link himself to John Kennedy while separating himself from Edward and the Kennedy family. He instructed his speechwriter, Rick Hertzberg, about the precise approach he wanted for the dedication—"substantive with a high literary content." He intended to use the occasion to reassert his conservatism, to separate himself from the old Kennedy brand of liberalism; "it should underline the fact that spending is not the way out, that government cannot solve all our problems. Government should not raise people's expectations above the ability of government to handle them. The solutions of the 1960s are not the solutions of the 1980s." The occasion should also be used to promote the SALT II negotiation efforts and the administration's energy legislation. Carter then gave Hertzberg a confusing set of instructions: "The speech should clearly set a Presidential tone, i.e., the incumbent President referring to a previous President, involving a special relationship that no one else can approach. The speech should clearly separate the President from the library itself and the family."[22]

Hertzberg missed the subtlety of the president's instructions. After speaking with several aides and outside advisers, he forwarded to Carter a four-page outline of the proposed speech. He began with a cryptic list of objectives. "Aims: To pay tribute to the memory of John F. Kennedy and to show the Carter Presidency as a lineal heir to that of Mr. Kennedy. Themes/Messages: President Kennedy's support of human rights and peace; the dark period that followed his death; the great changes since 1960; the essential identity of the goals of President Kennedy and President Carter despite very different changes." Hertzberg recommended that the tone of the speech be "gracious and warm," and written "*as if there were no such person as Edward Kennedy.*" Carter should "say what you would naturally say about John F. Kennedy at an occasion of this kind, without any concealed digs at his brother." "I agree," Carter wrote in the margin, underlining the recommendation. Hertzberg then noted that the "message" of the speech "would be that you are carrying out the essentials of [John Kennedy's] legacy and vision in a very different time." Hertzberg believed the president wanted to present himself as fulfilling John Kennedy's goals, a theme consistent with Carter's 1976 campaign rhetoric. Carter clarified his link to John Kennedy. "Rather, He and I both carry out legacy of America," he wrote in the margin, "—I'm not carrying out his legacy." The distinction was subtle, if not nebulous. Carter wanted to connect himself to John Kennedy only in the historical sense that they carried on the ideals of the nation. As presidents they shared "a special relationship," a higher sense of duty to which Edward Kennedy did not belong. As Carter read Hertzberg's outline, however, he became more agreeable to the idea that *he* was a more valid extension of John Kennedy's legacy than Edward.

Hertzberg's outline of the speech contained three layers. First, it would pay fitting tribute to John Kennedy. Aware of Kennedy's limited achievements, Carter worried about offering "faint praise," so he liked the idea of heralding Kennedy for what he "set in motion." In the second layer Hertzberg elaborated on the effort to depict Carter as John Kennedy's attendant. Carter's efforts on behalf of human rights would be related to John Kennedy's moral commitment to end discrimination. The SALT II negotiations would be tied to Kennedy's Nuclear Test Ban Treaty. Carter would depict himself as partly responsible for restoring "the ideals of decency, honor and service that the people of the United States believe in, and that John F. Kennedy exemplified." He would note, "The overarching purpose of John F. Kennedy's Presidency and mine—indeed the national purpose of the American people—remains the same. That purpose is the building of a just society, in an America living in peace and security with the other countries of the world." Carter had not instructed such parallels. He wanted only to publicize SALT II and human rights issues, not make them consistent with John Kennedy's goals. But now he raised no objections. In the third layer of the speech Hertzberg would present Carter as the more realistic agent of change for the 1980s than Edward Kennedy. Carter liked the quote that Hertzberg had found in which John Kennedy had stated that "change is the law of life." Since the Kennedy years, Hertzberg wrote, Americans had learned that economic prosperity does not alleviate social injustice; that the government is limited in its power at home and abroad; and that the nation faces energy problems unique to the 1980s.[23]

During the next two weeks Hertzberg, Stuart Eizenstadt, and Lloyd Cutler refined the central thrust of the speech. Partisan paragraphs were removed. Aides deleted subtle insults about John Kennedy's lack of achievement. Historical references were cautiously considered. Cutler was particularly irked by the promotion of the myth that Kennedy's murder had unleashed sinister forces that might have been avoided had he lived. Few questioned that America had suffered a series of political and social seizures since JFK's death. But one could argue, Cutler noted, that the nation had lost its innocence at the Bay of Pigs, not at Dallas.[24]

The speechwriters were careful not to overstate Carter's connection with John Kennedy. One omitted line alleged that if Kennedy were alive he would be "among SALT II's strongest supporters." Also struck was the assertion that Carter was "John F. Kennedy's compatriot and successor." The effort to show Carter as more attuned to the nation's problems than Edward Kennedy was addressed cautiously. Eizenstadt inserted into the text, "We cannot solve the problems of the 1980s with the ideas and programs of the early 1960s nor by looking back with nostalgia to that happier time." Hertzberg agreed with Eizenstadt's point, but he believed it was a "tactless elaboration on a point already made more subtly and gracefully in the speech." In the end, subtlety won out.[25]

Carter revised some of the wording of the finished draft, but the central points remained intact. He began his speech that day with a humorous anecdote that poked fun at the political overtones of the gathering. During a press conference, Carter recalled, John Kennedy was once reminded of his brother Ted's observation that after seeing the hardship of the presidency firsthand, he was not sure he ever wanted to be president. Asked if he recommended the job to others, President Kennedy had said he did not, "at least for a while." "As you can see," Carter added, "President Kennedy's wit and also his wisdom is certainly as relevant today as it was then."[26]

Carter added an important emotional layer to the speech. On a handwritten page he recalled how he had learned of John Kennedy's assassination. He had climbed down from a tractor, he told the audience, walked into his warehouse, and was told by a group of farmers that Kennedy had been shot. "I went outside, knelt on the steps, and began to pray," Carter wrote. "In a few minutes I learned that he had not lived. It was a grievous personal loss—my President. I wept openly for the first time in more than ten years—for the first time since the day my father died." Originally Carter wanted to minimize references to the grief following Kennedy's death. But the touching recollection was appropriate to the occasion and connected him more personally to Kennedy's spirit.[27]

Carter did not get lost in sentimentality. He toned down the assessment of the Kennedy administration, deleting from the text Kennedy's "very great" achievements and changing them to "admirable." At the dedication he lowered the estimation another notch to "notable." As planned, he identified himself with John Kennedy's commitment to moral imperatives, efforts to control nuclear weapons, and compassion for the poor and oppressed. He also empathized with

Kennedy's expressed frustration with the limitations of power. Carter then moved to the central point of his speech. "The carved desk in the Oval Office which I use is the same as when John F. Kennedy sat behind it," he noted, "but the problems that land on that desk are quite different. President Kennedy was right: Change is the law of life. The world of 1980 is as different from what it was in 1960 as the world of 1960 was from that of 1940. Our means of improving the world must also be different." He had balanced his respect for Kennedy with the suggestion that it was time to move on. After detailing the issues unique to the 1980s, Carter returned to his point. "The problems are different," he repeated, "the solutions, none of them easy, are also different." Still, he noted, "the essence of President Kennedy's message—the appeal for unselfish dedication to the common good—is more urgent that it ever was."[28]

Carter's speech was less a dedication than it was a sermon on the changing nature of the presidency, one reflective of his own leadership style. Originally he intended to articulate that the problems of the 1980s could not be solved with solutions of the 1960s. But Hertzberg had found credible links between Carter and John Kennedy, connections that Carter himself had not seen but that he was willing to draw upon. At an idealistic level, he identified himself with John Kennedy's moral commitment to equality and peace, renewing a promise to Kennedy's deeper spiritual essence. At a practical and realistic level, Carter let it be known that John Kennedy's policies were anachronistic—a fact, Carter implied, that Kennedy himself would appreciate if he were alive. The subtext of the speech, which aides had carefully crafted, argued that Jimmy Carter, not Edward Kennedy, had adapted more readily to changing events since 1963. And if John Kennedy's solutions had no place in the 1980s, then neither did Edward Kennedy's. Carter was both an agent of the past and the future, one who could be entrusted to accommodate John Kennedy's idealism to new political realities.

After Carter spoke, Edward Kennedy also called upon his brother's legacy. In direct contrast to the president's belief in the limitations of government, Edward reminded the audience of John Kennedy's faith in power. "He could make lightning strike on the things he cared about," he told the gathering. "He was an irresistible force that made immovable objects move.... There was a sense of progress and adventure, a rejection of complacency and conformity. There was a common mission, a shared ideal, and above all the joy of high purpose and great achievements." Thus Carter and Kennedy had charted two distinct views as to how the nation should emulate John Kennedy. Edward harkened back to a dream that would never die, asking the audience to sail against the wind and to have faith in vital programs guided by a strong leadership. Carter called upon the legacy to support moderation and pragmatic departures from traditional liberalism. Not knowing what John Kennedy would make of all this, Camelot's defenders could only disparage Carter's assessment as saying more about his own failures and limitations than about changes in the presidency.[29]

Lyndon Johnson had once lamented that because John Kennedy was dead, a person could make him do anything he wanted just by saying so. Rather than resign himself to this force, Carter turned it to his advantage. He shrewdly and cleverly molded the Kennedy image in a manner that his predecessors had not, diminishing Edward's blood connection by affirming his own unique historical linkage. In case the point was missed, Carter clarified himself during an interview with Boston correspondents after the dedication. He was asked by a reporter if Edward Kennedy was, by his name, any more worthy of the Kennedy legacy than he? "I don't think so," Carter replied. He and John Kennedy were part of a small "family of Presidents," he explained. "I've seen and studied about the decisions that President Kennedy made under the most trying and difficult circumstances... some of the decisions he made have affected my life as a President very profoundly.... So, I feel a political kinship with President Kennedy that's very intense and also very personal. And obviously, the name and the family relationship—blood kin—is a very strong and powerful force in the minds of American people." But, Carter added, in terms of understanding the office of the president, "I feel a very close kinship with President Kennedy also." A few days later he extended his connection. Asked if he thought he was "closer to John Kennedy than Edward Kennedy is," Carter replied, "Philosophically. I think so. I don't believe the Federal government ought to do everything." He reminded the interviewer that he opposed massive programs, demanded tight fiscal management, and wanted existing programs to be more efficient. "I believe that John Kennedy would have agreed with all those things." In short, if voters wanted to elect John Kennedy, they already had him.[30]

The Kennedy Library dedication was a defining moment for Carter and marked an important transition in the political use of the Kennedy myth. For the first time a politician with no personal connection to the Kennedys tried to deny a Kennedy access to his family's legacy by portraying himself as a more legitimate heir. Curiously, Carter never again laid such a heavy claim to the Kennedy legacy. Knowing that the occasion would invite comparisons between his presidency and John Kennedy's, he approached the dedication with typical ambivalence, one that perhaps reflected a struggle between his self-esteem and practical political considerations. His first and perhaps most authentic impulse was to reject the notion that he was JFK's lineal heir, a notion that threatened his pride. Gradually he accepted deeper parallels, claiming a kinship at personal, historic, and philosophical levels. If he adjusted his conclusion for political reasons, he was practicing the type of dishonest, insincere politics that he professed outwardly to be against. If he truly came to view himself as an authentic extension of the Kennedy legacy, he was a victim of self-persuasion. What began as a political ploy perhaps ended with deeper implications; in Jimmy Carter's mind the image had become the reality.

II Edward Kennedy's campaign was over before it began, a consequence of bad planning, bad timing, and unclear motives. Shortly before he declared his candidacy on November 7, 1979, Kennedy gave an awkward television interview to Roger Mudd, fumbling on the issue of Chappaquiddick and faring worse on the question of why he wished to be president. To make matters worse, three days before Kennedy announced his candidacy, American hostages were seized in Iran, prompting the nation to rally behind a president whom Kennedy charged was ineffective. "The flame under the charisma has been turned so low that it seems almost to have gone out, and the motivation seems muffled," columnist Mary McGrory wrote just days into the campaign.[31]

Despite the reversal of fortune, the Carter White House feared the Kennedy flame could be quickly rekindled. "Many people have pointed out that much of what the public seems to believe about Senator Kennedy is, in fact, based on impressions of his brothers and not of the Senator himself," Caddell reported to Carter in November. He recommended future polls probe the specific source of public feelings for Kennedy. Aides were confident that a close examination of Kennedy's character would separate him from myth—but unsure whether nostalgia for Camelot might compensate for his handicaps. "Kennedy also offers charisma—and with it hope," Rafshoon wrote Carter. "There is a sense among the supporters of [Kennedy and Jerry

Brown] that perhaps a totally different and unorthodox approach or a return to the 'magic' of John Kennedy will lift us out of our national doldrums. We should not underestimate the potential appeal of this approach."[32]

The Carter campaign developed three basic strategies to undercut Kennedy's image. First, Carter would defeat him in early caucuses. Jordan ordered a concerted effort to achieve decisive victories in the coming Florida and Iowa challenges. "Kennedy's [sic] are supposed to win, not to ever come in second," he wrote Carter, "again, this makes the early tests in both Iowa and Florida critical early tests of our strength and his weakness." Confident that Carter would win these contests, Jordan advised him to "hype it up as much as possible." Carter should pour massive resources into Florida, even at the risk of appearing obvious. Better to overdo it, he advised, "than to hold back on anything and possibly lose." Greg Schneiders concurred. "For a candidate running on charisma—not record, ideology, or personal characteristics," he wrote, "a loss in the first major contest could be very serious. Nothing will take the shine off charisma faster than the image of a loser." A few days before the Kennedy Library dedication, Carter won decisively in Florida, prompting boasts of confidence from the White House. Schneiders's memo was leaked to the press to underscore the significance of the victory.[33]

A second strategy was initiated at the library dedication: Carter portrayed the senator's liberalism as nostalgic and inappropriate to current problems. Specifically, Kennedy would be attacked as a "big spender" who was "weak on defense," had "poor leadership qualities and record," and was "not in tune with the times." "Senator Kennedy stands for the solutions of the 1960's . . . his proposals and ideas do not fit with the new realities of the 1980's," read one theme paper. Preparing for a scheduled debate in Iowa, Carter intended to argue that Kennedy "has failed to recognize that *we cannot afford to live in the past, to ask memories to solve our problems.*"[34]

The third means to attack the "mystique" was to publicize Kennedy's character as inconsistent with memories of John and Robert. Aides planned to contrast Carter's character with Edward Kennedy's. They were pleased when Kennedy initially emphasized the need for strong leadership rather than disagreeing with the president's policies. Such emphasis made it easier for the president to shift the attention to "personal character," which aides regarded as "an area of high vulnerability for [Kennedy]." While polls indicated that Kennedy was perceived as a stronger and more effective leader, Carter's advisers saw leadership as multifaceted and tried to separate its various strains. "You dominate the most important personality characteristics," Caddell reported to Carter, "—honest, truthful, forthright, moral, etc. Kennedy dominates the minor personality attributes—better speaker, better personality, dynamic, attractive, etc." Caddell reminded the president that Kennedy still "dominates all the leadership questions" in areas of knowledge, experience, vision, effectiveness, "and even handling a crisis." If the election was determined by moral character, however, Carter would win. He urged Carter to demonstrate more forceful leadership so that voters who eventually grew disillusioned with Kennedy's character would have even greater reason to turn to Carter.[35]

Using the blade of character, Carter planned to deny Edward the assets he had inherited from John. Jordan, Powell, Rafshoon, and Caddell drew up a list of ten "Characteristics for Success" to associate with Carter, three of which entailed issues of trust and steadiness during crisis. The trust theme was derivative of the 1976 campaign and reflected Carter's success in restoring faith in government. Against Kennedy, however, it took on new meaning. One memo cited the importance of contrasting Kennedy with Carter's "obvious integrity, character, and even morality." The task was to do so without appearing "unctuous and offending some people." "Create doubts about the opposition," Rafshoon instructed Carter in another memo. "Each of our likely opponents has major weaknesses. Negative advertising does not have to be heavey-handed [sic], personal, or unfair to be effective. You will not be personally involved in this aspect of the campaign. It will be done entirely through media. It must be done early."[36]

Like Nixon in 1960, Carter intended to portray himself as a "high road" candidate while allowing others to diminish his opponent's character. Advisers planned to refer obliquely to Kennedy's "lack of trustworthiness," noting that he did not have Carter's "overriding sense" of being "accurate and candid." Rafshoon advised Carter to respond to Kennedy's candidacy by noting that voters will in time "take the measure of Senator Kennedy and myself—to assess our *record*, our *position* on the issues and our *character*." "No amount of rhetoric, no amount of talk about leadership, no amount of charisma or nostalgia for simpler times will make these issues go away," Rafshoon wrote. He also urged Carter to campaign with Rosalynn and Amy, and to talk about the importance of family. "You're the only candidate in the Democratic primaries who's got one to brag about," he noted. In preparing Carter for his television interview with

Howard K. Smith, Powell recommended that he discuss "the importance of telling the people the truth" as well as citing John Kennedy's observation of the need for courage, sound judgment, integrity, and dedication. Powell wanted to turn the character issue against Edward by invoking memories of John.[37]

After Kennedy declared his candidacy, reporters sensed in Carter a renewed competitiveness. The head-to-head contest gave him a chance to achieve a degree of legitimacy he felt had been questioned by those who had long thought that a Kennedy properly belonged in the White House. He was confident that public support for Kennedy would evaporate with the actual possibility that he would become president. When Iranian militants seized the U.S. embassy in Teheran, Carter was given the opportunity to demonstrate the forceful leadership he was accused of lacking. In the months that followed, he confined his activities largely to the White House, acting presidential and using administrative surrogates to campaign on his behalf. In late November he canceled a planned six-state political tour. The Soviet Union's invasion of Afghanistan in December rallied additional national support and further compelled his challengers to suspend criticism of his foreign policies. Unable to resolve the hostage problem, Carter transformed it into a melodrama. Rather than pledge to do what he could to resolve the crisis and continue governing, he glumly exaggerated the crisis by comparing it to the Civil War, darkening the national Christmas tree, and harping on its seriousness.[38]

Carter declared his own candidacy on December 4, speaking in the East Room of the White House. He returned to the theme he had articulated at the Kennedy Library, reminding supporters that "the world of the 1980's will be as different from the world of 1960 as the world of 1960 was from that of 1930." In a show of restraint, he deleted an observation that the nation should not pursue "fantasy" or "self-delusion." But he noted emphatically that the American people could find in Carter the "truth." In the last twenty sentences he mentioned "truth" eight times. "Just as in 1976, the TRUTH is a major issue in 1980," Rafshoon wrote Carter. "Kennedy's lack of ability to answer questions is another issue."[39]

Throughout December and January Carter received news summaries about Kennedy's growing "character problem" and his difficulty in answering questions related to Chappaquiddick. Carter's aides compiled dozens of articles on the scandal and looked to publicize other unsavory moments in Kennedy's life dating back to his college years. Carter received updated polls showing his challenger suffered greatly on the character issue. White House staff circulated a political cartoon that appeared in the *Boston Globe* depicting John and Robert Kennedy walking among the heavenly clouds. "Teddy's running," Robert says. "What's he done this time?" John asks.[40]

In December Carter told the *Des Moines Register* that he thought Kennedy's reversal of support was a result of him moving from "a vision of perfection" to "a real flesh-and-blood candidate." Kennedy, he noted, had failed to meet high expectations. "That was almost inevitable," Carter said during a news conference, "and I don't say that in derogation of him." He noted his own initial frustration in being compared to idealized presidential images. "But I think once it got down to a matter of me versus specific human beings who also sought the Presidency, that factor was minimized." Carter knew that each mistake made by Kennedy distanced him further from myth. He perused articles disparaging the nostalgia behind Kennedy's campaign. Aides continued their efforts to separate Edward from John's image. When Kennedy criticized the Shah of Iran for having conducted "one of the most violent regimes in the history of mankind," the White House collected positive quotes that John Kennedy had made on behalf of the shah during his presidency. These were then given to the Washington bureau chief of the *Boston Herald American*, Robert E. Thompson, who wrote a front-page story contrasting President Kennedy's glowing assessments of the shah with Edward's insults.[41]

The hostage crisis provided Carter with short-term political benefits as the nation rallied around the president. From October to mid-December his approval rating doubled from 30 to 61 percent. With a 20 percent lead over Kennedy among Democratic voters, Carter now considered pulling out of the planned Iowa debate with Kennedy and Jerry Brown. Schneiders advised against the debate, noting that Carter "is now in the position of Kennedy before he announced: he is the repository of all the hopes of those disillusioned with others. At this point, he can only disappoint." Eizenstadt, however, warned Carter that he would appear to be "hiding behind Iran" and held captive by the crisis, a ploy that would wear thin in a matter of months if he did not actively seek votes.[42]

The White House soon announced that the president would not appear at political events while seeking nonpartisan support for the hostage crisis. In his memoir Carter maintained that it would have been a "mistake" for him to have debated in Iowa during the hostage crisis. By postponing political activities he "let the world know how seriously we continued to view these disturbing circumstances." For a man who professed self-confidence, who was supposedly "willing, even eager" to run against Kennedy, Carter did not have to dig deeply to find lofty excuses. He was not about to make the same mistake Nixon did in 1960. In Carter's last debate in 1976 he barely broke even against Gerald Ford, a candidate with the telegenic appeal of a sofa. Ted Kennedy was no Gerald Ford. He was the brother of a president who once reversed his entire political fortune with one debate. Despite Kennedy's rough start, Carter knew his rival had more personality and appeal than he did. He would campaign safely from the White House, granting interviews and holding news conferences. Comfortably leading in the polls, he chose to heighten a crisis mentality.[43]

Kennedy, meanwhile, self-destructed in Iowa. He was poorly organized, spent too much money, and often behaved as if the presidency was owed him. Throughout the early campaign he seldom shied from invoking his brother's legacy. But he was ultimately overshadowed by the myth that had given rise to his candidacy. Compared to his brothers, he was less eloquent, articulate, inspiring, graceful, and witty. On the stump he spoke too loud, laughed too hard, had no clear message, read his speeches woodenly, and rambled incoherently when speaking impromptu. Kennedy anticipated the high expectations that came with the "mystique," but not the degree of hostility that his campaign unleashed. "I felt the mystique in the middle '60's," a lawyer commented in Iowa. "But then the revelations came out about the Kennedy family—Chappaquiddick, John Kennedy's personal life. To me the mystique was shattered." Edward seemed accountable for all the sins of the family—the infidelity, the deceptions, and the opportunism—and he became a convenient target for those frustrated after two decades of reexamination of the Kennedy image.[44]

The Carter campaign subtly encouraged public uneasiness about Kennedy. Volunteers were urged to note that Carter was "a father who is providing the moral leadership to create a better world." "I don't think there is any way you can separate the responsibility of being a husband or a father or a basic human being from that of being a good President," Carter said in one advertisement. "What I do in the White House is to maintain a good family life, which I consider crucial to being a good President." From November 1979 to April 1980 the percentage of people who thought Kennedy had lied about Chappaquiddick almost doubled. Carter defeated Kennedy decisively in Iowa, winning by a two-to-one margin just eleven weeks after public opinion polls showed Kennedy to have a 34 percent advantage over Carter. It was the first defeat for Kennedy in his eighteen years in politics and the family's second defeat since Robert lost to McCarthy in the Oregon primary of 1968. With Kennedy's help, the Carter campaign had achieved exactly what it had planned. The senator appeared vincible, anachronistic, and flawed.[45]

In the following months Carter went on to defeat him in twenty-four of thirty-four primaries. To invigorate his failing effort and put more distance between himself and the president, Kennedy began chiding Carter for his poor leadership in world affairs, from Afghanistan to Iran. Carter was increasingly criticized for manipulating the political process through foreign-policy events. After losing the crucial New York primary to Kennedy, Carter learned that the character issue was being muted. Kennedy was now viewed as a gutsy and gracious loser. In Pennsylvania the Carter campaign reemphasized Kennedy's flaws. A half-hour television commercial showed Carter helping Amy with her homework: "Husband, father, President; he's done all three jobs with distinction." "The ads spoke of the perceptions of Kennedy that people already had in their minds," Rafshoon later explained. "We needed to remind people, that's all." Caddell was pleased that Rafshoon's ads "made Kennedy the issue again."[46]

Although polls consistently showed that Carter benefited greatly from the character issue, Kennedy narrowly won in Pennsylvania as well as in Michigan a few days later. Carter remained comfortably ahead in delegates, but his advisers sensed that his delegate count did not reflect the mood of the nation. The Rose Garden strategy, which had helped Carter appear presidential, now looked like an excuse to avoid a direct confrontation with the Kennedy myth. Following the failed rescue attempt of the hostages in Iran on April 25, Carter lifted his self-imposed ban on campaign travel, claiming the crisis was now more manageable.[47]

Kennedy and his advisers sensed that issues were catching up with Carter. Inflation and the nagging hostage crisis renewed questions about his leadership. Policy issues, rather than personality, were beginning to dominate the dialogue. In California Kennedy called on Carter to meet him in a televised debate, noting that Humphrey had debated McGovern there in 1972, Robert Kennedy had debated Eugene McCarthy in 1968, and John Kennedy had debated Lyndon Johnson during the Democratic convention. If Carter accepted the offer and then won the majority of votes in the June 3 primary,

Kennedy vowed he would concede the nomination to the president. Carter rejected the offer, knowing that the June 3 primaries virtually guaranteed him the number of delegates he needed to win the nomination on the first ballot.[48]

Carter arrived at the Democratic convention with 60 percent of the delegates pledged to him. To the president's obvious displeasure, Kennedy made a last-ditch, unsuccessful effort for an open convention, trying to change a party rule that required delegates to vote on the first ballot for the candidate to whom they were pledged. Addressing the convention the next night, Kennedy gave the speech of his lifetime. For months he had been ridiculed as ineffective, buffoonish, a loser who paled in comparison to John and Robert. Not this night. He began with a joke, noting that "things worked out a little different from the way I thought." But he quickly turned serious. "I have come here tonight not to argue as a candidate but to affirm a cause," he began. He called for unity, but he also articulated clearly his differences with Carter, something he should have done in November. Disheartened by conservative and moderate trends, he reminded followers about the party's heritage and called upon them to "sail against the wind." Kennedy distinguished between liberal values and liberal programs, implicitly refuting Carter's charge that he espoused outdated solutions from the 1960s. "The commitment I seek is not to outworn views, but to old values that will never wear out," he said. "Programs may sometimes become obsolete, but the ideal of fairness always endures. Circumstances may change, but the work of compassion must continue." He closed by associating himself with the courage, strength, and compassion of his brothers, drawing upon nostalgia to give final meaning to his campaign: "For all those whose cares have been our concern, the work goes on, the cause endures, the hope still lives, and the dream shall never die."[49]

The next day Carter called the address "one of the greatest speeches I have ever heard." The delegates interrupted Kennedy fifty-one times with applause. Five times they chanted, "We Want Ted." In the end they responded with a forty-minute demonstration on the convention floor. It was the most powerful evocation of the Kennedy aura since Robert Kennedy's appearance in Atlantic City in 1964. Even Carter delegates openly wept. The speech, Hamilton Jordan, later wrote, "triggered open the floodgates of memories: Camelot, magic rhetoric, and the shock of assassinations." Ironically, of course, the delegates rejected the old notions of liberalism they applauded. They were cheering collective, idealized memories, wanting to perpetuate John Kennedy's values even as they rejected Edward Kennedy. The convention was about to renominate a Southern moderate who advocated limited government, but the delegates wanted reassurance, to convince themselves that they were not forsaking John Kennedy's values in the process. It was both the last hurrah for Kennedy liberalism and a rekindling of Camelot.[50]

The next night Carter won the nomination on the first ballot, but Kennedy continued to hold hostage the convention's soul. For weeks Carter's speechwriters had considered a proper way to reach out to Kennedy during the acceptance speech. In the original drafts Carter intended simply to congratulate Kennedy on his "courageous campaign" and to note briefly that, while they differed in means, they shared common values and goals. As tensions increased, however, Caddell advised Carter to insert a statement intended to "nail EMK to the wall and make you gracious." After complimenting Kennedy on his hard-fought campaign, he should pressure Kennedy to support him by invoking John and Robert and implying that Carter was an extension of their cause. "There is no doubt that greatness lies ahead of you," the draft read, "but we need your strong voice now in the larger cause for which your brothers became martyrs and to which your own long life of public service has been dedicated." Hertzberg assured Carter, "Invoking his brothers this way will put him on the spot like nothing else could, and it is *not* in bad taste."[51]

After Kennedy's appearance, however, Hertzberg warned Carter that he now had "a tough act to follow." But he also had a unique opportunity to further unify the party. Because of the "emotional catharsis" prompted by the speech, Hertzberg sensed that "the Kennedy fever has broken." "You can now reach out to his people more openly than be[fore]." New drafts of Carter's speech were more deferential. Carter personally deleted the calculated reference to Kennedy's martyred brothers. He heralded Edward as "a tough competitor and a superb campaigner—I can attest to that." He congratulated "Ted" on his "magnificent speech" which defined the deeper meanings of the party. "I reach out to you and to those who supported you in your valiant and passionate campaign," Carter said. "Ted, your party needs—and I need—your idealism and dedication working for us. There is no doubt that even greater service lies ahead of you—and we are grateful to have your strong partnership now in the larger cause to which your own life has been dedicated." Delegates responded by chanting, "We Want Ted."[52]

Carter had originally intended to insult Kennedy while appearing gracious. Now, appreciating Kennedy's emotional hold on the convention, he reduced himself to a supplicant. "We've whipped his ass," a supporter told Rafshoon, "and now we're going to kiss his ass." Carter's appeal to Kennedy was just one of several awkward moments that night. His nomination received only a ten-minute demonstration. Unlike his 1976 convention speech, Carter was tense, evidenced in his high, shouting voice and perspiring visage. He recalled the great Democratic nominee of 1968, Hubert Horatio "Hornblower." The teleprompter failed. The audience seemed cheerless. Firecrackers were set off during the speech. And in the end, the balloon net atop the ceiling failed to open.[53]

Carter never looked more lonely than during the "celebration" that followed his speech. When Kennedy finally appeared on the podium, the roar of the crowd was louder than it had been for Carter's address. He appeared sober and unsmiling, determined not to clasp Carter's hand and raise his arms in the traditional unity salute. He shook Carter's hand, patted his back with his left hand, and quickly moved to the side. Carter looked pained. Television commentators noted the coldness. Kennedy wandered away from Carter, shaking hands and speaking with Arkansas Governor Bill Clinton. As the delegates chanted, "We Want Ted," Kennedy came onto the podium a second time, and Carter followed him off the stand, looking, as one Carter intimate said, "like a puppy dog." Kennedy offered a left-handed fist in the air. Reflexively, Carter duplicated the gesture with his right fist, desperate for even the semblance of unity. The interactions served as a metaphor of Carter's relationship with the Kennedy myth; he was both part of the Kennedy legacy and separate from it.[54]

After the convention Kennedy made a more concerted effort to support Carter, but the damage had been done. On the stump Carter called Kennedy "a great man," thanking him profusely in private letters for his strong support and for infusing into the campaign his "ideals," "vigor," and "spirit." Moved by political self-interest, Carter now praised the senator as the living embodiment of the Kennedy legacy. "Despite all the changes that have taken place since the early 1960s," he told an audience in Detroit, "the spirit of dedication and the spirit of idealism that marked John Kennedy's life is even more urgent today than perhaps it was then. Ted Kennedy personifies to me that spirit, and I'm glad to be working with him. . . ." Carter was also sensitive to avoiding any hint of character attack against Kennedy. In the draft of a speech for a Boston fund-raiser, he removed a joke that referred to a local dignitary's swimming skills. "No! No! No!" Carter wrote in the margins. [55]

Late in the campaign Carter made a final attempt to link himself to the traditions of Roosevelt, Truman, and John Kennedy. In Boston he recalled the dedication of the John F. Kennedy Library, "a day that brought back memories to my heart and to my mind that were almost overwhelming." Urging the public to vote, he repeatedly recalled John Kennedy's close victory in 1960. He criticized his opponent Ronald Reagan's insincerity for invoking John Kennedy and Franklin Roosevelt. He spoke at Bedford-Stuyvesant, describing the restoration project proposed by Robert Kennedy as a success that "would have made him very proud." During the last day of his campaign Carter quoted extensively from Robert Kennedy on the last day of *his* campaign. But such references were barely noticeable in the glare of Carter's own failures. If anyone projected optimism and idealism, it was Reagan. [56]

John Kennedy had helped elect Carter in 1976. Four years later Edward Kennedy helped defeat him. In many ways Carter's experience with the "mystique" mirrored Lyndon Johnson's. Both men were Southern incumbent Democratic presidents accused of a failure of leadership. Both found their nominations threatened by a "living and breathing" heir to the Kennedy legend. Both were deeply intimidated by the image Robert and Edward embodied. Like Johnson, Carter saw his nemesis as an opportunist, impatiently ambitious, morally flawed, and the benefactor of an inflated legacy. And like Johnson's absorption with Robert Kennedy, Carter devoted precious resources to neutralize Edward's ambitions. Although Johnson chose not to compete against the "mystique," and Carter won renomination, both presidents were escorted from office by a Kennedy. [57]

Edward Kennedy, meanwhile, seemed personally liberated from the myth of his brothers. From the beginning of his campaign, reporters and campaign aides had suspected he was merely playing out a sense of obligation to the Kennedy legend. By May he was poking fun at his defeats. He showed up at rallies wearing a rumpled suit with torn and mended pockets, greeting supporters in cracked and worn leather shoes. He gained weight. His face grew pasty and blotchy. John Kennedy had been meticulous, if not obsessed, with his physical appearance. Now, the last brother resembled Crazy Guggenheim. Like the Frank Fontaine character, Teddy could still belt out a political song when he had to. But he seemed comfortable with defeat and free from the expectations of perfection. In a way, he showed himself to be the most developed of all the Kennedy brothers. He was less compelled to hide behind façades. He learned to accept limitations, flaws, defeat, and folly in ways that his brothers never could. Ted Kennedy was different. He was real. He lost. John and Robert Kennedy had gone to great lengths to hide their imperfections. Edward seemed to define himself by them. In the process he was able to walk away from the torch he had dropped at Chappaquiddick.[58]

The status of the Kennedy myth remained indefinite by the fall of 1980. As a political symbol, the "mystique's" limitations were illustrated by Edward Kennedy's failure. "Running as a Kennedy doesn't always work," he later recalled. "I tried that once myself." The problem in his case, however, was less the message than the messenger. Edward Kennedy was not a credible torchbearer for the idealized standards that John symbolized. In addition to his character flaws, he represented outmoded liberal beliefs than even JFK had not embraced. But the Kennedy myth too was becoming less an ideological force than a purely symbolic one. Carter's invocations of John Kennedy in moving the party to the right pointed to the malleability of the Kennedy legacy. Because JFK's intentions were unclear and sometimes contradictory, he could be invoked to support moderation and limitation as easily as he could be used to entice voters to "sail against the wind." Indeed, the next president would use the Kennedy legend to move the nation even farther right.[59]

After losing to Ronald Reagan in 1980, Jimmy Carter retired to Plains, Georgia. For several years he was largely ignored by the news media and his contemporaries. He devoted himself to Habitat for Humanity, a volunteer organization that constructs housing for the needy. In the fall of 1986 the Carter Presidential Center was dedicated in Atlanta. Carter's good intentions and selflessness gained respect by the end of the decade. When he left office his approval rating was 34 percent. Ten years later 74 percent of the public had a favorable opinion of him. As part of his rehabilitation process, Carter wrote several books about his career and presidency. The Kennedys, however, remain a chapter in his career which he neither discusses nor has ever written about substantially.[60]

Jimmy Carter was never sure how to respond to the durability of the Kennedy legend, never able to come to authentic terms with its personal meaning. His uncertainty led to inconsistencies. In 1976 he encouraged memories of John Kennedy, tailoring himself to fill a vacuum felt since 1963. Once elected he abandoned any pretense of carrying out the Kennedy legacy. Three years later, pressed by political circumstances, he redefined the legacy in the context of his own inadequacies. Given the chance to compete against Edward Kennedy, Carter vacillated, avoiding his opponent while claiming he was eager to confront him. He made an issue of Kennedy's character while professing not to. He preferred to appear undaunted by the Kennedy legend, but White House memos revealed a president who nervously juggled myth, pride, and self-interest. For a man who claimed to embody the truth, he could be surprisingly devious. His relationship with the Kennedy legend exposed qualities of hypocrisy, opportunism, pettiness, insincerity, and fear in ways that few other challenges in his presidency did. He was not tormented as Johnson and Nixon were. Still, whether threatening or fortifying Carter, the "mystique" challenged his idealized self-image, revealed his shortcomings, and at times betrayed aspects of himself he would rather not recall.

7
Reinvention:
Ronald Reagan

WITH JIMMY CARTER's successful emulation of the Kennedy image in 1976, JFK was gradually becoming accessible to politicians of all ages, ideologies, and personality types. Young and old, conservative and liberal, male and female, realist and idealist, Northerner or Southerner—by 1984 almost any candidate could find something in John Kennedy to relate to his or her campaign. A politician could link idealized memories of JFK to his own innate qualities, or reinvent Kennedy or himself to bring him in closer alignment. The malleability of the Kennedy image became strikingly apparent that year when Ronald Reagan, Gary Hart, and the Democratic ticket of Walter Mondale and Geraldine Ferraro each claimed to be the true embodiment of the Kennedy past. That these candidates, as well as others, could feasibly draw on the Kennedy myth showed how universal—if not empty—the legacy had become. The remarkable political mileage that Hart got from emulating Kennedy, Reagan's conservative redefining of the Kennedy legacy, and the Democrats' resulting frustration pointed to the myth's value, appeal, and resiliency. The style of John Kennedy endured, even if his substance did not.

"Politics," Ronald Reagan once said, "is just like show business." As an actor and politician, Reagan liked to please his audience, to appeal to his listeners' expectations by playing to their predisposed emotions. To inspire his audiences he drew upon stock characters, frequently invoking Washington, Lincoln, and Franklin Roosevelt. He constantly praised soldiers, athletes, celebrities, and achievers. He even quoted fictionalized dialogue, most famously that written for the role of George Gipp, the Notre Dame football player whom Reagan portrayed in the film *Knute Rockne—All American*. Such invocations associated Reagan with powerful national myths and reminded listeners of their imagined origins and destiny. "He has appropriated other American folk tales," biographer Garry Wills noted, "making it difficult at times to distinguish between the teller and the tale, between one American and America itself. That explains Reagan's intimacy with America's psyche. He came at it from within."[1]

By the time Reagan was elected president, John Kennedy's place in national mythology was perhaps never more prominent, nor superficial. Through television and film portrayals, Hollywood had thoroughly transformed him into myth, stereotype, and sentiment. Motion picture producers had never hesitated to market the nation's presidents. Theodore Roosevelt was once depicted as the hero in a silent-film version of *Goldilocks and the Three Bears*. The silver screen portrayed Abraham Lincoln and Woodrow Wilson with all the historical mindfulness of an afternoon soap opera. By the early 1970s television docudramas began shaping the historical perceptions of tens of millions of people who were increasingly turning away from print media. In the twenty years that followed the airing of ABC's "The Missiles of October" in 1974, the Kennedy family, collectively and individually, was the subject of more than a dozen television docudramas. Theoretically one could sit in front of a television set for more than forty-eight hours and watch the entire history of the family without seeing a repeated episode.[2]

The nature of docudrama mandated that entertainment values supersede accuracy. Film portrayals were left largely in the hands of hucksters—entertainers, producers, and directors untrained in history, whose intentions in this case were to merchandise the Kennedy name by exploiting the dramatic expectations of their audience. The Kennedy docudramas were largely morality plays, giving velocity to counterrevisionist trends by disputing or ignoring unflattering disclosures surrounding the family.[3]

One fictional television portrayal succinctly elucidated the Kennedy myth. In a 1986 episode of "The Twilight Zone" called "Profile in Silver," a Harvard historian, Dr. Joseph Fitzgerald, is sent to us from two hundred years in the future to record the events of the Kennedy years. Knowing that Kennedy is to die in Dallas, the historian travels there to record the assassination. Filming the motorcade, he is overcome by emotion and saves Kennedy's life, ignoring his directive not to intervene in the flow of history. A grateful president later thanks the hero but quickly becomes distracted by a series of horrifying events—tornados sweep through Texas, Khrushchev is assassinated, the world is suddenly on the brink of nuclear war—all because the "fabric of time has been bent" by the historian's action. Fitzgerald confronts Kennedy, convincing him that he is from the future and that history has been distorted by his deed. Kennedy slowly understands that events must be replayed if the world is to survive. He must return to Dallas and die. The historian assures the president that "the realization of your greatest dreams will come true in the future." At the last instant, however, Fitzgerald manipulates the mechanisms of time travel and courageously reverses roles with Kennedy. He sends himself as a surrogate Kennedy to Dallas where he is shot, and transports the "real" Kennedy to two hundred years in the future where he, rather than Fitzgerald, will teach at Harvard.[4]

The episode brought to the fore some of the strongest themes of the Kennedy myth. Kennedy's martyrdom is Christ-like as he sacrifices himself to save humankind. The historian's willingness to trade roles with Kennedy allows the viewer to fantasize whether he or she would take a bullet for Kennedy. In the end, the docudrama both reaffirms Kennedy's goodness and rescues him from death. He is alive and well and living in the future—where he rightfully belongs. Add to such "histotainment" the countless sentimental documentaries on the Kennedys, and it becomes clear that television has encouraged the public to ignore history and to seek comfort in illusions. The heartwarming renderings have helped transform John Kennedy from a historical figure into a popular-culture icon.

Despite scholarly revisions, despite the disclosures of covert actions and sexual affairs, Kennedy was never more popular than during the Reagan presidency. A *Newsweek* poll in 1983 indicated that no president in American history was close to matching his appeal. Thirty percent of the public wished he were then president. A 1985 Harris survey showed that Kennedy was rated best among the preceding nine presidents in areas concerning confidence, personality, trust, ability to get things done, domestic affairs, and the setting of high moral standards. That same year a *USA Today* survey of 434 women indicated that more women chose JFK than any other celebrity or historical figure as the man they would most like to father their next child. Kennedy's posthumous fame and status as a celebrity enhanced his value as a political symbol, albeit at a highly superficial level. It was far less Kennedy's ideas that attracted attention than his emotive qualities—charm, energy, youth, excitement, and idealism. The fictional Kennedy had become a surrogate reality.[5]

Like the blending of history and entertainment, Ronald Reagan's election in 1980 illustrated that politics and show biz too were often indistinguishable. Since the 1950s media critics had lamented the troubling decline of political discourse. The infusion of television and advertising into the political process, they argued, had resulted in a greater premium on entertainment than on enlightenment. By the 1960s national candidates seemed increasingly assessed by their movie-star aura. "The Democrats," Norman Mailer wrote in his famous article on the 1960 Democratic convention, "were going to nominate a man who, no matter how serious his political dedication might be, was indisputably and willy-nilly going to be seen as a great box-office actor, and the consequences of that were staggering and not at all easy to calculate." After Kennedy it was increasingly common for politicians to use entertainment programs to promote themselves. By the 1970s the sketch-comedy program "Saturday Night Live" was the first television show to regularly induce political figures to appear as guests or hosts. In the 1980s Tip O'Neill, Gary Hart, and Michael Dukakis each made cameo appearances on the popular NBC comedy "Cheers." President Reagan starred in his own prime-time television special, "All Star Party for 'Dutch' Reagan." The program included songs and tributes from Frank Sinatra, Dean Martin, and Charlton Heston.[6]

The fusion of entertainment and politics had come full circle. With Kennedy, the American people had elected a president who wanted to be an actor; with Reagan, they elected an actor who wanted to be president. It was perhaps only natural, then, that Reagan and Kennedy, as storyteller and myth, developed a symbiotic relationship. The celebrification of JFK complemented Reagan's existing world of myth, fantasy, and imagination. As Reagan embarked on his presidency, he would do for the Kennedy legend what the docudramas did; he would tap into the dramatic expectations of the audience by invoking Kennedy, making people feel good about themselves, their nation, and their president. As a pitchman for national myths, he bridged the worlds between fact and fiction, history and entertainment. His invocations reflected and reinforced the superficiality of the Kennedy legacy, confusing its meaning and broadening its accessibility.

II On June 5, 1981, the thirteenth anniversary of Robert Kennedy's assassination and just two months after surviving an attempt on his own life, Ronald Reagan presented the Robert F. Kennedy medal to his widow, Ethel, in a late morning Rose Garden ceremony. The medal was authorized by Congress in November 1978, but Jimmy Carter had found cause not to present it. Reagan's willingness to participate in the ceremony said as much about his grace and political astuteness as it did about Carter's avoidance. The scene was plainly ironic. Unlike Carter, who professed a personal and philosophical association with John Kennedy, Reagan had a long history of expressed contempt for the Kennedys. Robert had campaigned on behalf of California Governor Edmund Brown against Reagan in 1966. When Kennedy ran for president in 1968, Reagan mocked RFK's law-and-order appeals to blue-collar voters and accused him of renouncing his brother's pledge not to lose South Vietnam to the Communists. After Robert lost the Oregon primary to McCarthy, Reagan cheerfully noted that the defeat dispelled the Kennedys' "myth of invincibility."[7]

The Kennedy legend proved invincible even if the living Kennedys were not. That summer morning Reagan displayed his ability to use personality and acting skills to appeal to those with whom he had little in common. Speaking of Robert Kennedy, he heralded his "service to his country, his commitment to his great ideals, and his devotion to those less fortunate." "He roused the comfortable," Reagan eulogized. "He exposed the corrupt, remembered the forgotten, inspired his countrymen, and renewed and enriched the American conscience." Reagan acknowledged his "philosophical differences" with Kennedy, but he noted that he "always appreciated his wit and his personal grace." "And may I say," he added, "I remember very vividly those last days of the California primary and the closeness that had developed in our views about the growing size and unresponsiveness of government and our political institutions." Speaking on behalf of Ethel, Edward Kennedy thanked the president. "It is appropriate that he should receive it from you," he said, "for he understood so well that the common love of our country transcends all party identification and all partisan differences."[8]

The ceremony was vintage Reagan. Perhaps better than any modern president, he understood intuitively the power of myth to unify diverse groups. Thirteen years earlier Robert Kennedy had been a leading spokesperson for everything Reagan disliked about liberal Democrats: big-spending government programs and failure of nerve against Communist aggression. While Reagan was praising Robert's "devotion to those less fortunate," his administration was making broad cuts in the social programs RFK had once advocated. He heralded Robert for remembering the forgotten people that Reagan himself was accused of neglecting. He praised Kennedy's selflessness while presiding over an administration accused of fostering greed and neglect. Never one to let facts stand in the way of history, Reagan drew on selective evidence to suggest implicitly that more elements linked him with Kennedy than separated the two men. By the end of his first term, Reagan would show such skill at associating himself with the Kennedy legend that Paul D. Erickson, a scholar familiar with Reagan's rhetoric, pronounced him "a conservative reincarnation" of John Kennedy.[9]

That a conservative Republican could convincingly associate himself with the Kennedy myth was a consequence of several characteristics unique to Reagan. From the time he was a boy growing up in Tampico, Illinois, he had been drawn to myth and fantasy. "As a kid," he recalled, "I lived in a world of pretend." While working as a sportscaster in Des Moines during the 1930s, he learned the trick of covering Chicago Cubs baseball games without being at the ball park. He took wire service teletype relays of the game, which gave only bare outlines of the plays, and translated them into vivid radio accounts. As a speaker for General Electric in the 1950s, he drew on acting skills to mold his image and rhetoric to suit conservative audiences. "Reagan believes in what he says," biographer Lou Cannon wrote, "and he wound up believing what he was saying. More than anything, it is his GE experience that changed Reagan from an adversary of big business into one of its most ardent spokesmen." Numerous biographers have pointed to Reagan's inability at times to separate fact from fiction. He often told the story of a World War II pilot who was awarded posthumously the Medal of Honor when he ordered his crew to bail out of the crippled bomber while he went down holding the hand of a wounded airman trapped in the ball turret. No such event ever occurred, except in a scene from Dana Andrews's war movie *A Wing and A Prayer*.[10]

Before his famous televised commercial on behalf of Republican nominee Barry Goldwater in 1964, Reagan had been involved in politics for some twenty years. He had been president of the Screen Actors Guild, campaigned on behalf of liberal Democrats until the late 1940s, and gradually articulated conservative themes on behalf of GE through the early 1960s. The 1960 presidential campaign marked an important transition in the development of his political consciousness, a point at which he claimed to have "completed a process of self conversion." His feelings for Kennedy were expressed in a letter he wrote to Nixon shortly after the Democratic convention. In it he noted that he had heard in Kennedy's acceptance speech "a frightening call to arms." Reagan had an uncomfortable appreciation for JFK's image: "Unfortunately, he is a powerful speaker with an appeal to the emotions." Disturbed by Kennedy's proposed programs, which translated into bigger, more expensive government, Reagan offered a strained comparison: "One last thought—shouldn't someone tag Mr. Kennedy's bold new imaginative program with its proper age? Under the tousled boyish haircut is still old Karl Marx—first launched a century ago. There is nothing new in the idea of a Government being Big Brother to us all. Hitler called his 'State Socialism' and way before him it was 'benevolent monarchy.'" Reagan was soon at the forefront of "Democrats for Nixon," delivering more than two hundred speeches on behalf of the Republican nominee.[11]

After Kennedy's election Reagan's talks for General Electric became more apocalyptic. He was particularly strident about Kennedy's alleged failure of nerve against Communist aggression. He also felt in competition with Kennedy's image. "During this time," he later wrote, "I was told that I was the most popular speaker in the country after President Kennedy." He suspected that the administration was countering his appearances by sending cabinet officials to the cities where he spoke. And he further suspected that he was being harassed by the Justice Department over his negotiation of an agreement between the Screen Actors Guild and the MCA talent agency. Reagan's reaction to Kennedy's assassination is unknown. He is the only president since Kennedy never to have spoken of or written about it. His daughter Patty Davis, however, recalled that she was the only person in her family to follow the events on television that weekend.[12]

In 1964 Reagan served as cochairperson of California Republicans for Goldwater. In the final week of the campaign he delivered a powerful pretaped televised speech on behalf of Goldwater, stimulating enormous contributions. Lou Cannon contends that it was the culmination of Reagan's political growth, fully transforming him from a celebrity into a conservative spokesperson. Unlike Goldwater, Reagan offered apocalyptic warnings without appearing terrifying. In 1966 a group of wealthy California businessmen sponsored him in a bid for governor. During the campaign Reagan drew on his affable personality, quick-study skills, and acting techniques. "All eyes were on him," Sander Vanocur recalled. "I've only seen this kind of magnetism in one other public figure—Jack Kennedy." Reagan won with 58 percent of the vote, becoming the new rising star of the Republican party.[13]

Just four months after being sworn in as governor, Reagan crossed paths with Robert Kennedy in what some pundits speculated might foreshadow the 1968 presidential contest. The two men appeared together on May 15, 1967, on the CBS program "Town Meeting of the World." A clear consensus of reporters agreed that Reagan bested Kennedy. He appeared poised, paternal, and serene as he defended America's involvement in the war. Kennedy, on the other hand, was defensive, unwilling to condemn a war his brother had initiated. Reagan took political communication to a new, more interactive level, one unintimidated and unencumbered by the Kennedy image.[14]

As governor, Reagan remained a leading spokesperson for the right wing of the Republican party and even made a brief, ill-conceived effort to win the Republican presidential nomination in 1968. During the Watergate scandal, he argued that Nixon had done nothing more criminal than Johnson and Kennedy. He was not hurt by his defense of Nixon. Indeed, as Cannon observes, "Reagan profited from Watergate because it encouraged voters to look at the human dimensions of their leaders, a yardstick by which Reagan is better measured" than by his substantive knowledge of issues. From 1972 through Nixon's resignation, Reagan offered encouragement and optimism to party regulars. In 1976 he fell just sixty delegate votes short of denying incumbent Gerald Ford the nomination. By 1980, with the failure of Jimmy Carter, the nation wanted desperately to believe that the presidency could be restored to a viable institution. Reagan's optimism, idealism, and unabashed hero worship contrasted with Carter's glum piety.[15]

Reagan's most valuable presidential symbol in 1980 was his first political hero, Franklin Roosevelt. He sustained his appeal with conservatives in 1980 by railing against big government; meanwhile, he appealed to moderate Democrats by presenting himself as a true Roosevelt Democrat. His boldest invocation came during his acceptance speech at the Republican National Convention in Detroit when he concluded with a lengthy quotation citing Roosevelt's desire for a less costly and more manageable federal government. Through errors of omission, he exploited Roosevelt for conservative ends. As the historian William Leuchtenburg noted, Reagan's Roosevelt image came from his promise to bring to the presidency a new coalition, an imaginative domestic agenda, a bold foreign policy, a sense of vision, strong leadership, and an inner strength. Such images associated

Reagan with a widely regarded "great" president while avoiding
unflattering comparisons to Nixon or Goldwater. Democratic leaders
such as Edward Kennedy and Walter Mondale protested Reagan's use
of Roosevelt, but they missed the point. The link between Reagan
and Roosevelt was impressionistic, not substantive. Moderate Democrats who had grown skeptical of liberalism were less mindful of the
philosophical differences than they were of the emotive similarities,
particularly as Reagan clouded FDR's philosophy. Later he would do
the same with the Kennedy image.[16]

During the 1980 campaign Reagan occasionally drew on John
Kennedy's memory. He charged that the Carter administration was
"dominated" by the "McGovernite wing of the party" and that it had
"broken sharply with the views and policies of Harry Truman, John
Kennedy, and many contemporary Democratic leaders." He vowed to
protect American prestige abroad by restoring the Truman-Kennedy
tradition in areas of national security and foreign policy. Quoting
from the speech Kennedy could not deliver in Dallas on November
22, 1963, Reagan pledged that America would once again serve as
"the watchman on the wall of world freedom."[17]

After the election Reagan's invocations shifted markedly from
Roosevelt to John Kennedy. During his first term he cited JFK more
than he cited any other former president. And he quoted Kennedy
more frequently than had any president since Lyndon Johnson.
According to Paul Erickson's calculations, Reagan invoked Kennedy
on 133 occasions, compared with seventy-six times that he quoted
Roosevelt. He referred to Calvin Coolidge only thirty-four times, to
Richard Nixon sixteen times, and to Herbert Hoover just once.
Initially Reagan did not speak at length about Kennedy; his recollections were seldom sentimental and usually employed to generate
support for specific measures. He sought to attract liberal support for
his economic package by frequently quoting John Kennedy's observation, "A rising tide lifts all boats." To gain support for cuts in social
service programs, he cited JFK's calls for volunteerism and his plea to
"Ask not what your country can do for you . . ." When he turned his
attention to foreign policy, he invoked Kennedy's name to procure
increased defense spending and to pursue aggressive policies in
Central America.[18]

Reagan's use of Kennedy soon inspired a political cartoon entitled
"New Frontier, 1983," depicting Reagan with a Kennedy-style haircut
amid a parody of quotes: "Ich bin ein Grenadian"; "Ask not what
your government can do for you. Period"; "We can't dismantle the

federal government in the first thousand days. But let us begin." As with his use of Roosevelt, Democrats charged Reagan with quoting Kennedy out of context and drawing evidence in a highly selective fashion. Edward Kennedy reminded reporters that, unlike Reagan, John Kennedy spoke out on behalf of "those who don't have an effective and forceful spokesman." Theodore Sorensen too criticized conservatives who used Kennedy to support the U.S. invasion of Grenada. When citing Kennedy's toughness, Sorensen wrote, they neglect to note that Kennedy negotiated the Cuban missile crisis without firing a shot. "By rejecting an 'either-or' approach, [Kennedy] built a record not easily categorized under any ideological label," Sorensen explained.[19]

Although both Reagan and Kennedy projected elements of optimism and idealism, their public images differed sharply. Reagan was termed "the political embodiment of the heroic westerner," an image augmented by his California ranch, his tall, rugged appearance, and his innocent sincerity and optimism. Reagan's antiintellectualism, his commonsense reasoning, and his effort to dismantle the New Deal drew comparisons to Andrew Jackson. Likewise, his calm, affable nature, his ability to simplify complex issues and events, and his grandfatherly reassurance evoked Warren G. Harding and Dwight Eisenhower. Kennedy was perceived as "great" because he seemed better than most people. He was more articulate, more intelligent, more poised, and better-looking than the average person. Reagan's popularity stemmed, on the other hand, from his common-man, commonsense image. He seemed similar to everyone and thus easy to relate to. He spoke in simple homilies, provided anecdotal assessments of the nation's ills, and heralded myths that, even if not exactly real, he obviously believed.[20]

Their personalities, too, were studies in contrast. Reagan was only six years older than Kennedy, but he seemed ancient compared to the late president, who remained frozen in time and forever young. Kennedy was Harvard-educated and a Pulitzer prize–winning author. His rhetorical style was in the lofty tradition of Winston Churchill. Reagan was a gifted raconteur who wove stories into his speeches with the ease of Will Rogers. Kennedy had a sardonic wit. Reagan's humor was usually more corny and scripted on a four-by-five index card. Kennedy worked on just a few hours of sleep, saw himself as the hub in a managerial wheel, and had an insatiable appetite for information. Reagan was passive, disengaged, impatient with details, and delegated authority. There was a qualitative difference in their idealism. Kennedy described himself as an idealist without illusions. He would have cringed at Reagan's sentimentality. Reagan was an idealist seemingly lost in illusion. Like Kennedy, he initiated covert operations, but he deluded himself into believing that he never traded missiles for hostages—he was pursuing a noble policy to gain the release of American hostages while opening relations with anti-Khomeini factions in Iran. The factions, it turned out, did not exist. Like Kennedy, Reagan talked of "sacrifice" and "requirements." But unlike Kennedy, he made no real demands of his audience. Mary Stuckey, a student of Reagan's rhetoric, observed that Kennedy had asked Americans to give of themselves to public service, to participate in making the nation more vital and responsive. Reagan merely asked Americans to believe "in ourselves . . . our capacity to perform great deeds." The audience could participate in Reagan's heroic quest for a greater America by doing nothing. [21]

But such contrasts had little effect in separating Reagan from Kennedy. Reagan was able to associate himself with presidents with whom he had little in common because his invocations seemed consistent with who he was. Indeed, given his long history of evoking myths, he seemed perfectly in character. Likewise, Reagan shared fundamental qualities with Kennedy and Roosevelt. He too urged the nation to break free of the doldrums; his personality offered the promise of greatness; he appealed to higher possibilities and pledged to restore vitality to the office. He was appealing even to those who opposed his ideas and programs. His invocation of the heroic Kennedy fit naturally with his own worldview and style of leadership. He had consistently heralded strength, leadership, courage, and the capacity to inspire. Like an actor, Reagan came at Roosevelt and later Kennedy not with facts but with feelings. His inner calm, meanwhile, made him immune to fears of comparisons. Like Ford, Reagan was undaunted by Kennedy's memory. Nor was he concerned with the presidential ambitions of Edward Kennedy. During his first term he was once asked what he would do if Edward became a presidential candidate. "I guess I'd just have to point out that I used to be a lifeguard," he replied. [22]

Given John Kennedy's sustained popularity by 1984, other national politicians, particularly Democrats, appreciated the obvious value of reclaiming the Kennedy legend. When John Kennedy died, he left behind a generation of politicians who were moved by his message and image. One candidate in particular came remarkably close to seizing the presidential nomination in large measure because he reminded voters of John Kennedy. Like Reagan, he was raised in a small, conservative, Midwest town, had a lower-middle-class up-bringing, and was identifiable as a Westerner. Like Reagan, he was an idealist, lost in his own set of myths. Like Reagan, he appealed to those who wanted to be seduced. Unlike Reagan, however, he seemed to use Kennedy less to fill a void in the national spirit than within himself.

The Rise and Fall of Gary Hart

CAMPAIGNING IN NEW HAMPSHIRE in the winter of 1984, Gary Hart appeared to be the quintessential Kennedy "clone." A man in his mid-forties, he displayed chiseled features, a tall, lean build, a full, thick head of hair cut in an Ivy League style, and a youthful smile. During speeches he chopped the air with his forefinger and hand. He went coatless and hatless during freezing weather. In public settings he appeared physically uncomfortable, fiddling nervously with his tie and sport-coat buttons, and brushing back his hair. When he walked he put his left hand in his jacket pocket with one thumb on the outside. Moreover, he repeatedly invoked John Kennedy's name, quoted Kennedy's words, and echoed Kennedy's themes.[1]

After his stunning victory in the New Hampshire Democratic primary, Hart was besieged by the news media. Who was this new, young candidate who upset conventional wisdom by defeating both Walter Mondale and John Glenn, the presumed front-runners for the nomination? Reporters rummaged about Hart's hometown in Ottawa, Kansas, questioning old classmates, neighbors, and relatives. It was soon learned that Hart had changed his name in the early 1960s, shortening it from Hartpence. His signatures had varied noticeably throughout his life. He had been unclear as to his date of birth. Such peculiarities raised fundamental questions about Hart's self-identity and fueled jokes that he was copying John Kennedy. Speaking at the White House correspondents' dinner, President Reagan remarked about impersonator Rich Little's guest appearance: "I was a little disappointed tonight, because you should really see him when he impersonates Gary Hart imitating Jack Kennedy."[2]

More than ten years have passed since Hart narrowly lost the

Democratic nomination. Questions surrounding his identity were later overshadowed by the image of Donna Rice on his lap on a Bimini dock. In the long reach of history, Hart will be remembered more for his political self-destruction than for his achievements. But his rise and fall illustrate the fickleness of the Kennedy myth as a symbolic force. Perhaps no national politician who was not a flesh-and-blood Kennedy benefited so greatly from reminding voters of JFK than Hart. And none suffered as much from comparisons. In the end, reality intruded upon illusions, both for the public that realized that Hart was no Jack Kennedy, and for a candidate who never fully understood how much he had lost himself in Kennedy's image.

Defining Gary Hart had long been a source of frustration for friends and reporters alike. "He's been a friend of mine for twenty-five years," Hal Haddon, Hart's Senate campaign manager, observed, "and I've never got to the bottom of him." Popularly described as mysterious, complex, and remote, Hart responded to such character-izations with a mixture of humor and defensiveness. "I used to be cold and aloof. Now I'm just enigmatic. Give me another 25 years and I'll be transparent," he said in 1987. Some of his difficulties in projecting a public image stemmed from his aversion to political theatrics. "Phoniness drives me nuts and politics is loaded with phonies," he once noted. "I constantly try to avoid what turns people off about politics—hypocrisy and shallow emotionalism. I am not an entertainer." Hart was not above show-biz politics, evident from his walk-on in an episode of television's "Cheers." But it would be difficult to imagine him cooking up barbecue with Bryant Gumbel on the "Today Show," or talking about his inner-child in a teary-eyed interview with Barbara Walters. Even within the confines of relatively private settings he was ill at ease. During dinner parties he hated playing games like charades. "I hate anything where you have to make a fool out of yourself," he explained.[3]

Hart was raised in Ottawa, a small, conservative, Republican town that voted three-to-one against Kennedy in 1960. "My childhood was as happy as one can be in not plush economic circumstances," he recalled. "My parents were mainly interested in loving us, in giving us the best start they could, in letting us be whatever we could be." Hart was a well-mannered, intelligent, and introverted kid. His strict religious upbringing provided a fundamental layer of idealism that drew him to John Kennedy. The Church of the Nazarene was extremely conservative, formed at the turn of the century as an offshoot of mainstream Methodism. "I got my values from my family and the church and the schools I went to and they were . . . service oriented," Hart recalled in 1992. "It was that you weren't here on earth just to make money or just to aggrandize yourself or just to be a cog in the social wheel or just live in comfort. You had an obligation and a duty. And in my [early] life, that had always had a church or religious or spiritual overtone."[4]

Hart attended Bethany Nazarene College in Bethany, Oklahoma, where he planned to study for the ministry. There J. Prescott Johnson, a philosophy teacher, introduced him to ideas outside the Nazarene mainstream, particularly the writings of Plato and Kierkegaard. After graduation Hart moved to New Haven, Connecticut, where he attended Yale Divinity School to pursue a career in either teaching or the ministry. But by 1960 he felt "adrift" in terms of his goals and ambitions. He still wished to pursue social service, but he no longer felt pulled to a religious vocation. Although he was drawn to academic pursuits, he did not want to teach. In short, he felt "a huge, big vacuum, professional and career vacuum, and I didn't know what to do." In the spring of 1960 he came closer to his calling. With the advent of the Democratic primaries, the conversation on the Yale campus turned to Kennedy's candidacy. Before then Hart had been generally indifferent about politics. During a social ethics course at Yale, however, students debated whether a Catholic could become president. Hart was struck by the degree to which his liberal classmates believed Kennedy would be barred from the presidency based on religious grounds. "That was my first real memory of him as a figure," he noted. "And then I began to pay attention."[5]

On a trip to New York City with three classmates several months later, Hart saw Kennedy speak in the ballroom of the Waldorf-Astoria Hotel. "Gary was in awe of him," recalled Joe Jones, who was with Hart that day. "It was in a way Gary's revelation." Hart later dismissed Jones's description as an exaggeration. "I don't trust even my closest friends to describe my emotions," he said, laughing. But he did remember "enormous electricity" and "a magnetism" coming from Kennedy. In 1993 he wrote of also being drawn to Kennedy's existential qualities, sense of irony, and detachment. He became active in the Kennedy campaign, working as a volunteer. When Kennedy made a final campaign swing through New England on the weekend before the election, Hart saw him again and remembered "enormous excitement in the air." It was Kennedy's presence, not just his rhetoric, that impressed Hart. Caught up in the euphoria, he overestimated Kennedy's chances for victory. "The shock to me on election night wasn't that he won," he recalled. "It was that he won so narrowly."[6]

The Kennedy campaign helped fill an important void in Hart's life. Although he was raised to view politics as worldly, vain, and corrupt, Hart recalled that Kennedy gave "direction and purpose" to his own impulse for service and reform. "It was an idealistic message," he explained. "It was a legitimizing message. For the first time in my lifetime, somebody in authority and power said it is not only acceptable to go into government or public service, it is desirable to do so. And noble." Hart no longer felt at odds with himself about how to pursue service-oriented goals in a manner consistent with his religious upbringing as well as his new philosophical and intellectual awareness. Kennedy served as "a bridge to the real world, an idealistic and honorable bridge," Hart recalled. Temperamentally, Kennedy reflected Hart's own cool detachment. Philosophically, Kennedy was consistent with Plato's emphasis on a rational approach to politics free of crude emotionalism. Spiritually, Kennedy pushed Hart toward self-actualization. Kierkegaard had emphasized that a person arrived at a stage of authentic existence not only through intellect but through a conscious decision and an act of commitment—a leap of faith. Through Kennedy, Hart made a decision, committing himself to a political life. He changed his academic focus, deciding to attend Yale Law School and to pursue a career related to public service as a government lawyer. No one in politics, he recalled, ever influenced him as Kennedy did.[7]

In the summer of 1963 Hart joined the fringes of the New Frontier, becoming a summer intern at the Justice Department, then headed by Robert Kennedy. Hart had a memorable meeting with the attorney general when, as student chairman of Yale's moot court program, he invited him to the university to preside over the prize argument case. He remembered that Kennedy's demeanor belied his popular image as "ruthless." "He spoke so softly you could barely hear him," he recalled. "Extremely shy." Kennedy asked Hart about his legal interests and joked about not being accepted at Yale. "He couldn't have been nicer, but I was shaking all the time," Hart remembered. Kennedy tentatively agreed to participate in the moot court program scheduled for December 1963.[8]

Hart was at his New Haven apartment preparing for an interview with a Denver law firm when he heard that John Kennedy had been shot. "Oh, it was horrible, horrible," Hart remembered. "It was horrible, horrible, horrible." He traveled with his wife to his sister-in-law's home in New Jersey for a planned family reunion, but he could not shake off his feelings of devastation. "I thought about it a lot in the sense of why the impact?" Hart recalled. "Why this huge emotional impact for somebody who was not a member of the family? And it was like he was a member of the family. I can't explain it."[9]

According to his professor at Yale, William Lee Miller, Hart came to his office after the assassination to express his grief. "I did not realize how much of a spiritual investment I had in that man," Hart allegedly told Miller. Nearly thirty years later Hart did not specifically recall the comment. "I don't think I would have said 'spiritual' because I'm pretty careful about keeping my politics and my religion separate," he noted. "And I never got Kennedy *that* far out of proportion." Whatever the degree of Hart's grief, it is clear Kennedy had served as an important vehicle in Hart's impulse to pursue idealistic and noble goals deeply rooted in Christian values. In committing himself to the New Frontier, he fused secular intentions with spiritual ideals so that they were not easily distinguishable.[10]

It was hardly surprising, then, that the utter senselessness of Kennedy's death challenged Hart's faith in politics. "I gave up," he recalled. "I literally gave up after the first assassination." Hart graduated from Yale in 1964. He returned to Washington where he worked for two years as an attorney in the Department of the Interior. He determined to complete his time in Washington and then return to Denver to get on with his life. "The sense of hope and the sense of optimism and unboundless [sic] American spirit suddenly was crushed," he recalled. "All the rules changed. All the rules. Life. It made people fatalistic. It made people vulnerable. It made people insecure about their own physical safety." Although he still intended to be a government lawyer, his dream of actively reforming society seemingly died at Dallas. When Hart spoke and wrote about America having lost its innocence, he echoed a sentiment felt by millions of people. But, on another level, what he really meant and what only he could know was that *he* had lost the youth and innocence he had experienced through Kennedy.[11]

Hart struggled to work through his period of trial. "That was a choice, too," he recalled. "A kind of important one in my life, I guess. Because the question became if the reason for doing this is gone, I mean the personal reason for doing this, why do it? And then I thought, well no, that's not what it's about. It wasn't about the person." It was, as Hart implied, about doing good through public service. A truly political person would not have seriously considered rejecting his profession. But Hart was less a politician than he was a devotee. The day before moving back to Colorado in 1966, he visited John Kennedy's grave for the first time, an observance he repeated "a number of times" throughout his career. Each time Hart felt a personal connection between his own life and the Kennedys. "It all comes back," he noted. "And you can't go up there and separate Robert from John. Then it's a whole decade or a whole lifetime."[12]

Hart returned to Denver where he worked for a prestigious law firm. Despite the vast social legislation passed under Lyndon Johnson, he could not shake the hopelessness he felt from Kennedy's death. The Vietnam War, Hart recalled, renewed his sense of activism. But he did not go to work in politics until Robert Kennedy declared his candidacy. The next day Hart and about a dozen young Denver lawyers set up a Kennedy for President headquarters. "I was almost the first one in the door," he recalled. Asked how much of his affection for John was transferred to Robert in 1968, Hart laughed. "About 110 percent," he said. Robert was younger and more accessible than John, Hart explained. "He was less the kind of remote, idealized figure, but still a figure of some consequence."[13]

In April Kennedy traveled to Denver to speak. Standing behind him with other campaign volunteers, Hart was surprised by two details. First, Kennedy needed to read from a text in order to give a rather predictable and well-rehearsed speech. Second, Kennedy's hands shook as he turned the pages. "It really told me about 10,000 words about *him*," Hart recalled. "Here was a guy [who was never] comfortable in that position [as a public speaker]. Here was a guy who was thrust into a role that fate and circumstances had not equipped him for." Robert, Hart observed, did not have his brother's self-confidence, grace, and style, and he knew it. "There he was. I mean, his hands were shaking," Hart repeated. "Here's a real vulnerable human being."[14]

In many ways John Kennedy, as a "remote, idealized figure," had represented Hart's ideal self—the part of Hart that wanted to do good in the world, that longed not to be vulnerable, that could be smooth in public, seemingly in control and infallible. Robert was closer to Hart's private self. The characteristics that he noticed in Robert were also part of himself—soft-spoken, shy, awkward and nervous in front of an audience. Hart could readily empathize with Kennedy's difficulty of being put in a position for which he was temperamentally unsuited. Neither Robert Kennedy nor Hart was a natural politician.

Each in his own way was an ill-equipped conveyer of the ideals of a more splendid man from a more splendid time.

Robert Kennedy's death affected Hart at an even more personal level than John's. "I said, 'No. This is too much,'" Hart recalled telling himself. "'This is not a system that makes any sense.' And I gave up again." He and several other more committed Colorado volunteers attended the funeral mass at Saint Patrick's Cathedral and the burial at Arlington Cemetery. Like many Kennedy volunteers at the time, he hoped that Edward Kennedy might continue Robert's campaign in 1968. Instead South Dakota Senator George McGovern picked up the fallen mantle and stood in for Kennedy during an eighteen-day campaign for the Democratic nomination. Hart did not involve himself in McGovern's brief, unsuccessful effort. He returned to Denver to practice law. Two years later McGovern's office contacted Hart, asking him to help organize the senator's scheduled appearance in Denver. Hart eventually became McGovern's national campaign director. He had been impressed with McGovern's direction of the Food for Peace program, his opposition to the war, and his role in reforming the Democratic party. But he remembered that his attraction to McGovern was based "a great deal" on his identification with Robert Kennedy. "That was it for me," he recalled, "and I think a culmination for about 90 percent of us who went to work for him—[McGovern's] representation of Robert Kennedy at the convention, number one."[15]

Hart soon found himself working closely with former Kennedy aides who were helping McGovern. He was particularly thrilled when Ethel Kennedy invited him to play tennis at her home. The young college student who had once admired John Kennedy in a crowded hotel ballroom was now, twelve years later, playing doubles at Hickory Hill with Edward Kennedy as his partner. The 1972 campaign represented for Hart an important rite of passage. He had moved from being a distant fan of the Kennedys to becoming a full-fledged operative for the man who personified the goals and ideals of John and Robert Kennedy. In some ways the effort proved disappointing. McGovern's landslide defeat that fall reminded Hart of the saying popularized by John Kennedy: "Victory has a thousand fathers, but defeat is an orphan." Yet he also emerged as a national figure in his own right. Campaign accounts credited him for his organizational and motivational skills. And he found himself becoming a part of the Kennedy world. By 1972 Ottawa, Kansas, must have seemed a light year away. Both of Hart's parents had died during the campaign, placing even greater distance between himself and the past. "It was a very bad year," he recalled—devastating in some ways, but in other ways liberating, moving this "orphan" from one community which he had been eager to escape into another that offered acceptance and purpose.[16]

After the McGovern campaign Hart recalled that he again "gave up." "I've given up on politics more times than anybody I know," he laughed. This time, however, his political hiatus was short-lived. In 1973 he published his first book, *Right from the Start*, a chronicle of the failed McGovern campaign. Late that year he became a long-shot candidate for the U.S. Senate from Colorado against two-time Republican incumbent Peter Dominick. He won an upset victory. Because Dominick had been involved with illegal dairy industry contributions in connection with Nixon's 1972 campaign, Hart effectively linked his opponent to Watergate, emphasizing issues of public trust and reform in campaign financing. His campaign literature called for "a new kind of representation," contrasting old-style politics with what Hart called "new ideas, new directions, youthful and responsible leadership."[17]

Unlike his national campaign ten years later, Hart did not quote Kennedy, nor did he rely on Kennedyesque campaign themes. Fred Brown, who covered the campaign for the *Denver Post*, recalled that the press sometimes mentioned that Hart was influenced by Kennedy, "but not in the sense of his looking like Kennedy or his acting like Kennedy [rather] as his being a child of the Kennedy 'mystique.'" Hart never concealed his affection for the Kennedys, but no one thought he was overly nostalgic. Hal Haddon, Hart's campaign manager, vaguely remembered newspaper articles comparing Hart physically to Kennedy, "good looking, dark hair, that sort of stuff." "But the Kennedy connection wasn't discussed in any detail then," Haddon recalled.[18]

Still, there was a connection between Hart and the Kennedy "mystique" that Denver reporters never explicitly addressed. Carl Hilliard, who covered Hart's Senate campaigns for the Associated Press, believed Hart always projected a strong Kennedyesque persona. Hilliard remembered, when Hart declared his candidacy, his "rather tweedy Kennedy look, and his hair kind of combed like Kennedy's." "All of us who were there commented, 'Well, here's another Kennedy for Colorado to take another look at.'" According to Hilliard, Colorado politics in the early 1970s was inundated with politicians who were "wrapped up in the Kennedy 'mystique,' the Kennedy imitators."

They included Richard Lamm, Tim Wirth, Rich Gephardt, and others who, like Hart, had been inspired by the Kennedys. "They damn well were Kennedy imitators and they were not embarrassed by it," Hilliard alleged. Fred Brown also remembered the wave of Kennedy impersonators, but neither he nor Hilliard ever wrote that Hart imitated Kennedy because reporters did not believe Hart mimicked Kennedy in order to deceive voters, and many of them were sympathetic to his campaign. Hart's public image soon became "more woodsy and outdoorsy." After winning election to the Senate, he started being photographed in "Man of the West" scenes, wearing a cowboy hat and Western-style clothes, often riding horseback.[19]

During his Senate career Hart had a unique opportunity to draw closer to the last Kennedy brother, developing what he termed a "very good" relationship with Edward. Hart's legislative assistant, Kathy Bushkin, remembered that the two men seemed "extremely friendly." "They were always standing around telling jokes, talking about women they saw on the Floor," she recalled. "Yuking it up." His relationship with Edward Kennedy likely broadened his perspective of the Kennedy legend, transcending the idealized, innocent view he had once had of John and Robert. Being with Edward almost daily, he was less likely to be awed by the Kennedy "magnetism" that had attracted him to John. He grew accustomed to the contrast between the image and the real person that had surprised him when he saw Robert. Edward Kennedy's well-known philandering and carousing made him a more acceptable target of jokes than either John or Robert. "When people would say that [I reminded them of Kennedy]," Hart recalled, "I used to say, 'Edward?' And of course that would get a laugh."[20]

The realities behind the Kennedy myth were revealed to Hart when in 1975 he was part of the Church Committee investigation of CIA-sponsored assassination plots against foreign leaders. Central to the investigation were John and Robert Kennedy's alleged attempts to use the CIA and the Mafia to kill Fidel Castro. Pained by the task of having to examine the underbelly of the Kennedy years, Hart forced himself to be detached. Among the revelations disclosed by the committee was Kennedy's long-standing affair with Judith Exner, the mistress of Sam Giancana, a mob boss cultivated by the CIA to arrange the killing of Castro. While Hart thought Kennedy's personal life was irrelevant to his ability to govern, he acknowledged that the president's affair with Exner was "a problem," for he potentially endangered national security. The committee concluded that there was no evidence linking the Kennedy brothers to the plots to kill Castro, either through their actions or knowledge, but Hart suspected they were compliant.[21]

As part of the Church Committee investigations, Hart and Senator Richard Schweiker headed a subcommittee that looked into the performance of intelligence agencies during the Warren Commission investigation of the Kennedy assassination. "I came to conclude that there was insufficient evidence to believe that anybody but Oswald was the shooter," Hart recalled. "But there was enough evidence to believe that somebody put him up to it." He speculated that anti-Castro forces were likely behind the assassination because they were angered by Kennedy's promise not to invade Cuba after the Cuban missile crisis. Hart's conclusion, however, said more about his therapeutic needs than it did about his studied examination of the evidence, which offers little serious confirmation of a conspiracy. Twelve years earlier Hart had wanted to abandon public service because of Kennedy's death. Now, as a U.S. senator, he found a larger explanation. Searching for answers and seeking a "system" that made sense, he cast himself in the role of helping to uncover the forces responsible for his hero's death.[22]

As Kennedy's reputation suffered revisionist assessments in the 1970s, Hart found himself having to acknowledge JFK's shortcomings. "I don't consider myself a kind of mindless, blind Kennedy acolyte," he noted in 1992. "The man had weaknesses," he was "pretty full of himself." Hart sensed that early in his administration Kennedy was "a little too heady in the use of power." He suffered from "the overconfidence of wealth and power, but," Hart added, "he was in the process of probably becoming a real human being by his defeats." Not surprising, perhaps, Hart felt that Kennedy's sexual affairs were irrelevant to historical judgment. "My response is twofold," he noted. "One, we will never know what is factual and what is not. And two, even if we did, it's none of our business." Hart had personal reasons for holding to this opinion. But like many Kennedy admirers, as well as people disturbed by the infatuation with the private lives of public people, he maintained that Kennedy's sexuality did not impair his performance of public duties.[23]

Hart never felt disillusioned or betrayed by the man who had inspired him to enter politics. He argued that one had to consider "what you leave behind, what I would call empowerment." In Kennedy's case, it was his ability to legitimize politics and to make it noble, thus inspiring an entire generation to pursue public service.

"You can't assess the person from the day they're sworn in to the day they leave office, standing up or not," he explained. "It is also what happens afterwards. And his impact is being felt even today." What remained forever etched in Hart's political spirit was Kennedy's idealistic call to public service. "I tried, frankly, all the time I was in office, both in the Senate races and in the national races, to carry that message on, particularly to young people—duties, responsibilities, and obligations of citizenship."[24]

By the time Gary Hart ran for president in 1984, the Kennedy brothers had come to represent for him a trinity of sorts. John exemplified idealism and youth—and his death a fall from innocence for both Hart and the nation. Whatever twists and turns Hart faced in his career, he would remain the idealistic kid from Ottawa who, through JFK's example, sought to form a more perfect world. Robert emphasized the human dynamics of politics, representing that part of Hart that was ill-prepared for public life. He showed that one could be "a real vulnerable human being" yet still pursue a political career, transcending his shortcomings by committing himself to a higher cause. And finally there was Edward—the dark side of the Kennedy "mystique"—the philanderer, the carouser, a walking symbol of the discrepancy between the public and private self. So too could Hart identify, consciously or not, with the shadowy elements of the Kennedy ideal, a part that needed to be hidden and denied if he intended to embody JFK's inspirational legacy.

II As the 1984 presidential campaign appeared on the horizon, Hart began to consider his possibilities. He studied the 1960 campaign, particularly in terms of developing a winning theme. In 1982, speaking to *Washington Post* correspondent Richard Cohen, Hart recommended he read Theodore White's *The Making of the President 1960*. Kennedy's victory, Hart told Cohen, was not an ideological triumph but a generational one. Part liberal and part conservative, Kennedy outmaneuvered old-guard Democrats because the times demanded new, youthful, postwar leadership. By late 1983 Hart believed the upcoming election would be determined in part by who could capture the generational theme. Bill Bradley and Joseph Biden, he noted, refused the generational "torch" when they decided not to run. Front-runner Walter Mondale was a throwback to the New Deal. Jesse Jackson was unique more for his race than his youth. In terms of personal image, John Glenn seemed closer to

Eisenhower than to Kennedy. Hart understood his own advantage, as did others. As early as May 1982 John Kennedy's secretary, Evelyn Lincoln, remarked before a group of Colorado Democrats that she was struck by how much Gary Hart reminded her of the late president.[25]

Often in search of new ideas, Hart talked with Patrick Caddell, the pollster who had tried to identify Jimmy Carter with the Kennedy myth. In November 1983, during the twentieth anniversary of Kennedy's assassination, Caddell had completed research suggesting that voters would be attracted to a young, imaginative, "new generation" candidate who called for new ideas. An overwhelming plurality (49 percent) wanted "a president who would be a new youthful leader, who would inspire the country with bold ideas and programs for a better future—say like John Kennedy." Caddell circulated a 150-page analysis outlining his thesis, and he found a willing accomplice in Hart. Three months later while speaking in Iowa, Hart echoed verbatim Caddell's winning themes. Given his own predisposition for generational politics and his faith in the Kennedy spirit, Hart found in Caddell's research a blueprint for victory.[26]

Although Reagan had had success among moderate Democrats in identifying himself with John Kennedy's legacy, liberal Democrats and Kennedy admirers generally rolled their eyes at his invocations of JFK, passing them off as a cynical effort to take advantage of the public's poor knowledge of history. For all of Reagan's appeal, much of the public still yearned for the idealism and hope associated with the Kennedy years. Throughout most of 1983 Reagan's public approval was below 50 percent. By the spring of 1983 a majority of Americans polled considered him intelligent, likeable, moral, interesting, and sincere, but only one of three people thought he was imaginative, had exceptional abilities, or was "a man you can believe in." And fewer than one in four people thought Reagan sided with the average citizen or was sympathetic to the poor, the two greatest shortcomings of his personal image. Hart's inclination to evoke Kennedyesque themes proved insightful and timely.[27]

Questioned by reporters in New Hampshire about his frequent invocations of Kennedy, Hart spoke knowingly of voter sentiment. "For a lot of people the world stopped in 1963, and everything since then is bad," he noted. "They want someone to go back to 1963 and pick it up from there." Aware of the power of nostalgia, he distinguished between the man and the ideal. "It's not the person the people want," he explained. "It's what the person represented, what Kennedy represented. And for twenty years, people have wanted to get that back. It is Kennedy's idealism. It's his appeal to nobility in the best sense of the word." Hart acknowledged that his goal in the upcoming election was to connect viscerally with the Kennedy years. "I'm trying to tap the broad-based energy that Kennedy found and that's been latent since his death."[28]

Hart's access to the Kennedy mantle was accommodated by Edward Kennedy's announcement in December 1982 that he would not seek the nomination. Former Vice-President Walter Mondale had little connection to the Kennedy legend. He had supported Hubert Humphrey over the Kennedy brothers in 1960 and 1968. And he was the polar opposite of charismatic, telegenic, youthful leadership. Hart's only serious competition for rights to the Kennedy myth was Ohio Senator John Glenn. As a former Mercury astronaut, he had had a close association with John and Robert Kennedy, and his aides were anxious to identify him with the determination and optimism of that era. When Edward Kennedy withdrew, Glenn proclaimed himself the natural heir to John. Edward Kennedy, however, had a poor relationship with Glenn and was reportedly miffed by his presumption. Glenn soon abandoned the strategy, admitting it was a mistake.[29]

With no serious Kennedyesque challenger, Hart openly enunciated themes derived from the 1960 campaign. He repeatedly referred to "new ideas," "new vision," "new agenda," "new leadership," and "new approaches," reminding voters, "We can do better." Hart borrowed heavily from Kennedy's call for sacrifice, hoping to excite voters with the same message that had inspired him. He also hired Theodore Sorensen as a speechwriter and cochairman of his campaign. "I think his goal was very much to recreate the sense of enthusiasm, momentum, feeling about one's country, all those things he felt Kennedy had created twenty years before," Hart's press secretary, Kathy Bushkin, recalled eight years later. "The truth is he loved Kennedy quotes, and he loved Ted Sorensen. . . . And I think he also thought they were quotes that had come back in terms of their meaning." Dorothy Lynch, a Hart pollster, conducted focus groups on Kennedy's slogans. "A lot of people volunteered that that's what John Kennedy had said, what he stood for, and that they wanted that to come back," she noted, "and that they were glad someone was saying those things." Hart repeatedly asked voters for their help, "not just for a candidate or not just for a campaign, but for a cause. The cause is the redemption of this land." Thus he presented himself as the embodiment of John Kennedy's promise, a disciple who promised to deliver the nation from the sins it had accumulated since 1963.[30]

During conversations with reporters, Hart used the Kennedy years as a reference point for his own campaign. He noted that both he and Kennedy lacked the support of the more traditional factions of the Democratic party. When asked about his lack of magnetism, Hart defended himself by noting that "John Kennedy didn't become charismatic till he started winning elections." A television commercial in California showed Hart walking along the beach, skipping rocks into the ocean. Radio advertisements in Texas called Mondale "los enimigos" of the Kennedy brothers. A biographical video reminded voters that Hart's career was inspired by John Kennedy. A spot advertisement showed Hart working in Robert Kennedy's Justice Department.[31]

After Hart's upset victory over Mondale in the New Hampshire primary, polls suggested that his surge was largely a result of the campaign's Kennedyesque elements. A *Newsweek* poll showed that 38 percent of the public was drawn to Hart because of his "new ideas theme." Sixteen percent of those polled were attracted to his "youth oriented campaign." And 8 percent liked Hart because "He reminds people of Kennedy." In addition to his physical and gestural similarities, Hart seemed cool and aloof. He projected vigor, toughness, and an appetite for life. He was physically active and enjoyed taking risk. He had earned a law degree from an Ivy League school, loved literature, and was considered to be more cerebral than emotional. Like Kennedy, he called himself "an idealist without illusions," despised political phoniness, and was perceived as a Washington outsider, even though he had been a U.S. senator for ten years. Such traits had a cumulative and subliminal effect. According to Gallup, 40 percent of the public thought Hart reminded them of John Kennedy.[32]

After New Hampshire, reporters sought to break through the veneer of the candidate's image to discover the "real" Hart. By the Super Tuesday primaries of March 22, the new front-runner had developed a serious "character issue." In addition to questioning Hart's name, birthday, and signature changes, reporters cited a contrast between his small-town upbringing and his "up-town," fast-track life-style, complete with Hollywood parties with actor Warren Beatty and rumored affairs. As part of the identity issue, Hart was criticized for conducting a campaign derivative of the Kennedy years. The press accused him of having studied Kennedy's mannerisms and of inventing "a Kennedy look." Journalists derided him as "the fourth

Kennedy brother," and some speculated he had supplanted his personality with JFK's. One said confidentially that Hart's emulation of Kennedy indicated "schizophrenic tendencies."[33]

The Kennedy problem, Bushkin soon realized, "had taken on a life of its own." Sinister motives were implied when Hart reportedly watched tapes of the Kennedy-Nixon debates before his own debate at Dartmouth. Questions were raised why Hart was reading Kennedy biographies. Political opponents contributed their own jabs. "I'm not trying to imitate anyone," Glenn commented strangely, "but John Glenn." Jackson criticized both Hart and Mondale for being trapped in the past. "One leans on Humphrey and the other leans on Kennedy which is even further back," Jackson commented. "Both of them are talking forward but walking backward."[34]

According to Bushkin, the staff wanted to "backtrack" on Hart's invocations of Kennedy. As early as the Dartmouth debate, John McEvoy warned Hart in a memo, "Everyone expects you to be JFK. That cuts two ways. They're disappointed when they find out you're not." Keith Glaser, a young staff member, lamented in a memo, "Gary overevokes the Kennedy image. People resent it because Gary does not seem authentic. He cannot win by draping himself in another's mantle. He must act himself. Moreover, if Gary seeks positive comparisons with JFK, he can't avoid negative ones as well—e.g., compassion, charm, humor." Hart's staff understood that each time he evoked Kennedy, he drew attention to his own icy exterior. Glaser recommended more subtle evocations. "Gary must not blatantly force the comparison," he wrote; "through his actions and style he can suggest it." Pollster Dorothy Lynch understood the essence of the danger. "What we've got to watch is that we don't create a standard that Gary can't live up to," she told a reporter.[35]

From the beginning of his campaign, Hart thought twice about being compared with Kennedy. "It would be bad if I tried to become Kennedy," he said to a reporter. "If I did, I'd be politically dead." The public, Hart noted on more than one occasion, can sense a "phony." Repeatedly he argued that he had never swayed from his own agenda or personality. "But now, as I become successful," he explained, "people will watch me on television and bring their own memories to what they see." Despite warnings from his staff, he refused to reduce his references to Kennedy or to alter the themes of his campaign. "There was no way he was going to change that message," Bushkin recalled. "That was the message for him."[36]

Eight years later Hart vehemently denied that he ever imitated

Kennedy. First, he explained, he had become a figure in his own right. "I had been in the public arena for thirteen years, and you don't start at the night of the New Hampshire primary pretending you're somebody else," he noted. "Second, it's not my style." Third, it would have been counterproductive for him to have imitated Kennedy because the voters would have considered him a phony. "I think this whole business about trying to be Kennedy is nonsense," Hart said, "because it assumes in a way you can kind of delude the voters. But I never, never, never, never believed that. And it's folly to even try."[37]

Hart maintained that his invocations of JFK were not as heavy-handed as the press reported. He professed to have limits. "I would never say anything like 'Let's get the country moving again.'" The Kennedyesque slogans, he argued, were "embroidery around some fairly heavy duty policy stuff." If he had miscalculated the attention that such features received, he was a victim of political naiveté. When he hired Sorensen, he recalled, he did not consider whether he was linking himself too closely to the Kennedy years. "I'm not a good politician. . . . I calculated that Sorensen would add value and weight. He was a figure of consequence, a figure of substance, a figure of value, and I admired him. It just gave me a lot of self-confidence to have him on board." But Hart admitted that he did not consider whether the press might view Sorensen's employment as an excessive attempt to identify with the "mystique." "I just don't operate that way. Never did."[38]

Hart's "Kennedy problem" rested with his failure to realize that by continuing his invocations of Kennedy and Kennedy-styled themes, he drew attention to similarities in mannerisms and looks, opening himself further to the charge that he was an imitator. He assumed that the public distinguished between his pledge to Kennedy's ideals and the charge that he was trying to imitate Kennedy. "If I said, 'Ask not what your country can do for you,' I'd be dead. I don't think I'll ever step over that line," he had told a reporter in early March. Yet a week later, speaking before the Alabama state legislature, Hart said, "We must once again have a President who will ask us what we can do for our country." Hart insisted that there was "a light year" of difference between calling for a recommitment to public service and quoting Kennedy without direct attribution. "I assume anytime you use phrases like that everybody knows that you know what you're doing," he recalled, "that you're not trying to pull the wool over their eyes, that you think you're somebody you're not." Perhaps. But the distinction was clearer in Hart's mind than in the perception of journalists who reported the speech as yet another example of Hart imitating Kennedy. Such rhetoric, in light of other evocations and gestural similarities, begged further discussion about the authenticity of Hart's public self.[39]

Bushkin too differentiated between Hart's call for renewal and the pretense behind his public image. "I don't think he saw that the [invocations and mannerisms] went together, necessarily," she explained. "I think he saw that everybody had the shared love of the Kennedy quotes or the Kennedy references and that he was evoking a time and not a person." Hart did not allow for the possibility that the public or press would interpret his invocations one step further; by invoking a time and spirit, he recalled a person with whom he also shared physical features and characteristics. "He was sort of surprised and shocked that [the Kennedy connection] became problematic," Bushkin recalled. Knowing Hart as well as she did, she was sure that he was "baffled why it would ever hurt to be called Kennedyesque."[40]

In general, Bushkin believed that Hart "both suffered and benefited" from comparisons. "I think to the degree he evoked Kennedy, it never hurt him," she recalled. "To the degree that people felt he did it artificially, it did hurt him. And that's a huge distinction." A dangerously fuzzy distinction, however. When a candidate invokes the past, he or she hopes to rekindle memories in voters' minds which they will transfer to the candidate's own cause. While the candidate's motives may be sincere, the evocation is premeditated and contrived. Hart had little room to maneuver, for it was highly difficult to determine where sincerity ended and pretense began. This line was irrevocably crossed on the evening of the Super Tuesday primaries during a televised interview with NBC correspondent Roger Mudd. It was a moment, Bushkin recalled, "when things got really ugly."[41]

In the weeks before, Hart had been innocently imitating Edward Kennedy for the private amusement of reporters and staff members. Bushkin recalled that Hart's Teddy Kennedy impersonation was "a great tension reliever." But she sensed that the press was anxious to "take him down a peg." Since the 1970s candidates had been subject to harsher scrutiny as they gained momentum. "He was ripe for the picking," Bushkin recalled. "Gary was totally unprepared, extremely tired, and very testy about personal things anyway. He couldn't understand why people gave a rat's ass about his handwriting, his name, all that jazz."[42]

On Super Tuesday early returns indicated that Hart would win three of the five most important primaries, including those in Massachusetts and Florida, the two largest states at stake. He was invited to appear on NBC television for what he assumed would be a postprimary victory interview with Roger Mudd. During the live conversation Mudd asserted that, despite Hart's victories, Mondale was "on his way back." "Back from where?" Hart asked. The interview degenerated from there. In an exchange that even seasoned campaign reporters termed "bizarre," Mudd pointedly asked Hart why he imitated John Kennedy so much. They then awkwardly discussed whether politicians were phony. Mudd concluded the interview by requesting that Hart impersonate Edward Kennedy. Hart declined. Mudd pressed on: "I've heard it's hilarious." "I don't think it is," Hart responded icily.[43]

Bushkin recalled that Hart was "furious," "confused," and "hurt" by the Mudd interview. According to Hart, Mudd's line of questioning had its roots twelve years earlier in the fall of 1972 when they had both attended a dinner party at Ethel Kennedy's house. Mudd had entertained guests with a humorous impersonation of Edward Kennedy. "I had told that story after I was in the Senate about the night Roger Mudd did his Kennedy imitation," Hart recalled. "And I do a fair Kennedy imitation. . . . So lo and behold, I win Tuesday, seven out of nine states, and I go on NBC . . . and Mudd makes a fool out of—tries to make a fool out of me and makes a fool out of himself in a way that no one knew what he was doing. . . . It was a stupid, frivolous thing that went back to 1972. . . . I was as dumbfounded as anyone, because I thought this was about running for president. And he was trying to make a fool out of me."[44]

Mudd's question marked a pivotal moment in the political use of the Kennedy myth. For the first time a candidate was taken to task for using the "mystique." Johnson, McGovern, Carter, and even Nixon had each tried to various degrees to pass himself off as Kennedyesque. Hart, however, was the first to be openly accused of imitating Kennedy. He was an easy target, given the issue of his character and the extent of his emulation and invocations. But as hostile as Mudd's question was, it was also legitimate. He had asked Hart about an issue that his own staff members recognized.

After the Mudd interview, the Kennedy problem became impossible for Hart to shake off. "When [the Kennedy comparisons] served us, we were happy to have him do it," Bushkin recalled. "When it didn't serve us we couldn't figure out what the hell had happened." Hart faced another round of press reports emphasizing his identity problem, further stalling his campaign's momentum. The Kennedy problem, Bushkin concluded, "went to the question of what his identity was and whether he was creating it out of whole cloth. I think if [the Kennedy issue] had been on its own, it wouldn't have been [damaging]."[45]

Hart suffered from other overriding problems during the 1984 primaries. He lacked the necessary organization to take advantage of his New Hampshire victory. His campaign sunk heavily into debt. He made two serious gaffes just before the Illinois and New Jersey primaries. And Mondale, backed by traditional factions in the party, recovered quickly after New Hampshire, proving to be a tenacious challenger. During a debate two days before the Super Tuesday primaries, he subtly raised the character issue and accused Hart of being more style than substance. "We don't elect images," Mondale told the audience. "We elect a human being." In what proved to be a devastating sound bite, Mondale raised a question that would be repeated throughout Hart's campaign. "When I hear your new ideas," Mondale told Hart, "I'm reminded of that ad: Where's the beef?" Hart failed to appreciate the effectiveness of the attack and the seriousness of the questions about who he was and what he stood for.[46]

In his concession speech at the 1984 Democratic convention, Hart continued to evoke the Kennedy legend, linking his failed campaign to the idealism associated with John and Robert. Sounding much like Edward Kennedy at the 1980 convention, Hart declared, "I see an America too young to quit, too courageous to turn back, with a passion for justice and a program for opportunity, an America with unmet dreams that will never die.... If not now, someday we will prevail." To those critical of the allusions to Kennedy, Hart seemed stubborn, if not delusional. To those who yearned for a return to Camelot, Hart reaffirmed their faith, letting them know that they would again have an opportunity to pursue a noble endeavor.[47]

Reflecting on his Kennedy problem eight years later, Hart blamed the national news media for being "overly hung up" on the issue. "I didn't hide behind [the Kennedy legacy], nor did I think I featured it," he argued. He was frustrated that reporters who had not covered his earlier Senate campaigns assumed that he contrived a Kennedy-style persona. "The one thing you cannot do in politics is change personas or styles from the state to national level," Hart explained. "If I had gone out and done some kind of an eerie Jekyll and Hyde thing about Kennedy when I ran for president in '84, [the reporters of Colorado] would have gone berserk." Hart disputed numerous press accounts about the Kennedy problem. The "pop-psychologists" who alleged that he supplanted his personality with Kennedy's obviously did not know him, he said. He denied having watched tapes of the Kennedy-Nixon debates during the campaign. "It's like saying I read the Lincoln-Douglas debates," Hart said, laughing. "It would have about as much applicability." He did not recall ever being warned by his staff about evoking Kennedy themes. Nor was he aware of any poll that compared him to Kennedy.

Hart recalled having worried "a whole lot" about press comparisons to Kennedy. "How would you like to be compared to one of the most beloved presidents of your lifetime," he explained. "It's not the kind of thing you go looking for. If you suffer, you're going to suffer any way you slice it." He understood the impossibility of measuring up to myth, "because, first of all, Kennedy's not Kennedy. It's too grand an ideal." Hart also felt "very uncomfortable" about comparisons because he did not believe he shared *any* personal or political traits with John Kennedy. Those who associated him with Kennedy's idealism, pragmatism, and self-confidence were projecting what they wanted to be true. "Our lives were about as totally different as you can imagine," Hart argued. He distinguished between how the press and voters responded to the Kennedy issue. Voters, he thought, made only fleeting comparisons. They might have said, "'Well, I wish he were,' or 'He's got some qualities like [him], but he ain't Kennedy,'" Hart recalled. "A lot of [the Kennedy parallel] has to do with appearance. In those days, anybody who had teeth and hair and was six feet tall reminded people of Kennedy."

In short, Hart dismissed the Kennedy problem, contending that among all the handicaps he faced during the campaign, it hurt him "very, very little." "I think the voters who voted for me voted for me because I was me. I think the voters who voted against me, voted against me because I was me." He never felt it was politically dangerous to recall the Kennedy past—"nor did I think it was very politically advantageous." The Kennedy problem was simply an unwarranted distraction from the better nature of his campaign.[48]

Hart's recollection was burdened with contradictions. As early as 1982 he had been mindful of a spiritual void stemming from Kennedy's death, and he repeatedly publicized his desire to rekindle his hero's idealism, quoting Kennedy and evoking his themes while focus groups and polls confirmed their viability. In retrospect he suggested that the Kennedy themes were inconsequential, and that those people who identified him with Kennedy suffered from an overimagination. He had been seriously hurt by the accusation that he imitated Kennedy, and he could not accept responsibility for having invited and encouraged comparisons.

Hart's temperament was not well suited to a political life. Shy, intellectual, reserved, and despising phoniness, he would have been more comfortable in the ministry or in academia. To enter a world that required making speeches, kissing babies, and projecting personality, Hart needed to make certain outward adjustments if he wished to be successful, especially in an age of television and personality-oriented journalism. He needed to find a way to participate in politics while maintaining his sense of self. His solution may have been unconsciously to wear a Kennedy mask, less to manipulate the public than to protect himself, to hide his own shortcomings by "picturing in his head" an ideal character-type. By doing so, Hart emulated what he wanted to be, not who he wanted to be. He did not want to be Kennedy. He wanted to play the public role of Kennedy. Hart suggested as much when asked why he had incorporated so many Kennedyesque themes, quotes, and slogans. "It was just a shorthand way of self-definition," he replied.[49]

Jung might have noted that the Kennedy mask represented Hart's ideal self, not a false self. It was composed of characteristics he admired in Kennedy as a public figure—his idealism, commitment, intelligence, pragmatism, inspiration, and compassion. Yet Hart would not have been drawn to Kennedy unless he perceived and admired those elements within himself. Kennedy gave Hart direction, not definition. But as this shy, reserved man entered the political arena, he may have manifested the image of the man whose spirit had touched him so deeply, just as someone entering any profession might incorporate the words, mannerisms, or temperament of a favorite role model. If so, it would help to explain Hart's defensiveness. He denied he imitated Kennedy because he did not know that he did.[50]

Today Hart continues to view himself as part of a vanguard of those who have remained faithful to Kennedy and what he represents. The years before and during Kennedy, he asserted, were "better times," "the last good time, really." The television program "Happy Days" pretty well captured life in those days. "It was simpler," he explained. "It was better, clearer. People thought at least that the races got along. Everybody had a job and a little house on Elm Street and the kids went to school." Everything since the Kennedy assassination has been "bad." "Life had become a lot more complicated and sinister, conspiratorial. We lost optimism. We lost *a lot* of optimism. We lost a lot of hope. We lost a sense of perfectibility and reform and change."

Hart is disturbed by critical Kennedy biographies. "Why?" he asked, sounding much like a victim. "Why? What forces are there at work in the world that still want to kill this guy? That's what amazes me. This desire to drive a silver stake through his heart and destroy not only idealism but any favorable notion about him and to paint him as the blackest kind of person." His aversion to such biographies may explain in part the exceedingly generous treatment Hart devoted to Kennedy in his 1993 book, *The Good Fight*. Privately Hart concluded that Kennedy was simply too good a person. "It's the Billy Budd syndrome from Melville," he contended. "That somebody's too perfect, too good can't be tolerated. And I suppose for two hundred or five hundred years, people will be writing books about what a horrible man he was. . . . What is there about human beings that can't stand that [goodness]?"[51]

If Hart seemed romantic about the past and cynical about the present, perhaps it is because for him life has indeed become less hopeful, more complicated, and less perfect. In 1987 he moved from "Happy Days" to *Peyton Place*, destroyed by sinister forces similar to those that assaulted Kennedy's reputation. The arguments that Hart used to defend Kennedy are the same ones he would use to defend himself against questions about his sexual ethics: investigators should not probe into areas of private conduct that are unimportant and none of our business. As a thoughtful and intelligent person, Hart must know that illicit affairs suggest a person's capacity for deception. How a political figure's character strikes a person's gut is as important as how his ideas appeal to the head. After all, it was not Kennedy's position papers that attracted Hart, it was Kennedy's style and spirit. But when it came to judging Kennedy, Hart seemed divided between knowledge and faith. Intellectually he could separate himself from the Kennedy legacy. Emotionally he remained the young graduate student who was awed by Kennedy and his idealistic message, who could not detach himself from the feelings that Kennedy inspired in him.

A part of Hart wants to remain idealistic even though he must *know* that the Kennedy era was neither "Happy Days" nor Camelot. Perhaps Hart would prefer to remember the best of the Kennedy years because he would like to think the best of himself. By minimizing Kennedy's flaws, he can overlook his own. By accentuating Kennedy's idealism, he can reaffirm his own. By believing in a time of innocence, he can ease the pain of reality. His lasting faith in Kennedy is his final and most essential connection to the "mystique." Today Gary Hart recalls the Kennedy past not as a means of reminding voters but as a way of reminding himself—as a way, perhaps, of rekindling his faith.

9

1984:
Reagan Redux

FOR ALL OF Ronald Reagan's optimism, there was an undercurrent of discontent in 1984, a sense that a significant segment of America and its problems were being neglected in the interest of selfish pursuits. From 1983 through 1985 critics accused Reagan of lacking compassion, neglecting the poor, and doing little to help minorities. To counter such perceptions, Reagan's media team launched a "feel-good" television campaign, the slickest in the history of American politics. Part of Reagan's reelection strategy was to blend him into the national mythology. "Paint Mondale as . . . soft in his defense of freedom, patriotic values, American interests," Richard Darman advised. "Paint RR as the personification of all that is right with or heroized by America. Leave Mondale in the position where an attack on Reagan is tantamount to an attack on America's idealized image of itself—where a vote against Reagan is in some subliminal sense, a vote against myth 'AMERICA.'" Reagan subsequently heralded American myths, equated liberalism with irresponsibility, and encouraged contempt for the liberal media and Congress. The Mondale-Ferraro ticket was portrayed as an extension of the gloomy Carter years. As part of his appeal to crossover Democrats, the seventy-three-year-old candidate invoked John Kennedy, associating himself with images of toughness, progress, and heroes.[1]

The first serious indication that Reagan intended to challenge the Democrats' claim to Kennedy came at the end of the Democratic primaries in 1984. Trying to secure funding for the Nicaraguan *contras*, Reagan cited Kennedy's reference to America's "long twilight struggle" to defend freedom around the world and quoted Kennedy's expressed resolve not to jeopardize U.S. security in the

Western Hemisphere. Kennedy, Reagan argued, had received over-whelming support from the Senate and House while he, Reagan, had not. "Were John Kennedy alive today," he added, "I think he would be appalled by the gullibility of some who invoke his name."[2]

In June 1984 Reagan identified himself with Kennedy at a sentimental level when he traveled to Ireland. Speaking before both houses of the Irish Parliament as JFK had in the summer of 1963, he closed his address by recalling what Kennedy had said during his last day in Ireland: "I certainly will come back in the springtime." "It was a promise left unkept for a spring that never came," Reagan concluded. "But surely in our hearts there is the memory of a young leader who spoke stirring words about a brighter age for mankind, about a new generation that would hold high the torch of liberty and truly light the world." Reagan dedicated himself to such a task. The trip was also marked by an interesting discovery among the church records where Reagan's great-grandfather had been baptized. His Irish genealogical history "showed that I was distantly related not only to Queen Elizabeth II," Reagan later wrote, "but also to John F. Kennedy."[3]

Once the fall campaign was under way, Reagan began freely associating himself with Kennedy as he had done with Franklin Roosevelt in 1980. In September he traveled to Waterbury, Connecticut, to recall Kennedy's memorable visit there in 1960. Reagan devoted a quarter of his speech to reaching out to old Kennedy supporters. He told them a story: "Over there on the balcony of the Elton one night in 1960 . . . young John Kennedy stood there in the darkness. It was almost 3 o'clock in the morning. His campaign was near ending, and he was exhausted. But the night was bright with lights, and they lit the faces of the tens of thousands of people who had showed up to cheer John Kennedy on. And he stood there— looked down at them. He smiled in the glow, and even though it was fall, it seemed like the springtime, those days. I see our country today, and I think it is springtime for America once again—so many new beginnings. And I think John Kennedy would be proud of you and the things you believe in, proud of the stoutness of your hearts and the vision in your soul."[4]

Reagan, of course, had no way of knowing the details of the setting the night Kennedy spoke. Like the broadcaster reading the bare teletypes of a baseball game, he recreated the scene with such skill that it seemed as if he had been staring up at Kennedy and cheering him on himself. That day he went on to recall the "wrenching" difficulty he had experienced in breaking his affiliation with the Democrats. "You feel as if you're abandoning your past," Reagan explained. "But I tell you truly, the only abandoning I see is that the Democratic leadership has abandoned the good and decent Democrats of the JFK, FDR, and Harry Truman tradition—people who believe in the interests of working people, who are not ashamed or afraid of America standing up for freedom in the world." Such Democrats had a "home with us," Reagan told them. With the crowd chanting "Four more years," Reagan left them with a final reminder: "Waterbury's made a real difference in my campaign, just as it did in John Kennedy's, and I will always remember."[5]

Geraldine Ferraro, the Democrats' vice-presidential nominee, was angered by Reagan's presumptuousness. Ferraro admired John Kennedy. She had met him briefly in May 1952 at her high school graduation, which Kennedy attended because a classmate of Ferraro's, Ann Gargan, was his cousin. "We were a bunch of high school girls," Ferraro recalled forty years later. "We all thought he was the best thing going. He was gorgeous." Although they shared only a passing hello, Kennedy left a lasting impression. She followed his political career when she went to college. Being Catholic, she was especially mindful of his removal of religious barriers from elected office. Teaching full time and raising a family, she did not have time to devote to Kennedy's campaign, but her sentiments were with him.[6]

Like millions of Americans, Ferraro watched intently on television the events surrounding the assassination in 1963. "You kind of felt that what was happening to them was happening to a friend," she recalled. "When they buried him they buried a part of you, too, as a young person at that time." Kennedy's death was particularly painful because he was the first national figure she had ever met. "I never, ever touched a national prominence like that," she recalled. She had little recollection of what Kennedy had achieved while he was alive. What she recalled of him was largely impressionistic—his style, charm, and good looks. She refused to allow later disclosures about his personal life to shake her opinion of him. "Kennedy was human," Ferraro explained. As with Hart, Kennedy had made an indelible imprint on Ferraro in her youth, and nothing could change it.[7]

While Ferraro admired Kennedy, her mother and Eleanor Roosevelt were far greater influences on her political career. Politically she was a late bloomer. Her dedication to her family and to her private law practice kept her from getting involved in local politics. In 1974 she became assistant district attorney in Queens. By 1978 she had won a seat in Congress in the conservative, ethnically diverse Ninth Congressional District in Queens. Like Kennedy, Ferraro was Catholic, a tough Democrat, nonideological, pragmatic, proud of her ethnic heritage, and intent on breaking barriers. Did anyone ever describe her as Kennedyesque? "No," she replied, laughing. "But I wouldn't mind if they did."[8]

When Mondale won the Democratic nomination in 1984, he wanted a running mate who would generate excitement and media exposure for his long-shot campaign against Reagan. He chose Ferraro as the first woman vice-presidential nominee of a major political party. As part of a broad range of strategies to neutralize Reagan, Ferraro was assigned the task of challenging the president's claim to Kennedy and other Democratic presidents. "I get slightly crazed whenever I hear Republicans singing the praises of Roosevelt, Truman, and Kennedy," she noted nine years later, "because the Reagan and Bush policies were really so opposed to the viewpoint of both Roosevelt and Kennedy, even more so than to Truman. I don't mind them taking their Republican heroes; leave us our Democrats."[9]

As a representative of an ethnically diverse, blue-collar, Catholic district, Ferraro had a unique appreciation for Reagan's appeal to moderate Democrats. Reagan, she noted, understood Kennedy's popularity among ethnic Catholics who, when they voted for JFK in 1960, based their choice more on religious affinity than on his policies. "They still loved him twenty years later," she recalled. "So, Reagan was doing precisely what he should have been doing; appealing to those who he knew he had to keep in '84 in order to be reelected. And he kept them." Irish, Italian, and Polish Catholics had grown more conservative since Kennedy's death, Ferraro observed, particularly on abortion, government spending for social welfare programs, and affirmative action. "It was not so much that Ronald Reagan was claiming the Kennedy Democrats," she reasoned. "What was happening was that the Kennedy Democrats had changed over the twenty years to become Reagan Democrats. Although they had changed in their policies and in their viewpoints, Kennedy—because he was a Catholic—was still a hero. So, why not claim John Kennedy if [Reagan] could possibly do so?" Ferraro rejected the notion that Reagan attracted Kennedy Democrats at an impressionistic level. His appeal, she believed, was based solely on substantive issues.[10]

One week after Reagan's appearance at Waterbury, Ferraro set out to reclaim the memory of John Kennedy. The occasion came in Boston before ten thousand voters on a rainy afternoon. Edward Kennedy was standing by her side. The setting, she remembered, begged that she answer Reagan's invocations and "deal with it." Ferraro told the crowd that day that she "resented" Reagan associating himself with John Kennedy at Waterbury, and charged that he "portrays himself as a friend of the very things he undermines." "The more I think about it," she said, "the angrier I get. I resent it when Ronald Reagan lays claim to the memory of President Kennedy and pretends that he has anything in common with that good man. The people of Massachusetts know what John Kennedy stood for." Where Kennedy had sent the Peace Corps to Latin America, she noted, Reagan sent "secret military aid to help Latin Americans kill each other." Whereas Kennedy emphasized a "cultivated mind," Reagan's "idea of helping education is to launch a teacher into space." "President Kennedy freed the skies of nuclear explosions with the nuclear test ban treaty," Ferraro continued. "Reagan is the first President since Herbert Hoover not to meet with his Soviet counterpart." Edward Kennedy joined Ferraro in chastising Reagan. "I wonder why he doesn't quote Richard Nixon," he told the crowd. "After all, Mr. Reagan was leader of 'Democrats for Nixon' in 1960."[11]

The event was particularly memorable for Ferraro. To this day, the only picture of the campaign that she displays in her home is one taken of her standing next to Edward Kennedy at that rally. "It embodies the campaign," she explained. "It was exciting. There was rain. There was enthusiasm. There was this Kennedy that was very much a part of my campaign as well." Ferraro was well aware that, like Reagan, she was "totally selective" in the data she drew from the Kennedy past. The ritualism of a political rally in Boston mandated that she do so. "This is not delivering a lecture for a college course," she emphasized. Her aim was to appeal to voters' emotions and to win a sound bite on the evening news. Although Kennedy had been subjected to considerable revisionism during the preceding twenty years, Ferraro knew he remained a valuable political symbol. "As far as Democrats are concerned, they can have all kinds of revisionist exposure," she noted pointedly, "and he's still going to be a hero to a lot of us Democrats."[12]

After Ferraro's volley, Mondale took Reagan to task during their first televised debate. In what was regarded by analysts as Mondale's most intense moment during the event, he challenged Reagan's assertion that he left the Democratic party because it changed. He reminded the audience that Reagan had "decided we had lost our way" in 1960. "I was chairman of Minnesotans for Kennedy," Mondale noted. "Reagan was chairman of a thing called Democrats for Nixon. Now maybe we made the wrong turn with Kennedy, but I'll be proud of supporting him all my life." Reagan sought to deflect Mondale's point by noting that he had earlier supported Eisenhower.[13]

Reagan could only be encouraged by Mondale's and Ferraro's response. Their frustration was evidence that his appeal had worked. It illustrated Reagan's advantage in competing for Kennedy's image. Mondale appreciated the attraction of Reagan's rhetorical style and his infusion of Kennedyesque themes, but he had difficulty infusing his own style with the required sentiment and romance. Three years earlier Mondale's speechwriter, Bernie Aronson, had urged him to create a set speech that offered "a statement of hope; an evocation of basic American values and idealism; a celebration of American possibilities; a summoning up of the energies of the nation to meet a challenge, and a call to action." Aronson understood that Mondale had a "strong aversion" to such rhetoric. "You call it 'dawnism,'" he wrote. "You identify it with Bobby Kennedy. And you tend to reject it more often than not. . . . John Kennedy created a presidency largely around the rhetoric of his speeches and in certain ways Ronald Reagan is doing the same." While Reagan's rhetoric was "corny and hokey," it was nevertheless persuasive. "Reagan projected an image of himself and of America that was larger than life," Aronson explained. "He unabashedly summoned up America's idealism. He invoked his image of a City on a Hill. And while I would not suggest that you ape Reagan in any particular way, his evocation of universal themes of hope and activism is the basic winning model for presidential candidates from Roosevelt to Kennedy." Unlike Mondale and Ferraro, Aronson fully appreciated a visceral line from Roosevelt to Kennedy—to Reagan.[14]

In projecting an image, Reagan had a clear advantage over Mondale. He was indeed larger than life, a man who had taken a bullet (like Kennedy) and lived (like Theodore Roosevelt and Andrew Jackson). While Mondale promoted failed liberalism with all the flair of a political science professor, Reagan heralded "universal truths," advocated change, beckoned the nation to get moving again, promised boldness in America's role in the world, and spoke convincingly of America's call to greatness. Mondale faced a difficult task to begin with. He was challenging Reagan at a time of economic prosperity and peace. But he could not bring himself to speak of "dawnism," and he was going against a candidate who embodied it. "The fact of the matter is," Mondale acknowledged after the election, "President Reagan's ability to communicate—even things that I think are demonstrably not accurate—verges on genius. I don't think anybody accused me of the same capability."[15]

The Mondale-Ferraro effort to reclaim Kennedy not only failed but seemed to inspire Reagan. After the first debate Reagan laughed off the Democrats' charge of symbolic kidnaping, gleefully noting that when he quoted their presidents, "my opponents start tearing their hair out." "They just can't stand it," Reagan said to college students. "Well, of course they can't, because it highlights how far they, the leadership today of the Democratic Party, has strayed from the strength of the Democratic political tradition." Reagan appealed again to the "rank and file" Democrats who are "clear-eyed about the world." Kennedy, he said, "didn't push a program of dreary mediocrity with endless tax increases on those who dreamed of better days. He challenged Americans, just as we're challenging you today." Sounding much like Kennedy in 1960, he appealed to the students to join the Republicans: "We need your new blood, your ideas, your enthusiasm, and your energy." "[Mondale] promises Camelot," Reagan said on another occasion, "but he would give us a reign of error."[16]

The day before his second debate with Reagan, Mondale learned of the letter that Reagan had written to Nixon in 1960, comparing Kennedy to Marx and Hitler. He disclosed Reagan's true feelings for Kennedy while campaigning in Youngstown, Ohio. "Over this last campaign," Mondale said, "Mr. Reagan has been trying to steal our Democratic heroes. He's been saying he's for Kennedy, he's even for Hubert Humphrey. He's for any Democrat that's dead. Well, what did he say about Kennedy when he was alive?" Mondale then read passages from the letter. Reagan's press secretary, Larry Speakes, said that the president was "pleasantly surprised to find the difference between Kennedy the candidate and Kennedy the President." "If you read the letter," Reagan told reporters, "you will find there is nothing wrong with it."[17]

For the next few days Reagan avoided mentioning Kennedy and focused instead on Truman. It was soon clear, however, that the letter would have little consequence. "In a close election," Jack Germond and Jules Witcover wrote, "the letter about JFK might have been a bombshell, bringing Democrats 'home' in droves. In this one, it was an amusing sidelight." Because Democrats thought Mondale had no chance of winning, voters had no great incentive to rally to his cause. Indeed, it was Mondale who soon found himself on the defensive when asked by reporters if his use of a twenty-four-year-old letter was a cheap shot. "Any adult that tried to compare John Kennedy with Karl Marx and Adolf Hitler isn't going to improve with age," he replied. His charge fell flat. "Mondale convinced us that, yes, he had voted for Kennedy," Sidney Blumenthal wrote. "But he never showed us why he deserved JFK's endorsement."[18]

Like other criticisms of Reagan, the old letter ran up against the well-established "Teflon" factor: Reagan seemed immune to factual challenges, whether from his political opponents or the press. "Part of it was because of Reagan's masterful ability to sell himself as a nice, well-meaning guy," Witcover recalled in 1994. "The whole 'feel-good' atmosphere could not have been created for somebody else. The other attitude was, we all know the guy is a dumbbell. What's the use of pointing it out?" In this case Reagan promoted fantasies about Kennedy with all the affable charm of a grandfather telling his grandchildren about Santa Claus the night before Christmas. It was Mondale who seemed Grinch-like, trying to destroy the illusion. Reagan never pretended to offer a discourse on Kennedy's policies. He did not address at any length or with any degree of logic the subtleties of Kennedy's rhetoric or the intricacies of his programs. Kennedy served the dramatic purposes of Reagan's commercial for America. He was metaphor, not history. As with any story or commercial, no serious claims were made by Reagan except those brought by the listener.[19]

A week later, with a landslide victory virtually assured, Reagan resumed his invocations of Kennedy during a rally at Boston city hall. Interrupted by hecklers, he silenced them with their own icon: "I would think that even they would have the respect to listen to the words I'm going to say in quoting John F. Kennedy." He went on to invoke Kennedy's name twelve more times during the last five days of the campaign, citing him as often as three times a day. In his address to the nation on election eve, Reagan spoke of heroes. After quoting John Wayne, he returned one last time to Kennedy. "Well, sadly, our opponent's team is not in the tradition of President Kennedy and his predecessors, Truman and Roosevelt," Reagan noted. "*Their* policies never sent out an S.O.S. They proudly proclaimed U.S.A.!"[20]

Reagan's invocations successfully attracted moderate Democrats while denying his opponents a legacy they had claimed exclusively in every presidential campaign since 1964. His margin of victory showed clearly that he did not need to use Kennedy to entice votes. But, as Paul Erickson's study of Reagan's rhetoric showed, his invocations added confusion to the Democrats' identity and made them seem divided among themselves. Mondale and Ferraro tried to portray themselves as more consistent with Kennedy's philosophy. But Reagan showed that Kennedy's emotional appeal and personal qualities made it possible to quote him from either side of the political spectrum—to support increases or cutbacks in defense spending or social welfare programs; to support counterinsurgency in Latin America or advocate benevolent social reform for the region. Those who protested Reagan's invocations failed to appreciate that the substance of Kennedy no longer existed. Like Jefferson, Lincoln, and FDR, Kennedy was an icon, a representative of "universal truths of hope and activism" deeply enmeshed in the American psyche. His memory, like all memorials, was subject to a variety of national myths, ideals, and political needs. He had become part of the usable past, as accessible as apple pie or the American flag.[21]

The distinctions between Reagan's and Hart's use of Kennedy were important. In their own way, each was an idealist and romantic who yearned to return to simpler times and used the Kennedy legend to coax the nation, to different degrees, to the right. But Reagan's portrait of Kennedy was done in the texture and sentiment of a Norman Rockwell illustration. His glassy-eyed sketch blended Kennedy into widely assumed American beliefs. Hart's portrait of Kennedy was more personal, more visceral, like a Jacques Lowe photograph—moody, private, detailed, and inspiring for its seeming honesty. Reagan's invocations likely appealed to those with less historical mindfulness of Kennedy. True Kennedyites like Theodore Sorensen dismissed Reagan and found in Hart a more credible extension of John Kennedy's legacy.

In trying to reclaim the Kennedy legacy, Mondale and Ferraro underestimated Reagan's skill at blurring fact and fiction. Ferraro understood that "political campaigns are mostly a lot of hot air" and not an "intellectual discourse." But her idealized view of John Kennedy and her hostility for Reagan caused her too readily to dismiss the symbiotic relationship between the two presidents. "Kennedy and Reagan were totally different people," she argued. True. But the Kennedy myth and Reagan were similarly heroic. Dismissing Reagan as "very superficial," Ferraro ultimately failed to understand how her campaign was more burdened than blessed by the Kennedy myth. "I didn't pay too much attention to Ronald Reagan," she admitted. "But I guess the people did, huh?"[22]

Six months after his second inauguration, Reagan paid tribute to the Kennedy legacy, just as he had six months after his first inauguration. This time the occasion was a reception for a fund-raiser for the Kennedy Library held at the home of Edward Kennedy. The president and the senator had developed a personally amiable relationship. Although Kennedy was among Reagan's harshest policy critics, he appreciated Reagan's skills at symbolic leadership and his willingness to fuse the memory of his brothers with national mythology. Earlier, on the twentieth anniversary of John Kennedy's assassination, Reagan had attended a memorial service at Georgetown's Holy Trinity Church. On that occasion Edward began his eulogy by thanking Reagan for his "gracious presence" and citing his kindness to the family. In addition to presenting the Robert Kennedy Medal to Eunice Kennedy Shriver, Reagan had invited Rose Kennedy to the White House. And he had awarded Eunice the Medal of Freedom for her work in mental retardation.[23]

Standing before John Kennedy's brother, widow, two children, and three sisters, Reagan captured the Kennedy mythology more vividly than any previous president or national candidate. He noted how Kennedy fused "very American contradictions." He was self-depreciating but proud; philosophical but pragmatic; literary but earthy. Reagan praised Kennedy for understanding the world's harsh realities, then cited Kennedy's capacity to summon young people to public service, noting that his own White House employed men and women who were moved by this call. "Which is not to say I supported John Kennedy when he ran for President; I didn't," Reagan added. "I was for the other fellow." Sitting in the audience, Jacqueline Kennedy Onassis smiled. "But you know, it's true, when the battle's over and the ground is cooled, well, it's then that you see the opposing general's valor."

Reagan then moved to an almost poetic description of Kennedy as one who saw life as "one fast-moving train, and you have to jump aboard and hold on to your hat and relish the sweep of the wind as it rushes by." The country remembered "his joy—and it was a joy he knew how to communicate." "And when he died, when that comet disappeared over the continent a whole nation grieved and would not forget," Reagan said. "A tailor in New York put up a sign on the door: 'Closed because of a death in the family.' . . . They put his picture up in huts in Brazil and tents in the Congo, in offices in Dublin and

Warsaw. That was some of what he did for his country, for when they honored him they were honoring someone essentially, quintessentially, completely American." Reagan continued, recalling how he was sure that each of the five presidents since Kennedy had thought of him during their tenure. "I've been told that late at night when the clouds are still and the moon is high, you can just about hear the sound of certain memories brushing by." After evoking images of Franklin Roosevelt and Theodore Roosevelt, Reagan spoke of JFK: "Walk softly, now, and you're drawn to the soft notes of a piano and a brilliant gathering in the East Room where a crowd surrounds a bright young President who is full of hope and laughter." In this way, Reagan concluded, Kennedy was still with us. "A life given in service to one's country is a living thing that never dies."[24]

Unlike Carter's speech at the Kennedy Library or Lyndon Johnson's remarks at the dedication of the USS *Kennedy*, there were no hidden agendas or political overtones to Reagan's appearance. Like most of his finest speeches, he fused death, heroes, memorials, fantasy, and myth. He anticipated precisely the emotions brought by the Kennedys to the occasion. "Mr. President," Jacqueline said to him afterward, "nobody ever captured him like that. That was Jack." Speaking before the gathered guests, Edward Kennedy praised Reagan for having "restored the presidency as a vigorous, purposeful instrument of national leadership on issues. I suspect the two of you would not have always agreed, but I know he would have admired the strength of your commitment and your capacity to move the nation." The next day Kennedy wrote a heartwarming thank-you letter: "I only wish Jack could have been there too last night." Like voters in 1984, the Kennedys found themselves drawn to a storyteller whose capacity to romanticize the past transcended partisan differences.[25]

Although their goals conflicted, Reagan, Hart, and to a lesser extent Mondale and Ferraro perpetuated romantic notions of the Kennedy myth and played upon the memories, hopes, and imagination of the public. Twenty years after his death, John Kennedy was still running for reelection, a ghost who reappeared on the balcony in Waterbury, Connecticut, or in the political soul of a boy from Ottawa, Kansas. Like Dr. Fitzgerald in the "Twilight Zone" episode, each national contender promised in his or her own way to straighten "the fabric of time," to move the nation into a more promising future by drawing upon the spirit of an idealized past. In their effort to get elected, to make voters feel better about themselves, these leaders reinvented Kennedy to suit their own ambitions. In the process they heightened unrealistic expectations, burdened the political process with nostalgia, and added to the vacuousness of the Kennedy legacy.

10 Re-creation: The Sentimental Journey of Michael Dukakis

BY THE END OF his second term in office, Ronald Reagan seemed old and out of touch. Jokes about his senility and propensity for naps pointed to a lack of vigor and energy. While much of the public appreciated the sense of pride and confidence he had restored to the nation, disclosures surrounding the Iran-Contra scandal affirmed the image of a president who was disengaged, delusional, and not particularly smart. Reagan was popular but not widely respected. His cuts in social programs seemed increasingly cruel, associating his administration with the catchwords greed, selfishness, and neglect. In January 1987 commentator John Chancellor reflected on John Kennedy's inauguration, noting "now, twenty-six years later, the hope and idealism of the early '60s is gone." Reagan refuted the observation in his State of the Union Address, criticizing "last week's commentary downgrading our optimism and idealism." His defensiveness suggested that something was indeed amiss. [1]

During the 1988 presidential campaign no fewer than six candidates, most Democrats, some Republicans, sought to capture voter support by claiming the Kennedy mantle. Gary Hart announced his candidacy in April 1987, continuing to hold firm to the Kennedyesque themes he had articulated three years before. Since Mondale asked him the fateful question, "Where's the beef?" he had proven himself through his writings, speeches, and proposals to be the most substantive candidate in the Democratic field. "He has for the most part outgrown the mannerisms of Jack Kennedy," *Newsweek* decided, "and the hair that artfully hides his ears is graying." Some reporters noted that, in an age of sound bites and personality profiles, Hart's disdain for celebrity politics was refreshing. He understood, however, that as the front-runner he would face close scrutiny. "People didn't examine Franklin Roosevelt, or even John Kennedy, the way they examine us today," Hart told *Newsweek* in April, referring to two presidents whose private lives conflicted dramatically with their personas. "Now there are more strands to pull."[2]

Hart was not in the race long enough to test whether he would draw on the Kennedy myth as he had in 1984. In the spring of 1987 the Donna Rice scandal shattered the image of the "new" Gary Hart, amplifying the character issue that had earlier burdened him. The man who had always sought to protect his privacy and who hated to appear foolish now suffered from an avalanche of public ridicule. The negative elements of the Kennedy past conspired against Hart just as its positive components had once lifted him. He now found himself compared to JFK in ways he never intended. His uncle told a reporter that Gary's womanizing might be a result of "trying to keep the Kennedy image." Like John Kennedy, Ellen Goodman wrote, Hart enlightened voters "about impulsiveness, self-control, and even the ability to compartmentalize ethics." Some reporters thought Hart suffered widespread condemnation partly because of pent-up frustration toward the Kennedys for their sexual improprieties. It was tasteless to criticize John and increasingly pointless to attack Edward. But Hart was a readily assailable target for those who felt angered by twenty-five years of deception and hypocrisy.[3]

Announcing his withdrawal before reporters and supporters at a Denver hotel, Hart denounced the nomination process as "a mockery" that "reduces the press of this nation to hunters and presidential candidates to being hunted." "I haven't spent a lot of time creating an image," he claimed. "I am what I am. Take it or leave it." Ironically, if he felt victimized by a new journalistic ethic that made a politician's sexual conduct fair game for investigation, the Kennedys bore considerable responsibility for advancing such transformations. Hart's closing statement underscored the totality of his career: he reaffirmed himself as "an idealist" who wanted nothing more than to serve the country he loved. "I would say to the young people of this country, the torch of idealism burns bright in your hearts," Hart concluded. "It should lead you into public service and national service. It should lead you to want to make this country better. And whoever you are, and whatever you do in that cause, at least in spirit, I will be with you."[4]

That morning Gary Hart perhaps spoke as much to himself as he did to his young volunteers. He could not bring himself to admit any wrongdoing, just as he had denied responsibility for his troubled campaign four years earlier. Instead he recalled the idealistic spirit that had attracted him to Kennedy and that, in turn, had drawn so many people to his own campaign. In a different time under different circumstances, it could well have been Hart standing in the audience as a Kennedy volunteer, listening to JFK answer to a sex scandal that threatened to destroy his career. Now Hart tried to keep faith with those who had believed in him. Knowledge of Kennedy's sexual dalliances had never disillusioned Hart. Perhaps he hoped similar understanding could be extended to him. When he reentered the Democratic primaries in December 1987, he continued to evoke the Kennedy past, holding fast to the last remaining threads of idealism. "I want to encourage a shift from being like Ivan Boesky to being the way my generation was under John Kennedy," he told a crowd in Exeter, New Hampshire. The evocations of Kennedy rang hollow. Only the truly delusional or faithful saw in Hart the embodiment of the Kennedy ideals. He still reminded people of Kennedy, but it was a part of Kennedy that they would just as soon forget.[5]

With Hart gone, other candidates looked to draw the sword from the stone. Tennessee Senator Al Gore reminded audiences that he too came from a Democratic family dynasty. His father had been friends with John Kennedy. Like Kennedy, Gore was young and Harvard educated, had served in a generational war, married an attractive woman, and flirted with a career in journalism before being elected to the House and Senate. Speaking at American University, Missouri Congressman Richard Gephardt extensively quoted Kennedy and told the audience that he "strongly felt" his presence. Arizona Governor Bruce Babbitt also reflected on the Kennedy years, telling hushed audiences of "an unfinished agenda everywhere in society." Babbitt, however, understood the limits of recalling the past. "Thirty years later, you don't rekindle the sense of change by simply repeating the words of the past," he noted. Other candidates were less cautious.[6]

As early as 1986 the news media had likened Delaware Senator Joseph Biden to John and Robert Kennedy. His rhetoric, passion, and even his laugh were described as Kennedyesque. Biden aides forewarned reporters that their candidate intended to recapture the Kennedy idealism of the 1960s. But even before he declared his candidacy, Biden's Kennedyesque persona had grown thin. Appearing on CNN's "Larry King Live," he was compelled to defend himself when a telephone caller accused him of pretending to be Kennedy. "In the spirit of another time," Biden said in declaring his candidacy, "let us pledge that our generation of Americans will pay any price, bear any burden, accept any challenge, meet any hardship to secure the blessings of prosperity and the promise of America for our children." By July Gephardt playfully mocked Biden, claiming that when his rival had spoken to an Oklahoma audience, he had said, "Ich bin ein Sooner."[7]

In September Biden's campaign unraveled with the disclosure that his comments in an Iowa debate had been lifted from a speech by Britain's Labor party leader, Neil Kinnock, without attribution. Further rhetorical analysis showed that Biden had copied phrases and imagery from the speeches of John and Robert Kennedy as well as Hubert Humphrey. Biden's press secretary considered the Kennedy parallel as having a particularly serious impact because it was tailor-made for television coverage. Networks showed a split screen of Biden echoing Robert Kennedy word for word. "That's when it started to get perverse," his press secretary recalled. Biden soon withdrew from the race.[8]

Before the primaries even began the news media featured excessive attempts by candidates to associate themselves with Kennedy's memory. Bruce Morton of CBS News devoted a piece to Kennedy's twenty-five-year-old coattails. "Ask not what a candidate can do for a Kennedy," he concluded. "Ask what a Kennedy can do for a candidate." Some columnists hoped that Biden's demise might finally "end the two-decade attempt by Democratic strategists to take promising politicians . . . and mold them into ersatz Kennedys." One pundit wrote that while strategists were correct in sensing a public desire for inspirational leadership, they were wrong in thinking that "all that was needed was to take a current Democrat, douse him with eau de Kennedy and give a script of JFK's inaugural."[9]

The jostling for rights to the Kennedy myth seemed counter-productive in light of the news media's criticism of its saturation and cynicism. The "cloning" of JFK also seemed incongruous with recent disclosures about John Kennedy's private life. Some revelations were gossipy, such as his alleged affair with Marilyn Monroe. Others, however, were well documented. The historian Herbert Parmet provided convincing evidence not only of Kennedy's numerous sexual dalliances but of his accepting a Pulitzer prize for a book he did not write. He also raised questions about Kennedy's drug use and poor health. Still, Kennedy continued to be admired more than any president in recent history. A 1988 *Wall Street Journal*/NBC News poll found that 34 percent of Americans believed that Kennedy had been the most effective president since the end of World War II. He had twice as many devotees as runner-up Harry Truman, and he outdistanced Ronald Reagan by twenty percentage points. Thomas Brown concluded that by 1988 Kennedy's popular image contained regressive fantasies. Kennedy was perceived by the public as someone who would have spent more money on the poor, confronted the Soviet Union, helped harmonize the races, and infused the country with goodwill and style. "The image of Kennedy that emerges . . . is not merely heroic," Brown wrote, "it is almost messianic." It was an image that complemented Michael Dukakis's memory.[10]

II   While numerous candidates walked and talked like JFK in 1988, the man who ultimately carried the torch was oddly unimpassioned. Dukakis was among the most well-intentioned, dutiful public figures to try to carry on the Kennedy legacy. Growing up in an upper-middle-class environment in Brookline, Massachusetts he was instilled with a strong, independent character and an equally powerful sense of civic duty. "I'm a fairly simple guy," he recalled, "whose parents came over on the boat, who had a very happy childhood, fortunately did well academically, athletically, have always been interested in public service, love my wife, and have three terrific kids." Teaching at Northeastern University four years after his defeat in the 1988 presidential election, Dukakis impressed his students by his dedication and passion for government. But they also sensed his coldness. When journalists tried to analyze him during the 1988 campaign, Dukakis's standard response was, "Look, what you see is what you get." More accurately, what you saw was *all* you got. Dukakis was an extremely self-contained person. He earned the label "The Iceman."[11]

Because both he and JFK were born in Brookline, Dukakis felt "a kind of special connection" to his hero. "I've been inspired by some people in public life," he recalled, crisply, "but not like him." Interested and active in local politics, he remembered first seeing Kennedy at the 1952 state Democratic convention "when he was at least nationally a kind of rising young star." Kennedy was not altogether popular that night. The audience was more enamored of Massachusetts Governor Paul Dever. Watching Kennedy, a woman in the gallery turned to Dukakis and commented, "Ah, get that Harvard boy out of there." "The sense you had, or at least I had," Dukakis recalled, "was that it was the old, kind of hard urban Democrats like

Dever who had the allegiance of the party machinery, such as it was. Kennedy was a relative upstart."[12]

Two years later, as a junior at Swarthmore, Dukakis wrote to Kennedy, urging the senator to oppose the Bricker Amendment, "an attempt to legislate isolationism, pure and simple." And he commended Kennedy for supporting the construction of the Saint Lawrence Seaway. Despite the issue's unpopularity in "our home state," Dukakis wrote, Kennedy's position was "extremely well-taken," for it benefited the national economy. In retrospect, Dukakis was unsure why he had contacted Kennedy; it was not his habit to write members of Congress. "I was impressed with this guy, thought he was gutsy," he recalled, "willing to put the country above the region." Characteristically he was drawn to Kennedy's sense of duty.[13]

In the fall of 1954 Dukakis attended American University as part of an internship. There he interviewed Robert Kennedy for a brief thesis he was writing on congressional staffing. Kennedy was then a minority counsel to the Senate Permanent Subcommittee on Investigations. Dukakis remembered him as young, nervous, and impatient. "He didn't spend an awful lot of time with me," he recalled. While in Washington, Dukakis also witnessed the Senate's censure of Joe McCarthy. John Kennedy had abstained from voting against McCarthy, a failure that Dukakis had difficulty reconciling with Kennedy's earlier "gutsiness" on the Saint Lawrence Seaway initiative.[14]

Attending Harvard Law School in the late 1950s, Dukakis became more active in local politics, winning a seat on the Brookline town meeting. At about the same time he became seriously impressed with Kennedy when he heard him speak at Harvard's Young Democrat Club in 1959. "He just walked in, about four hundred law students in the room—a tough audience—and he walked in and said, 'I'm not going to make a speech. I'm sure you have lots of questions. We have an hour, let's go.' And I tell you, it was brilliant. I'd never seen anyone handle an audience that way." Kennedy was witty, intelligent, direct, and candid. It was, Dukakis recalled, "one of the most impressive hours and a half I had ever spent with a political figure."[15]

By 1960 Dukakis was so inspired by Kennedy that he set out to reform the state Democratic party in a manner consistent with Kennedy's ideals. He remembered how Kennedy had risen above a party faction that was "urban, overwhelmingly Catholic, ethnic, and had a reputation for a certain degree of, if not corruption, a certain amount of sleaziness, particularly around the statehouse." Impressed by Kennedy's idealism and his rise to national prominence, Dukakis wondered why he and others of his generation could not follow Kennedy's example. "A lot of us, I think, looked at Kennedy and said, 'Jesus. If he can do it, why can't we? Why can't we transform the Democratic party in Massachusetts into a party which is very much in Kennedy's image? And why aren't there more Kennedys?' Obviously, you can't duplicate a John Kennedy. But why aren't there more folks like him who are rising in a position of leadership in the party?"[16]

Dukakis had an idealistic, if not naive, perspective on Kennedy's rise in Massachusetts politics. Behind the scenes Joseph Kennedy wielded considerable power, invested vast sums of money, and orchestrated sleazy strategies in each of his son's campaigns. Still, Kennedy projected a young, stylish, Harvard manner that contrasted sharply with the colorful backroom world imagined in the novel *The Last Hurrah*. Jonathan Rowe has noted in a brief history of Massachusetts politics that "It was Kennedy, more than anyone else, who provided a bridge between the tribal Irish politics of his grandparents and the suburban, managerial Democratic polity that Dukakis has come to represent." Perceived as a "rational, problem-solving, consensual politician," Kennedy helped make it respectable to vote Democratic, bringing to the party an image of integrity that Dukakis valued. So in 1960 Dukakis and others formed the Commonwealth Organization of Democrats, a group designed to infuse the party with the energy and idealism that Kennedy had projected at a national level. The organization later served as the springboard for Dukakis's career, and its origins showed him to be much in Kennedy's image—a gutsy, relative upstart in pursuit of higher ideals.[17]

In the spring of 1960 Dukakis graduated from Harvard Law School. After taking the bar exam, he and a friend drove west for the Democratic National Convention. They arrived in Los Angeles in time to see Kennedy make a surprise appearance at the convention hall on the night he won the nomination. Dukakis remembered feeling "very troubled" when he learned Kennedy had nominated Lyndon Johnson as his vice-president. "Johnson was Johnson," Dukakis explained glibly. In retrospect, however, he thought the selection was "a good one." It allowed Kennedy to carry important Southern states pivotal to his victory in the fall.[18]

Kennedy gave Dukakis an inspirational boost as he advanced in his career in Boston politics. Like Gary Hart, he was profoundly inspired by Kennedy's call to public service. "For guys like me," he recalled, "it was marvelously reaffirming to have somebody in the White House from our state with the kind of intelligence and strength that

guy had, saying, 'This is the most noble thing you can do.'" During
the Kennedy years he enmeshed himself in local Democratic
organizations and joined a law firm. Running on themes involving
change, youth, and reform, he won his first election to the
Massachusetts House of Representatives in 1962.[19]

During his first term in the House, Dukakis did not let his
admiration for the Kennedys undermine his principles. When Edward
Kennedy ran against Edward McCormack for the Democratic nomination to the United States Senate in 1962, Dukakis campaigned and
voted for McCormack. McCormack had paid his dues, Dukakis
explained, and had been a good attorney general. Dukakis himself
had been doing a great deal of traveling and organizing on behalf of
the Democratic party, trying to reform its structure and image. "And I
think I had this strong sense that you had to earn your spurs a little
bit," he recalled. "You know, we're out there kind of slugging away,
and Ted ought to do the same thing, run for a seat in the state
legislature and help to clean up the mess around here."[20]

Politically the Kennedys were never ones to "earn their spurs." For
decades Joseph Kennedy had used his wealth and influence to
shortcut the system, to find unique and at times unsavory avenues to
power. The idea that Edward Kennedy, the brother of the President of
the United States, was expected to pay his dues was so naive as to be
almost endearing. There was as much chance he would serve in the
state House of Representatives as on the Brookline Redevelopment
Authority. Dukakis had advanced himself through hard work,
perseverance, and commitment. That he expected the same of the
Kennedys showed how unsuspecting he was about the way they
played politics.

Dukakis was returning to his law office from lunch when he
learned that President Kennedy had been assassinated. That December,
in his monthly column for the *Brookline Chronicle Citizen*, he
praised Kennedy for having served as a living example of what
"competence, integrity, and dedication really mean in public life."
Privately he was more emotional. "Our [son] John was five," Dukakis
recalled thirty years later. "It was the first time I think he'd ever seen
me cry. He sat there watching Kitty and me with tears rolling down
our faces. I mean, hour after hour. We couldn't stop." The entire
weekend surrounding the assassination, Dukakis recalled, was a
mixture of "crazy" and "brutal."[21]

During the 1960s Dukakis served eight years in the Massachusetts
House. He was an early supporter of Eugene McCarthy in 1968, but

he switched predictably to Robert Kennedy after he entered the race. Dukakis remembered being "enormously impressed" with Robert Kennedy's "growth and transformation," believing he emerged into "an extraordinary figure." He rejected the notion that Kennedy's evolving liberalism was a result of political expediency. "The Bobby Kennedy who spoke the night of Martin Luther King's assassination, there was nothing contrived about that," Dukakis argued. "I don't think there was anything mannered or contrived about anything." Dukakis was impressed with Kennedy's "very gutsy position" on the war. In general he thought "Bobby" was even more "gutsy" than John. Contrary to most historical judgments, Dukakis believed Kennedy would have become president in 1968 had he not been killed. "Jesus, that campaign was something," he recalled. "And he was going to win. He was coming out in a very gut sense, I think. At least, that's my impression."[22]

The 1970s were a period of great highs and lows for Dukakis. He lost a bid for lieutenant governor in 1970. He then honed his television skills and became a popular moderator for the PBS program "The Advocates." In July 1973 his brother Stelian died. In October Dukakis announced his candidacy for governor, winning the election a year later. During his first term he was accused of being self-righteous and stubborn, alienating many of his close political allies. After losing to Ed King in his bid for reelection, he felt humiliated and fell into a deep depression that lasted two to three months. Less than three weeks after leaving office in January 1979 he accepted a teaching post at the John F. Kennedy School of Government at Harvard.[23]

Dukakis reentered the political arena in 1980 when he campaigned for Edward Kennedy in his bid to defeat President Jimmy Carter for the Democratic nomination. The Carter administration had considerable regard for Dukakis, and the president was reportedly hurt by his endorsement of Kennedy. Some pundits suspected that Dukakis supported Kennedy because he did not wish to jeopardize his political future in the state. But Dukakis rejected the assertion: "I just kind of felt a special responsibility to Ted." Dukakis may have also been enticed by Edward's potential to complete John's unfinished presidency. "It was a special time, a special association," he recalled.[24]

As Ed King bumbled away the Massachusetts governorship, Dukakis eyed a comeback. During the 1982 race for governor the "new" Michael Dukakis admitted his past managerial mistakes. More relaxed and humble, he projected an amiable yet aggressive political style.

Ten days before the primary Dukakis's aides informed Edward Kennedy that their candidate was struggling. No great fan of King, Kennedy reciprocated Dukakis's earlier support. While Dukakis benefited from a number of conditions, he believed that Kennedy's endorsement was "very important" to his victory. "He was a very gutsy guy to do it," he recalled. "There was no reason why he had to do that, to step into that situation. . . . And I've never forgotten it." Dukakis now appreciated the Kennedys at a pragmatic level.[25]

During his second term as governor, Dukakis professed to have a close working relationship with Edward. He acknowledged, "Ted Kennedy and I have never been social buddies. At six o'clock weekday nights I was home, not out drinking with the boys. That's just Mike Dukakis." His admiration, he contended, was based less on Kennedy's name than on his accomplishments. "I know he's got personal problems, but as a public servant, he's very tough to beat." Like many people in Massachusetts, Dukakis was willing to overlook Kennedy's personal flaws. Unable to view him as an extension of the Kennedy myth, Dukakis praised Edward for his legislative and managerial skills, traits to which Dukakis could readily relate.[26]

As Dukakis considered national office, he weighed his own ambitions against Kennedy's. He had been flirting with the idea of running for president since 1983. But his ambitions were contingent on Edward Kennedy's intentions. Challenging Kennedy for the presidential nomination would not have been "a sensible or practical thing to do," Dukakis recalled. They were both Massachusetts liberals who shared many of the same allies. Unmentioned was the fact that Kennedy's name, legacy, wealth, and influence would have vastly overshadowed Dukakis. "If he wanted another shot at it, I certainly would have said fine, terrific, and I would have supported him." If Dukakis felt ambivalent about the Kennedy legacy, he did not show it.[27]

Fortunately for Dukakis, Kennedy announced in December 1985 that he would not seek the presidency in 1988, declaring that "the pursuit of the presidency is not my life." Conventional wisdom held that the new front-runners for the Democrat nomination were Gary Hart and New York governor Mario Cuomo. Low on the list of potential candidates was Michael Dukakis. Undaunted by his lack of name recognition, and freed from the threat of a Kennedy campaign, Dukakis announced his candidacy in April 1987. His effort was less a campaign than a sentimental journey.[28]

For a man accused of being cold and demeaned as a technocrat,

Dukakis had strong feelings for John Kennedy. "I'm not a guy that goes up and down the emotional scale," he admitted, "[but] I never go to the Kennedy Library, I never watch those films without getting filled up." Appropriately, many of the exhibits at the Kennedy Library are accompanied by video compilations of Kennedy's career, depicting his campaigns, the space program, press conferences, and the like. "Of course, you'd pay money to watch his press conferences," Dukakis noted, "I mean, God! It was the greatest show on earth." Other occasions related to the Kennedys were often emotional for Dukakis, particularly the 1979 Kennedy Library dedication. At a dedication of a park in Kennedy's honor in May 1987, he sat between Edward Kennedy and Jacqueline Kennedy Onassis. He was photographed brushing away a tear.[29]

Dukakis was not sure why memorials to John Kennedy evoked such strong feelings in him. "I think part of it is the man," he said, "part of it is kind of recalling one's youth, both personally and politically." Part of Dukakis's feelings were also linked to the "profound impact" he believed Kennedy's death had on the course of the nation. "And I'm not somebody who gets that emotional about things," he clarified. "And I don't want to overdo it. I mean, I didn't walk around my entire political career carrying John Kennedy's picture in my wallet. But there's something about it." When interviewed in 1992, he noted that he and his wife would soon be attending a celebration of John Kennedy's seventy-fifth birthday held at the library. "We're gonna go and there's going to be a lot of emotion in that room," he noted. "It isn't going to be just Kitty and Mike Dukakis. And for all the same reasons"—reasons he struggled to articulate.[30]

Dukakis's feelings for John Kennedy caused him to view his presidency through a stained-glass haze. He had a "gut sense" that Kennedy would have "skillfully disengaged" America from the Vietnam War. He acknowledged that the Bay of Pigs was "a big mistake" but added that Kennedy had grown from the experience, learning not to trust military advice. "We all make mistakes," he repeated. "Nobody is perfect." Dukakis blamed Kennedy's involvement in CIA-sponsored assassination attempts and the wiretapping of Martin Luther King on the cold war temperament of the times. Kennedy would have "evolved" in his thinking, Dukakis said. On social issues, he believed that Kennedy felt "very strongly" about "those basic, gut domestic issues" pertaining to civil rights and poverty. "When that guy went into Appalachia, he wasn't just singing ragtime. He felt it. You could tell that," Dukakis noted. Had Kennedy lived, America might not have suffered from the civil rights violence of the 1960s. "I don't have any doubt that he would have been reelected," he noted. "And we would have had a very solid second four years." There was also no question in Dukakis's mind that America would have been better off had Kennedy lived. "I mean, my God! The possibilities are infinite," he noted. He acknowledged that Kennedy was "less than successful" in passing his legislation in Congress. This was his "one moderate weakness." But when asked to grade Kennedy on his ability to get substantive legislation through Congress, Dukakis responded, "B minus—to be objective about it."

Like Gary Hart, Dukakis believed that Kennedy's greatest strength was his ability to inspire the nation, giving "this country a sense of who we were and where we were heading." He admitted that he had read none of the revisionist assessments of Kennedy, and he offhandedly dismissed almost all charges about Kennedy's personal character. He did not know of "any evidence" that Kennedy stole the 1960 election. The notion that Kennedy accepted the Pulitzer prize for a book he did not write disturbed Dukakis "if it's true." "Guys are getting good money to write this drivel," he argued. "So, I'm always a little skeptical about the revisionist types." He dismissed the assertion that Kennedy contributed significantly to the blending of Hollywood and politics, rejecting the argument that Kennedy manipulated his image. "That was the genuine article out there," he insisted. "It was a palpable kind of joy at being at the helm. And there's nothing mannered about that. You can't rehearse that." Asked about Kennedy's least admirable personal quality, Dukakis maintained that Kennedy was "very tough to fault. I don't see any weaknesses."

Dukakis did not challenge the conclusion that he was an apologist for the Kennedys. And he readily conceded that his sentimental attraction to Kennedy clouded his judgment. Indeed, he justified his sentimentality: "Why do all of us by the millions look back on those years and say, 'Those were good years for America. They were years when we felt good about ourselves—when there was a sense of the future'?" he asked. "Well, I think because the reality is that they did." Today's nostalgia for the Kennedy presidency, he argued, was a consequence of our stumbling as a nation since Kennedy's death. The Kennedy years were the last time we felt "old fashioned American optimism" and believed "we were moving ahead and moving forward." "And it was based on something real," Dukakis concluded. There was "a very strong and genuine sense that this country had its act together." "Overall, those were exceedingly good years for the country. And the guy in the White House had a good deal to do with it, in my judgment."[31]

While Kennedy's positive attributes were surely admirable, Dukakis's appraisal gave one the impression that he had spent the past thirty years in a time capsule. He assessed Kennedy less from knowledge than from personal memory, using as his sources his "gut," his "sense," or his "impression." No amount of evidence, no degree of historical revisionism could penetrate his belief system. Indeed, he assumed responsibility for his hero's upkeep. Regardless of how one feels about Kennedy, serious scholarly evidence has raised legitimate questions about his character and his excessive attention to marketing an image that clashed with his authentic self. Many historians have illustrated his penchant for clandestine operations, a resistance to the civil rights movement, and an inability to transcend a cold war mentality. Dukakis, however, viewed Kennedy in terms of what he wanted to be true—even though his beliefs had little to do with the reality of the man and his achievements. He did not "see" any weaknesses in Kennedy because he never looked for them. As a devotee of the Kennedy legend, he focused on aspects of it that reaffirmed his opinions.

Dukakis's affection for the Kennedy years and his belief that things were better, happier, more hopeful then seemed purely nostalgic. In his book *Yearning for Yesterday: The Sociology of Nostalgia*, Fred Davis defines simple nostalgia as "the celebration of now ostensibly lost values, the sense of some ineffable spirit of worth or goodness having escaped time. . . . The emotional posture is that of a yearning for return, albeit accompanied often by an ambivalent recognition that such is not possible."[32]

When acting upon a nostalgic impulse, as Dukakis did in 1988, a person seeks continuity. Davis relates the story of a man who fondly remembers an old tweed coat he wore when he was young. Seeing a new tweed coat, the man decides to buy it to renew pleasant memories of the past. He does not transform himself by cutting his hair short, buying argyle socks, and so forth. Instead he incorporates the coat into his current reality. In the 1988 presidential campaign, Dukakis too wore Kennedy like an old tweed coat, but stylistically it did not fit him. His nostalgia for Kennedy caused him to evoke the myth in ways that were often self-defeating.[33]

III From the beginning of his campaign, Dukakis cloaked himself in the Kennedy legend. In the early primaries he reminded audiences of how Kennedy had inspired him to pursue a political career. He urged voters to "ask more of your candidates, because the next President will be asking more of you." By December 1987 he began speaking of "the Next Frontier," a slogan aides admitted was designed to improve his image. "A few months ago he was cold, almost aloof," a campaign adviser noted. "Today, he is much warmer, almost Kennedyesque. Almost." Campaigning in West Virginia, Dukakis repeatedly noted that twenty-eight years earlier, voters there had helped nominate "another son of Massachusetts" who went on to defeat a Republican vice-president in the fall. "History will repeat itself," he promised.[34]

As part of his effort to align himself with the Kennedy myth, Dukakis invited Edward Kennedy to Iowa to stump on his behalf. Speaking before larger than usual crowds, Kennedy worked to transfer affection for him and the Kennedy legacy onto Dukakis. While he enjoyed this added attention to his campaign, Dukakis was overshadowed by the accompanying "mystique." Crowds seemed less interested in hearing Dukakis speak than in catching a glimpse of the last Kennedy brother. Stories also circulated that Kennedy did not take Dukakis's campaign seriously. He reportedly rolled his eyes in disbelief when he introduced the governor as the next President of the United States. Dukakis was unruffled, maintaining that Kennedy was unequivocal in his support. "Kennedy's presence always overshadows people," he added. "It didn't bother *me*. I was pleased and delighted to have him there. I don't mind basking in a little reflective glory from time to time. It was terrific."[35]

While Dukakis may have seen himself as basking in "a little reflective glory," reporters saw him as diminished by the Kennedy shadow. His willingness to be momentarily obscured by Kennedy's presence forewarned of his enthrallment with the "mystique." Throughout the early primaries he extended the historical parallels. One week before the Democratic convention, in his most obvious attempt to recall the 1960 election, he brought Texas Senator Lloyd Bentsen onto the ticket. "Jack Kennedy and Lyndon Johnson beat that incumbent Republican vice president in 1960," he announced in Boston, "and Mike Dukakis and Lloyd Bentsen are going to defeat him in 1988." The geographical similarities generated anticipated headlines and feature stories about the re-creation of the Boston-Austin axis.[36]

Dukakis hoped that Bentsen might appeal to Southerners, centrists, conservative Democrats, farmers, and the business community. But he was also enticed by history. Before he made his choice, Dukakis was shown a copy of a memo that John Kennedy had drawn upon when he selected Lyndon Johnson. Several Dukakis advisers believed that the memo encouraged Dukakis to see himself as mystically linked to the Kennedy campaign. Dukakis disputed such claims, later asserting that if Bentsen had been from Nebraska, "I think I still would have picked him." The desire to recreate the Boston-Austin axis, he said, was "lower on the scale" of considerations. Bentsen's stature in the Senate, his Southern appeal, and his political skills weighed more heavily. Still, Dukakis noted that the historic parallels were "an extra added something" and "a nice little bonus." "And no question, in some ways a reflection of feelings about 1960 and so forth," he recalled. "And I felt good about it. I think Bentsen felt good about it. I think a lot of people felt good about it."[37]

That Dukakis considered Kennedy-Johnson parallels at all was testimony to the growing derivativeness of his campaign. The conditions that allowed Johnson to carry important Southern states crucial to Kennedy's victory did not apply in 1988. Bentsen did not have broad Southern appeal; as it turned out, he could not even carry his own state on behalf of the ticket. Unlike Richard Nixon in 1960, George Bush could claim Texas as his home state. And, as many political commentators correctly predicted, Texans were more likely to put one of their own in the White House than in the vice-presidency. Moreover, Dukakis based his decision on a seriously flawed understanding of how Kennedy came to select Johnson. Kennedy intended only to give Johnson the right of first refusal, and worked frantically to remove him from the ticket. "That's not the history I've been reading," Dukakis replied. It probably wasn't.[38]

Other actions by Dukakis suggested that he had become fixated on the Kennedy past. The 1988 Democratic National Convention was so purposeful in its intent to reinforce memories of the Kennedy years that one comedian likened it to a colorized version of the 1960 convention. John Kennedy, Jr., made his first national political appearance. During his brief speech he recalled how his father had inspired many delegates to pursue public service. "Because of you," he told them, "he is with us still." He introduced his uncle, Edward

Kennedy, whose most memorable moment was his taunting mockery of Bush's role in the Reagan administration, repeatedly asking, "Where was George?" But Kennedy also waxed nostalgic, linking Dukakis with the Kennedy tradition. He recalled the "continuity" of "commitment" between the Dukakis-Bentsen ticket of 1988 and the Kennedy-Johnson ticket of 1960. "For Michael Dukakis and Lloyd Bentsen, like John Kennedy and Lyndon Johnson, believe that we cannot be content with things as they are. That there are newer frontiers to be crossed and a greater society to be built." Recalling the memory of John and Robert Kennedy, as well as Martin Luther King, Kennedy linked Dukakis with "the trustees of a dream."[39]

If Edward Kennedy rolled his eyes at the thought of Dukakis as president, the idea of such a technocrat being the trustee of the Kennedy legacy might have caused a facial tic. Nevertheless, Dukakis believed that Kennedy's comparisons that night were politically and personally valuable, and not contrived. During his acceptance speech, Dukakis reinforced his Kennedy identity, envisioning "the next American frontier" and pledging "to recapture the spirit of energy and confidence and of idealism that John Kennedy and Lyndon Johnson inspired a generation ago."[40]

After the convention Dukakis unabashedly compared the election to 1960, when "after eight sleepy but amiable years of a Republican administration, a son of Massachusetts challenged the incumbent vice president." He cited Kennedy frequently, as many as five times in a single speech. In speeches written by Theodore Sorensen, he promised to "get America moving again," demanded "a new call to greatness," asserted "we can do better," pledged to "pay any price" to assure the defense of liberty, and, while speaking at the Camelot Hotel in Little Rock, Arkansas, described an America "with new horizons to reach and new frontiers to conquer." Aides conceded that their candidate was trying to conjure images they hoped would be transferred to Dukakis. "A great many voters are too young to remember those years," Sorensen noted. "But it gives Dukakis a place among the older politicos who remember what it was like then."[41]

Preparing for his debates with Bush, Dukakis watched excerpts of the Kennedy-Nixon debates. Aware that he was not "Mr. Warmth and Charm," Dukakis was pleased to see that Kennedy too seemed "very serious" and "nervous." Dukakis felt particularly nostalgic when he traveled to Ann Arbor, Michigan, where Kennedy had announced his pledge to create the Peace Corps program. Speaking on the steps of the student union at the University of Michigan, Dukakis noticed a plaque commemorating Kennedy's appearance. "So here I was speaking to thousands [of students]," he recalled. "Lots of enthusiasm. And basically I'm retracing John Kennedy's steps . . . that was an emotional moment." Looking at himself and laughing, Dukakis remembered having said to himself, "What am I doing here?" Dukakis knew he lacked Kennedy's charismatic appeal. Still, he identified himself with those elements of the myth that were part of his natural makeup—duty, confidence, and integrity. Mindful of how history might have been different had John Kennedy lived, perhaps, too, he believed that with Edward Kennedy's departure from presidential politics, he might in his own technocratic way complete the unfinished Kennedy presidency.[42]

Four years after the 1988 campaign Dukakis freely admitted that he had tried to associate himself with the Kennedy myth. "Look," he noted, "I didn't discourage [comparisons to Kennedy]. Not because I had any pretensions of being another Jack Kennedy, certainly. But because you [could not be] a young Democratic politician coming of age in Massachusetts in the early sixties, who suddenly in the eighties finds himself running for the presidency with a running mate from Texas, and not feel that [connection] very powerfully." Dukakis saw natural parallels between his campaign and Kennedy's. As in 1960, America had completed eight years of a Republican president. Like Eisenhower, Reagan was "running out of gas." And like Vice-President Nixon, Vice-President Bush represented the stagnation and thinking of the past. "So the similarities were there," he argued. "And you don't have to reach for them." He believed the issues of 1960 were similarly relevant. "I don't mean that we're going to find another Kennedy," he qualified. "They don't come along very often. But we needed some of that sense of renewal. And I very inadequately hoped that somehow in my candidacy in 1988 we could recapture that."[43]

Dukakis was partly correct. The parallels between 1960 and 1988 were there, and the press would have raised them with or without his encouragement. The impulse for renewal, for a return to the idealism, hope, optimism, and compassion embodied in the Kennedy myth, was indeed an energy waiting to be tapped. But the practical differences between the two campaigns ran far deeper than Dukakis perhaps appreciated. By 1988 television was more dominant. Polling had become more sophisticated. The ground rules of journalism had changed dramatically, and public examination of a candidate's character was commonplace. Since 1960 America had experienced important demographic changes. The growth of suburbia, the rise of the Sunbelt, and a vast increase in the number of black and Hispanic voters demanded major adjustments to campaign strategies. The average age of the American voter was younger. Americans were less optimistic; many had lost faith that government could solve national problems. Liberal Democratic programs had become highly discredited. The credibility gap between the public and their representatives seemed impassable. The primary concern in 1988 was not atomic war but economic stagnation due to foreign competition. With the advent of a high-tech service economy, voters worried about long-term health care, the affordability of homes, and whether their children would have the same opportunities they had.[44]

But when he was asked what was original about his campaign, what distinguished it from John Kennedy's, Dukakis laughingly replied, "I wish I could tell you." He returned to comparisons with the 1960 campaign, recalling how Bush attacked him for being too timid and inexperienced in foreign policy. Nixon had done the "same kind of stuff" to Kennedy, he noted. Dukakis's sentimentality, his seeming seance with Camelot, clouded his perspective of the 1988 campaign much as it affected his judgment of JFK. He was so enamored of the "mystique" that years after his defeat to George Bush he had not reconciled its delibitating effect on his campaign.[45]

For his part, Bush devoted implicit homage to Kennedyesque ideals. He understood the need to separate himself from the greed and neglect associated with Reagan. At the Republican National Convention he presented himself as a sincere public servant whose life since World War II had been a series of missions completed. He criticized the selfish pursuit of wealth and called upon government and the private sector to bring about "a kinder, and a gentler nation." During the fall campaign he periodically associated himself with Kennedy's tough cold war actions while linking Dukakis with the failed liberalism of the 1960s. Like Reagan in 1984, Bush professed that he, not Dukakis, was more akin to Kennedy in standing tough against communism. Like Reagan, Bush accused Dukakis of repudiating the foreign policy vision of John Kennedy. Unlike "today's liberals," he would boldly meet America's foreign policy challenges.[46]

Wanting it both ways, Bush disparaged Dukakis as a "typical, New Deal, Northeastern Kennedy-type liberal." He tried to exploit the vague and evolving meaning of "liberalism." Franklin Roosevelt had been more a pragmatist than a liberal, and was initially regarded with suspicion by liberal writers. Under Harry Truman, left-wing New

Dealers had split early with his administration and formed the Progressive party. John Kennedy had been viewed suspiciously by the liberal wing of the Democratic party in 1960. During the fall campaign, Kennedy had addressed the term's negative connotations. "If by 'liberal,'" he told the New York State Liberal Party, "they mean someone who looks ahead and not behind, someone who welcomes new ideas without rigid reactions, someone who cares about the welfare of the people.... If that is what they mean by 'liberal,' then I'm proud to say that I'm a liberal."[47]

By 1988 Bush and the Republicans had redefined liberalism to mean soft on crime, captured by special-interest groups, and unpatriotic. When Bush attacked Dukakis as a Kennedy-type liberal, he was referring not to John or Robert but to Edward, who had long served as a lightning rod for conservative Republicans. For them, Edward Kennedy represented everything that was wrong with America— big-spending government initiatives, failed social welfare programs, neglect of the middle class, and special treatment of minorities, as well as hypocrisy and immorality.

Dukakis was not surprised that Bush sought to blunt his association with the Kennedy legend by tagging him as a Kennedy-type liberal. "I'm sure one of the things the Republicans did not want to see was lots and lots of people reflecting nostalgically on Kennedy and saying, 'Yeah, Dukakis and Bentsen. That's the same thing.'" He rejected the claim that Edward Kennedy's involvement in the campaign facilitated Republican attacks. "No," Dukakis recalled. "It was terrific. I thought he was terrific. It was great." But he recognized that he never effectively addressed the "liberal" issue. Referring to Kennedy's 1960 speech before the Liberal party, he recalled, "I must have [made the same argument], or something like that, hundreds and hundreds of times. Obviously I didn't say it very well." He also said it only during the closing days of the campaign. "I just think in many ways we failed to do what [John] Kennedy was able to do in 1960," he noted, and part of that failure was his inability "to frame the liberalism issue in the way that Kennedy had. He did it much more effectively than I did." "Thinking back on it," he added, "on that particular issue, I probably should have invoked Kennedy's name as well as the response much more frequently than I did." After conceding his mishandling of the liberalism issue, Dukakis drifted into an imaginary speech: "Well, you know, Richard Nixon accused Jack Kennedy of exactly the same thing. And let me tell you what Kennedy said...." "Now in that case," Dukakis concluded, "I think it would have been far, far

more effective to have put it in those terms. And we should [have].
Don't ask me why we didn't do it that way."[48]

Thus Dukakis acknowledged that he tried to copy Kennedy,
measured himself against Kennedy's success, and chastised himself
for not having been as effective. The problem, he thought, was not
that he tried to mimic Kennedy in a manner that was inappropriate to
the times, but that he had not copied Kennedy well enough.
Preoccupied by the 1960 campaign, he failed to appreciate that the
term "liberal" was more reminiscent of the failures embodied by
Edward Kennedy than the nobleness associated with John.

Bush, however, was also guilty of misconstruing the Kennedy
myth. At the Republican convention he accepted the advice of
strategists Roger Ailes and Robert Teeter who urged him to nominate
forty-one-year-old Indiana senator Dan Quayle for the vice-presidency.
Among the main reasons for Quayle's selection was the belief that he
would appeal to the eighteen-to-forty-five-year-old generation as
Kennedy had in 1960. Bush advisers were convinced that Quayle had
a Kennedyesque appeal, and they imagined him riding in an open
convertible with young women reaching for him and tearing off his
cuff links. Both Kennedy and Quayle brought a youthful, attractive
physical presence to their respective tickets. Both came from wealthy
families. Neither Kennedy nor Quayle had served in the House of
Representatives with distinction; in the Senate, Quayle was regarded
as more effective than Kennedy had been.[49]

But instead of "screamers" and "jumpers" yearning to lay hands on
Quayle, there were only questions regarding his military service, his
lack of intellectual depth, and his capacity to hold higher office. In
late September 1988, while on the political stump, Quayle responded
to criticism of his academic skills, legal talents, and youth by
recalling historical figures who had suffered from similar judgments.
Winston Churchill, he noted, was a mediocre student. Franklin
Roosevelt had failed his bar exam. And "Jack Kennedy was about my
age when he ran for President." Hearing of Quayle's allusions to
Kennedy, Dukakis and Bentsen were irritated. "For Quayle to invoke
Jack Kennedy's name was ludicrous," Dukakis recalled. To those who
fondly recalled the Kennedy years, Quayle lacked not only Kennedy's
ideology and political values but his wit, charm, intelligence,
articulateness, telegenic appeal, and war record. At best he was a
Kiwanis Club version of Kennedy.[50]

Voters got their first sustained view of Quayle during the televised
debate against Lloyd Bentsen. In preparation, advisers had implored

Quayle not to mention Kennedy, anticipating that Bentsen would turn the reference against him. Standing next to the courtly Texan, Quayle was nervous and painfully scripted. Any illusions about him being Kennedyesque had vanished as a result of what many called his deer-in-the-headlights expression. Asked about his qualifications, he repeatedly avoided mention of Kennedy. On the fourth occasion he wandered off his mental teleprompter. "I have as much experience in Congress," Quayle said, eager to get past the question, "as Jack Kennedy did when he sought the presidency." A wide-angle camera shot showed Bentsen licking his lips and raising his eyebrows, looking, as one reporter noted, like a dog who had seen a squirrel in the backyard. Since Kennedy's death, presidential contenders from Lyndon Johnson to Pat Robertson had referred to Kennedy as a means of bolstering their appeal. Reporters and pundits may have questioned such parallels, but no political figure had ever chastised another publicly for the gambit—until now. "Senator, I served with Jack Kennedy," Bentsen said steadily. "I knew Jack Kennedy. Jack Kennedy was a friend of mine. Senator, you're no Jack Kennedy."[51]

On the surface Bentsen's response was devastating. The audience gasped, howled, and applauded, as if watching the impact of a left hook or a low blow, depending upon one's perspective. "I think it was a damn good moment for Lloyd Bentsen," Dukakis recalled. "I think it was a good moment for us." Newspapers headlined the retort. The exchange proved to be among the most memorable moments of the campaign, and it would haunt Quayle during his four years as vice president. ("What did Marilyn Quayle say to Dan after making love?" one popular joke went. "'Senator, you're no Jack Kennedy.'") Bush supporters tried arguing that Bentsen and Kennedy had never been all that friendly. Some Quayle supporters took a different, revisionist approach. "Dan's a Better Man than Jack," read a hand-held sign in Springfield, Missouri.[52]

Bentsen had struck a powerful nerve that voters could easily understand. Two forces had converged—one, a candidate whom many people felt had no right to be a heartbeat away from the presidency; the other, a mythic ideal. Not since Roger Mudd asked Gary Hart why he imitated John Kennedy had a candidate been so quickly diminished by the Kennedy aura. Negative comparisons to Kennedy usually came slowly and subtly. With Quayle they were swift and embarrassing.

Yet Bentsen's response was somewhat unfair. Quayle's evocations of Kennedy were far less strained than those of other candidates. Some

Republicans had gone to unusual lengths to identify themselves with Kennedy. Jack F. Kemp made note of his identical monogram, as if the Kennedy legacy could be transferred by alphabetical coincidence. Suffering from weeks of scrutiny about his qualifications, Quayle had only tried to argue that he and Kennedy had served the same number of years in Congress. Bentsen ignored Quayle's mathematical parallel (which was wrong anyway), and instead effectively twisted Quayle's meaning to suggest he was inappropriately trying to claim the Kennedy mantle.[53]

Unexpectedly, the "you're no Jack Kennedy" retort placed Dukakis in an uncomfortable position, begging the question, if Dan Quayle was no Jack Kennedy, who was? Earlier Dukakis had suffered inevitable comparisons with the myth he perpetuated. A political cartoon pictured a miniature Dukakis sitting in a huge JFK rocking chair next to a miniature Lloyd Bentsen who straddled a giant pair of LBJ cowboy boots. Columnist Mike Royko, meanwhile, drew on revisionist trends to disparage Dukakis's use of Kennedy romanticism. While Dukakis hoped to make voters "burst into a chorus or two of 'Camelot,'" Royko reminded readers that Kennedy bore responsibility for Vietnam and was reluctant to advocate civil rights. "So Dukakis and Bentsen can spare me any further reminders," he wrote. "I've never been able to get nostalgic about body bags and tear gas."[54]

After the Bentsen-Quayle debate, journalists wondered if it was any less "ludicrous" for Dukakis to invoke Kennedy than it was for Quayle. One widely circulated political cartoon pictured Bentsen holding aloft a doll-sized version of Dukakis, proclaiming, "*This* is a Jack Kennedy!" David Broder reported that Dukakis "may be even more vulnerable to a self-promoted Kennedy comparison" than Quayle. He accused Dukakis of having failed to capture the spirit and desire for change that had marked Kennedy's campaign. "[A]s of today," Broder concluded, "[Dukakis] is losing even more vital ground in the Kennedy comparison than Quayle did the other night." The stylistic contrasts between Dukakis and Kennedy were elaborated. Dukakis trudged while Kennedy strode. Dukakis pleaded while Kennedy challenged. Kennedy sparkled on television while Dukakis looked into a television camera like he was looking into a refrigerator. "The Duke isn't JFK either," columnist Joe Klein concluded.[55]

Broder and Klein pointed to a fundamental shortcoming of Dukakis's campaign—its lack of passion, excitement, and vision. After the election such critics as Sidney Blumenthal continued to chastise him for his failure to recapture Kennedy's poetry and imagination. Speaking at Yale University four months after the election, Edward Kennedy assailed the Democratic party for being devoid of ideas and vision. Democrats needed to "move beyond the New Deal and the New Frontier and the Great Society," Kennedy said. He charged that there was "no compelling Democratic message." "Competence was not enough," Kennedy said, referring to one of Dukakis's major campaign themes. "Ideology—which is about ideas—was missing and our opponents filled the gap with appeals to fear, only lightly sprinkled with the kinder, gentler seasoning of his perorations." He urged Democrats to emulate former President Ronald Reagan's capacity to bring to the presidency vigor and single-mindedness. He credited Reagan's success and effectiveness to the fact that "he stood for a set of ideas" that were infused "into the national consciousness." "Ronald Reagan may have forgotten names, but never his goals," Kennedy said. "He was a great communicator, not simply because of his personality or his teleprompter, but mostly because he had something to communicate."[56]

Asked about Kennedy's rebuke a few years later, Dukakis conceded that despite his intentions he was never able to rekindle the idealism and passion associated with the Kennedy campaign. "I think our failure in some ways was in failing to capture much of that spirit," he said. Early in the campaign he believed "there was a real possibility, a potential for doing that which we kind of blew." Dukakis knew that he could not rekindle the spirit by exclusively or endlessly invoking the Kennedy past. He thought he had tried to balance his linkage with the Kennedy legacy with efforts to project his own identity, values, and goals. "You've got to kind of provide a good deal of that yourself, and I'm sorry to say that for a variety of reasons I wasn't able to do that."

Dukakis dismissed critics who asserted that he was lost in nostalgia. "I don't want to sound like old granddad," he replied, "but Sid [Blumenthal] wasn't *there* in the early 1960s. So he can't understand this. You can't unless you were *there*. It was an extremely powerful force and in many ways it becomes more powerful." Dukakis's response suggested he had been swept by forces beyond his control, and that his political roots gave him special insight into those years. Ironically, he failed to understand that he wasn't *there* either. He was a fan, a distant bystander, like millions of Americans including Blumenthal, who was an impressionable fifteen-year-old when Kennedy was killed. But consistent with his heroic view of Kennedy, Dukakis felt closer to Kennedy than he really was.

In retrospect, Dukakis never thought he overreached himself in trying to identify his campaign with the Kennedy past. He recalled having urged his speechwriters to find references to Kennedy as well as to Franklin Roosevelt and Harry Truman. He conceded, however, that he emphasized and preferred the Kennedy quotes. Characteristically, he justified his use of Kennedy quotes by noting that Kennedy too had infused his speeches with historical references. Sorensen's contributions as a speechwriter were "valuable," Dukakis noted, although he had "a style which sounded a lot better coming out of a John Kennedy than it did a Mike Dukakis." He eventually had second thoughts about his forced rhetorical style. "Finally in that last month I just threw the script away," he recalled, "which I should have done months earlier to tell you the truth."

Indicative perhaps of his infatuation with the Kennedy image, Dukakis had no recollection being compared unfavorably to JFK. "I'm Mike Dukakis. I'm not John Kennedy. Everybody knew that," he said rapidly. "[Comparisons to Kennedy] may have been a problem that Lyndon Johnson had, but it wasn't a problem Mike Dukakis had." When shown a political cartoon of Bentsen holding up a doll-sized version of his running mate, Dukakis smiled vainly. Did he understand its message that he paled in comparison to Kennedy? "Well, I suppose," Dukakis conceded. "Folks that invoked Franklin Roosevelt were never going to be Franklin Roosevelt. I mean, you know, what are you going to do?" A second cartoon pictured him holding a Kennedy mask in front of his face. After a pause, he responded cheerfully, "That doesn't bother me."[57]

Dukakis implied that he was helpless to ward off comparisons. Yet it was *he* who chose a Texas Senator as a running mate, who called for the "Next Frontier," who used Kennedy-like catchphrases, who "basked" in Edward Kennedy's aura, who belabored historical parallels, and who admitted that he did not wish to discourage comparisons. Far from being embarrassed by his Kennedy façade, as Gary Hart was, Dukakis seemed honored. He did not wear the Kennedy mask as a means of placing himself on the political stage, but because he hoped that others would see him as he wanted to see himself—as a legitimate extension of the Kennedy legacy. He never understood that the Kennedy façade distracted voters from seeing and judging him on his own terms. He failed to appreciate how the Kennedy image drew attention to his own inability to project vision, idealism, and hope. In the end he was neither Jack Kennedy nor, it seemed, fully Michael Dukakis. He was a guy clutching proudly and hopefully at a mask.

During the Democratic primaries in the spring of 1992, Dukakis hoped that Bill Clinton could evoke Kennedy's spirit better than Dukakis had in 1988. "I don't think the yearning after a Kennedy-like president is the worst idea in the world," Dukakis noted. Clinton's use of the "mystique" was "perfectly understandable" given the degree to which John Kennedy had influenced him as a teenager. He predicted the Kennedy nostalgia would serve Clinton well. "I don't think it's debilitating at all. It *was* a very important time," he said, falling deeper into the nostalgia trap. He now saw "parallels" between the 1992 and 1960 campaigns. The country, he explained, was still in need of "new ideas, new vision, new energy, a commitment to public service, a president who can energize the government and make government an instrumentality for progress."[58]

In noting the nation's shortage of vision, energy, and new ideas, Dukakis was not so much pointing out "parallels" as he was confessing his own limitations and needs. Certainly he was not alone. Part of the initial widespread appeal of the Hart and Dukakis campaigns was their call for the renewal associated with the Kennedy years. But even Edward Kennedy understood that neither John Kennedy nor Ronald Reagan inspired the American people by pretending to be someone else. While the yearning for a Kennedy-like candidate may not have been the worst idea in the world, the successful candidate had to wear the Kennedy tweed coat and still be himself.

11

Bill Clinton
and the Laying
On of Hands

THE DAY BEFORE his inauguration, Bill Clinton visited John Kennedy's grave at Arlington National Cemetery to pay respects to the man who thirty years earlier had inspired him to pursue public service. He was accompanied that cold January day by members of the Kennedy family, including the last Kennedy brother, the widow and son of Robert Kennedy, and the only son of the late president. The short, informal ceremony cemented symbolically the president-elect to his hero—a connection he had consciously cultivated throughout the 1992 campaign. That evening Clinton was shown on the nightly news placing a single white rose by the eternal flame before kneeling in prayer. The footage brought to mind the final scene of Brian DePalma's 1976 horror film *Carrie*, when a young woman classmate of the maligned protagonist lays flowers at Carrie's grave. Suddenly a bloody hand lunges from the dirt, grabs the devotee's wrist, and pulls her into the grave. The young woman awakes hysterically from her nightmare, tormented by memories of the person she had come to honor. Given the way the Kennedy legend has often haunted the presidency, one could imagine Clinton becoming a casualty of the myth to which he paid tribute. If Kennedy could reach from beyond the grave, however, he would not terrorize Clinton. The slain president would more likely extend a hand of gratitude, for Clinton has helped to rehabilitate the Kennedy legend as much as he has been enhanced by it.[1]

After the 1988 election, Edward Kennedy and the Kennedy family became a source more of titillation than inspiration. In December 1990 rumors about Edward Kennedy's womanizing and carousing received widespread attention in GQ, a magazine which twenty-eight years earlier had heralded John Kennedy for his fashion sense. Now the last Kennedy brother was pictured in deteriorating physical condition, lying on top of a woman in a boat off Saint-Tropez, and was described copulating with a congressional lobbyist in an exclusive Washington restaurant. On Easter weekend in 1991 the debauchery became more serious when Kennedy's thirty-year-old nephew, William Kennedy Smith, was accused of raping a woman at the Kennedy compound in Palm Beach. As details of the evening became known, the senator's behavior seemed pathetically delinquent. To assure a fair trial, Smith's attorney, Roy Black, asked potential jurors their opinions about the Kennedy family. Not surprisingly, most of those questioned respected Edward the least of the Kennedy brothers. A seventy-eight-year-old woman was asked by Black what she knew about the case. She remembered hearing "somebody was running around without his pants. I think it was Kennedy, the fat [pause]—the senator. He's idealistic, but maybe a little horny." By December Smith could state with some degree of accuracy that, although he was the person on trial, "in some strange way I'm on trial for my family."[2]

By the end of 1991 Edward Kennedy had become the Fatty Arbuckle of American politics. Stories and jokes about his purported alcoholism and womanizing were widespread. Political satirist Mort Sahl recalled how Democratic fund-raisers had repeatedly asked him for donations by recalling the Kennedy legend. "People would say, 'Dukakis, he was just like Kennedy,' 'Clinton, he's just like Kennedy,'" Sahl noted. "Finally, in exasperation, I turned to a waiter and asked, 'Is there anyone in the Democratic Party who isn't like Kennedy?' And he said, 'Yeah, Ted.'" Supporters argued that Edward Kennedy was still among the hardest working and most effective lawmakers of this century. John and Robert had long suffered criticism that they were more style than substance. The last Kennedy brother seemed sustained by his achievements. Some journalists appreciated the larger historical context of Edward's fate. "His older brothers were martyred before their sins caught up with them," *Newsweek* explained. "Now Kennedy must bear the brunt of resentment from a public that feels betrayed, not only by his highly publicized indiscretions, but by the revelations about Jack and Bobby." Faced with declining popularity in his own state, Kennedy spoke at the John F. Kennedy School of Government at Harvard in October 1991. He apologized for unspecified behavior and suggested that he would better himself in the future. Kennedy may have helped stem his political slide in Massachusetts, but he remained a chronic source of vitriolic attacks by conservatives and a ready target of humor for late-night talk show hosts.[3]

Meanwhile, the Kennedy "mystique" continued to have a paradoxical appeal. In November 1990 a Gallup poll indicated that John Kennedy was more popular than any of the past nine presidents; 84 percent of Americans approved of his administration. In the spring of 1991 an NBC/*Wall Street Journal* poll indicated that one in three Americans would add John Kennedy's face to the portraits on Mount Rushmore. Kennedy received further deification in Oliver Stone's popular film *JFK*. Audiences were led to believe that Kennedy had been murdered by evil forces within the military and government to assure America's commitment in Vietnam. The protagonist pleaded with audiences not to forget its "fallen king," and the film's subtext reminded viewers of how much better life would have been if Kennedy had lived. Despite the lack of credible evidence, nearly nine in ten people believed in 1993 that Kennedy was killed by a conspiracy.[4]

The mythical dimensions of John Kennedy's life and death seemed more potent than they had thirty years before. By the 1992 election millions of Americans, alarmed perhaps by the nation's economic decline, increased violence, and unresponsive government leaders, still looked to the Kennedy myth for reassurance. Unable to find embodiment in Edward Kennedy, the "mystique" had wandered about the political landscape, finding inadequate refuge in Gary Hart and Michael Dukakis. In 1992 Bill Clinton became a more viable outlet for lingering fantasies. For the World War II generation, Bush was their contemporary, a veteran of the Good War just like John Kennedy. For those inspired by the Kennedy of their youth, however, Clinton spoke to their better nature. "The Kennedy's are the one face you can put on all our lost youth," recalled Tom Campbell, a college roommate of Clinton's who sought to explain Clinton's appeal. For those with no actual memories of Camelot, those post–baby boomers who learned history via television, Clinton could be readily cast as Kennedy, a fictionalized player in a prime-time docudrama.[5]

II Like a television docudrama, Clinton's early life offered a fairytale connection to the Kennedy legend. Raised in a middle-class family in Hope, and later Hot Springs, Arkansas, Clinton suffered through numerous hardships as a boy. His father was killed in a freak automobile accident four months before he was born. After his grandfather died when Clinton was ten, he had no satisfactory male role models in his life. His mother Virginia, married an alcoholic who physically and psychologically abused the family. Her optimism, ambition, and love compensated for much of her son's pain. Still the turmoil forced him to grow up quickly.[6]

Television politics offered a diversion from family tensions. Clinton's interest in national politics was sparked in 1956 after the family bought its first television set. That summer nine-year-old Billy watched both national conventions, including John Kennedy's failed bid for the vice-presidency. "I was fascinated by it," he recalled in 1987. "I was the only person in my family who sat there and watched it all." Like most people, Clinton was struck by television's capacity to dramatize politics, creating a sense of immediacy and intimacy. Drawn more to personality than ideology, he was attracted to Eisenhower, referring to him as the "father figure."[7]

Friends recalled that Clinton was uniquely aware of social issues while he was growing up. Mauria Aspell, a childhood friend of Clinton's, remembered that the integration of Central High in Little Rock during the 1950s sparked a serious interest in social conditions. "Bill was always more involved in and thinking about politics and issues than we ever were," recalled another friend, Joe Newman. David Leopoulis remembered "feverish pitched" political conversations at Clinton's home. School, meanwhile, provided him with a sense of stability and accomplishment in a sometimes disorienting home life. He was a remarkable student, earning impressive recognition. "He was brilliant," Aspell recalled. "He was very competitive. You just always knew that he could be successful in politics. He could run or run for someone else a very successful campaign in the ninth, tenth, and eleventh grade. So you started to associate him with that." Less admiring peers referred to him as "Billy-vote Clinton."[8]

In 1960 Clinton followed the Kennedy-Nixon campaigns while taking a ninth-grade civics class. He remembered that he and his civics teacher were the only Kennedy supporters in the class. "Presidential politics began with Kennedy for us," Aspell remembered. "I remembered how excited people like Bill were that Kennedy had won." Watching the campaign on television, Clinton could readily identify with Kennedy. "That was the first president that we thought of as a human being rather than as an old man," Aspell noted.[9]

In July 1963 Clinton's life changed dramatically when he traveled to Washington, D.C., as a delegate to Boys Nation. The highlight of the trip came when President Kennedy addressed the delegates in the

Rose Garden of the White House. The representatives from each state were arranged alphabetically on the White House lawn. Bigger than the other boys, Clinton muscled his way to the front of the Arkansas delegation. "I made sure I got to shake hands with him," he recalled. "And I remember just thinking what an incredible country this was that somebody from a little town in Arkansas who had no money, no political position, or anything, would be given the opportunity to meet the President." Thirty years later he recalled the moment while walking past the Rose Garden with Dan Rather. Excited by the memory, he pointed to his exact position when he had met Kennedy. "And I never will forget that," he reflected. He paused, gazed at the spot, and bit his lower lip.[10]

Friends noticed that when Clinton returned to Hot Springs he seemed changed by the experience. "I remember him just *raving* about Kennedy when he came back from Boys Nation," Aspell recalled. "I just remember how excited he was and how in awe he was of John Kennedy. . . . We kind of wanted to touch the man who had touched the man. You didn't see Bill Clinton get awe-struck with very many people." The photograph of him shaking hands with Kennedy was hung on the wall of his home beside family photographs. Friends playfully referred to the display as Virginia's "shrine," but Clinton himself was not one to brag about meeting Kennedy. His response was more internal. "He ingested it in some way," Leopoulis remembered.[11]

Later, Arkansas political columnist John Brummett speculated on the lasting influence of the handshake. "One can only wonder," he wrote, "what might have happened if young Billy had not been elected to the Arkansas Boys State to represent the state at Boys Nation, and if, just suppose, he had met Elvis Presley instead of JFK that summer." But the Kennedy handshake merely pulled Clinton down the path he was headed. "Kennedy, if anything else, put him over the top, like a crescendo," Leopoulis argued. "It was just the ultimate of all the emotions. Kennedy was like a booster rocket." Aspell concurred. "I do think Kennedy changed him. He changed that day. I think he started thinking bigger. National politics became a real reachable thing for him or a possibility then, rather than state politics." If he had met President Nixon in 1963, Aspell noted, his reaction "would have been a shrug." "I know for Bill Clinton it didn't take Kennedy's death to make him feel sanctified. It took meeting him. He was just somebody that Bill just totally looked up to."[12]

Clinton's impulse for public service was likely intensified by the

Kennedy assassination just four months after he had shaken the president's hand. He remembered the events of the day vividly and wondered about the future. "I was afraid that Kennedy's potential to benefit our nation and the world would never be realized," he recalled. His friends remembered how he checked his emotions. His pain, however, was not concealed from everyone. Aspell saw Clinton after classes were abruptly canceled. He was sitting on the wall by the front steps of the school and crying softly. "It really, really hit him hard. He was just staring off with tears and he held his head. . . . I think Bill had a personal sense about Kennedy," Aspell noted. "I think that when he died, while most of us took it very hard and certainly grieved, Bill almost took it personally. It was like a personal loss."[13]

After graduating from high school in 1964, Clinton attended Georgetown University, largely because of its foreign-service program and its location in Washington. Among a handful of students with whom he developed a close, lasting friendship was Thomas Caplan. Caplan had worked informally for the Kennedys since the summer of 1963 and, during his freshman year at Georgetown, was a volunteer in Robert Kennedy's Senate office. Having entered Georgetown just a year after John Kennedy's assassination, Clinton and his classmates, many of whom were Irish Catholics and interested in public service, remained mindful of John Kennedy's example. "The halo of John Kennedy and the memory of him had an enormous effect on all of us," Caplan recalled. "It was a place where the Kennedy influence was very strong at that point in particular." Through Caplan, Clinton met Robert Kennedy for the first time in May 1965 when, as class president, he attended a campus gathering organized by Caplan. "He liked Bobby a lot," Caplan recalled. Caplan was also involved in a tour of Kennedy memorabilia organized to raise money for the John F. Kennedy Library. One night he and Clinton visited Evelyn Lincoln, John Kennedy's secretary, whom Caplan knew well. They went to the archives where they examined John Kennedy's desk and other Kennedy artifacts.[14]

During his junior year Clinton began working part-time for Senator William Fulbright. He had met and spoken with Fulbright when he participated in Boys Nation, providing another important layer to his political consciousness. The distinguished Arkansas senator was a source of pride for a kid who lived in a state widely disparaged for its poverty, backwardness, and resistance to integration. On a practical level, Fulbright's impact on Clinton was far greater than Kennedy's. Kennedy was an idealized figure held at arm's length; his influence was personal but remote, providing Clinton with a valuable source of inspiration in his youth. Fulbright, on the other hand, was a living, breathing example of what it was to be a politician.[15]

Because of his work in Fulbright's office, Clinton was not permitted to campaign for any presidential candidate in 1968. Although Tom Campbell, his college roommate, vaguely remembered that Clinton favored Eugene McCarthy, Caplan thought he was sympathetic to Robert Kennedy. Just a few days before graduation Clinton watched Kennedy's victory speech on television on the night of the California primary and then went to bed. "I introduced him to Robert Kennedy," Caplan recalled, "and I woke him up and told him that he was shot." Clinton was stunned, particularly because Kennedy's murder came on the heels of Martin Luther King's death. "There was a general feeling that things were getting out of control," Caplan noted. "Our college career began sort of punctuated by the death of one [Kennedy] and then ended with the death of another."[16]

Clinton remained on the fast track, attending prestigious schools, collecting degrees, and ever mindful of his dream to return to Arkansas and pursue a political career. Despite the upheavals of the late 1960s, he held fast to his idealism. "The good [thing] was that people really caught up in the '60s cared about one another," he recalled, "cared about civil rights and poverty and making things better, and saw themselves as part of a larger whole, with responsibilities not only to themselves but to others. . . . There was a great sense of possibility of hope—a sense that the system could be made to work." At Yale Law School he worked for an antiwar candidate running for the U.S. Senate from Connecticut. He supported George McGovern's campaign in 1972, managing his general election campaign in Texas. And while teaching at the University of Arkansas Law School at Fayetteville, he ran for the U.S. Congress against a popular four-term incumbent, losing by only four percentage points. Reporters were struck by his good 'ol boy, baby-faced charisma, referring to him as the "boy wonder." Three months shy of his thirtieth birthday in 1976, Clinton won his bid for attorney general of Arkansas in a walk. Two years later, at age thirty-two, he became the youngest governor in the nation and was touted as one of a "new breed of Southern governors." "The foundation was laid for the establishment of Camelot at the Capital," Arkansas journalist John Robert Starr wrote.[17]

Like Gary Hart's connection to Kennedy during his early career in Colorado politics, Clinton's youth, charm, and articulate speaking style inspired natural comparisons. Stephen Smith, a friend and political advisor to Clinton during this time, recalled that voters thought of Kennedy in reference to Clinton as early as 1974. "It wasn't anything that he was doing intentionally or anything that he said," Smith recalled twenty years later, "but a lot of the people responding to him after he'd give a speech would say, 'This guy reminds me of John Kennedy.'" Like Governor Jimmy Carter, Clinton did not fully exploit his Kennedyesque image. The photograph of him shaking hands with Kennedy was displayed in his office, but it was not used in campaign publicity. "I don't think [the Kennedy linkage] was something that he tried to push," Smith recalled. Clinton would occasionally reflect on Kennedy's influence on him, particularly when speaking to youth groups. And in his 1978 campaign for governor, a five-minute campaign film included a section in which Clinton spoke of his lonely support of Kennedy in 1960.[18]

Although Arkansas was conservative and predominantly Protestant, Smith thought that the Kennedy aura, minor as it was, translated well there. Voters associated the late president with the hope and optimism shaken by Vietnam and Watergate. The image complemented progressive trends to move Arkansas beyond the backwardness associated with the governorship of Orval Faubus. Moreover, the Kennedy reminders and his work for Fulbright neutralized criticism that Clinton was too inexperienced to hold office. "Because he was such a young candidate," Smith noted, "you needed something to give it legitimacy.... Having that relationship ties in and gives credibility to the fact that this guy is real young but knows what's going on—experience by osmosis." Generally, however, the Kennedy allusions were subliminal and so subtle that many friends and political allies had no recollection of Kennedy-Clinton parallels during the 1970s. For political purposes, Clinton emphasized instead his work for Senator William Fulbright. Still, Smith recalled, the existing Kennedy comparisons were welcomed. "I didn't think it was completely off base," he noted, "but it was not anything that I would have generated on my own."[19]

Like Jimmy Carter, with whom Governor Clinton had a sound relationship, he combined fiscal conservatism with progressive views on matters of race. He may have been criticized for being arrogant and out of touch with his constituents, but the national news media promoted Clinton as a Golden Boy. In 1980 Clinton supported Carter's renomination over Edward Kennedy's challenge. Unlike Dukakis, who supported Kennedy in 1980, Clinton was not torn by his decision or enamored by the Kennedy legend. "It was easier to be for John Kennedy in the fall of 1960 than it was to be for Ted Kennedy in the spring of 1980," Smith recalled. "Ted Kennedy had a lot more negative baggage to carry around." Clinton meanwhile lost his 1980 bid for reelection to Republican Frank White, who, according to Starr, "brought Camelot down around Clinton's ears." At the age of thirty-four he became the youngest ex-governor in U.S. history.[20]

Demonstrating remarkable resiliency, Clinton ran against White in a rematch in 1982. Like Dukakis, he admitted his mistakes and vowed to listen more and to set more realistic goals. Clinton used his personality more effectively, reinventing himself slightly to distance himself from his negative image of the late 1970s. After winning the Democratic run-off, he defeated White handily and went on to win reelection three more times. He drew on a new, informal, personal touch while building popular support for his programs.[21]

Clinton considered running for president in 1988 but hesitated for a number of reasons. Given the press scrutiny surrounding Gary Hart's involvement with Donna Rice, he was well aware that he might face a similar onslaught of questions about his own indiscretions. During the 1988 campaign he traveled extensively with Dukakis, serving as his adviser and promoter. At the convention that year he hoped to gain important national recognition when he placed Dukakis's name in nomination. But his nominating speech dragged on for more than half an hour, much to the ridicule of the political press. The next day he accepted an invitation to appear on the "Tonight Show." He joked with Johnny Carson that Dukakis requested he give a similar type of nominating speech for George Bush. He then played the saxophone with Doc Severinsen and the NBC Orchestra. He successfully turned a national embarrassment to his advantage, using warmth and self-deprecation to schmooze with Carson and the television audience. Bill Clinton may have been a child of the Kennedy "mystique," but that night he showed he was a uniquely contemporary politician.[22]

III The struggle for rights to the Kennedy "mystique," like the neverending quest for the Holy Grail, began in 1992 where it left off in 1988. Nebraska Senator Bob Kerrey had the youthful looks, rhetorical style, and war record of Kennedy, but not his energy and charm. Iowa Senator Tom Harkin presented himself as the last of the Kennedy-Johnson liberals, but he had the presence of a small-town hardware salesman. Former Massachusetts Senator Paul Tsongas understood his charismatic limitations, so he recalled the Kennedy past by reminding audiences of his service in the Peace Corps. Robert Kennedy's oldest son, Congressman Joe Kennedy III, campaigned with Tsongas during the early primaries. "People say I don't have any charisma," Tsongas told audiences, "so I brought some."[23]

During the early primaries the more charismatic Clinton also presented himself in the Kennedy tradition even as he articulated a decidedly moderate, New Democrat agenda. As a national candidate he drew more deliberately on presidential symbols than he had as governor. For the first time his television commercials featured the photograph of him shaking hands with John Kennedy. Like Kerrey and Tsongas, he openly claimed the fallen Kennedy brothers as his heroes and repeatedly invoked their memory during speeches. After Tsongas suspended his campaign, Clinton welcomed Joe Kennedy's support, and they appeared together regularly on the stump. Well before the Democratic convention, voters connected Clinton to the Kennedy image. In a survey of 250 New Yorkers, Clinton's fourth most attractive quality was that he "reminds people of John F. Kennedy." Random interviews with voters in other states frequently alluded to his Kennedyesque aura. In Illinois a Reagan Democrat told a reporter that Clinton made him more agreeable to vote for a Democrat for the first time since Kennedy.[24]

Boyhood friends of Clinton who had never associated him with Kennedy began sensing a vague Kennedyesque aura. Aspell traveled to New Hampshire on Clinton's behalf during the New Hampshire primary. She had never been impressed with her friend's public appearances. But one day in New Hampshire, standing behind Clinton as he spoke in a gymnasium, she was reminded of another era. "I watched him start talking to those people and it was electrifying," she remembered. "You felt that same feeling. I turned and I said to David [Leopoulis], 'It's like listening to John Kennedy.'" Clinton was especially articulate that day, speaking in shirt-sleeves before a captivated audience. "For me, from then on I really did see Kennedy personally. I was in awe. Not of him but of this candidate. I felt, my God, who is he? And I remember wondering, is he going to change? Is he not going to be himself?"[25]

Clinton evoked Kennedy for both personal and political reasons. Stephen Smith, who guided Clinton's earliest campaigns and is still a friend of the president, sensed Clinton was nostalgic for the Kennedy years. "He looks at [his presidency] as a chance to sort of bring back

Camelot in a way," he recalled in 1994. "I think he finds the Kennedy analogy useful just because it was a time of hope and enthusiasm about the future and what we could do." The invocations, he believed, were not contrived or artificial. "On some things I don't think it would be beyond him to do that," Smith conceded, "but in this case I don't think it is at all." Leopoulis and Newman sensed that Clinton was moved by personal memories of growing up in Hot Springs in the early 1960s. "It was good times for everybody," Newman recalled. "So when you evoke that memory, he's trying to bring back those good-time, feel-good, you-know-everything-is-right-with-the-world sort of feelings." Clinton's boyhood, of course, was not so ideal. Like Hart and Dukakis before him, he was not immune to fantasy as he sought to restore the confidence and hope imagined in the Kennedy years.[26]

Comparisons between Clinton and Kennedy were strained at several levels. Physically Clinton lumbered about like a young Lyndon Johnson. His geographic origins invited comparisons with Jimmy Carter. His personal demeanor suggested Phil Donahue more than JFK. Kennedy was aloof; Clinton hugged. Kennedy hated "couch" questions; Clinton sounded like a self-help book. Kennedy connected with audiences from afar; Clinton was interactive, at his best when engaging questioners intimately. Kennedy was modern; Clinton was postmodern. "His breakthrough insight is that power resides with the host, not the guest," journalist Joe Klein observed. "He is equal parts master of ceremonies, televangelist, and group therapy facilitator. You tell him your problem; he tells you his twelve-step program—with appropriate body language, concerned lip-biting, caring nods and clucks."[27]

Still, Clinton was able to project innate qualities that connected him with his hero and obscured their geographical, social, and philosophical differences. At an obvious level he conjured images of youth, energy, and idealism—qualities that had long been a part of his political makeup but which took on new meaning in a national campaign. Clinton and Kennedy both seemed sincerely devoted to public service and addressing the nation's problems. His Ivy League education, as well as his ability to think on his feet and to recall and articulate complex data, brought to mind the Kennedy image of intelligence. He enjoyed politics and power, and displayed a similar detached irony that allowed him to laugh privately at his own success. Both men were pragmatists, moderates who challenged the party establishment and pros. Clinton was short on Kennedy's good looks, grace, mystery, and wit. But in his own Southern way he was charming, easygoing, friendly, and sexy. Indeed, thousands of women around the country reported having sexual dreams involving Clinton.[28]

Clinton's great advantage over Kerrey, Tsongas, and other Democratic contenders for rights to the Kennedy mantle was not only his pleasing personality but an ability to convey empathy. In some ways Clinton's public image seemed derived from Reagan. He heralded middle-class values, promoted national myths, and waxed poetic at times about traditional American heroes. Likewise he could project warm emotions through television. Unlike Reagan, however, Clinton seemed compassionate toward the underprivileged. "I feel your pain" was a Clintonian cliché, but it succinctly captured perhaps his strongest asset in 1992. Caplan, who is a novelist, thought Clinton's empathy reflected a unique gift uncharacteristic of most politicians. "Though he is a politician, his personality is in many fundamental ways artistic," he explained. "He is able to put himself through his imagination into the role of another person."[29]

Clinton's empathy, too, was reminiscent of Kennedy's. "Whenever I see any Kennedy, I feel good," a sixty-one-year-old retired schoolteacher told a reporter, "and whenever I see Bill Clinton, I get a little of that Kennedy feeling. These are people who care about people and give you hope, and there's hope." John Kennedy was never one to bite his lower lip and get teary-eyed. And Robert Kennedy worked hard to overcome his "ruthless" reputation. Still, whether talking quietly to West Virginia coal miners or speaking in Indianapolis on the night of Martin Luther King's death, John and Robert projected compassion. Although Clinton's body language and the clip in his voice was uniquely his own, he too connected at a visceral level.[30]

The parallels between Clinton and Kennedy were not always beneficial. Early in the 1992 campaign it appeared he would suffer the same fate that had humiliated and destroyed an earlier Kennedy-styled candidate. In January, Gennifer Flowers sold a story to a tabloid magazine describing her alleged twelve-year affair with the governor. Reporters scrutinized Clinton's personal background, examining not only the womanizing issue but draft-dodging charges as well. The so-called character issue proved cumbersome and embarrassing, fueling Clinton's reputation for evasiveness and confirming for many the image of "Slick Willie." As it had with Hart, the infidelity issue invited unwelcome comparisons with the Kennedys. *Newsweek*'s "Conventional Wisdom" section observed about Clinton, "Old CW: Hooray, the new JFK. New CW: Uh-oh, the new JFK."

"Tonight Show" host Jay Leno noted in his monologue that when Clinton was fifteen years old he imitated John Kennedy by playing football on his front lawn. "As he got older," Leno noted, "he found other ways to emulate Kennedy."[31]

But Clinton overcame the issue when he finished strongly in the New Hampshire primary. The sex scandal became old news, a warmed-over replay of Hart's unraveling in 1987. An ABC News survey indicated that 80 percent of voters did not think Clinton's sexual indiscretions were a legitimate issue in the campaign. Flowers was a self-promoter who invited suspicion and ridicule. And Clinton adeptly handled allegations, particularly during an appearance with his wife, Hillary, on "60 Minutes." Accusations about character assassination inspired a political cartoon of Clinton in a limousine beneath the Texas School Book Depository. The cartoonist placed a "tabloid reporter" on the sixth floor, with "2nd tabloid reporter spotted on grassy knoll offering women money to say they did it with Bill."[32]

In a left-handed way the Kennedy "mystique" helped salvage Clinton. A focus group of five men was asked if Clinton's morals hurt him politically. Mindful of their own flaws, each man distinguished Clinton as being more like John Kennedy than Edward. Clinton, in other words, was given greater leniency than Edward Kennedy. Edward was perceived as having "killed" a woman and then lying to authorities. Clinton, however, responded to charges with greater perceived candor, a plus in an age of confessional politics. And like the public's response to John Kennedy's infidelity, voters seemed willing to overlook Clinton's transgressions. "Now, Bill Clinton may be 'no Jack Kennedy' any more than Dan Quayle is," the *Christian Science Monitor* speculated. "But Kennedy's success proves that politics is more than just bookkeeping, more than just tallying pluses and minuses. If a candidate, for whatever unquantifiable reason, electrifies voters, they will overlook defects that would doom other candidates. Clinton appears to have some of that spark."[33]

As Clinton clinched the nomination, he grew bold in making parallels with the 1960 campaign. His selection of Al Gore as his running mate underscored what Gore termed the need for "a new generation of leadership." Unlike Dukakis, who was so enamored of the Kennedy past that he duplicated the Boston-Austin axis, Clinton chose a fellow youthful Southerner—but it was a choice that augmented the Kennedyesque aura of his campaign. Gore was young, Harvard-educated, and part of a political family dynasty. One popular cartoon showed Clinton standing beside Gore at a podium. "Just remember," Clinton says to Gore. "I'm the one doing the Kennedyesque stuff."[34]

Before the convention, one of Clinton's key media advisors, Hollywood producer Harry Thomason, studied tapes of the 1960 Democratic National Convention with the intention of duplicating appropriate moments. So, on the second night of the convention the party paid tribute to John and Robert Kennedy. Seated in the audience were John Kennedy's daughter and son, several of his sisters, and Ethel Kennedy with several of her children. Clint Holmes began the Kennedy celebration by singing a rendition of "Abraham, Martin, and John." A "Bobby" verse was duly added, and photographs of John and Robert Kennedy materialized on cue on a large screen monitor above the convention podium. Speaking in tribute to his father, Joe Kennedy cited Robert's compassion, moral prerogatives, efforts at inclusion, and desire to protect the middle class. Bill Clinton and Al Gore, he said, were part of the Kennedy tradition. After the showing of a sentimental film biography of RFK, Edward Kennedy called for a return to the compassion, activism, and hope associated with his brothers, and he praised Clinton for his ability "to heal, to oppose hate, to reach across the divide and make us whole again." When he finished, John Kennedy, Jr., appeared on television waving a Clinton sign.[35]

Under Thomason's direction, Clinton then broke with tradition and did what John Kennedy had done in Los Angeles in 1960. After he won the nomination in the roll-call vote, he made a "surprise" appearance at the convention hall to thank the delegates for their support. In case anyone missed the point, he reminded the audience that "thirty-two years ago another young candidate who wanted to get this country moving again, came to the convention to say a simple thank you." Typical of Clinton's use of the Kennedy legend, however, the appearance was consistent with his personality and his expert understanding of television. "Anybody who knows Bill Clinton knows that his natural personality would not have been to sit in that hotel suite," Caplan explained. "What would have been less authentic would have been to say, 'Hey, there are all these people down there for you but let's just sit here and have a pizza.'"[36]

Before Clinton accepted the nomination the next evening, delegates watched his film biography. Its most emotional moment came with the black-and-white footage of young Bill Clinton shaking hands with John Kennedy. Although a photograph of the handshake was given much exposure, film of the event had only recently been discovered in the archives of the Kennedy Library. For dramatic purposes the film was edited into a close-up of Clinton and Kennedy. It was also shown in slow motion and in reverse, so that Kennedy moves into Clinton rather than sweeping past him. In the original clip Clinton looks down briefly to see Kennedy's hand before reaching to shake it. Played in reverse, however, Clinton appears to bow humbly and avert his eyes *after* shaking Kennedy's hand. It was a dramatic subtlety that only a Hollywood production team could catch. In a voice-over, Clinton recalled the moment for viewers, noting, "That's when I decided that I really could do public service because I cared so much about people." As anticipated, the scene brought a huge ovation from the audience. The film biography concluded with a replay of the archival footage, and Clinton saying to the swell of music, "I still believe in a place called Hope." At the end of the film he walked unannounced to the podium and accepted the party's nomination. His speech combined the themes of John Kennedy's acceptance speech and inauguration, pledging a "New Covenant... based not simply on what each of us can take, but what all of us must give to our nation."[37]

Other Democratic conventions had recalled the Kennedy legend, but never more dramatically. Reagan's former speechwriter, Peggy Noonan, disparaged the sentimentality but conceded its effectiveness. "It is almost three decades since his passing," she wrote, "but JFK was the most popular man at the convention, RFK the most beloved." The emotional power of the tribute was unmatched, owing to high-tech graphics, the enthusiasm of the Kennedys themselves, and the tear-jerking lyrics of a 1960s song lamenting lost heroes. Unlike Hart or Dukakis, Clinton had the full blessings of the Kennedy family. Edward Kennedy had never endorsed Hart, and his obligatory pronouncements on behalf of Dukakis entailed suspicious eye-rolls of disbelief. In 1992 the Kennedys seemingly relinquished the myth to a more credible heir than themselves. Watching the campaign in retirement, another presidential candidate who twenty-four years earlier had run against Robert Kennedy, was struck by the symbolism. "Our blessing is on you," Eugene McCarthy commented, "inheriting the crown not in blood lines but by a laying on of hands."[38]

The footage of Clinton shaking hands with John Kennedy was an image-solidifying breakthrough. Arkansas journalist John Brummett, who had pondered what might have happened if Clinton had met Elvis in 1963 rather than Kennedy, could have asked what might have happened if photographers had never filmed the Rose Garden ceremony. The still photograph and film footage conveyed a level of authenticity that no previous Kennedyesque candidate had projected. No candidate had ever found an intergenerational image as powerful as the Clinton-Kennedy handshake. The grainy black-and-white pictures blended him into the legend itself, fusing neatly the past with the present.[39]

Clinton faced minor criticism for his use of the "mystique." His acceptance speech was criticized by some as derivative and less engaging than John Kennedy's. A political cartoon lampooned him for the contrast between his Southern heritage and the Kennedy image, proclaiming, "Ich bin ein Bubba!" One reporter charged him with purposely gesturing like Kennedy. (Clinton scoffed at the suggestion that he watched old Kennedy videos before the campaign.) Critics lamented another candidate exploiting voter fantasies. "One's heart sinks," George Will wrote. "Is Clinton another politician spoiled at a tender age by exposure to the politics of manufactured glamour and the pursuit of power for its own sake?"[40]

But such criticisms were rarer than they had been with Hart or Dukakis. After years of witnessing a series of Kennedy impersonators, reporters who covered the 1992 campaign seemed neither surprised nor highly critical of Clinton's Kennedy motif; more often they accommodated him. Publications confirmed his "Kennedy aura." The eye-catching photographs of him shaking hands with the late president graced many of the early articles on his campaign. By 1992 such symbolic exploitation was accepted practice, generating a collective yawn among campaign reporters. Younger journalists were caught up in the "mystique," attracted to Clinton's Kennedyesque aura. "A lot of these journalists who think that maybe this will be their Camelot gave him a head of steam before any vote was cast," Bill Kovach, head of the Nieman Foundation at Harvard, observed.[41]

Criticism of Clinton was also muted because he did not appear to rely heavily on the Kennedy legend. Unlike Hart and Dukakis, he projected a unique persona and a message distinct from the Kennedy image. Jules Witcover, who for twenty-eight years had observed the political usage of the "'mystique," defended Clinton. Although people often compared Clinton to Kennedy, the overriding voter sentiment was that Clinton "really sounded like he wanted to do something." Witcover recalled, "Clinton made an appeal to the better nature of people that was similar to what Kennedy did but in his own context." His campaign had contemporary features, including moderate appeals to middle-class Americans. Fleetwood Mac music, bus tours, MTV appearances, Larry King interviews, and saxophone recitals. His campaign theme song, "Don't Stop Thinking About Tomorrow," balanced calls to recapture yesterday. His political persona was both nostalgic and contemporary as he incorporated the spirit of John Kennedy into his larger, touchy-feely, New Age self.[42]

Clinton's unique personality made his use of the Kennedy myth seem less transparent. Hart made many voters uneasy—he was too cold, too weird, as if he had been secretly programmed to be JFK. Dukakis was Kennedy absent of charm, charisma, and sex appeal—in essence, not a Kennedy at all except geographically and somewhere in the real estate of his mind. Each acknowledged that he was not good at projecting his personality, a severe handicap in an era of talk-show politics. Uncomfortable with their public selves, they put on a Kennedy halo that ultimately blurred their authentic selves. Clinton, however, was open to self-disclosure, giving him definition and distinctiveness. He did not seem to rely on the "mystique" to fill a void within himself. "In the case of Bill Clinton," Caplan noted, "it's just a case of enrichment. [The mystique is] a guide, but there is a person there to begin with."[43]

Clinton's invocations of Kennedy therefore did not overshadow him. They seemed in keeping with his personality, blending with qualities he already possessed. Witcover sensed that the press did not accuse Clinton of imitating Kennedy as they did Hart because Clinton was "*seemingly* more authentic." Clinton's emulation was not as forced as Hart's. "The contrast between what Hart really was and what he professed to be in terms of imitating Kennedy was more jarring than it was with Clinton," Witcover recalled. Clinton was an extrovert while Hart was reserved and guarded. "Kennedy," he noted, "was the kind of guy who was in the middle of those two." He was aristocratic but he was also a product of Boston politics, which required a degree of glad-handing. "Hart took a lot of heat for [emulating Kennedy] because it was so blatant. It didn't square with his personality as much as it squared with Clinton's personality and style."[44]

To be sure, Clinton had problems with his public image. For all his self-revelations, he seemed vague and contradictory. He was part Yuppie, part Bubba; part Hope, part Yale; part Elvis, part JFK. He remained an elusive entity, suspected of seducing the public just as effectively as he supposedly did the women he was accused of bedding. John Kennedy, too, was elusive. But what was mysterious for Jack was "slick" for Willie, a consequence perhaps of the greater scrutiny of private lives, the growing cynicism about the manipulation of public images, and Clinton's lapses into evasiveness. Still, Clinton held a unique advantage over other Kennedy "wannabes." A key to Clinton's success in evoking the "mystique" was that he could remind people of Kennedy while still being himself.[45]

The Clinton camp pretended that the Kennedy connection was spontaneous. "It's not really that we promote a Kennedy mystique, or even that the ideas are similar," Bruce Reed, Clinton's issues director noted. "It's that many people believe Bill Clinton has the same potential that Kennedy did." While the assertion was partly true, Clinton seldom spoke at a rally without mentioning John Kennedy. He carried with him a collection of Kennedy speeches to which he frequently referred. Like Kennedy, he pledged to move the nation past its economic stagnation, and renewed calls for sacrifice and volunteerism. Witcover sensed that Clinton got considerable mileage out of his advocacy of a national service program because it reminded voters of the Peace Corps. "No matter what he talked about on domestic and foreign policy," Witcover recalled, "that was the one thing that always got the biggest crowd reaction."[46]

Symbolically, Clinton was further connected to Kennedy through campaign buttons that pictured the now famous handshake and proclaimed, "The Torch is Passed to a New Generation" and "The Dream Lives On!" He spoke at rallies standing beside busts, plaques, and statues commemorating John Kennedy. Such symbolism fed and reflected voters' imagination. "He is the first since Kennedy," a Hispanic man commented in south Texas. "We have waited all these years." One campaign sign read simply, "1960 1992." In France, editors spliced together films of Clinton and Kennedy to accommodate public fantasies.[47]

In the campaign Bush tried to paint Clinton as a latter-day Jimmy Carter, but he could do little to separate Clinton from the Kennedy myth. Addressing the Boys Nation delegates on the White House lawn, Bush cited the names of past delegates who had gone on to distinguished careers in public service. He made no mention of Clinton. Some Republican media strategists argued that Bush was truly of John Kennedy's generation; both men had served heroically during World War II. The reminder was part of Bush's shrill effort to portray Clinton as a radical holdover from the 1960s. For his part, Bush tried to portray himself as a Truman-like underdog, taking advantage of a recent resurgence in the former president's popularity.

The effort was lame and duly disparaged by surviving members of the Truman family. As economic issues dominated and Bush's campaign fell apart, some Republicans looked forward to the 1996 election when they could nominate their own JFK—former Congressman Jack F. Kemp.[48]

Upon Clinton's victory, the news media unleashed a wave of headlines and stories promoting him as the elected heir to the Kennedy legacy. The metaphor of the torch being passed to a new generation of leadership was vastly overplayed. When *Time* named Clinton "Man of the Year" it announced "The Torch Is Passed" and dramatically pictured Clinton with a clenched fist superimposed over the photograph of him shaking hands with Kennedy. The "Today Show" devoted four minutes to parallels between Clinton and Kennedy, noting how both men evoked similar feelings of idealism, activism, and hope. Some differences were cited. Clinton assumed office as America suffered through economic and spiritual decline, making his call for sacrifice more strained. Writing for *Time*, Lance Morrow predicted that Clinton would likely come to physically resemble W. C. Fields or Tip O'Neill. Hillary, meanwhile, was widely regarded as the antithesis of Jacqueline Kennedy. But her intelligence, ambition, toughness, and role as an informal adviser to the president inspired comparison to Robert Kennedy.[49]

The morning after the election, a caller proclaimed to a radio talk-show host, "I voted for the reincarnation of John F. Kennedy!" No one can know for certain to what degree the urge to reelect John Kennedy played a role in Clinton's victory. The campaign was marked by fresher considerations—widespread hostility toward elected incumbents, frustration with legislative gridlock, a faltering economy. Issues unique to the 1990s dominated the political dialogue. Clinton was no more in the liberal, Kennedy tradition than Jimmy Carter had been. He advocated government intervention to stimulate growth and opportunity but avoided calls for new programs and increased federal funding for social programs. Ross Perot's popularity showed the extent of voter contempt for all Washington-styled politicians. Most political analysis concluded that the election was more a referendum against Bush than a vote for Clinton.[50]

Yet, at a subliminal level, voter desire for change and renewal was fundamental to Clinton's appeal. As in the Hart and Dukakis campaigns, the Kennedy "mystique" played a recurring role, providing a historic context for the candidate's youth, vigor, and new-generation image. Clinton successfully blended a moderate philosophy with the compassion, confidence, and optimism reminiscent of the Kennedy years. He worked to redefine the role of government as one that provided security to people willing to make sacrifices for the greater good of the nation. This idealistic call for sacrifice had laid dormant for much of the 1980s, a potential force that both Hart and Dukakis understood but failed to harness. Clinton was better able to claim that spirit, echoing more loudly and credibly the message he had heard as a teenager. *Gallup Poll Monthly* reported in January 1993 that 57 percent of those polled believed the Clinton administration would "create a new spirit of idealism in this country." "You ought to read my mail," Clinton told a gathering of reporters from *Rolling Stone,* "people my age writing me, saying they haven't felt this way since Kennedy was president or since Bobby Kennedy was killed. All those polls mean is people desperately want this country to work again." He convinced untold numbers of voters to believe he could cut a path to renewal. His use of the myth may not have been an overriding factor in his victory, but it commanded occasional attention and reminded voters of a time of perceived greater promise.[51]

Clinton was so effective in projecting a contemporary version of Kennedy that the past and present converged in the public's imagination. He became part of the Kennedy legend itself, an interchangeable essence expressed in tabloid magazines shortly after his inauguration. The cover story of a Mexican magazine offered "evidence" that Clinton was in fact the reincarnation of John Kennedy. An American tabloid offered photographic "proof" of Kennedy's ghost attending Clinton's inauguration. Another claimed Kennedy was still alive and had met with Clinton for two hours at Camp David to advise him on his presidency. Fantasies involving Bill Clinton and John Kennedy reached an unprecedented level. Since the late 1960s there had been recurrent rumors that John Kennedy was alive, but no one had ever suggested that he appeared at Lyndon Johnson's barbecues, or that Jimmy Carter was holding prayer breakfasts with the dead president.[52]

During his first year in office Clinton continued to blend the Kennedy image into his own identity. He also incorporated other presidential icons such as Thomas Jefferson, Franklin Roosevelt, Abraham Lincoln, Andrew Jackson, and Harry Truman. Still, much of his recall centered on Kennedy, beginning with his visit to Kennedy's grave before his inauguration. The images surrounding the ceremonies the next day were so decidedly Kennedyesque that a "Saturday Night Live" television parody depicted the Clintons sitting in a presidential box and listening to Madonna, à la Marilyn

Monroe, sing, "Happy Inauguration, Mr. President." The themes of his Inaugural Address echoed Kennedy's call for sacrifice. He moved John Kennedy's desk into the Oval Office. The historic linkage was accommodated by those who hosted the new president. Touring a computer graphics plant in Seattle, Clinton was treated to a demonstration on a computer screen whereby Franklin Roosevelt's face was morphed into John Kennedy's, which was then reconstructed into Bill Clinton's.[53]

With mixed assessments, the news media invariably compared Clinton to Kennedy in his rhetorical style, record of achievement, staff selections, managerial style, and such personal qualities as pragmatism, intelligence, disorganization, carelessness, commitment, love of gossip, susceptibility to allergies, and affinity for telephones and Hollywood stars. A parody published in *Spy* magazine mocked the absurd lengths of the parallels. "John Kennedy could never have been elected without the help of a man named Martin Luther King," it reported. "Bill Clinton could never have been elected without the help of a man named Larry King."[54]

To a degree, Clinton invited such comparisons. He appointed John Kennedy's sister, Jean Kennedy Smith, ambassador to Ireland. Sargent Shriver appeared with the president when he announced the National Service Program, giving Clinton's version of the Peace Corps a stamp of approval. The new president wrote a foreword to a book of photographs commemorating Robert Kennedy's last campaign. On the thirtieth anniversary of John Kennedy's assassination, he allowed Yousuf Karsh to photograph him in the identical pose and lighting that Karsh had once used to photograph Kennedy. Taking questions and answers from citizens of Russia during his trip there in early 1994, he was asked by a young boy if his handshake with John Kennedy had inspired him to become president. Clinton invited the boy to the stage. "Come shake hands with me," he said, "and maybe you'll be President of Russia someday."[55]

The comparisons between Clinton and JFK gradually diminished after his first few months in office. The campaign, the transition, and his first hundred days as president inspired parallels partly because there was no frame of reference; Clinton was still a relatively unknown entity. For better or worse, he then came into his own, inevitably bringing his own personality and style to the office. His struggle for substantive achievements had obscured stylistic demands. "There are too many important things on the plate now that people are aware of that touch on their lives, such as health care," Witcover explained. "And that's what they are going to be thinking about, not whether Clinton reminds them of John Kennedy."[56]

Still, during his first year and a half in office, on several occasions Clinton plainly associated himself with the Kennedy legend. In June 1993, when he paid tribute to Robert Kennedy, his fledgling administration had already experienced early setbacks. There was criticism that he had lost his way, that he lacked a cohesive vision of how he wanted to move the nation. Speaking to eighteen thousand Kennedy devotees during a memorial service at Arlington National Cemetery, he sought to define the meaning of Robert Kennedy's life and career. The laughter and tears of those present, he said, reminded him that "the memory of Robert Kennedy is so powerful that in a profound way we are all in two places today. We are here and now, and we are there and then." While the nation suffered terribly from his passing, if Kennedy were alive "he would dare us not to mourn his passing but to fulfill his promise and to be the people that he so badly wanted us all to be." Clinton evoked Robert Kennedy to admonish the nostalgic impulse he promoted and from which he benefited. He seemed to be intuitively working through the "mystique's" distortion of time and events. Perhaps it was not coincidental that in the aftermath of "getting right" with Bobby, Clinton seemed rejuvenated, articulating more clearly his goals, setting priorities, and shaping the future. Before the year was out he secured a national service corps, gun-control legislation, and the North Atlantic Free Trade Agreement.[57]

Clinton's second well-publicized appearance with the Kennedys occurred two months later in an entirely different setting. In August, the president took his first vacation since entering the White House, traveling to Martha's Vineyard off Cape Cod. News media attention to the obvious Kennedy parallels reached a crescendo when the Clintons joined Edward Kennedy, Jacqueline Kennedy Onassis, Caroline Kennedy Schlossberg, and others for a five-hour luncheon cruise aboard a seventy-foot yacht. Television news editors predictably spliced black-and-white footage of John Kennedy sailing off Hyannis Port with images of Bill and Jackie cruising about the sea. From her visit with him afterward, Mauria Aspell remembered how thrilled her old friend was, and how he was struck by the irony surrounding the mutual admiration; he had admired the Kennedys for so long and now they seemed admiring of him. "He reminisced about [John] Kennedy and what a powerful, wonderful man he had been," Aspell recalled, "how sad it was that the world had lost him; its personal impact on the people who had been out on that boat; what could he have done; what would have happened to all of their lives and all of our lives if he had lived." Like the public, Clinton was not immune to the fantasies connected to Kennedy's death, even as he beckoned the nation to move on.[58]

The image of Clinton cruising into dock, waving to bystanders with Jacqueline at his side, seemed like a virtual reality program, a bridging of memories that had Clinton frolicking not only with Jackie but with Jack as well. Just as he had in the photograph of him shaking hands with John Kennedy, he transcended the past, present, and future. Had Jacqueline Kennedy Onassis not been present, Clinton might have been open to ridicule. He would have been cruising about the Martha's Vineyard waters with Teddy Kennedy— within walking distance of Chappaquiddick. Indeed, when Clinton returned to Martha's Vineyard a year later, three months after the death of Jacqueline, the Kennedys did not host the president. The presence of John Kennedy's widow had allowed Clinton to reach back to a deeper, nobler past, winning him an imagistic coup. Nixon's dinner with Jacqueline in 1969 had been quiet and dark, more a therapy session than a social occasion. Lyndon Johnson would have renamed the vacation spot John F. Kennedy's Vineyard could he have gotten the kind of pictures Clinton did.[59]

In October 1993 Clinton spoke at a rededication ceremony of the Kennedy Library. The president greeted Jacqueline by kissing her on the cheek; this time she did not wince as she had when Jimmy Carter pecked her cheek at the 1979 dedication. Edward Kennedy praised Clinton for supporting issues that John Kennedy championed. Joe Kennedy asserted that both John and Robert Kennedy would have approved of Clinton's presidency. Clinton, meanwhile, laced praise of John Kennedy with unembarrassed assertions that he was carrying forth his legacy in the areas of civil rights, national service, space exploration, health care, and the control of nuclear weapons. To promote his North American Free Trade Agreement, Clinton playfully invoked John Kennedy, knowing that Edward had been wavering in his support of the measure. "I believe," he said, "if President Kennedy was still . . . in Congress, he would endorse it as well." The assertion prompted Joe to clap his hand on his uncle's shoulder; Edward responded by grabbing his own necktie and pretending to hang himself with it.[60]

Both Lyndon Johnson and Jimmy Carter had been painfully self-conscious when preparing their tributes to the Kennedys. But Clinton, like Reagan, was unemcumbered by political considerations as he wove the Kennedy myth into a larger national mythology. Absent from his speech were hidden agendas that had marked other dedications. He did not fear comparisons with John Kennedy; he invited them. He did not avoid the Kennedy family; he hugged them. He was not as poetic as Reagan was when he spoke at the Kennedy Library fund-raiser in 1985. But unlike Carter or Johnson, Clinton displayed no remote conflict with the Kennedy legacy. With the support of the Kennedy family, he promoted himself as its legitimate extension.

Clinton's relationship with the Kennedys reflected changing dynamics within the "mystique." For years politicians had cultivated the Kennedys to enhance their stature. Now the Kennedys used Clinton in part to elevate their fallen reputation. Speaking at Jacqueline's funeral in May 1994, Edward Kennedy recalled that she had suggested he greet the president when he arrived that summer day to go yachting. Kennedy balked, passing on the responsibility to Maurice Tempelsman, Jacqueline's longtime companion. "Teddy, you do it," she insisted. "Maurice isn't running for reelection." Clinton's ability to evoke memories of an idealized past offset the Kennedys' problems in the present. For the Kennedys, the new president was a respectable embodiment of the Kennedy legacy and fulfilled their imagined standards of idealism, compassion, and style. "[Jacqueline] loved that the Clintons loved the Kennedys," a friend of the late First Lady recalled. "And she was intrigued with the continuity, the idea that her husband in some way launched Bill Clinton's political career." Let others write scathing accounts of the family; here was a young man who, like Reagan, relished the mythic ideals they had long promoted, and who advertised the best of what they wanted remembered of themselves. The Kennedys embraced Clinton like an adopted son who now had significant authority over the family fortune.[61]

During his second year in office Clinton showed himself to be mindful of the lessons of his predecessors. "It's impossible to be in this job without feeling a special bond with the people who have gone before," he commented when he announced Richard Nixon's death in the spring of 1994. Since becoming president, he had consulted with Nixon by telephone, invited him to the White House, and sought his advice on policy toward Russia. As might be expected, Clinton's relationship invited comparisons about the resiliency and self-determination he shared with the former president. Like the

Kennedys, Nixon too appreciated how Clinton enriched his own influence and stature. When Nixon died, Clinton spoke generously about the need to consider Watergate in the larger context of Nixon's career. He offered the Nixon family the option of a state funeral. And he attended and spoke movingly at the burial in Yorba Linda. Like his enhancement of John Kennedy's memory, Clinton, by praising Nixon, deflected the lies and deceptions that had earlier destroyed him.[62]

Clinton was also compared to Reagan, particularly in his rhetorical style and expressed vision. He spoke openly of Reagan's effectiveness in coming to office with a plan and a goal, and of taking charge. He took a page from Reagan's book in appearing presidential. He used the same regal press conference setting as Reagan did, and the White House borrowed from the Ronald Reagan Library a videotape of the former president's speech at Normandy in preparation for Clinton's own visit there on the fiftieth anniversary of the D-day invasion. Republicans were irritated by the president's Reaganesque skill of wrapping himself in traditional middle-class values to advance his so-called liberal agenda. With poetic justice, Clinton, the "reincarnation" of JFK, borrowed Reagan just as Reagan had once pirated John Kennedy.[63]

John Kennedy's memory has always been a double-edged sword, and Clinton was not immune to its dangers. While speaking at the Brandenburg Gate in Berlin in July 1994, he borrowed from JFK by interjecting a German phrase into his speech. In doing so he crossed the delicate line between reminding people of John Kennedy and inviting unfavorable comparisons. Just as the news media once heralded Clinton as the next Kennedy, so too they began the predictable process of deconstruction. The only surprise was that it had taken two years to do so. Clinton was particularly vulnerable at the time. Congressional hearings on the Whitewater episode were about to begin; he was busy fending off a lawsuit for sexual harassment; and his push for national health care was stalled in Congress. After his Berlin appearance he was pictured in cartoon form holding a Kennedy mask in front of his face, just as Dukakis once was. Columnist Joel Achenbach concluded that "Clinton isn't Kennedy. . . . Clinton lacks that Kennedy sparkle, that Kennedy magic." Such lamentations showed how little the mind-set toward the Kennedy myth had changed in thirty years. As long as journalists and the public wanted and expected "magic" from their leaders, presidents, including Clinton, were bound to disappoint.[64]

Clinton might be more cautious in the future, but he could be expected to evoke the Kennedy legend regardless of its liabilities. The "mystique" spoke to something deep within him. Corresponding with the author in the fall of 1994, he continued to express an abiding faith in his idol's altruistic message. "Though he was President for only a thousand days," he wrote, "he changed the way we think about our country, our world, and our own obligations to the future. He dared Americans to join him on an adventure he called 'The New Frontier.' He inspired millions of us to take a very personal responsibility for moving our country forward and for advancing the cause of freedom throughout the world. He convinced us that our effort would be both exciting and rewarding, and he reminded us that our democracy, at its best, is a bold and daring adventure." Clinton linked some of his more noble accomplishments during his first two years in office with those of the New Frontier. He associated passage of the Motor Voter Act in 1993 and the racial diversity of his administration with Kennedy's commitment to civil rights. The National Service Corps, he wrote, had a "common thread" with the Peace Corps. Kennedy's call for religious tolerance had partly inspired the Religious Freedom Restoration Act. So too Clinton perceived his commitment to the space program and efforts to stem the proliferation of nuclear weapons as an extension of JFK's ideals. And in terms of symbolic leadership, often a weak point for the president, he nevertheless felt that he had learned from Kennedy that "vigor and determination and confidence are great ingredients of success. That humility is important."[65]

Clinton and Kennedy had become kindred spirits. Although he rarely linked himself to the Kennedy image during his first eighteen years in politics, Clinton now confidently and openly articulated the imagined goals and viewpoints of the martyred Kennedy brothers. Stephen Smith, who served as Clinton's campaign adviser in the 1970s, speculated that he might have fallen victim to self-persuasion. Having repeatedly recalled the influence of John and Robert Kennedy, he now saw it as a more powerful force than it really was. Whatever its source, the sincerity behind Clinton's commitment to Kennedy's memory made future invocations inevitable, just as pundits would surely continue to lament that he was no Jack Kennedy.[66]

12 The Prison of the Past

DURING THE 1992 CAMPAIGN, Bill Clinton benefited greatly from his celebration of JFK. Two years later, though, he seemed close to joining the ranks of Lyndon Johnson, Richard Nixon, Jimmy Carter, Gary Hart, and Michael Dukakis. Like others drawn to JFK's personal style and the allure of restoring Camelot, he had become a casualty of failed expectations. True, he had avoided certain pitfalls of his predecessors. Unlike Johnson, Nixon, and Carter, Clinton was unencumbered by the threat of another Kennedy denying him access to the myth. Unlike Gary Hart and Michael Dukakis, he did not appear infatuated with the Kennedy image. His openness to revisionist accounts of JFK's presidency suggested a level of detachment similar to Gerald Ford's and George McGovern's. Clinton nevertheless emerged as a victim of the Kennedy mystique in large measure because its emotive underpinnings set politicians up for failure. What JFK left in the way of ideas, programs, or policies was vague and contradictory. He was more feeling than fact. "History will remember not so much what [John Kennedy] did as what he was," Lance Morrow wrote in 1983, "a memory kept in some vault of the national imagination. In the end, the American appreciation of Kennedy may come to be not political but aesthetic, and vaguely religious." The history of the Kennedy mystique suggests that when his style and spirit are substituted for politics, disappointment inevitably follows. [1]

To be sure, public disillusionment with Clinton reflected larger political trends. Since Vietnam and Watergate, voter cynicism about politics has been symptomatic of the age of the antiheroic; the media and the people are drawn incessantly to the personal flaws of public figures. Presidents no longer enjoy honeymoon periods and are quickly eviscerated by a discourse of meanness that seems unprecedented. After deconstruction of their leaders, voters soon develop high expectations and romantic notions that the next president will somehow solve the nation's seemingly insurmountable problems. "Asking for the impossible, we are bound to be disappointed," Anthony Lewis explained in the fall of 1994. "And as in a failed romance, we turn bitterly on the one who has failed us."[2]

As part of this trend, the Kennedy image has played a subliminal role. The perpetual longing for the style and spirit of JFK has helped stall the political process and encourage disenchantment. Part of the reason, of course, can be traced to Kennedy himself. His colleagues, friend and foe alike, agreed that he owed his political advancement not to his meager accomplishments but to his charm, eloquence, good looks, and intellectual aura. His telegenic appeal, lofty rhetoric, and noble intentions obscured his personal foibles and policy failures. In later years voters yearned for John Kennedy for good reason: he was a dynamically appealing politician, especially when compared to those who followed.

It would be wrong to think, however, that JFK's attractiveness rested solely on celebrity and style. For Carter, Hart, Dukakis, and Clinton, as well as for millions of Americans, the Kennedy presidency encompassed idealism, excitement, and energy. If the real JFK was not all he was imagined to be, at least outwardly he championed freedom and activism, and expressed compassion for those traditionally neglected by government. The impression was real enough for those who acted upon his call to give something back to their nation. Even Ronald Reagan and Richard Nixon understood that the qualities heralded by Kennedy—excellence, optimism, confidence, and courage—had universal appeal. His rhetoric served as a conductor, making unattainable abstractions seemingly concrete and possible. Kennedy did not create his myth as much as did the voters and politicians who misassigned to him a sense of hope. His death, meanwhile, clothed him in spiritual robes, imparting greater "religious" thrust to his words and purpose. At "The Sixth Floor" in the Texas School Book Depository, those visitors who write in the journals provided by the museum do not reflect on his charm and good looks. They record their devotion and hope. "May God help us carry out the ideals we still associate with him," wrote one person. "I'll remember you forever," wrote another. "The nation still waits for another cry, 'We can do it.'" Even the popularity of Ronald Reagan could not diminish the longing for Camelot, in part because Kennedy's message of compassion and sacrifice was absent.[3]

To fill the void left by Kennedy's passing, presidents and contenders promised or implied that JFK's term could be completed if only voters would turn to them. On more than one occasion the offer of restoration became the centerpiece of a campaign. But the quest for Camelot and the heralding of Kennedy's spirit often diminished candidates and cheapened JFK's memory in the process. The best features that Kennedy embodied—his ideals and vision—were often reduced to formula. Short on inspirational qualities of their own, politicians parroted Kennedy, reworking old scripts with a seeming conviction that the awakening could be attained by properly arranging phrases and repeating them like a mantra. Too often American leaders appeared desperate, as if trying to compensate for something lacking in themselves. With slight modifications they echoed the mythic past—Let us continue . . . a new spirit . . . the next frontier . . . a new covenant. While some may have been sincere and well intentioned, they evoked Kennedy with such regularity that his once uplifting message became meaningless.

The more politicians promised restoration, the deeper voters became entrapped by fantasies of the past. The elusiveness of the mystique made it difficult to distinguish where memory ended and imagination began. There seemed to be no Jack Kennedy, because, as Gary Hart appreciated, Jack Kennedy was not even Jack Kennedy. The ideal JFK, one born of the nation's desires and needs, obscured the reality of who he was and set standards no mortal could achieve. The failure of the Johnson, Nixon, and Carter presidencies, and the disappointment of the Hart and Dukakis campaigns, only elevated JFK's stature and encouraged greater longings for his qualities. Issues and ideology might evolve, but emotionally much of American presidential politics remained frozen at Dealey Plaza. The search for JFK prevented the nation, as George McGovern understood, from confronting its own problems in its own way.

The political process was similarly burdened by Kennedy's style. The power of his personality and public image created an aura of leadership that presidents and candidates worked as diligently to evoke as his vision. Even Nixon, who routinely demeaned Kennedy as more style than substance, plainly understood that his winning personality not only sustained his popularity but was substituted in the public's mind for accomplishment. Anyone could attain greatness by accomplishing great deeds, but to attain greatness without accomplishing anything significant seemed a sign of true genius. Henceforth the personality of the performer seemed as important as the performance itself. With little subtlety, candidates aped selected Kennedyesque features. Johnson hobnobbed with intellectuals; Nixon walked by the water; Carter rolled up his shirt-sleeves; Hart jabbed his index finger into the air; and Clinton played touch football. Kennedy could not be blamed for the imitations that followed. He simply proved so effective at presenting himself that he transformed the way his successors saw themselves. While politicians would have manipulated their image whether Kennedy had come about or not, the appeal of the Kennedy style drove them to distraction. They altered their personas and rhetoric in ways that were often confusing or artificial, and sometimes embarrassing. Greater attention to personal image took energies away from the real work at hand. Like bad Elvis impersonators, they only made fans of Camelot yearn for the real thing.

Gradually the Kennedy image no longer belonged to the Kennedys. With an optimistic message, proper physique, and energetic persona, anyone, from a moderate Southerner to an elderly conservative Republican, could be construed as "Kennedyesque." Edward Kennedy's struggle to win reelection to the Senate in 1994 illustrated the irony of this development. Old, bloated, and a symbol of entrenched incumbency, he was so lacking in Kennedyesque qualities that his challenger, Mitt Romney, reminded voters of John Kennedy more than did his sixty-two-year-old brother. Romney was a handsome, energetic, forty-seven-year-old newcomer, a wholesome family man who challenged the status quo. Fighting for his political life, Edward surrounded himself with his young nephews, John Kennedy, Jr., and Joe Kennedy III, as well as his new forty-year-old wife, Victoria Reggie Kennedy, all of whom sought to infuse his struggling campaign with youth, charm, and energy reminiscent of John and Robert. In the end, Edward seemed sustained less by the living Kennedys than by his deceased brothers. When Romney questioned the senator's personal finances during a televised debate, Edward did not hesitate to draw upon the memory of John and Robert. "Mr. Romney," Kennedy said stonily, "the Kennedys are not in public service to make money. We have suffered too much for that." In this case the Kennedy name and memory ultimately triumphed over aesthetics. "You know, I'm going to stick with Kennedy," a mother of two told a reporter just before the election. "JFK, Bobby K., Joe K., and Teddy K."[4]

Although time erodes all legends, the ongoing fusion of politics and entertainment assures that the Kennedy image will remain readily exploitable to politicians who, like tourists who have their picture taken with cardboard cutouts of the president, will find it irresistible to associate themselves with an established crowd-pleaser. Television docudramas as well as tabloid programs and magazines will continue their trivial pursuit of JFK. In many precincts he will always be viewed more as a celebrity than an historic figure, identified less with the promise and hope of the 1960s than with Marilyn Monroe. Authentic memories of him may fade, but the fantasy seems secure. A 1993 Gallup poll showed that Kennedy's retrospective approval rating was essentially the same among eighteen- to twenty-nine-year-olds, a generation unborn when Kennedy came into office, as among older Americans who remembered the so-called golden age. The perpetuation of JFK's appeal assures that there will likely be politicians who jab their index finger into the air or walk coatless about the streets of Concord, New Hampshire, in February. And there will be those anxious to quote Kennedy or who promise to "get the country moving again." At its most meaningless level, the Kennedy image will endure. How much it endures may rest upon the fate of the Clinton presidency.[5]

With Clinton's election, the "mystique" came close to exhausting itself as a presidential campaign device. The transference was so thorough, the bridge between man and myth so clear, that Clinton's victory perhaps served as a catharsis. Presidential politics will not likely produce another intergenerational candidate so convincingly inspired by and committed to John Kennedy's memory. Clinton's election was a realization of the "mystique" that could perhaps be surpassed only if John F. Kennedy, Jr., pursued elected office.

The fantasies that accompanied Clinton's victory—the hope and promise—dissipated with the growing realities of governing. Although he achieved more substance in his first two years in office than did his idol, accomplishments, as Lyndon Johnson realized, measure poorly against myth, especially when they are not accompanied by affection for the person. By the spring of 1994, polls indicated that only one in three people felt that Clinton had kept his promises. Although most people believed he cared about their needs, fewer than half the people thought he inspired confidence. The post-modernist candidate was perceived as a bland, evasive, and waffling president, absent of true convictions. Too often he seemed to have lost his moorings. "Clinton isn't a leader," humorist Fran Lebowitz commented. "He's a prom king. He's a boy."[6]

The apparent repudiation of his presidency during the mid-term elections in 1994 was partly a reflection of what happens when a candidate promises Camelot and then fails to deliver. Recalling the Clinton-Gore 1992 bus tour two years later, a middle-aged woman told *Newsweek*, "It reminded me of the night I went to Springfield to see Jack Kennedy. Electricity was in the air." Now, she said, she felt disappointment more than anger. "I'm floundering. I'm searching for honest politicians, and I'm having a lot of difficulty."[7]

When Clinton spoke of Kennedy in 1992, surely some supporters knew he was invoking the ideal Kennedy, not the philanderer and underachiever. "People in this country don't seem to be looking for living, breathing human beings," a seventy-four-year-old woman commented during the Pennsylvania primary. "They're looking for fables like John Kennedy, who, it turns out, bought his nomination." Voters were not oblivious to the deception taking place, any more than Clinton surely knew he was no Jack Kennedy. Both they and the candidate entered into a symbiotic relationship, one based on a pleasant and accepted falsehood. Enough voters welcomed "Slick Willie" as a surrogate for myth, and Clinton pulled it off because he seemed sincere. The mutual delusion was agreeable and reaffirming as long as there were no negative repercussions. Once Clinton inevitably failed to fulfill the expectations that accompany myth, the public felt damaged by the deception and turned against him. It has always been easier and more assuring to dismiss leaders as "no JFK" than to question the assumptions of the myth.[8]

In some ways, Clinton represented the best and worst of the Kennedy legacy. He too exploited voter fantasies about resurrection. He mimicked, manipulated, and deceived with the best of them— combining elements of Lyndon Johnson's promise of legislative completion, Jimmy Carter's offer of restoration, Gary Hart's call to activism and volunteerism, and Michael Dukakis's faith in the Kennedy past. His skill and seeming sincerity at evoking the Kennedy legend in 1992 did not diminish his role as huckster. To his credit, however, Clinton did not seem entrapped in the past. He did not approach his presidency as a historical reenactment. Rather, he incorporated the values and lessons of Kennedy, as well as other presidents, into a contemporary context uniquely his own. If the Kennedy myth inspired Clinton, if it moved him to achieve agreeable consequences, then JFK's contribution to the American presidency would not consist simply of cheap slogans and false personas. The spiritual component, one founded on truth and deception, offers a path to greater meaning.

By a process of default and elimination, Bill Clinton became the "keeper of the flame," the custodian to the noblest essence of the Kennedy myth. Fifteen months after his inauguration he found himself again at Arlington National Cemetery, this time to help bury Jacqueline Kennedy Onassis. For those old enough to recall the Kennedy presidency, the funeral prompted a burst of memories and recollections. For the younger generations, the news media fed the Camelot myth, praising her courage, grace, and dignity. Television commentators repeatedly referred to her as "Mrs. Kennedy," as if she had remained exclusively John Kennedy's widow. If the funeral made people yearn for an era that now seemed more distant, so too did it suggest continuity. "With admiration, love, and gratitude, for the inspiration and the dreams she gave to all of us, we say goodbye to Jackie today," the president eulogized at her graveside before the small gathering of friends and Kennedy family members. "May the flame she lit so long ago burn ever brighter here and always brighter in our hearts. God bless you friend, and farewell."[9]

With the blessing of the Kennedy family, Clinton assumed a role anxiously pursued by others ever since Lyndon Johnson stood at the same burial site thirty years earlier. For many of those inspired by John Kennedy, Clinton, like "The Sixth Floor" museum in Dallas, housed both their memories and their dreams. Certainly more important things were riding on the Clinton presidency, but the most worthy part of the Kennedy legacy also rested in his hands. Clinton could never live up to the Kennedy myth. But if he attained Kennedy's ideals, then JFK might be recalled as an inspirational force that helped move a president to improve the lives of people into the next century. The fantasy of what was and what might have been may subside, and with it perhaps the need or desire for John Kennedy. The final irony is that a successful Clinton presidency might help lay to rest the Kennedy past while giving his life a more dignified meaning. Clinton's success or failure might determine whether we remember the best of John Kennedy or the worst; whether we are liberated from the past or remain imprisoned by it.

Notes

INTRODUCTION

1. The entries were recorded by the author at "The Sixth Floor Museum: John F. Kennedy and the Memory of a Nation," on August 15, 1993.

2. *Gallup Poll Monthly*, December 1991, 40–41. *Ibid.*, November 1993, 2–4.

3. George W. Hunt, "Of Many Things," *America*, November 26, 1988. Dr. Frederick Goodwin, *Washington Post*, November 13, 1988. The past-future dialectic of the Kennedy myth is noted in Vincent L. Toscano, *Since Dallas: Images of John F. Kennedy in Popular and Scholarly Literature, 1963–1973* (San Francisco, 1978), 47–48.

4. Thomas Brown, *JFK: History of an Image* (Bloomington, Ind., 1988).

5. Barry Schwartz, *George Washington: The Making of an American Symbol* (New York, 1987). Merrill D. Peterson, *The Jefferson Image in the American Mind* (New York, 1962). John William Ward, *Andrew Jackson: Symbol for an Age* (New York, 1955). Merrill D. Peterson, *Lincoln in American Memory* (New York, 1994). William E. Leuchtenburg, *In the Shadow of FDR: From Harry Truman to Ronald Reagan* (Ithaca, N.Y., 1985).

6. Schwartz, *George Washington*, 91–92. Ward, *Andrew Jackson*, 110. Peterson, *Lincoln*, 165. Peterson, *Jefferson*, 264, 332, 355, 357–358. Leuchtenburg, *In the Shadow*, 209–235.

7. For a discussion of Edward Kennedy's use of the Kennedy myth, see Garry Wills, *The Kennedy Imprisonment: A Meditation on Power* (Boston, 1982). See also James MacGregor Burns, *Edward Kennedy and the Camelot Legacy* (New York, 1976).

1. LYNDON JOHNSON: THE INTERLOPER

1. Barbara Garson, *The Complete Text of MacBird* (New York, 1966). *JFK*, director Oliver Stone, 1991. LBJ to J. Edgar Hoover, November 29, 1963, Recordings of Conversations Related to the JFK Assassination (hereafter RC), K6311.04, Lyndon B. Johnson Library (hereafter LBJL).

2. Doris Kearns, *Lyndon Johnson and the American Dream* (New York, 1976), 37–40, 369–375. Robert A. Caro, *The Years of Lyndon Johnson: The Path to Power* (New York, 1983) 150–160, 174–201. William A. Degregorio, *The Complete Book of U.S. Presidents: From George Washington to Bill Clinton* (New York, 1993), 567–568.

3. Merle Miller, *Lyndon: An Oral Biography* (New York, 1980), 141–231. Kearns, *Lyndon Johnson*, 135–159. Theodore C. Sorensen, *Kennedy* (New York, 1965), 43–70. Paul K. Conkin, *Big Daddy from the Pedernales: Lyndon Baines Johnson* (Boston, 1986), 148–149.

4. See letters exchanged between LBJ and JFK in White House Name File—John F. Kennedy (hereafter WHNF-JFK), box 4, LBJL; Sorensen, box 9, John F. Kennedy Library (hereafter JFKL). See especially LBJ to JFK, August 3, 1956, Presidential Office Files (hereafter POF), box 30, JFKL. *Boston Herald*, August 18, 1956, 1. For JFK's appointment to Senate Foreign Relations Committee, see LBJ to JFK, December 3, 1956, WHNF-JFK, box 4, LBJL. JFK to LBJ, December 11, 1956, WHNF-JFK, box 4, LBJL. LBJ to JFK, December 17, 1956, WHNF-JFK, box 4, LBJL. JFK's letter of gratitude in JFK to LBJ, January 26, 1957, WHNF-JFK, box 4, LBJL.

5. Harry McPherson, Lyndon B. Johnson Library—Oral History (hereafter LBJL-OH), 41–42. Miller, *Lyndon*, 343. Bobby Baker, *Wheeling and Dealing: Confessions of a Capitol Hill Operator* (New York, 1978), 76–77. Theodore C. Sorensen, "Election of 1960," in Arthur M. Schlesinger, Jr., ed., *History of American Presidential Elections: 1789–1968*, iv (New York, 1971), 3449–3460. Kearns, *Lyndon Johnson*, 59, 88–89, 101, 125, 209, 378–379.

6. LBJ's newsletters, Pre-Presidential Papers (hereafter PPP), box 1046, JFKL. Rowland Evans and Robert Novak, *Lyndon B. Johnson: The Exercise of Power* (New York, 1966), 272. *Time*, July 18, 1960, 9. Harry McPherson, recorded telephone interview (hereafter RTI), May 17, 1994.

7. George Reedy to LBJ, March 5, 1960. Senate Political File (hereafter SPF), box 267, LBJL. Reedy to LBJ, n.d., SPF, box 267, LBJL.

8. LBJ to Amon Carter, May 12, 1960, Notes and Transcripts of Johnson Conversations, box 1, LBJL. Evans and Novak, *Lyndon B. Johnson*, 277. Peter Lisagor, John F. Kennedy Library—Oral History (hereafter JFKL-OH), 25–26. Hugh Sidey, JFKL-OH, 9. Hobart Taylor to LBJ Staff, n.d., SPF, box 254, LBJL. Folder, "Kennedy, Joseph: Documents on German Foreign Policy 1918–1945," SPF, box 264, LBJL. Walter Jenkins conversation with Lou Bouldes, June 28, 1960, Office Files of Walter Jenkins, box 2, LBJL. Don Cook to Walter Jenkins, July 5, 1960, SPF, box 76, LBJL.

9. *Time*, July 18, 1960, 10–11. Baker, *Wheeling*, 120–121. Evans and Novak, *Lyndon B. Johnson*, 285–286, 289–291. Horace Busby to LBJ, n.d., SPF, box 258, LBJL.

10. Kennedy-Johnson Debate, NBC News, July 12, 1960. John Roche, LBJL-OH, 3. Doris Kearns Goodwin, *The Fitzgeralds and the Kennedys* (New York, 1987), 780–781.

11. Hugh Sidey, "Boston-Austin Was an Accident," *Time*, July 25, 1988, 23. Evans and Novak, *Lyndon B. Johnson*, 298, 304–306. Herbert S. Parmet, *JFK: The Presidency of John F. Kennedy* (New York, 1984), 24–25, 28–29. Edwin O. Guthman and Jeffrey Shulman, eds., *Robert Kennedy in His Own Words: The Unpublished Recollections of the Kennedy Years* (New York, 1988), 19–26. Baker, *Wheeling*, 130.

12. See various letters between Joseph Alsop and LBJ, March 1964, Political Files, box 1, LBJL. Lyndon B. Johnson, *The Vantage Point: Perspectives of the Presidency, 1963–1969* (New York, 1971), 91–92.

13. Kearns Goodwin, *Fitzgeralds*, 781. Evans and Novak, *Lyndon B. Johnson*, 312.

14. Reedy to LBJ, September 9, 1960, SPF, box 267, LBJL. James Rowe to LBJ, August 25, 1960, "Notes and Transcripts of Johnson Conversations," box 1, LBJL.

15. Miller, *Lyndon*, 273. Baker, *Wheeling*, 133–134. Kearns, *Lyndon Johnson*, 165–167. Leonard Baker, *The Johnson Eclipse: A President's Vice Presidency* (New York, 1966), 28. Lee White, LBJL-OH, 12–13. Horace Busby to Sorenson [sic], March 20, 1961, White House Name File—Horace Busby, JFKL. George Reedy, *Lyndon B. Johnson: A Memoir* (New York, 1982), 21–22, 127.

16. LBJ to JFK, September 6, 1961, WHNF-JFK, box 4, LBJL. LBJ to JFK, August 30, 1963, POF, box 30, JFKL. LBJ to JFK, January 1, 1962, WHNF-JFK, box 4, LBJL. Reedy, *Lyndon B. Johnson*, 121, 127.

17. Guthman and Shulman, eds., *Robert Kennedy*, 417. Miller, *Lyndon*, 280, 305. Reedy, *Lyndon B. Johnson*, 4, 56–57, 63–64, 122, 124–125, 134. Arthur M. Schlesinger, Jr., *Robert Kennedy and His Times* (Boston, 1978), 623–624.

18. Richard Harwood and Haynes B. Johnson, *Lyndon* (New York, 1973), 139. Johnson, *Vantage Point*, 2.

19. LBJ to John McCormack, November 23, 1963, Transcript of Telephone Conversation, November 1963, Chronological File, LBJL.

20. See various letters of LBJ and Jacqueline Kennedy, WHNF—Mrs. John F. Kennedy (hereafter Mrs. JFK), LBJL. Mrs. John F. Kennedy to LBJ, February 4, 1962, WHNF-Mrs. JFK, LBJL. Jacqueline Kennedy, LBJL-OH, 4–5, 6–7, 13–14. LBJ to Jacqueline Kennedy, December 1, 1963, WHNF-Mrs. JFK, LBJL. LBJ to John Kennedy, Jr., November 22, 1963, WHNF-Mrs. JFK, LBJL. LBJ to Caroline Kennedy, November 22, 1963, WHNF-Mrs. JFK, LBJL. Jacqueline Kennedy to LBJ, December 6, 1963, WHNF-Mrs. JFK, LBJL.

21. Pierre Salinger, *With Kennedy* (Garden City, N.Y., 1966), 336. *New York Times*, February 26, 1964, 14; February 27, 1964, 18. LBJ to Frances Lewine, December 23, 1963, RC, K6312.16, LBJL.

22. Charles Roche to Jack Valenti, September 24, 1964, PL2, box 84, LBJL. Jack Valenti to Charles Roche, September 29, 1964, FG2, box 40, LBJL. Jacqueline Kennedy, LBJL-OH, 9. *New York Times*, October 15, 1964, 1.

23. William Manchester, *The Death of a President* (New York, 1967), 387. LBJ to David Lawrence, December 9, 1963, RC, K6312.05, LBJL.

24. Clark Clifford with Richard Holbrooke, *Counsel to the President: A Memoir* (New York, 1991), 395. Clifford to LBJ, December 4, 1963, RC, K6312.03, LBJL. LBJ to Stephen Smith, Office Conversation, December 11, 1963, RC, K6312.07, LBJL.

25. Schlesinger, *Robert Kennedy*, 628, 649. Guthman and Shulman, eds., *Robert Kennedy*, 326–327.

26. Kearns, *Lyndon Johnson*, 174–178. LBJ to Lawrence O'Brien, November 25, 1963, RC, K6311.02, LBJL. Arthur M. Schlesinger, Jr., LBJL-OH, 15–16.

27. Patrick Anderson, *The President's Men* (Garden City, N.Y., 1968). Pierre Salinger to Larry King, "November 22, 1963: Where Were You?" Turner Network Television, November 22, 1993. Andy Logan, "The Stained Glass Image," *American Heritage*, August 1967, 5–7, 75–78. McGeorge Bundy, "The History-Maker," *Massachusetts Historical Society* 90 (December 1978). 78.

28. Anderson, *The President's Men*, 245–275.

29. Brian VanDeMark, "A Way of Thinking: The Kennedy Administration's Assumptions About Vietnam, and Their Consequences"; William C. Gibbons, "LBJ: The First Months, October–December, 1963," Vietnam: The Early Decisions, 1961–1964, symposium October 16 and 17, 1993, LBJL.

30. Gibbons, "LBJ," Vietnam: The Early Decisions, October 17, 1993, LBJL. John M. Newman, "The Transition: The Case of Policy Reversal," Vietnam: The Early Decisions, October 17, 1993, LBJL. Larry Berman, "The Battle over Historical Interpretation: NSAM 263 and NSAM 273," Vietnam: The Early Decisions, October 17, 1993, LBJL.

31. LBJ to Don Cook, November 30, 1963, RC, K6311.06, LBJL. William Fulbright to LBJ, December 2, 1963, RC, K6312.02. LBJL. Larry E. Cable, "Dogma, Doctrine, and Distortion: The Influence of Intellectual Heritage upon Intelligence and Decisions, 1954–1965," Vietnam: The Early Decisions, October 16, 1993, LBJL.

32. Kenneth W. Thompson, ed., *The Johnson Presidency* (Lanham, Md., 1986), 50. Nelson Lichtenstein, ed., *Political Profiles: The Johnson Years* (New York, 1976), 75–77.

33. Thomas Brown, *JFK: History of an Image* (Bloomington, Ind., 1988), 6–49. Kent M. Beck, "The Kennedy Image: Politics, Camelot, and Vietnam," *Wisconsin Magazine of History* 58 (Autumn 1974), 45–55.

34. LBJ to George Smathers, November 23, 1963, RC, K6311.01, LBJL.

35. LBJ to Horace Busby, November 26, 1963, RC K6311.02, LBJL. LBJ to Lewis Seltzer, November 27, 1963, RC, K6311,03, LBJL.

36. Steven F. Lawson, "Civil Rights," in Robert A. Divine, ed., *The Johnson Years: Foreign Policy, the Great Society, and the White House* (Lawrence, Kans., 1987).

37. LBJ to Whitney Young, November 24, 1963, RC, K6311.02, LBJL. LBJ to Martin Luther King, November 25, 1963, RC, K6311.02, LBJL. LBJ to Katherine Graham, December 2, 1963, RC, K6312.01, LBJL. LBJ to John McCormack, December 5, 1963, RC, K6312.04, LBJL.

38. Thompson, ed., *The Johnson Presidency*, 143.

39. Bradley S. Greenberg and Edwin B. Parker, eds., *The Kennedy Assassination and the American Public: Social Communication in Crisis* (Stanford, Calif., 1965). Arthur M. Schlesinger, Jr., *A Thousand Days: John F. Kennedy in the White House* (Boston, 1965), 949. Brown, *JFK*, 8, 25. Guthman and Shulman, ed., *Robert Kennedy*, 210–212.

40. Miller, *Lyndon*, 357–358. Johnson, *Vantage Point*, 37. LBJ to Katherine Graham, December 2, 1963, RC, K6312.01, LBJL. *Public Papers of the Presidents of the United*

States: Lyndon B. Johnson, 1963–64 (Washington, D.C., 1965), 115. *New York Times,* February 27, 1964.

41. Richard Goodwin to LBJ, n.d., 1964, FG1, box 10, LBJL. LBJ to Walter Heller, December 23, 1963, RC, K6312.15, LBJL. Jack Valenti to LBJ, January 11, 1964, PR18, box 367, LBJL.

42. Nicholas Lemann, "The Unfinished War," *Atlantic,* December 1988, 47–49. Mark I. Gelfand, "The War on Poverty," in Divine, ed., *The Johnson Years,* 126–154. Richard Goodwin, *Remembering America: A Voice from the Sixties* (Boston, 1988), 260.

43. Lemann, "Unfinished War," 39. Schlesinger, *Robert Kennedy,* 637.

44. *Public Papers, 1963–64,* 1145, 1152, 1158–1159, 1248, 1275, 1287, 1466–1470, 1523–1529. *Public Papers,* 1965, 408–412. Kearns, *Lyndon Johnson,* 340–341.

45. LBJ to Robert Kintner, November 24, 1966, WE9, box 28, LBJL. Fred Panzer to Jake Jacobsen, November 26, 1966, CF FG/RS/PR18, box 16, LBJL. Eric F. Goldman, *The Tragedy of Lyndon Johnson* (New York, 1969), 26–27. John Roche, LBJL-OH, 4.

46. *Newsweek,* August 31, 1964, 27. Tom Wicker, "Lyndon Johnson vs. the Ghost of Jack Kennedy," *Esquire* (November 1965), 85ff.

47. Horace Busby to LBJ, January 14, 1964, Busby, box 53, LBJL.

48. Horace Busby to LBJ, April 1964, Busby, box 52, LBJL. Jack Valenti to LBJ, January 4, 1964, PR18, box 367, LBJL. Jack Valenti to LBJ, January 11, 1964, PR18, box 367, LBJL. *Time,* May 1, 1964, 17–21.

49. *U.S. News and World Report,* February 17, 1964, 60–63. *Newsweek,* April 13, 1964, 22–23. Miller, *Lyndon,* 342–346.

50. William Rivers, "The Correspondents After 25 Years," *Columbia Journalism Review,* Spring 1962, 4–10. Ben H. Bagdikian, "JFK to LBJ: Paradoxes of Change," *Columbia Journalism Review,* Winter 1964, 36.

51. Valenti, LBJL-OH, v, 27. Kearns, *Lyndon Johnson,* 315. Reedy, *Lyndon B. Johnson,* 62, 67–68.

52. Horace Busby to LBJ, January 23, 1964, FG/RS/PR18, box 9, LBJL. Horace Busby to LBJ, "Image Assessment and Suggested Activities, April 1964, Busby, box 52, LBJL. Horace Busby to LBJ, April 11, 1964, Busby, box 53, LBJL. Horace Busby to LBJ, May 14, 1964, Busby, box 52, LBJL. Horace Busby to LBJ, April 29, 1964, Busby, box 52, LBJL. Horace Busby to LBJ, April 30, 1964, Busby, box 53, LBJL. Eric Goldman to LBJ, June 16, 1964, FG1, box 10, LBJL. Jack Valenti to LBJ, January 8, 1964, PR18-2, box 374. Bill Moyers to LBJ, May 15, 1964, Moyers, box 190, LBJL. Milton Gordon, *Assimilation in American Life: The Role of Race, Religion, and National Origins* (New York, 1964), 224–232.

53. Horace Busby to LBJ, January 23, 1964, FG/RS/PR18, box 9, LBJL. Horace Busby to LBJ, July 19, 1964, Busby, box 52, LBJL.

54. Bill Moyers to LBJ, August 31, 1965, FG1, box 12, LBJL. *New York Times,* December 9, 1965, 73.

55. *Newsweek,* July 6, 1964, 24–26.

56. Goldman, *Tragedy,* 234. *Newsweek,* August 10, 1964, 19. Kearns, *Lyndon Johnson,* 199–200.

57. "Memorandum," n.d., White House Name File—Robert F. Kennedy (hereafter WHNF-RFK), box 6, LBJL.

58. Clifford, *Counsel,* 396. DT to vm, September 30, 1964, WHNF-RFK, box 6, LBJL. Johnson, *Vantage Point,* 98–100. Schlesinger, *Robert Kennedy,* 659–661. Goldman, *Tragedy,* 236. Miller, *Lyndon,* 389.

59. Douglass Cater to Bill Moyers, July 15, 1964, Cater, box 13, LBJL. Douglass Cater to LBJ, July 21, 1964, Cater, box 13, LBJL. Memorandum to Moyers, August 5, 1964, PL1, box 78, LBJL. Douglass Cater to Bill Moyers, August 5, 1964, Cater, box 13, LBJL. "Schedule for Atlantic City," August 31, 1964, Statements File, box 117, LBJL.

60. Democratic National Convention, NBC, August 27, 1964. "Dictated over phone RFK," August 26, 1964, text of speech, Attorney General File, Box 3, JFKL. "Final Draft," August 26, 1964, Attorney General File, box 3, JFKL.

61. *Public Papers, 1963–64,* 541.

62. *Public Papers*, 1963–64, 1049–1052. W. J. Jorden to Douglass Cater, September 18, 1964, PR3, box 11, LBJL.

63. Horace Busby to LBJ, October 1964, Busby, box 52, LBJL.

64. For LBJ's invocations of JFK, see *Public Papers*, 1963–64, particularly 1260, 1315–1316, 1324, 1352, 1414, 1469–1470, 1498, 1507, 1522, 1534, 1550. Dick Scammon to Douglass Cater, September 10, 1964, FG2, box 40, LBJL. Clark Clifford to LBJ, September 11, 1964, Busby, box 52, LBJL. Horace Busby to LBJ, September 11, 1964, Busby, box 52, LBJL.

65. Horace Busby, "The Campaign," October 1964, Busby, box 52, LBJL. *New York Times*, October 15, 1964, 1, 30. *Newsweek*, October 19, 1964, 30–31. *New York Times*, October 14, 1964, 30. *New York Times*, October 20, 1964, 1.

66. Johnson, *Vantage Point*, 100. Schlesinger, *Robert Kennedy*, 674. *Public Papers*, 1963–64, 1337–1340, 1341–1347.

67. Milton C. Cummings, Jr., ed., *The National Election of 1964* (Washington, D.C., 1966), 261–262. *Public Papers*, 1963–64, 1580.

2. JOHNSON AS HIS OWN MAN

1. *Public Papers of the Presidents of the United States: Lyndon B. Johnson*, 1964 (Washington, D.C., 1965), 1624–1625. Jack Valenti to LBJ, November 16, 1964, FG2, box 40, LBJL. RFK to LBJ, November 17, 1964, WHNF-RFK, box 6, LBJL.

2. Horace Busby to LBJ, December 9, 1964, Busby, box 52, LBJL. *New York Times*, January 4, 1965, 18. *Newsweek*, February 1, 1965, 11–12.

3. See index to *Public Papers*, 1964. William E. Leuchtenburg, "A Visit with LBJ," *American Heritage*, May/June 1990, 47–52ff.

4. Horace Busby to LBJ, December 4, 1964, Busby, box 52, LBJL.

5. Douglass Cater to LBJ, December 16, 1964, Cater, box 13, LBJL. Jack Valenti to LBJ, February 13, 1965, PR18-2, box 375, LBJL. Douglass Cater to LBJ, February 4, 1965, Cater, box 13, LBJL. Jack Valenti to LBJ, March 10, 1965, Moyers, box 9, LBJL. Douglass Cater to LBJ, November 27, 1964, Cater, box 13, LBJL. "Report to the President," February 19, 1965, PR18, box 367, LBJL.

6. Robert Kintner to LBJ, February 18, 1967, PR18-1, box 368, LBJL. *Broadcasting*, "The Brand That's Being Burned in TV," November 8, 1965, 54–56, 58.

7. Harry McPherson to LBJ, July 13, 1965, McPherson, box 52, LBJL. Harry McPherson to George Christian, February 28, 1967, McPherson, box 22, LBJL. Ben Wattenberg to LBJ, January 6, 1967, McPherson, box 51, LBJL.

8. Harry McPherson to LBJ, June 24, 1965, McPherson, box 52, LBJL. Harry McPherson to LBJ, "Thoughts on Bobby Kennedy and Loyalty," June 24, 1965, McPherson, box 21, LBJL. Harry McPherson, LBJL-OH, III, 22. *Newsweek*, August 2, 1965, 20. Richard Goodwin, *Remembering America: A Voice from the Sixties* (Boston, 1988), 400–401.

9. Doris Kearns, *Lyndon Johnson and the American Dream* (New York, 1976), 313–317.

10. Harry McPherson, recorded telephone interview (RTI), May 17, 1994. George Gallup, *The Gallup Poll: Public Opinion, 1935–1971* (New York, 1972), 1972–1973.

11. McPherson, RTI. Harry McPherson to LBJ, June 24, 1965, McPherson, box 21, LBJL.

12. Eric F. Goldman, *The Tragedy of Lyndon Johnson* (New York, 1969), 20.

13. RFK to Anthony Lewis, July 19, 1965, RFK SF/PC, box 2, JFKL. RFK to Mr. President, Speech, July 9, 1965, SF, box 47, JFKL. McGeorge Bundy to RFK, May 9, 1965, SF, box 12, JFKL.

14. Horace Busby to LBJ, March 5, 1965, Busby, box 52, LBJL. See press conferences in *Public Papers*, 1965, March 13, April 27, June 1, July 13, July 28, and August 9. McGeorge Bundy to LBJ, March 28, 1965, NSF:VN, box 15, LBJL.

15. Horace Busby to LBJ, July 20, 1965, Busby, box 51, LBJL. Goldman, *Tragedy*, 518.

16. Harry McPherson, LBJL-OH, III, 23–25. McPherson, RTI.

17. *Newsweek*, February 15, 1965, 62–63. LBJ to Bob, September 21, 1966, CF PR18, box 83, LBJL.

18. *Time*, August 6, 1965, 18–22. *Time*, August 13, 1965, 10. Allen Otten, *Wall Street Journal*, July 6, 1965, 16.

19. *Gallup Poll*, 1945, 2027. *Newsweek*, January 17, 1966, 17–20, 25. Arthur M. Schlesinger, Jr., *Robert Kennedy and His Times* (Boston, 1978), 732–737. *Public Papers*, 1966, 213–214.

20. Moyers to LBJ, June 9, 1966, Moyers, box 12, LBJL. Bill Moyers to LBJ, September 10, 1966, Watson, box 25, LBJL. Liz Carpenter to LBJ, April 1, 1966, WHNF—RFK, box 6, LBJL.

21. *Newsweek*, June 13, 1966, 35. Joseph Califano to George Smathers, January 22, 1966, FG2, box 41, LBJL.

22. *Newsweek*, January 17, 1966, 17–20, 25. *Newsweek*, October 24, 1966, 30, 35–38. *Life*, November 18, 1966, 40. Frederick Dutton to RFK, December 8, 1966, RFK SF/PC, box 3, JFKL. Frederick Dutton to RFK, April 6, 1966, RFK SF/PC, box 3, JFKL.

23. Roger Stevens to Bill Moyers, December 27, 1965, FG2, Box 40, LBJL. *New York Times*, May 31, 1966, 1. Robert Kintner to LBJ, May 30, 1966, CF FG/RS/PR18, box 16, LBJL. Marvin Watson to LBJ, August 19, 1966, FG2, box 41, LBJL.

24. *Newsweek*, September 5, 1966, 17.

25. *Newsweek*, January 17, 1966, 25.

26. *Gallup Poll*, 2023. Louis Harris, "State of the LBJ Image," *Newsweek*, January 9, 1967, 18–19. *Newsweek*, October 24, 1966, 30, 35–38. Harry McPherson to LBJ, September 22, 1966, McPherson, box 22, LBJL. *Life*, November 18, 1966, 39.

27. Schlesinger, *Robert Kennedy*, 761. William Manchester, *Controversy: And Other Essays in Journalism*, 1950–75 (Boston, 1976), 5–76.

28. LBJ to Nicholas Katzenbach, December 5, 1966, Recordings of Conversation Related to the JFK Assassination (hereafter RC), K66.01, LBJL. LBJ to Abraham Fortas, December 16, 1966, RC, K66.01, LBJL. LBJ to Abraham Fortas, December 17, 1966, RC, K66.01, LBJL.

29. LBJ to Bill Moyers, December 26, 1966, RC, K66.02, LBJL. LBJ to Nicholas Katzenbach, January 25, 1967, RC, K67.01, LBJL.

30. LBJ to Nicholas Katzenbach, January 25, 1967, RC, K67.01, LBJL. LBJ to Jacqueline Kennedy, December 16, 1966, WHNF–Mrs. JFK, box 5, LBJL.

31. LBJ to Nicholas Katzenbach, January 25, 1967, RC, K67.01, LBJL. See also LBJ to Ramsey Clark, January 25, 1967, RC, K67.01, LBJL.

32. *Newsweek*, December 26, 1966, 19–20.

33. LBJ to Ramsey Clark, January 25, 1967, RC, K67.01, LBJL. *Newsweek*, February 13, 1967, 34–35. Nicholas Katzenbach, LBJL-OH, 27–29.

34. Schlesinger, *Robert Kennedy*, 767–769. *Time*, March 17, 1967. Victor Lasky, *Robert F. Kennedy: The Myth and the Man* (New York, 1968), 385. David Wise, *The Politics of Lying: Government Deception, Secrecy, and Power* (New York, 1973), 86.

35. *New York Times*, March 3, 1967, 1. Chalmers Roberts, *The First Rough Draft: A Journalist's Journal of Our Times* (New York, 1973), 250. Jack Valenti to Jack Watson, May 2, 1967, SP, box 3, LBJL. Memorandum to the President, March 20, 1967, PR18-2, box 376, LBJL.

36. Lasky, *Robert F. Kennedy*, 392. *Newsweek*, March 20, 1967, 26. Schlesinger, *Robert Kennedy*, 774.

37. Harry McPherson to LBJ, May 12, 1967, FG1, box 14, LBJL. Harry McPherson to LBJ, May 4, 1967, McPherson, box 53, LBJL. Harry McPherson to LBJ, May 17, 1967, McPherson, box 53, LBJL. *Boston Globe*, February 5, 1967, FG1, box 13, LBJL. Tom Cronin to Harry McPherson, March 24, 1967, McPherson, box 18, LBJL.

38. Ben Wattenberg to LBJ, May 19, 1967, Wattenberg, box 22, LBJL.

39. Christening Speech, May 27, 1967, ST, box 238, LBJL. *Public Papers*, 1967, 579–580.

40. *Newsweek*, September 4, 1967, 17–21. Schlesinger, *Robert Kennedy*, 784, 789, 797. Fred Panzer to LBJ, November 27, 1967, Panzer, box 398, LBJL.

41. Fred I. Greenstein, ed., *Leadership in the Modern Presidency* (Cambridge, Mass., 1988) 147. Marvin Watson to LBJ, September 6, 1967, FG1, box 15, LBJL. Walter Rostow to LBJ, September 15, 1967, NSF:VN, box 97, LBJL.

42. LBJ did not mention JFK during a highly publicized press conference on November 17, 1967, or during the December airing of "A Conversation with the President."

43. *Newsweek*, November 27, 1967, 25–29. Schlesinger, *Robert Kennedy*, 827. Merle Miller, *Lyndon: An Oral Biography* (New York, 1980), 506. John Roche to LBJ, January 26, 1968, Watson, box 25, LBJL. Ben Wattenberg to LBJ, November 21, 1967, Wattenberg, box 22, LBJL. James Rowe to LBJ, January 16, 1968, Watson, box 25, LBJL. John Roche to LBJ, December 18, 1967, Watson, box 29, LBJL. John Roche to LBJ, December 4, 1967, CF PL2, box 76, LBJL.

44. Kearns, *Lyndon Johnson*, 335–336. Schlesinger, *Robert Kennedy*, 842–844. Lloyd Hackler to Jim Jones, March 15, 1968, PL/Kennedy, box 26, LBJL.

45. Evelyn Lincoln, *Kennedy and Johnson* (New York, 1968), 205–206. Marvin Watson to LBJ, February 19, 1968, WHNF-JFK, box 4, LBJL. Marvin Watson to Horace Busby, February 20, 1968, FG2, box 41, LBJL.

46. Lyndon B. Johnson, *The Vantage Point: Perspectives of the Presidency, 1963–1969* (New York, 1971), 538. *New York Times*, March 14, 1968, 1; March 15, 1968, 1. Harry McPherson to LBJ, March 18, 1968, McPherson, box 53, LBJL. Memorandum to the President, March 16, 1968, CF PL/ST, box 77, LBJL. Roscoe Drummond article, March 30, 1968, FG2, box 41, LBJL. Bill McSweeny to John Criswell, March 18, 1968, Watson, box 25, LBJL. Bill Crook to Marvin Watson, March 27, 1968, PL/Kennedy, box 26, LBJL. George Reedy to LBJ, March 16, 1968, Watson, box 28, LBJL. Lloyd Hackler to LBJ, March 25, 1968, PL/Kennedy, box 26, LBJL.

47. *Newsweek*, April 8, 1968, 36–37. Douglass Cater to LBJ, March 28, 1968, FG1, box 18, LBJL. *New York Times*, February 28, 1968, 1.

48. Drew Pearson, *Washington Post*, April 3, 1968, 19. *Public Papers*, 1968, 475–477.

49. Kearns, *Lyndon Johnson*, 343. James Jones, "Behind LBJ's Decision Not to Run in '68," *New York Times*, April 16, 1988, 17.

50. Eugene McCarthy, RTI, February 10, 1994. See also, Eugene J. McCarthy, *Up 'Til Now: A Memoir* (San Diego, Calif., 1987), and Eugene J. McCarthy, *Year of the People* (Garden City, N.Y., 1969).

51. Eugene McCarthy, RTI. Jeremy Larner, *Nobody Knows: Reflections on the McCarthy Campaign of 1968* (New York, 1970), 63–64.

52. "Vietnam and the JFK Legacy," RFK Papers—1968 Campaign/Research Division, box 59, JFKL. Eugene McCarthy, RTI.

53. Eugene McCarthy, RTI. See also Jules Witcover, "McCarthy and Kennedy: A Study in Styles," *Progressive*, May 1968, 17–20.

54. LBJ's meeting with RFK is drawn from two summaries. One was written by Walter Rostow, April 3, 1968, WHNF-RFK, box 6, LBJL. Another was written by Rostow and/or Murphy on April 4, 1968, WHNF-RFK, box 6, LBJL. See also Theodore C. Sorensen, *The Kennedy Legacy* (New York, 1969), 146–147.

55. Johnson, *Vantage Point*, 539–542.

56. Joseph Califano, Jr., *The Triumph and Tragedy of Lyndon Johnson: The White House Years* (New York, 1991), 298–302. Kearns, *Lyndon Johnson*, 350.

57. Michael W. Schuyler, "Ghosts in the White House: LBJ, RFK, and the Assassination of JFK," *Political Science Quarterly* 17 (Summer 1987), 503–518. Califano, *Triumph*, 318–321.

58. Johnson, *Vantage Point*, 539. *Public Papers*, 1968, 938, 964, 1026, 1044–1045, 1089, 1153, 1204–1205, 1270.

59. Joseph A. Califano, Jr., *Governing America: An Insider's Report from the White House and the Cabinet* (New York, 1981), 90. *New York Times*, May 3, 1970, 1, 79; April 26, 1975, 12; June 25, 1976, 12. Bobby Baker, *Wheeling and Dealing: Confessions of a*

Capitol Hill Operator (New York, 1978), 273–274. Kearns, *Lyndon Johnson*, 178. Johnson, *Vantage Point*, 19, 41.

60. Richard Harwood and Haynes B. Johnson, *Lyndon* (New York, 1973), 137.

3. RICHARD NIXON: THE ANTI-KENNEDY

1. Dan Rather and Gary Paul Gates, *The Palace Guard* (New York, 1974), 243–245.

2. American Experience, "Nixon," PBS, 1990. Richard Nixon, *RN: The Memoirs of Richard Nixon* (New York, 1978) 14–25. William A. Degregorio, *The Complete Book of U.S. Presidents: From George Washington to Bill Clinton* (New York, 1993), 582–595. See also Stephen E. Ambrose, *Nixon: The Education of a Politician 1913–1962*, (New York, 1987); Bruce Mazlish, *In Search of Nixon: A Psychohistorical Inquiry* (New York, 1972); Fawn M. Brodie, *Richard Nixon: The Shaping of His Character* (New York, 1981); Herbert S. Parmet, *Richard Nixon and His America* (Boston, 1990), 117.

3. Nixon, *RN*, 42–43. Ambrose, *Nixon*, 584–587. Parmet, *Richard Nixon*, 118–119.

4. *Time*, November 7, 1960, 27.

5. Eric F. Goldman, "The 1947 Kennedy-Nixon 'Tube City' Debate," *Saturday Review*, October 16, 1976, 12–13. Nixon, *RN*, 42–43.

6. Victor Lasky, *JFK: The Man and the Myth* (New York, 1963), 129. James MacGregor Burns, *John Kennedy: A Political Profile* (New York, 1960), 184. *New York Times*, March 31, 1960, 16. *New York Times*, July 26, 1960, 18. Nixon, *RN*, 75. RN to JFK, August 23, 1958, Pre-Presidential Papers (Hereafter PPP), Series 78, box 5, Richard Nixon Library and Birthplace (hereafter RNLB).

7. "An Analysis of a Trial Pairing of Vice President Richard M. Nixon vs. Senator John F. Kennedy," October 1957, PPP, Senate Files, box 819, JFKL.

8. Arthur M. Schlesinger, Jr., *A Thousand Days: John F. Kennedy in the White House* (Boston, 1965), 64–65. Arthur M. Schlesinger, Jr., *Kennedy or Nixon: Does It Make Any Difference?* (New York, 1960), 27.

9. "Analysis of Voter Attitudes Toward Nixon," 1956, Vice President's General Correspondences (hereafter VPGC), Series 320, box 647, National Archives, Pacific Southwest Branch, Laguna Niguel (hereafter NARA-LN). Charles Robinson to RN, June 17, 1959, VPGC, Series 320, box 647, NARA-LN. Charles Robinson to RN, December 31, 1959, VPGC, Series 320, box 648, NARA-LN.

10. RN to Herbert Klein, May 4, 1960, PPP, Series 77, box 6, RNLB. RN to Robert Finch, July 18 and July 19, 1960, Robert Finch Papers (hereafter RFP), box 5, RNLB.

11. RN to Robert Finch, July 18 and July 19, 1960, RFP, box 5, RNLB.

12. "First Draft Acceptance Speech," n.d., Series 45, box 1, NARA-LN.

13. See various drafts of acceptance speech in Series 45, box 1, NARA-LN. Transcript of Nixon's Address, *New York Times*, July 29, 1960, 9.

14. RN to Robert Finch, August 1, 1960, RFP, box 5, RNLB. RN to Robert Finch, August 1, 1960, RFP, RNLB. *New York Times*, August 3, 1960, 14.

15. Claude Robinson to RN, September 1, 1960, VPGC, Series 320, box 648, NARA-LN. RN to Robert Finch, September 7, 1960, RFP, box 5, RNLB. *Freedom of Communications: Final Report of the Committee of Commerce, United States Senate* (Washington, D.C., 1961–62), 610, 648, 712, 722, 732, 825, 919. RN to Fred Seaton, September 21, 1960, PPP, Series 45, box 1, NARA-LN.

16. John Ehrlichman to Robert Finch, July 22, 1960, RFP, box 5, RNLB. Florence Mary Kater letter, n.d., RFP, box 5, RNLB. Coke Prentice to Robert Finch, August 26, 1960, RFP, box 5, RNLB. Lincoln Zonn to RN, October 21, 1960, RFP, box 5, RNLB. Memorandum, October 17, 1960, RFP, box 5, RNLB. "Richard Nixon Reflects," PBS, May 5, 1990.

17. RN to Robert Finch, July 14, 1960, RFP, box 5, RNLB. RN to Robert Finch (three memos), July 18, 1960, RFP, box 5, RNLB. RN to Robert Finch, August 29, 1960, RFP, box 5, RNLB.

18. Parmet, *Richard Nixon*, 432–433.

19. Rather and Gates, *Palace*, 101. Brodie, *Richard Nixon*, 61, 416, 419. Ambrose, *Nixon*, 576.

20. Tom Wicker, *One of Us: Richard Nixon and the American Dream* (New York, 1991), 445. Brodie, *Richard Nixon*, 420–421. Theodore C. Sorensen, *Kennedy* (New York, 1965), 183. Ambrose, *Nixon*, 586–587. *Time*, September 19, 1960, 22. *Time*, October 3, 1960, 18. *Time*, November 7, 1960, 27. *Time*, September 5, 1960, 11. *Time*, November 7, 1960, 27. *Freedom*, 405, 861, 947. Richard Nixon, *Six Crises* (New York, 1962), 335–336. Rita E. Hauser to Robert Finch, October 9, 1960, PPP, Series 45, box 1, NARA-LN.

21. Claude Robinson to RN, September 22, 1960, PPP, Series 77, box 6, RNLB. RN to Speech Team, October 11, 1960, PPP, Series 45, box 1, NARA-LN. *Freedom*, 723, 724, 768, 1061. Ambrose, *Nixon*, 589. Charles Lichenstein to RN, September 14, 1961, PPP, Six Crises Manuscript (SCM), box 1, NARA-LN.

22. Claude Robinson to RN, August 1, 1960, VPGC, Series 320, box 648, NARA-LN. Claude Robinson to RN, September 1, 1960, VPGC, Series 320, box 648, NARA-LN. Claude Robinson to RN, September 22, 1960, PPP, Series 77, box 6, RNLB.

23. RN to Robert Finch, August 1, 1960, RFP, box 5, RNLB. Index Cards, PPP, Series 77, box 6, RNLB. "Debate Preparation," PPP, Series 77, box 6, RNLB. RN to Robert Finch, September 7, 1960, RFP, box 5, RNLB. RN to Robert Finch, August 29, 1960, RFP, box 5, RNLB. Ted Rogers to Robert Finch, September 29, 1960, RFP, box 5, RNLB. Ambrose, *Nixon*, 570–571. "The Making of the Great Debate," Arts and Entertainment Network, 1988. Nixon, *Six Crises*, 324.

24. Nixon, *Six Crises*, 340–341. Carroll Newton to Leonard Hall, October 19, 1960, PPP, Series 45, box 1, NARA-LN.

25. Ambrose, *Nixon*, 594. Claude Robinson to RN, November 10, 1960, PPP, SCM, box 1, NARA-LN. Wicker, *One*, 234. Nixon, *Six Crises*, 357–358.

26. Nixon, *Six Crises*, 298, 344. Wicker, *One*, 25–26. Six Crises Manuscript, 99–100, PPP, SCM, box 1, NARA-LN.

27. Rene J. Muller, "The Fictional Richard Nixon," *The Nation*, July 6, 1974, 6–11.

28. David S. Kaufer, "The Ironist and Hypocrite as Presidential Symbols: A Nixon-Kennedy Analog," *Communication Quarterly* 27 (Fall 1979), 20–26. Wicker, *One*, 445.

29. Nixon, *RN*, 214, 225–226.

30. *Time*, February 17, 1961, 17. Nixon, *RN*, 232–235. George Gallup, *The Gallup Poll: Public Opinion, 1935–1971* (New York, 1972), 1717. Victor Lasky to RN, April 17, 1961, VPGC, Series 320, box 440, NARA-LN.

31. Nixon, *Six Crises*, xv. "Second Insert with Regard to Issues," Six Crises Manuscript, n.d., PPP, SCM, box 1, NARA-LN. RN to Herbert Klein, August 24, 1961, VPGC, Series 320, box 416, NARA-LN. RN to Charles Lichenstein, August 27, 1961, PPP, SCM, box 1, NARA-LN. Charles Lichenstein to RN, September 14, 1961, PPP, SMC, box 1, NARA-LN.

32. RN to Charles Lichenstein, September 12, 1961, PPP, SCM, box 1, NARA-LN. "Tape 8," PPP, SCM, box 1, NARA-LN. "Tape 12," PPP, SCM, box 1, NARA-LN. RN to Charles Lichenstein, October 18, 1961, PPP, SCM, box 1, NARA-LN. RN to Charles Lichenstein, August 26, 1961, PPP, SCM, box 1, NARA-LN. RN to Charles Lichenstein, August 21, 1961, PPP, SCM, box 1, NARA-LN.

33. Douglas Robinson, "Nixon in Crisis-Land: The Rhetoric of 'Six Crises,'" *Journal of American Culture* 8 (Autumn 1985), 79–85. *Time*, October 6, 1961, 20. *Newsweek*, October 8, 1961, 61. Nixon, *RN*, 239.

34. Parmet, *Richard Nixon*, 428. Ambrose, *Nixon*, 666, 670. Nixon, *RN*, 244. *Newsweek*, November 11, 1962, 32. Ambrose, *Nixon*, 670. Jules Witcover, *The Resurrection of Richard Nixon* (New York, 1970), 19, 31. Garry Wills, *Nixon Agonistes* (Boston, 1970), 379.

35. Paul Keyes to RN, "First Notes," PPP, Series 77, box 6, RNLB. RN to Paul Keyes, February 25, 1963, PPP, Series 77, box 6, RNLB. Paul Keyes to RN, n.d., PPP, Series 77, box 6, RNLB. "Question Ideas," PPP, Series 77, box 6, RNLB.

36. American Experience, "Nixon," PBS, 1990. *Newsweek*, March 18, 1963, 24–25. "Telephone Call from Paul Keyes," March 13, 1963, PPP, Series 77, box 6, RNLB. RN to Jack Paar, March 11, 1963, PPP, Series 320, box 575, NARA-LN.

37. RN notes, PPP, Series 320, box 793, NARA-LN.

38. *Dallas Times Herald*, November 21, 1963, 1. *Newsweek*, October 28, 1963, 17–18. *U.S. News & World Report*, November 25, 1963, 34–35. *Time*, November 22, 1963, 18.

39. Witcover, *Resurrection*, 60–64. Nixon, *RN*, 253.

40. Parmet, *Richard Nixon*, 391. Stephen E. Ambrose, *Nixon: The Triumph of a Politician 1962–1972* (New York, 1989), 38. *Newsweek*, February 3, 1964, 18.

41. Witcover, *Resurrection*, 459. *New York Times*, March 31, 1968, 48.

42. Wills, *Nixon*, 19. *Time*, March 1, 1968, 14. William Safire, *Before the Fall: An Inside View of the Pre-Watergate White House* (New York, 1975), 152. Wicker, *One*, 270. Rather and Gates, *Palace Guard*, 102.

43. Witcover, *Resurrection*, 60–61.

44. *Newsweek*, March 18, 1968, 69. *Time*, March 1, 1968, 14. *Time*, April 26, 1968, 23. *Richmond Times Dispatch*, February 5, 1968. *Washington Daily News*, May 28, 1968. RFK Papers, '68 Campaign/Research Division, box 61, JFKL.

45. Joe McGinniss, *The Selling of the President 1968* (New York, 1969), 174, 179. Timothy Crouse, *The Boys on the Bus* (New York, 1972), 198–199. Safire, *Before*, 63–65. *Washington Post*, February 7, 1968. "Youth for Nixon" Pamphlet, RFK Papers, '68 Campaign/Press Division, box 11, JFKL.

46. *Time*, March 8, 1968, 23. Safire, *Before*, 82, 153–154. Stanley Kutler, *The Wars of Watergate: The Last Crisis of Richard Nixon* (New York, 1990), 131. Theodore H. White, *The Making of the President 1968* (New York, 1969), 152–153. Ambrose, *Nixon: Triumph*, 136–137.

47. *Time*, March 1, 1968, 14. McGinniss, *Selling*.

48. McGinniss, *Selling*, 70.

49. *U.S. News & World Report*, October 3, 1966, 62. Witcover, *Resurrection*, 262–263. Parmet, *Richard Nixon*, 502.

50. Ambrose, *Nixon: Triumph*, 146, 151. Rather and Gates, *Palace Guard*, 143–144, 172.

51. *Christian Science Monitor*, May 18, 1968, 10. Arthur M. Schlesinger, Jr., *Robert Kennedy and His Times* (Boston, 1978), 891. Witcover, *Resurrection*, 270.

52. Witcover, *Resurrection*, 262. *Washington Post*, May 17, 1968. *Time*, May 17, 1968, 23. *The Oregonian*, May 25, 1968, 12.

53. Nixon, *RN*, 305–306. Herbert Klein, *Making It Perfectly Clear* (Garden City, N.Y., 1980), 14–15. Witcover, *Resurrection*, 315, 372.

4. NIXON IN THE WHITE HOUSE

1. William Safire, *Before the Fall: An Inside View of the Pre-Watergate White House* (New York, 1975), 152.

2. Herbert Klein, *Making It Perfectly Clear* (Garden City, N.Y., 1980), 8. Garry Wills, *Nixon Agonistes* (Boston, 1970), 368–369. Safire, *Before*, 153. *Public Papers of the Presidents of the United States, Richard M. Nixon, 1972* (Washington, D.C., 1973), 36. RN to H. R. Haldeman, June 12, 1972, President's Office Files (hereafter POF), Annotated News Summaries (hereafter ANS), box 40, Nixon Presidential Materials Project, Alexandria, Va. (hereafter NPMP). *Public Papers, 1969,* 303, 755, 903, 932. *Public Papers, 1970,* 244, 409, 556, 604. *Public Papers, 1971,* 594, 1108.

3. RN to H. R. Haldeman, March 14, 1973, POF, ANS, box 47, NPMP. Harry R. Haldeman, *The Ends of Power* (New York, 1978), 70. Stanley Kutler, *The Wars of Watergate: The Last Crisis of Richard Nixon* (New York, 1990), 102–103. H. R. Haldeman, *The Haldeman Diaries: Inside the Nixon White House* (New York, 1994), 6.

4. Klein, *Making*, 323, 351. Safire, *Before*, 153. Kenneth L. Khachigian to Patrick Buchanan, September 27, 1971, Buchanan, box 3, NPMP. H. R. Haldeman to Charles

Colson, May 15, 1972, Buchanan, box 5, NPMP. Kenneth L. Khachigian to Patrick Buchanan, July 26, 1971, Buchanan, box 4, NPMP.

5. Safire, *Before*, 63. Stephen E. Ambrose, *Nixon: The Triumph of a Politician 1962–1972* (New York, 1989), 250. Haldeman, *Diaries*, 574. RN to H. R. Haldeman, October 7, 1970, POF, ANS, box 32, NPMP. Haldeman, *Ends*, 70.

6. Haldeman, *Diaries*, 58. RN to H. R. Haldeman, February, 1971, POF, ANS, box 32, NPMP. Ambrose, *Nixon: Triumph*, 375. Patrick Buchanan to Jeb Magruder, January 8, 1971, Buchanan, box 4, NPMP.

7. Klein, *Making*, 127. Tom Wicker, *One of Us: Richard Nixon and the American Dream* (New York, 1991), 442–443. RN to H. R. Haldeman, January 31, 1970, President's Personal Files (hereafter PPF), box 2, NPMP. RN to H. R. Haldeman, March 13, 1972, PPF, box 3, NPMP. RN to H. R. Haldeman, October 1, 1969, PPF, box 1, NPMP. RN to H. R. Haldeman, March 2, 1970, PPF, box 2, NPMP. RN to H. R. Haldeman, January 14, 1971, PPF, box 3, NPMP. RN to Ron Ziegler, July 1, 1972, POF, box 41, NPMP. Charles Colson to H. R. Haldeman, June 2, 1971, White House Special Files (hereafter WHSF), Colson, box 4, NPMP. See also, Patrick Buchanan to Charles Colson, February 4, 1971, Buchanan, box 3, NPMP.

8. RN to H. R. Haldeman, January 1970, POF, ANS, box 34, NPMP.

9. RN to John Ehrlichman, February 5, 1969, PPF, Memos to the President, box 1, NPMP. RN to John Ehrlichman, March 11, 1969, PPP, box 1, NPMP.

10. RN to H. R. Haldeman, April 29, 1972, PPF, box 3, NPMP. Charles Colson to Patrick Buchanan, October 20, 1971, Buchanan, box 3, NPMP. Patrick Buchanan to Charles Colson, June 22, 1972, Buchanan, box 5, NPMP.

11. Charles Colson to H. R. Haldeman, May 21, 1971, WHSF, Colson, box 4, NPMP. Patrick Buchanan to RN, September 17, 1971, Buchanan, box 4, NPMP. Ray Price to David Gergen, n.d., Gergen, box 2, NPMP. Ray Price to H. R. Haldeman, July 21, 1972, Gergen, box 2, NPMP.

12. Haldeman, *Diaries*, 287.

13. Fawn M. Brodie, *Richard Nixon: The Shaping of His Character* (New York, 1981), 119.

14. Richard Schickel, *Intimate Strangers: The Culture of Celebrity* (Garden City, N.Y., 1985), 147–148. Haldeman, *Diaries*, 125.

15. Thomas Brown, *JFK: History of an Image* (Bloomington, Ind. 1988), 50–69. Kent M. Beck, "The Kennedy Image: Politics, Camelot, and Vietnam," *Wisconsin Magazine of History* 58 (Autumn 1974), 45–55.

16. Brown, *JFK*, 65, *Newsweek*, February 1, 1971, 20–22.

17. Daniel Moynihan to RN, February 1, 1969, POF, box 1, NPMP. Ethel Kennedy to RN, February 3, 1969, POF, box 32, NPMP.

18. Charles Colson to H. R. Haldeman, July 30, 1971, WHSF, Colson, box 4, NPMP. See also Len Garment to H. R. Haldeman, August 9, 1971, Haldeman, box 133, NPMP.

19. Garry Wills clipping and RN's critique in Haldeman, box 187, NPMP. See also Patrick Buchanan to RN, June 24, 1969, POF, box 78, NPMP. RN to H. R. Haldeman, November 29, 1971, POF, ANS, box 36, NPMP. See also Ambrose, *Nixon: The Triumph*, 417.

20. Julie Nixon Eisenhower, *Pat Nixon: The Untold Story* (New York, 1986), 467–468.

21. Nixon, *RN*, 502–503. Jacqueline Kennedy Onassis to RN, February 4, 1971, Kennedy Folder, RNLB. John Kennedy, Jr., February 4, 1971 to RN, Kennedy Folder, RNLB. RN to John Kennedy, Jr., February 28, 1971, Kennedy Folder, RNLB. RN to Caroline Kennedy, February 28, 1971, Kennedy Folder, RNLB. Jacqueline Kennedy Onassis to RN, March 1971, Kennedy Folder, RNLB. The above materials were sent to the author by Olivia S. Anastasiadis, assistant curator, RNLB, April 8, 1992.

22. Mort Allin to H. R. Haldeman, February 4, 1971, Buchanan, box 4, NPMP. Robert Odle to H. R. Haldeman, February 4, 1971, Buchanan, box 4, NPMP.

23. RN to H. R. Haldeman, January 21, 1971, POF, ANS, box 32, NPMP. RN to Ron Ziegler, February 27, 1973, POF, ANS, box 20, NPMP. Henry Fairlie, "Camelot Revisited," *Harpers*, January 1973, 67–68, located in POF, box 20, NPMP. Haldeman,

Diaries, 567, 585–586. Patrick Buchanan to H. R. Haldeman, August 1, 1972, Haldeman, box 101, NPMP.

24. William Shannon, "JFK in Retrospect," *New York Times*, October 19, 1971. For compilation of notes and letter of response see WHSF, David Young, Subject Files, box 7, NPMP.

25. William Safire to H. R. Haldeman, August 4, 1970, WHSF, Klein, box 1, NPMP. H. R. Haldeman to Herbert Klein, August 5, 1970, WHSF, Klein, box 1, NPMP.

26. Haldeman, *Ends*, 160–162. "Richard Nixon Reflects," PBS, May 5, 1990. Nixon, *RN*, 509, 633, 844. John Dean, *Blind Ambition: The White House Years* (New York, 1976), 114–115. Brodie, *Richard Nixon*, 497–498. Bob Woodward and Carl Bernstein, *The Final Days* (New York, 1977), 336. Kutler, *Wars*, 112.

27. Nixon, *RN*, 513–514.

28. Charles Colson to H. R. Haldeman, June 25, 1971, WHSF, Colson, box 14, NPMP. Charles Colson to H. R. Haldeman, July 19, 1971, WHSF, Colson, box 4, NPMP. Haldeman, *Diaries*, 430.

29. Brodie, *Richard Nixon*, 493. J. Anthony Lukas, *Nightmare: The Underside of the Nixon Years* (New York, 1976), 79. Arthur M. Schlesinger, Jr., *Robert Kennedy and His Times* (Boston, 1978), 486. Haldeman, *Ends*, 26–27, 33, 38–40. Nixon, *RN*, 515.

30. *New York Times*, August 22, 1968. Dan Rather and Gary Paul Gates, *The Palace Guard*, (New York, 1974), 166–167. Kutler, *Wars*, 104. Lukas, *Nightmare*, 15. Nixon, *RN*, 357.

31. *New York Times*, July 26, 1969. See Haldeman's notes, July 19, 1969, Haldeman, box 40, NPMP. Haldeman, *Diaries*, 72. Haldeman, *Ends*, 60. Klein, *Making*, 110. Nixon, *RN*, 543.

32. Lukas, *Nightmare*, 16–17. Dean, *Blind*, 35. Rather and Gates, *Palace*, 293. Chappaquiddick Folders, WHSF, Ehrlichman, box 20, NPMP. John Caulfield to John Ehrlichman, April 30, 1970, WHSF, Ehrlichman, box 20, NPMP. Haldeman, *Diaries*, 72, 74, 79. Safire, *Before*, 154. Nixon, *RN*, 417–418. Theo Lippman, Jr., *Senator Ted Kennedy* (New York, 1976), 199. John Caulfield to John Ehrlichman, July 24, 1969, WHSF, Ehrlichman, box 20, NPMP. RN to H. R. Haldeman, July 1969, POF, ANS, box 3, NPMP. RN to Herbert Klein, July 1969, POF, ANS, box 3, NPMP.

33. RN to John Ehrlichman, October 3, 1969, POF, ANS, box 31, NPMP. Nixon, *RN*, 542–543.

34. RN to Herbert Klein and H. R. Haldeman, September 20, 1969, POF, ANS, box 3, NPMP. RN to John Ehrlichman, September 1969, POF, ANS, box 3, NPMP. See also Ambrose, *Nixon: Triumph*, 297–298. Lukas, *Nightmare*, 17.

35. RN to Alexander Butterfield, December 1969, POF, ANS, box 31, NPMP. December 22, 1969, POF, ANS, box 31, NPMP. RN to H. R. Haldeman, January 16, 1970, POF, ANS, box 31, NPMP. RN to H. R. Haldeman, February 5, 1970, POF, ANS, box 31, NPMP.

36. RN to Charles Colson and H. R. Haldeman, January 28, 1972, PPF, box 3, NPMP. RN to John Scali, April 6, 1972, POF, ANS, box 40, NPMP. News Summary, April 10, 1972, POF, ANS, box 40, NPMP. RN to Charles Colson, August 7, 1972, POF, ANS, box 42, NPMP.

37. Nixon, *RN*, 543, 665. RN to H. R. Haldeman, November 1970, POF, ANS, box 32, NPMP. Lukas, *Nightmare*, 179. Haldeman, *Ends*, 59.

38. Haldeman, *Diaries*, 237, 293. RN to H. R. Haldeman, March 15, 1971, POF, ANS, box 32, NPMP. Gallup poll cited in Patrick Buchanan to RN, April 19, 1971, POF, box 10, NPMP. Harris poll in *Boston Globe* clipping, July 15, 1971, WHSF, Colson, box 4, NPMP.

39. Charles Colson to H. R. Haldeman, May 10, 1971, WHSF, Colson, box 2, NPMP. May 29, 1971, POF, ANS, box 33, NPMP. Patrick Buchanan to RN, June 9, 1971, Buchanan, box 4, NPMP.

40. Patrick Buchanan to RN, June 9, 1971, Buchanan, box 4, NPMP. See also Bill Gavin to Frank Shakespeare, June 14, 1971, Gergen, box 2, NPMP.

41. RN to Charles Colson, October 15, 1971, POF, ANS, box 34, NPMP. Patrick

Buchanan to RN, September 25, 1971, Buchanan, box 4, NPMP. Charles Colson to H. R. Haldeman, November 4, 1971, WHSF, Colson, box 4, NPMP.

42. William Safire to H. R. Haldeman, November 16, 1971, Haldeman, box 87, NPMP.

43. Patrick Buchanan to RN, April 19, 1971, POF, box 10, NPMP. Patrick Buchanan to RN, June 9, 1971, Buchanan, box 4, NPMP.

44. George S. McGovern, *Grassroots: The Autobiography of George McGovern* (New York, 1977), 3–10, 17–20, 34–38, 52–70.

45. George McGovern, recorded personal interview (hereafter RPI), February 19, 1993. McGovern, *Grassroots*, 78.

46. McGovern, RPI. McGovern, *Grassroots*, 81–82.

47. McGovern, RPI.

48. McGovern, RPI. McGovern, *Grassroots*, 88–91.

49. McGovern, RPI.

50. McGovern, RPI.

51. McGovern, *Grassroots*, 101–102, 106, 110–114, 117. Schlesinger, *Robert Kennedy*, 899. McGovern, RPI.

52. McGovern, *Grassroots*, 117–118, 121. McGovern, RPI.

53. McGovern, RPI. McGovern, *Grassroots*, 126.

54. McGovern, *Grassroots*, 156–158. McGovern RPI.

55. McGovern, RPI.

56. RN to Charles Colson, January 27, 1972, POF, box 16, NPMP. RN to Charles Colson, March 24, 1972, POF, ANS, box 39, NPMP. Bruce Oudes, ed., *From the President: Richard Nixon's Secret Files* (New York, 1989), 409–410. RN to H. R. Haldeman, March 28, 1972, POF, ANS, box 40, NPMP. Nick Thimmesch, "Democrats Need 'Strong Man,'" April 4, 1972. Haldeman, box 95, NPMP.

57. RN to H. R. Haldeman, April 3, 1972, POF, ANS, box 40, NPMP. Patrick Buchanan, April 7, 1972, Buchanan, box 7, NPMP. Haldeman, *Diaries*, 435–436, 460.

58. Pat Buchanan and Ken Khachigian to John Mitchell and H. R. Haldeman, April 12, 1972, Buchanan, box 6, NPMP. *The Watergate Hearings* (New York, 1973), 494.

59. Nixon, *RN*, 622. McGovern, RPI.

60. News Summary, February 25, 1971, POF, ANS, box 32, NPMP. News Summary, February 9, 1972, POF, ANS, box 38, NPMP. News Summary, June 12, 1972, POF, ANS, box 40, NPMP. Ollie Atkins to H. R. Haldeman, July 20, 1972, Haldeman, box 101, NPMP.

61. McGovern, RPI. McGovern, *Grassroots*, 193–196.

62. McGovern, *Grassroots*, 196. McGovern, RPI.

63. News Summary, July 21, 1972, POF, ANS, box 41, NPMP. Nixon, *RN*, 654. Ron Ziegler, Memorandum for the President's File, July 16, 1972, POF, box 89, NPMP. RN to Patrick Buchanan, July 26, 1972, POF, ANS, box 41, NPMP.

64. McGovern, *Grassroots*, 212–215. McGovern, RPI. Ambrose, *Nixon: Triumph*, 583.

65. News Summary, August 2, 1972, POF, ANS, box 42, NPMP. McGovern, RPI. McGovern, *Grassroots*, 290. Charles Colson to Patrick Buchanan, September 5, 1972, WHSF, Colson, box 5, NPMP.

66. News Summary, September 12, 1972, POF, ANS, box 43, NPMP. Patrick Buchanan to H. R. Haldeman, September 13, 1972, Buchanan, box 7, NPMP. News Summary, September 14, 1972, POF, ANS, box 43, NPMP. News Summary, September 16, 1972, POF, ANS, box 43, NPMP. Kenneth Clawson, Memorandum for the President's File, September 21, 1972, POF, box 89, NPMP. Charles Colson to Nick Thimmesch, August 4, 1972, Haldeman, box 101, NPMP. Nixon, *RN*, 683.

67. McGovern, RPI.

68. McGovern, RPI.

69. Mike Royko, "Suppose a President Named Kennedy Did This," *Miami Herald*, October 12, 1971, POF, ANS, box 34, NPMP.

70. Nixon, *RN*, 226. Ambrose, *Nixon: Triumph*, 502. Lukas, *Nightmare*, 179, 181,

419, 431. Kutler, *Wars*, 105, 203. Haldeman, *Ends*, 154–155. Dean, *Blind*, 67. RN to H. R. Haldeman, January 1971, PPF, box 3, NPMP. RN to John Ehrlichman, March 4, 1973, PPF, box 4, NPMP. RN to Alexander Haig, July 7, 1973, PPF, box 4, NPMP. Woodward and Bernstein, *Final Days*, 38–41.

71. *New York Times*, November 22, 1973. *Newsweek*, October 7, 1974, 36.

72. Brown, *JFK*, 65–66. *New York Times*, December 18, 1974. *Variety*, December 18, 1974, 26.

73. Gerald Posner, *Case Closed: Lee Harvey Oswald and the Assassination of JFK* (New York, 1993), 453–454, 471. Carl Oglesby, *The Yankee and Cowboy War: Conspiracies from Dallas to Watergate* (Lawrence, Kansas, 1976). Paul D. Scott, *The Assassinations: Dallas and Beyond* (New York, 1976). Mark Lane, *Plausible Denial* (New York, 1991). Bruce A. Rosenberg, "Kennedy in Camelot: The Arthurian Legend in America," *Western Folklore* 35 (Autumn 1976), 52–59.

74. Olivia S. Anastasiadis, assistant curator RNLB, telephone conversation, April 8, 1992. *New York Times*, January 12, 1992, 12. *New York Times*, April 28, 1994, 11.

5. RESTORATION: GERALD FORD AND JIMMY CARTER

1. Gerald R. Ford, *A Time to Heal* (New York, 1979), 42–48. Robert Shogan, *The Riddle of Power: Presidential Leadership from Truman to Bush* (New York, 1992), 170–175, 180–183. William A. Degregorio, *The Complete Book of U.S. Presidents: From George Washington to Bill Clinton* (New York, 1993), 603. Bud Vestal, *Jerry Ford: Up Close* (New York, 1974), 18–19. John J. Casserly, *The Ford White House: Diary of a Speechwriter* (Boulder, Colo., 1977), 12, 39, 42, 138. Robert T. Hartmann, *Palace Politics: An Inside Account of the Ford Years* (New York, 1980), 58–59. James Cannon, *Time and Chance: Gerald Ford's Appointment with History* (New York, 1994), xiv–xv, 17, 393–395, 411–412.

2. Gerald Ford, recorded personal interview (RPI), August 25, 1992.

3. Ford, RPI.

4. Ford, RPI.

5. Ford, RPI.

6. Ford, RPI. "Your Washington Review," April 12, 1961, Congressional Papers (CP), box D2, Gerald R. Ford Library (hereafter GRFL). Speech, May 29, 1962, CP, box D15, GRFL. Speech, September 28, 1963, CP, box D16, GRFL.

7. Ford, RPI.

8. Ford, RPI.

9. Ford, *A Time*, 265–266.

10. William Casey to Gerald Ford, September 13, 1975, White House Central Files—Subject File (hereafter WHCF-SF), box 16, GRFL. Remarks by Gerald R. Ford, April 23, 1975, Subject Cards, GRFL. Ford, RPI.

11. Ron Nessen, *It Sure Looks Different from the Inside* (New York, 1978), 59–60. *Public Papers of the Presidents of the United States: Gerald R. Ford, 1976–1977* (Washington, D.C., 1978), 1801–1802. Hartmann, *Palace*, 42. Gerald R. Ford and John R. Stiles, *Portrait of an Assassin* (New York, 1965). Ford defended himself from critics that he profited from the Kennedy assassination in *New York Times*, November 6, 1973, 22. *Gallup Report*, February 1977, 1–3, reported that 81 percent of Americans believed that more than one person killed Kennedy.

12. Ford, RPI.

13. See GF to Edward M. Kennedy, September 20, 1974, Name File—Edward Kennedy (hereafter NF-EMK), GRFL. EMK to GF, July 22, 1975, NF-EMK, GRFL. James MacGregor Burns, *Edward Kennedy and the Camelot Legacy* (New York, 1976), 228, 240. GF to EMK, January 19, 1976, NF-EMK, GRFL. EMK to GF, March 12, 1975, NF-EMK, GRFL. President's Activities, April 19, 1975, GRFL. EMK to GF, December 22, 1976, NF-EMK, GRFL. Burns, *Edward Kennedy*, 266. Interview of President, November 2, 1975, Subject Cards, GRFL.

14. Ford, RPI.

15. Jimmy Carter, *Why Not the Best?* (Nashville, Tenn., 1975), 13–60. Bruce Mazlish and Edwin Diamond, *Jimmy Carter: A Character Portrait* (New York, 1979), 9–10, 15–17.

16. Carter, *Why*, 77–86. Hamilton Jordan, Carter Presidency Project—Oral History (hereafter CPP-OH), 70.

17. Jimmy Carter, *The Turning Point: A Candidate, a State, and a Nation Come of Age* (New York, 1992), xxiii, 62. Mazlish and Diamond, *Jimmy*, 142.

18. Shogan, *Riddle*, 210. Mazlish and Diamond, *Jimmy*, 143–149, 176–183. Carter, *Why*, 102.

19. Martin Schram, *Running for President: A Journal of the Carter Campaign* (New York, 1976), 30.

20. Betty Glad, *Jimmy Carter: In Search of the Great White House* (New York, 1980), 103. Victor Lasky, *Jimmy Carter: The Man and the Myth* (New York, 1979), 45–46, 99. Gerald Rafshoon, CPP-OH, 2.

21. *Newsweek*, January 25, 1971, 51. Blake Fleetwood, "The Resurrection of JFK," [MORE], March, 1976, 24–25. Cover Illustration, *Time*, May 31, 1971. *Time*, May 31, 1971, 15. Glad, *Jimmy*, 209.

22. Jordan, CPP-OH, 2–3, 15–16.

23. Jordan, CPP-OH, 17. Lasky, *Jimmy*, 134, 136. Glad, *Jimmy*, 208–209. Jules Witcover, *Marathon: The Pursuit of the Presidency, 1972–1976* (New York, 1977), 106. James Wooten, "Can Rafshooning Save Jimmy Carter?" *Esquire*, March 13, 1979, 33.

24. Gary M. Fink, *Prelude to the Presidency: The Political Character and Legislative Leadership-Style of Governor Jimmy Carter* (Westport, Conn., 1980), 19. *Newsweek*, May 10, 1976, 28–29. Glad, *Jimmy*, 219. Witcover, *Marathon*, 111–112. Schram, *Running*, 70.

25. Mazlish and Diamond, *Jimmy*, 15–16. Glad, *Jimmy*, 487–507.

26. Jerry Rafshoon, n.d., Rafshoon DHM, box 5, Jimmy Carter Library (hereafter JCL).

27. Hunter S. Thompson, *The Great Shark Hunt* (New York, 1979), 466–467, 474, 478, 486–495. Rosalynn Carter, *First Lady from Plains* (Boston, 1984), 108. Glad, *Jimmy*, 219–221, 498.

28. *Newsweek*, October 7, 1974, 35. Lasky, *Jimmy*, 138–139, 179. Witcover, *Marathon*, 120–121, 124–125.

29. Witcover, *Marathon*, 116, 132. Jody Powell, *The Other Side of the Story* (New York, 1984), 184. Glad, *Jimmy*, 221.

30. Lasky, *Jimmy*, 101, 181–184. *Newsweek*, May 10, 1976, 29. Degregorio, *Complete*, 622–623.

31. Elizabeth Drew, *American Journal: The Events of 1976* (New York, 1977), 191–192. Charles Bell to Jody Powell, March 27, 1976, Powell, Briefcase Contents, box 5, JCL. Glad, *Jimmy*, 256–257. Power, *Other*, 182–185.

32. Glad, *Jimmy*, 275, 376. Witcover, *Marathon*, 521, 589.

33. Drew, *American*, 36, 195, 203, 225. Witcover, *Marathon*, 150–152, 234, 250.

34. *Newsweek*, August 2, 1976, 77. "Florida TV Campaign," n.d., Powell, box 1, JCL.

35. *The Presidential Campaign 1976: Jimmy Carter* (Washington, D.C., 1978), 15, 453, 495, 901. Glad, *Jimmy*, 341.

36. *Presidential Campaign 1976*, 225, 503, 702, 995–997, 1087–1093. Democratic National Convention, NBC, July 15, 1976.

37. *Presidential Campaign 1976*, 702, 717–719, 1104. Robert S. McElvaine, "Franklin and Jack . . . and Jimmy?" *America*, October 23, 1976, 246–248. *New York Times*, June 16, 1976.

38. *Time*, May 10, 1976, 14. *Time*, September 6, 1976, 15. *Time*, October 18, 1976, 11. *Time*, November 22, 1976. *Newsweek*, July 19, 1976, 17. Fleetwood, [MORE], 24–25.

39. Drew, *American*, 18. Lasky, *Jimmy*, 102. Schram, *Running*, 30. Witcover, *Marathon*, 211. David Halberstam, "The Coming of Carter," *Newsweek*, July 19, 1976, 11.

40. Dorrance Smith to Michael Duval, September 3, 1976, Collins, box 1, GRFL. "Jimmy Carter—Impressions," n.d., Duval, box 30, GRFL. Kennedy Quotes, President Ford Committee Record (hereafter PFCR), box H23 & H27, GRFL. Bill Greener to Michael Duval, September 18, 1976, WHCF, PL7, box 86, GRFL. David Gergen to Ron Nessen, July 22, 1976, Nessen, box 36, GRFL.

41. Michael Duval to Richard Cheney, October 19, 1976, Duval, box 28, GRFL. "Presidential Visit to Bedford-Stuyvesant," n.d., Duval, box 28, GRFL.

42. Joseph Blatchford to GF, October 5, 1976, WHCF, PL7, box 86, GRFL. Jim Reichley to Michael Duval, September 29, 1976, Duval, box 27, GRFL. Bill Greener to Michael Duval, September 18, 1976, WHCF, PL7, box 86, GRFL.

43. *New York Times* clipping, August 30, 1976, PFCR, box E39, GRFL. Bill Carruthers to Michael Duval, August 30, 1976, Duval, box 29, GRFL. Bill Carruthers to David Gergen, August 30, 1976, Duval, box 29, GRFL. Bill Carruthers to Terry O'Donnell, August 24, 1976, Duval, box 30, GRFL. Bill Carruthers to Roy Hughes, September 20, 1976, Collins, box 1, GRFL. Handwritten Notes, Duval, box 29, GRFL. Handwritten Notes, September 10, 1976, Duval, box 30, GRFL. David Gergen to Richard Cheney, September 18, 1976, Duval, box 30, GRFL.

44. Handwritten Notes, September 10, 1976, Duval, box 30, GRFL. Ford, RPI.

45. Ford-Carter Debate, Videotape, F 696-97, GRFL. Mark Decker to Terry O'Donnell, September 24, 1976, WHCF PL7, box 85, GRFL.

46. *Time*, September 21, 1976. Witcover, *Marathon*, 572–573. Robert Kintner to Dejongh Franklin, August 23, 1976, Staff Secretary Files (hereafter SSF), box 1, JCL. Cambridge Survey Research, August 31, 1976, Powell, box 4, JCL.

47. Polls, September 1976, Nessen, box 35, GRFL. "Talking Points—Second Debate," n.d., Duval, box 27, GRFL. Michael Duval to Jerry Jones, September 6, 1976, Duval, box 31, GRFL. Witcover, *Marathon*, 637–639. "Feeling Good," Videotape, XXPF C756, GRFL.

48. Ford, RPI.

49. Ford, RPI.

50. Carter, *Why*, 9.

6. CARTER AND THE CHALLENGE OF EDWARD KENNEDY

1. Patrick Caddell to JC, January 5, 1977, SSF, box 2, JCL.

2. Jerry Rafshoon to JC, January 4, 1977, SSF, box 2, JCL. Jerry Rafshoon to JC, Inaugural Theme, n.d., SSF, box 4, JCL. Theodore Sorensen to JC, January 6, 1976 [sic], SSF, box 2, JCL. Harrison Wellford, January 6, 1977, SSF, box 2, JCL. *Public Papers of the Presidents of the United States: Jimmy Carter 1977* (Washington, D.C., 1978), 1–4.

3. Jimmy Carter, *Keeping Faith: Memories of a President* (New York, 1982), 24. See index to *Public Papers*, 1977. Rafshoon, Carter Presidency Project—Oral History (hereafter CPP-OH), 22–23.

4. Jody Powell, *The Other Side of the Story* (New York, 1984), 40. JC to Benjamin Bradlee, July 26, 1979, Powell, box 40, JCL.

5. *Time*, May 5, 1980, 19. Hugh Sidey, "Days That Call for Daring," *Time*, May 5, 1980, 25.

6. Patrick Caddell, Initial Working Paper on Political Strategy, December 10, 1979, Powell, box 4, JCL.

7. JC to Edward M. Kennedy, December 5, 1977, NF-EMK, JCL. JC to EMK, January 30, 1978, NF-EMK, JCL. JC to EMK, October 28, 1978, NF-EMK, JCL.

8. *Public Papers*, 1978, 400. *Newsweek*, January 29, 1979, 24. Powell, *Other*, 188–189. *Public Papers*, 1978, 2225–2226.

9. *Public Papers*, 1978, 1413–1414. JC to Benjamin Mays, October 25, 1979, SSF, box 153, JCL.

10. Robert Shogan, *The Riddle of Power: Presidential Leadership from Truman to Bush* (New York, 1992), 217.

11. Patrick Caddell, Cambridge Survey Research, May 25, 1979, Jordan, box 33, JCL.

12. Jerry Rafshoon to JC, n.d., Rafshoon, box 28, JCL.

13. Eleanor Randolph, "The 'Whip-His-Ass' Story," *Washington Monthly*, September 1979, 50–51. Powell, *Other*, 185. Carter, *Keeping*, 464. *Newsweek*, June 23, 1979, 40.

14. Patrick Caddell, Of Crisis and Opportunity, April 23, 1979, Powell, box 40, JCL. Shogan, *Riddle*, 218–219.

15. Jerry Rafshoon to JC, July 10, 1979, Speechwriters' Chronological Files (hereafter SCF), box 50, JCL. Greg Schneiders to Jerry Rafshoon, July 10, 1979, Rafshoon, box 28, JCL.

16. Speech Outline, July 11, 1979, SSF, box 139, JCL. Shogan, *Riddle*, 219–221. Jack W. Germond and Jules Witcover, *Blue Smoke and Mirrors: How Reagan Won and Why Carter Lost the Election of 1980* (New York, 1981), 52.

17. *Newsweek*, August 6, 1979, 20. *New York Times*, October 14, 1979, 1. *Newsweek*, August 27, 1979, 23. Germond and Witcover, *Blue*, 53. *Newsweek*, September 17, 1979, 28. *Newsweek*, September 24, 1979, 30.

18. Hamilton Jordan to JC, n.d., Jordan, box 78, JCL. Hamilton Jordan to JC, n.d., Jordan, box 78, JCL. *Newsweek*, September 24, 1979, 30.

19. Germond and Witcover, *Blue*, 54. *Public Papers*, 1979, 1750–1751, 1839–1840. *New York Times*, September 27, 1979, 1. *New York Times*, September 28, 1979, 27. *Newsweek*, October 8, 1979, 27.

20. *Newsweek*, November 5, 1979, 51. Betty Glad, *Jimmy Carter: In Search of the Great White House* (New York, 1980), 464–465. Robert Day, letter, *New York Times*, November 1, 1979, Press Powell, box 9, JCL.

21. JC to EMK, May 25, 1979, NF-EMK, JCL. Landon Butler to Hamilton Jordan, September 10, 1979, Jordan, box 78. Rafshoon, CPP-OH, 24.

22. Bob Meyers to Rick Hertzberg, October 3, 1979, SCF, box 57, JCL.

23. Rick Hertzberg to JC, October 15, 1979, Draft B-2, SCF, box 57, JCL.

24. See p. 12, Hertzberg, October 15, 1979, Draft B-2, SCF, box 57, JCL.

25. See especially Domestic Staff, Eizenstadt, Kennedy Library Remarks, box 229, JCL. Hertzberg, October 15, 1979, Draft B-2, SCF, box 57, JCL. Hertzberg, October 16, 1979, Draft B-3, Staff Office, Chronological Files, box 57, JCL. Hertzberg, October 16, 1979, Draft 1-3, SSF, box 152, JCL. Kennedy Library Remarks, P-1, SSF, President's Trip to Boston, October 21, 1979, box 152, JCL.

26. *Public Papers*, 1979, 1979.

27. *Public Papers*, 1979, 1981. Kennedy Library Remarks, P-1, SSF, President's Trip to Boston, October 21, 1979, box 152, JCL.

28. *Public Papers*, 1979, 1979–1982. Hertzberg, October 16, 1979, Draft 1-3, SSF, box 152, JCL.

29. *Washington Star*, October 21, 1979. Thomas Brown, *JFK: History of an Image* (Bloomington, Ind., 1988), 81–83.

30. *Public Papers*, 1979, 1987–1988, 2034–2035.

31. Germond and Witcover, *Blue*, 75. Murray B. Levin and T. A. Repak, *Edward Kennedy: The Myth of Leadership* (Boston, 1980), 134.

32. Patrick Caddell, Initial Survey Research Needs of the Campaign, November 26, 1979, Jordan, box 33, JCL. Jerry Rafshoon to Evan Dobelle, Themes, n.d., Rafshoon, box 24, JCL.

33. Hamilton Jordan to JC, n.d., Jordan, box 78, JCL. Greg Schneiders to Jody Powell, n.d., Powell, box 11, JCL. *Newsweek*, October 29, 1979, 32–33.

34. Themes, n.d., Press Powell, box 9, JCL. Summary of Kennedy Record, n.d., Press Powell, box 8, JCL.

35. Patrick Caddell to Hamilton Jordan, October 11, 1979, Jordan, box 80, JCL. Patrick Caddell to JC, November 6, 1979, Powell, box 13, JCL.

36. Themes, October 11, 1979, Jordan, box 80, JCL. Jerry Rafshoon to Evan Dobelle, Themes, n.d., Rafshoon, box 24, JCL.

37. Themes, n.d., Press Powell, box 9, JCL. Talking Points, November 1979, Moses, box 18, JCL. Jerry Rafshoon to JC, November 5, 1979, Press Powell, box 9, JCL. Jerry

Rafshoon to Evan Dobelle, Themes, n.d., Rafshoon, box 24, JCL. Jody Powell to JC, November 1, 1979, Powell, box 40, JCL.

38. Elizabeth Drew, *Portrait of an Election: The 1980 Presidential Campaign* (New York, 1981), 28–29, 122, 124. Jimmy Carter, *Keeping Faith: Memories of a President* (New York, 1982), 530–531. Shogan, *Riddle*, 222.

39. Hertzberg, Draft A-2, November 30, 1979, Announcement, December 4, 1979, SSF, box 158, JCL. Jerry Rafshoon to JC, December 20, 1979, SSF, box 161, JCL.

40. "Brushes with Law Stain Kennedy's Past," *Cavalier Daily*, November 19, 1979, in SSF, box 164, JCL. *Los Angeles Times Poll*, Summary, December 1979, Press Powell, box 10, JCL. *Boston Globe*, November 29, 1979, Press Powell, box 9, JCL.

41. Germond and Witcover, *Blue*, 88–89. *Presidential Papers*, 1979, 2241. *Presidential Papers*, 1980, 90. Barry Bingham, Jr., "Ted Kennedy," *Louisville Courier-Journal*, October 7, 1979 in SSF, box 153, JCL. Kennedy 1979–80, folder 1, Press Powell, box 9, JCL. Robert E. Thompson, "JFK vs. Teddy," *Boston Herald American*, December 4, 1979.

42. Austin Ranney, *The American Elections of 1980* (Washington, D.C., 1981), 44–45. Greg Schneiders to Jerry Rafshoon, December 28, 1979, Press Powell, box 8, JCL. Stu Eizenstadt to JC, December 26, 1979, SSF, box 161, JCL.

43. *New York Times*, December 29, 1979. Carter, *Keeping*, 473–474.

44. See L. Patrick Devlin, "An Analysis of Kennedy's Communication in the 1980 Campaign," *Quarterly Journal of Speech* 68 (November, 1982), 397–417. Steven V. Roberts, "Ted Kennedy: Haunted by the Past," *New York Times Magazine*, February 3, 1980, 56. Brown, *JFK*, 93–94.

45. Drew, *Portrait*, 54, 123–124. Stephen J. Wayne, "Public Perceptions about Ted Kennedy and the Presidency," *Presidential Studies Quarterly* 12 (Winter 1982), 87. Ranney, *American*, 199. Germond and Witcover, *Blue*, 144–145. *New York Times*, January 23, 1980, 1.

46. William A. Degregorio, *The Complete Book of U.S. Presidents: From George Washington to Bill Clinton* (New York, 1993), 643. Drew, *Portrait*, 144–145, 161–162. Ranney, *American*, 53–54. *Washington Post*, June 10, 1980, 8.

47. Hamilton Jordan, CPP-OH, 85–86. Germond and Witcover, *Blue*, 160–165.

48. Drew, *Portrait*, 163–164. Carter, *Keeping*, 532. Jerry Rafshoon, CPP-OH, 60.

49. Democratic National Convention, NBC, August 12, 1980, *New York Times*, August 13, 1980, II, 2.

50. *New York Times*, August 14, 1980, 1. *Presidential Papers*, 1980, 1528. Devlin, 415–417. Hamilton Jordan, *Crisis: The Last Year of the Carter Presidency* (New York, 1982), 326–327. Stephen P. Depoe, "Requiem for Liberalism: The Therapeutic and Deliberative Functions of Nostalgic Appeals in Edward Kennedy's Address to the 1980 Democratic National Convention," *Southern Communication Journal* 55 (Winter 1990), 175–192.

51. For early drafts, see SCF, box 75 and 76, JCL. Patrick Caddell to JC, August 8, 1980, SSF, box 199, JCL. Rick Hertzberg to JC, n.d., SCF, box 77, JCL. Draft P-1, August 10, 1980, SSF, box 199, JCL.

52. Rick Hertzberg to JC, August 13, 1980, SCF, box 78, JCL. Acceptance Speech, SSF, box 199, JCL. Garland A. Haas, *Jimmy Carter and the Politics of Frustration* (Jefferson, N.C., 1992), 150.

53. Drew, *Portrait*, 259. Rafshoon, JCL-OH, 71. Meg Greenfield, "The Hostage of the Convention," *Newsweek*, August 25, 1980, 90.

54. Democratic National Convention, NBC, August 14, 1980. *Public Papers*, 1980, 1532–1540. Germond and Witcover, *Blue*, 192–193. Powell, *Other*, 249–251. *Newsweek*, August 25, 1980, 30. Carter, *Keeping*, 552–553.

55. *Presidential Papers*, 1980, 1548–1549, 1557, 1762, 2340–2342. Jokes—Boston Fundraiser, SSF, box 210, JCL. See also, DNC Fundraiser (Jokes), September 22, 1980, SSF, box 206, JCL. Boston Meeting with Senior Citizens. October 14, 1980, SSF, box 210, JCL.

56. Remarks of the President, October 15, 1980, SSF, box 210, JCL. Houston Campaign Volunteers Rally, September 10, 1980, SSF, box 205, JCL. Mt. Zion Baptist

Church, September 1, 1980, SSF, box 203, JCL. Boston Meeting with Senior Citizens, October 14, 1980, SSF, box 210, JCL. Al Smith Dinner, October 15, 1980, SSF, box 210, JCL. Concord Baptist Church/Bedford-Stuyvesant, October 20, 1980, SSF, box 211, JCL. Meeting with Black Ministers, n.d., SSF, box 211, JCL. *Presidential Papers, 1980, 1956,* 2664.

57. Jordan, *Crisis,* 376.

58. Brown, *JFK,* 93–94. Drew, *Portrait,* 40–41. Meg Greenfield, "The Kennedy Puzzle," *Newsweek,* September 24, 1979, 114. Devlin, *Quarterly Journal of Speech,* 397–417. *Newsweek,* December 10, 1979, 56.

59. "CBS Evening News," CBS, August 25, 1987.

60. *New York Times,* January 14, 1993, II, 4. *New York Times,* October 2, 1986, 1. *Gallup Poll Monthly,* November 1990, 36. See also *Wall Street Journal*/NBC Poll. *Wall Street Journal,* March 16, 1990, 1.

7. REINVENTION: RONALD REAGAN

1. Neil Postman, *Amusing Ourselves to Death: Public Discourse in the Age of Show Business* (New York, 1986), 125. Paul D. Erickson, *Reagan Speaks: The Making of an American Myth* (New York, 1985), 51–71. William F. Lewis, "Telling America's Story: Narrative Form and the Reagan Presidency, *Quarterly Journal of Speech* 73 (August 1987), 280–302. Geoffrey S. Smith, "Memory and Aspiration in Recent Presidential Politics," *Queens Quarterly* 95 (Winter 1988), 797–811. Walter R. Fisher, "Romantic Democracy, Ronald Reagan, and Presidential Heroes," *Western Journal of Speech Communication* 46 (Summer 1982), 299–310. Frontline, "The Reel Life of Ronald Reagan," PBS, 1988.

2. Docudramas include "The Missiles of October" (1974), "Kennedy" (1983), "The Kennedys of Massachusetts" (1990), "Johnny, We Hardly Knew Ye" (1977), "JFK: Reckless Youth" (1993), "Young Joe" (1977), "Jacqueline Bouvier Kennedy" (1981), "A Woman Named Jackie" (1991), "Robert Kennedy and His Times" (1985), and "The Ted Kennedy, Jr., Story" (1986). See also Anthony Frewin, *The Assassination of John F. Kennedy: An Annotated Film, TV, and Videography, 1963–1992* (Westport, Conn., 1993).

3. Lance Morrow, "The History-Devouring Machine," *Horizon,* July 1978, 18–23. William Cohn, "History for the Masses: Television Portrays the Past," *Journal of Popular Culture* 10 (Spring 1976), 280–289.

4. Twilight Zone, "Profile in Silver," CBS, directed by John Hancock, written by J. Neil Schulman, September 12, 1986

5. *Newsweek,* November 28, 1983, 64. *Cleveland Plain Dealer,* April 15, 1985, 14. *USA Today,* October 3, 1985, 1D.

6. Richard Schickel, *Intimate Strangers: The Culture of Celebrity* (Garden City, N.Y., 1985), 135–208. Norman Mailer, "Superman Comes to the Supermart," *Esquire* (November 1960). *Detroit News,* "Politicians in Prime Time," April 10, 1986, 1B. "All Star Party for 'Dutch' Reagan," CBS, December 8, 1985.

7. Garry Wills, *The Kennedy Imprisonment: A Meditation on Power* (Boston, 1982), 196. *Los Angeles Times,* May 30, 1968; *Los Angeles Times,* March 28, 1968; *Hartford Courant,* May 12, 1968; *Washington Post,* May 21, 1968; *New York Times,* May 21, 1968, clippings available in Robert Kennedy Papers, 1968 Campaign/Press Division, box 11, JFKL.

8. *Public Papers of the Presidents of the United States: Ronald Reagan, 1981* (Washington, D.C., 1982), 488–489.

9. Paul D. Erickson, "The Once and Future President: John F. Kennedy in the Rhetoric of Ronald Reagan," Fourth Annual Presidential Conference, John F. Kennedy: The Promise Revisited, March 30, 1985.

10. "Reel Life of Ronald Reagan," 1988. Kurt Ritter and David Henry, *Ronald Reagan: The Great Communicator* (New York, 1992), 5–6, 99. Lou Cannon, *Reagan* (New York, 1982), 94.

11. William A. Degregorio, *The Complete Book of U.S. Presidents: From George Washington to Bill Clinton* (New York, 1993), 639–641. Mary E. Stuckey, *Getting into*

the Game: The Pre-Presidential Rhetoric of Ronald Reagan (New York, 1989). Ronald Reagan, *Ronald Reagan: An American Life* (New York, 1990), 132–134. *New York Times,* October 27, 1984, 31. Stephen E. Ambrose, *Nixon: The Education of a Politician 1913–1962* (New York, 1987), 541–542.

12. Anne Edwards, *Early Reagan: The Rise to Power* (New York, 1987), 475–477. Ritter and Henry, *Ronald Reagan,* 11–34. Stuckey, *Getting,* 11–17. Ronald Reagan, *Speaking My Mind* (New York, 1989), 23. Kitty Kelley, *Nancy Reagan: An Unauthorized Biography,* (New York, 1991), 129.

13. Reagan, *Speaking,* 22–36. F. Clifton White and William J. Gill, *Why Reagan Won* (Chicago, 1981), 88.

14. Ritter and Henry, *Ronald Reagan,* 95–96. Haynes Johnson, *Sleepwalking Through History: America in the Reagan Years* (New York, 1991), 53–54. *Newsweek,* May 29, 1967, 26–27.

15. Stuckey, *Getting,* 31–32. Cannon, *Reagan.*

16. William E. Leuchtenburg, *In the Shadow of FDR: From Harry Truman to Ronald Reagan* (Ithaca, N.Y., 1985), 209–235.

17. Frank Van Der Linden, *The Real Reagan* (New York, 1981), 238, 248.

18. Paul D. Erickson, "The Once and Future President," in *John F. Kennedy: The Promise Revisited* (New York, 1988), 313. *Public Papers, 1981,* 576, 882–883. *Public Papers, 1984,* 663.

19. A reprint of the cartoon by Ohman for the *Oregonian* appeared in the *Washington Post,* December 3, 1983. Ritter and Henry, *Ronald Reagan,* 98. Edward Kennedy Interview, *Los Angeles Times,* November 21, 1983, 21–22. Theodore C. Sorensen, "The Kennedy Complex," *New York Times,* November 22, 1983, 31.

20. Lewis, 285–286. Erickson, *Reagan,* 32–50. Mary E. Stuckey, *Playing the Game: The Presidential Rhetoric of Ronald Reagan* (New York, 1990), 31–45.

21. Stuckey, *Playing,* 37.

22. Lou Cannon, *President Reagan: The Role of a Lifetime* (New York, 1991), 126.

8. THE RISE AND FALL OF GARY HART

1. Michael Kramer, "Hart Stopper," *New York,* March 12, 1984, 32–38. Michael Kramer, "Falling in Love Again," *New York,* March 19, 1984, 28ff. Morton Kondracke, "Hart's Long March," *New Republic,* April 2, 1984, 15. Morton Kondracke, "Hart Line, Soft Line," *New Republic,* April 9, 1984, 12–13. *Time,* March 12, 1984, 16. *Time,* March 26, 1984, 19. George Will, "Jay Gatsby in Politics," *Newsweek,* March 12, 1984, 92. *Newsweek,* March 12, 1984, 21. *Newsweek,* March 26, 1984, 32. Susan Casey, *Hart and Soul: Gary Hart's New Hampshire Odyssey—And Beyond* (Concord, N.H., 1986), 304–305. Elizabeth Drew, *Campaign Journal: The Political Events of 1983–1984* (New York, 1985), 369.

2. *Newsweek,* March 26, 1984, 32–33. *Public Papers of the Presidents of the United States: Ronald Reagan, 1984* (Washington, D.C., 1985), 534–535.

3. Harold Haddon, RTI, October 21, 1992. *Newsweek,* April 13, 1987, 25–27. *Newsweek,* March 26, 1984, 26. *New York,* March 12, 1984, 32ff. Sidney Blumenthal, "Hart's Big Chill," *New Republic,* January 23, 1984, 21. Gary Hart, RTI, July 15, 1992.

4. *Time,* April 9, 1984, 21. Gail Sheehy, *Character: America's Search for Leadership* (New York, 1988), 37–74. Hart, RTI.

5. Garry Wills, *Under God: Religion and American Politics* (New York, 1990), 41–50. Gary Hart, *The Good Fight: The Education of an American Reformer* (New York, 1993), 55–56. Hart, RTI.

6. *Newsweek,* April 13, 1987, 26. Hart, RTI. Hart, *Good Fight,* 56–57.

7. *New Republic,* January 23, 1984, 18. Hart, *Good Fight,* 58. Hart, RTI. E. J. Dionne, Jr., "Gary Hart: The Elusive Front-Runner," *New York Times Magazine,* May 3, 1987, 28–34ff.

8. Hart, RTI.

9. Hart, RTI.

10. William Lee Miller, "Remembering Gary," *New Republic*, April 16, 1984, 11–12. Hart, RTI.

11. Hart, RTI. John B. Jovich, ed., *Reflections on JFK's Assassination: 250 Famous Americans Remember November 22, 1963* (North Manchester, Ind., 1988), 111.

12. Hart, RTI.

13. Hart, *Good Fight*, 73, 77. Hart, RTI. *Newsweek*, March 12, 1984, 32.

14. Hart, RTI. See also, Hart, *Good Fight*, 82–83.

15. Hart, RTI. *Newsweek*, March 12, 1984, 32. Robert M. Kaus, "Should This Man Be President?" *Washington Monthly*, October, 1981, 40. Gary Hart, *Right from the Start: A Chronicle of the McGovern Campaign* (New York, 1973).

16. Hart, RTI. Hart, *Right*, ix. *New York Times Magazine*, May 3, 1987, 32, 40.

17. Hart, RTI. Haddon, RTI. *Denver Post*, September 16, 1974; October 13, 1974; October 27, 1974.

18. Fred Brown, RTI, October 22, 1992. Haddon, RTI.

19. Carl Hilliard, RTI, October 22, 1992. Brown, RTI.

20. Kathy Bushkin, RTI, July 30, 1992. Hart, RTI.

21. Hart, RTI.

22. *New York Times*, October 10, 1975, 19. Hart, RTI.

23. Hart, RTI.

24. Hart, RTI.

25. Richard Cohen, "Why Nobody Knows Gary Hart," *Rolling Stone*, July 5, 1984, 25. *New York Times*, May 18, 1983, III, 13.

26. Peter Goldman and Tony Fuller, *The Quest for the Presidency 1984* (Toronto, 1985), 83–85, 398–401.

27. *Gallup Report*, May 1983, 3–15.

28. Sidney Blumenthal, *Pledging Allegiance: The Last Campaign of the Cold War* (New York, 1990), 121. *New York*, March 12, 1984, 35.

29. Goldman and Fuller, *Quest*, 59–70, 134.

30. Morton Kondracke, "Hart's Long March," *New Republic*, April 2, 1984, 15. *New York*, March 19, 1984, 30. *Time*, March 19, 1984, 17. *Newsweek*, March 19, 1984, 24–25. *New York Times*, March 19, 1984, 11. Bushkin, RTI. *New York*, March 12, 1984, 35. Drew, *Campaign*, 328–329.

31. *New Republic*, January 23, 1984, 21. *New York*, March 12, 1984, 38. *New York*, March 19, 1984, 30. Blumenthal, *Pledging*, 121. *Time*, June 11, 1984, 27. *Time*, May 14, 1984, 17. Drew, *Campaign*, 412. Sidney Blumenthal, "Hart Attack," *New Republic*, March 19, 1984, 15.

32. *Newsweek*, March 26, 1984, 22. Casey, *Hart and Soul*, 304–305. *New York*, March 12, 1984, 35. *Gallup Report*, April 1984, 28–30.

33. *Newsweek*, March 26, 1984, 26–27. Drew, *Campaign*, 360. *New Republic*, April 2, 1984, 15. *Newsweek*, March 12, 1984, 92.

34. Bushkin, RTI. Drew, *Campaign*, 360. *Time*, March 19, 1984, 8. Goldman, *Quest*, 160.

35. Bushkin, RTI. Goldman, *Quest*, 87, 101. *New York*, March 12, 1984, 35.

36. *New York*, March 12, 1984, 35. *Newsweek*, March 26, 1984, 26–27. Bushkin, RTI.

37. Hart, RTI.

38. Hart, RTI.

39. *New York*, March 12, 1984, 35. *Time*, March 19, 1984, 17. Hart, RTI.

40. Bushkin, RTI.

41. Bushkin, RTI.

42. Bushkin, RTI.

43. Goldman, *Quest*, 157. Jack W. Germond and Jules Witcover, *Wake Us When It's Over: Presidential Politics of 1984* (New York, 1985), 198–199.

44. Bushkin, RTI. Hart, RTI.

45. Bushkin, RTI. *Time*, March 26, 1984, 19. *New York*, March 26, 1984, 27.

46. Frontline, "So You Want to be President," PBS, 1984. Germond and Witcover,

Wake Us, 187–188, 208, 314–316. *Newsweek*, March 26, 1984, 20-24. In Illinois, Hart accused Mondale of running negative advertisements that questioned Hart's character. When it was learned that no such ads had been aired, Hart appeared disorganized and defensive. Shortly before the New Jersey primary, Hart lamented to a California audience about having to spend time in New Jersey.

47. Drew, *Campaign*, 544.
48. Hart, RTI.
49. Hart, RTI.
50. Ira Progoff, *Jung's Psychology and Its Social Meaning* (New York, 1955), 83.
51. Hart, RTI.

9. 1984: REAGAN REDUX

1. Jack W. Germond and Jules Witcover, *Wake Us When It's Over: Presidential Politics of 1984* (New York, 1985), 341–342, 467–468. Paul D. Erickson, *Reagan Speaks: The Making of an American Myth* (New York, 1985), 3, 99–101. Mary E. Stuckey, *Playing the Game: The Presidential Rhetoric of Ronald Reagan* (New York, 1990), 48.

2. *Public Papers of the Presidents of the United States: Ronald Reagan, 1984* (Washington, D.C., 1985), 663.

3. *Public Papers, 1984*, 811. Ronald Reagan, *Ronald Reagan: An American Life* (New York, 1990), 373.

4. *Public Papers, 1984*, 1316–1318.

5. *Public Papers, 1984*, 1316–1318.

6. Geraldine Ferraro, RTI, March 29, 1993.

7. Ferraro, RTI.

8. Geraldine A. Ferraro, *Ferraro: My Story* (Toronto, 1985). Ferraro, RTI.

9. Ferraro, RTI.

10. Ferraro, RTI.

11. Ferraro, RTI. *New York Times*, September 27, 1984, IV, 23.

12. Ferraro, RTI.

13. *New York Times*, October 8, 1984, B5. *Public Papers, 1984*, 1464.

14. Peter Goldman and Tony Fuller, *The Quest for the Presidency 1984* (Toronto, 1985), 387–388.

15. Stuckey, *Playing*, 35. *Cleveland Plain Dealer*, February 22, 1985, 20. *New York Times*, February 28, 1985, 16; April 8, 1985, 5.

16. *New York Times*, October 16, 1984, 24. *Public Papers, 1984*, 1491, 1531.

17. *New York Times*, October 24, 1984, 24.

18. *Public Papers, 1984*, 1655, 1658, 1661, 1672. Germond and Witcover, *Wake Us*, 537. Jules Witcover, RTI, March 24, 1994. *New York Times*, October 24, 1984, 24. Sidney Blumenthal, *Our Long National Daydream: A Political Pageant of the Reagan Era* (New York, 1988), 133.

19. Witcover, RTI.

20. *Public Papers, 1984*, 1718, 1795.

21. Paul D. Erickson, "The Once and Future President," *John F. Kennedy: The Promise Revisited* (New York, 1988), 313–320. Michael Kimmelman, "Horror Unforgotten: The Politics of Memory," *New York Times*, March 11, 1994, B1.

22. Ferraro, RTI.

23. Hugh Sidey, "An Unlikely Affinity," *Time*, August 12, 1985, 16. *Public Papers, 1983*, 1621. *Newsweek*, December 12, 1983, 68. *New York Times*, November 23, 1983, 18.

24. *Public Papers, 1985*, 814–816.

25. *Washington Post*, June 25, 1985, 1. Peggy Noonan, *What I Saw at the Revolution: A Political Life in the Reagan Era* (New York, 1990), 231–233.

10. RE-CREATION: THE SENTIMENTAL JOURNEY OF MICHAEL DUKAKIS

1. Mary E. Stuckey, *Playing the Game: The Presidential Rhetoric of Ronald Reagan* (New York, 1990), 51–52. Tom Shales, *Cleveland Plain Dealer*, January 19, 1987, 20.

2. *New York Times*, April 14, 1987, 10. E. J. Dionne, Jr., "Gary Hart: The Elusive Front-Runner," *New York Times Magazine*, May 3, 1987, 30. *Newsweek*, April 13, 1987, 25–27.

3. *New York Times*, April 14, 1987, 10. James Reston, "Hart Bets on the Cycle," *New York Times*, April 15, 1987, 21. *Time*, May 18, 1987, 16–20. *Newsweek*, May 18, 1987, 22–28. Hugh Sidey, "Upstairs at the White House," *Time*, May 18, 1987, 20. Lance Morrow, "Kennedy Going on Nixon," *Time*, May 18, 1987, 90. Jonathan Alter, "Sex and the Presidency," *Newsweek*, May 4, 1987, 26. Gail Sheehy, *Character: America's Search for Leadership* (New York, 1988), 37–74. *Rolling Stone*, March 24, 1988, 76. Suzannah Lessard, "The Issue Was Women," *Newsweek*, May 18, 1987, 34. Garry Wills, "Hart's Guilt Trick," *Newsweek*, December 28, 1987, 17–18.

4. Special Report, CBS, May 8, 1987. *New York Times*, May 9, 1987, 1.

5. *New York Times*, January 9, 1988, 9. *New York Times*, January 13, 1988, 10.

6. *Christian Science Monitor*, March 10, 1988, 15. *Chicago Tribune*, September 26, 1987, 3. *New York Times*, July 5, 1987, 11. *New York Times*, February 26, 1988, 8. Morton Kondracke, "Gephardt's Inside Moves," *New Republic*, June 1, 1987, 20. Mike Royko, "Simon: Candidate Who Is Not a Clone," *Toledo Blade*, May 16, 1987. Jack W. Germond and Jules Witcover, *Whose Broad Stripes and Bright Stars?: The Trivial Pursuit of the Presidency 1988* (New York, 1989), 225.

7. *Cleveland Plain Dealer*, November 3, 1986, 11. *New York Times*, March 4, 1987, 9. *New York Times*, June 10, 1987, 10. *New York Times*, June 14, 1987, 5. *New York Times*, July 5, 1987, 11.

8. *New York Times*, September 16, 1987, 1. *New York Times*, September 17, 1987, 1. Germond and Witcover, *Whose*, 233–234.

9. Bruce Morton, "CBS Evening News," CBS, August 25, 1987. *New York Times*, April 17, 1987, 26. *New York Times*, July 5, 1987, 1. *Newsweek*, September 28, 1987, 24. Robert S. McElvaine, "The Kennedy Complex," *New York Times*, September 27, 1987, 15.

10. Herbert S. Parmet, *JFK: The Presidency of John F. Kennedy* (New York, 1983). *Wall Street Journal*, July 15, 1988, 1. Jon Margolis, "A Symbol of Hope," *Chicago Tribune*, November 22, 1988, 17. Bob Greene, "It's Strange What Life Does to Dreams," *Chicago Tribune*, November 21, 1988, V, 1. Joan Beck, "Kennedy Myth Still Persists and Serves National Purpose," *Chicago Tribune*, November 7, 1988, 21. Pete Hamill, "JFK: The Real Thing," *New York*, November 28, 1988, 44–51. Nicholas M. Horrock, "The Kennedy Mystique," *Chicago Tribune*, November 20, 1988, IV, 1. Thomas Brown, *JFK: The History of an Image*, (Bloomington, Ind., 1988), 101.

11. Michael Dukakis, RPI, May 11, 1992. Jeff Fospan and select students at Northeastern University, RPI, May 15, 1992. *Boston Globe*, May 14, 1992, 81. Charles Kenney and Robert L. Turner, *Dukakis: An American Odyssey* (Boston, 1988). Richard Gaines and Michael Segal, *Dukakis: The Man Who Would Be President* (New York, 1988). Richard Ben Cramer, *What It Takes: The Way to the White House* (New York, 1992). Sheehy, *Character*, 222–251. *Time*, June 20, 1988, 14–16. *Newsweek*, July 25, 1988, 24–43.

12. Dukakis, RPI, May 11, 1992.

13. Michael Dukakis to Senator John F. Kennedy, January 19, 1954, PPP, Senate Files, box 650, JFKL. Kenney and Turner, *Dukakis*, 34. Dukakis, RPI, May 11, 1992.

14. Dukakis, RPI, May 11, 1992. Kenney and Turner, *Dukakis*, 39.

15. Dukakis, RPI, May 11, 1992. Gaines and Segal, *Dukakis*, 45. Kenney and Turner, *Dukakis*, 48–49.

16. Dukakis, RPI, May 11, 1992.

17. Dukakis, RPI, May 11, 1992. Jonathan Rowe, "Massachusetts Matrix," *Christian Science Monitor*, June 18, 1988, 16. Kenney and Turner, *Dukakis*, 50–52.

18. Dukakis, RPI, May 11, 1992. Kenney and Turner, *Dukakis*, 42.

19. Dukakis, RPI, May 11, 1992. Kenney and Turner, *Dukakis*, 59.

20. Dukakis, RPI, May 11, 1992. Gaines and Segal, *Dukakis*, 64.

21. Dukakis, RPI, May 11, 1992. Gaines and Segal, *Dukakis*, 69.

22. Dukakis, RPI, May 11, 1992.

23. Gaines and Segal, *Dukakis*, 125–127. Kenney and Turner, *Dukakis*, 73–77, 129–139. Cramer, *What*, 202–209.

24. Dukakis, RPI, May 11, 1992. Kenney and Turner, *Dukakis*, 143.

25. Dukakis, RPI, May 11, 1992. Gaines and Segal, *Dukakis*, 254. Kenney and Turner, *Dukakis*, 159–172.

26. Dukakis, RPI, May 11, 1992. *New York Times*, June 16, 1988, 14.

27. Dukakis, RPI, May 11, 1992. Kenney and Turner, *Dukakis*, 212.

28. Kenney and Turner, *Dukakis*, 212–223.

29. Dukakis, RPI, May 11, 1992. *New York Times*, May 30, 1987, 8.

30. Dukakis, RPI, May 11, 1992.

31. Dukakis, RPI, May 11, 1992.

32. Fred Davis, *Yearning for Yesterday: The Sociology of Nostalgia* (New York, 1979), 10, 18, 20.

33. Davis, *Yearning*, 34–35.

34. *New York Times*, July 5, 1987, 11. *New York Times*, November 1, 1987, 11. *New York Times*, December 18, 1987, 12. *Atlanta Constitution*, January 28, 1988, 6. *New York Times*, May 6, 1988, 8.

35. *New York Times*, January 22, 1988, 10. *New York Times*, June 16, 1988, 14. Dukakis, RPI, May 14, 1992.

36. "CBS Evening News," CBS, July 13, 1988.

37. Sidney Blumenthal, *Pledging Allegiance: The Last Campaign of the Cold War* (New York, 1990), 239. *Newsweek*, July 25, 1988, 16. Dukakis, RPI, May 14, 1992.

38. Dukakis, RPI, May 14, 1992. "CBS Evening News," CBS, July 13, 1988.

39. *USA Today*, July 22, 1988, 2D. Democratic National Convention, CNN, July 21, 1988.

40. Dukakis, RPI, May 14, 1992. Democratic National Convention, CNN, July 21, 1988. *New York Times*, July 22, 1988, 8.

41. *New York Times*, September 13, 1988, 10. *New York Times*, September 20, 1988, 10. *New York Times*, September 21, 1988, 11. *New York Times*, October 5, 1988, 15. *New York Times*, October 5, 1988, 15. *Time*, October 3, 1988, 16. Blumenthal, *Pledging*, 239.

42. Dukakis, RPI, May 14, 1992.

43. Dukakis, RPI, May 14, 1992.

44. "1960–1988: The Making of the Presidents," *Life*, September 1988, 50–58. "Election Comparisons: '60 vs. '88," *Christian Science Monitor*, June 23, 1988, 4. Sander Vanocur, "The Return of Political Reality," *Boston Globe*, July 19, 1988, 11.

45. Michael Dukakis, RTI, July 5, 1992.

46. Jack W. Germond and Jules Witcover, "Bush's JFK Script," *Boston Globe*, August 15, 1989, 33. Michael Kramer, "Trying to Go All the Way with JFK," *U.S. News & World Report*, October 3, 1988, 21. *New York Times*, August 5, 1988, 1.

47. *New York Times*, November 1, 1988, 27.

48. Dukakis, RPI, May 14, 1992. *New York Times*, October 31, 1988, 1.

49. Germond and Witcover, *Whose*, 441.

50. *New York Times*, September 28, 1988, 12. Dukakis, RPI, May 14, 1992.

51. The Vice-Presidential Debate, CBS, October 5, 1988. Germond and Witcover, *Whose*, 440–441. *USA Today*, October 10, 1988, 4A.

52. Dukakis, RPI, May 14, 1992. *Time*, October 17, 1988, 20–21. *Chicago Tribune*, October 6, 1988, 11. *Chicago Tribune*, October 10, 1988, 5. John Hughes, "Quayle as Kennedy," *Christian Science Monitor*, October 7, 1988, 16. Germond and Witcover, *Whose*, 441. *USA Today*, October 7, 1988, 4A.

53. Peter Goldman and Tom Mathews, *The Quest for the Presidency: The 1988*

Campaign (New York, 1989), 248. Edwin M. Yoder, "Robertson Can't Ride Kennedy's Coattails Too Far," *Atlanta Constitution*, February 12, 1988, 19. David B. Wilson, "Getting to the Facts in the Kennedy Comparison," *Boston Globe*, October 12, 1988, 19.

54. *Atlanta Journal*, July 22, 1988, 21. Mike Royko, "The Painful Days of Camelot," *Cleveland Plain Dealer*, July 16, 1988, 9. *Time*, September 19, 1988, 18.

55. Cartoon by BOK in *Akron Beacon Journal*, reprinted in *Newsweek*, October 17, 1988, 21. David Broder, "Quayle, Dukakis and the Kennedy Comparison," *Chicago Tribune*, October 7, 1988, 29. Joe Klein, "The Great Pretenders," *New York*, October 17, 1988, 16, 20. Roger Simon, "We Wouldn't Let Kennedy Be Kennedy," *Los Angeles Times*, October 7, 1988, 2.

56. Ellen Goodman, "What We Need Is Kennedy-Style Call to Public Service," *Atlanta Constitution*, November 18, 1988, 23. Victor Kamber, "When the People Wanted Vision, Dukakis Turned Out to Be No John F. Kennedy," *Atlanta Constitution*, November 22, 1988, 10. Blumenthal, *Pledging*, 239, 349. *New York Times*, March 7, 1989, 14.

57. Dukakis, RPI, May 14, 1992. BOK cartoon in *Newsweek*, October 17, 1988, 21. Ori Hofmekler cartoon in *New York Times*, August 5, 1988, 23.

58. Dukakis, RPI, May 11, 1992.

11. BILL CLINTON AND THE LAYING ON OF HANDS

1. *New York Times*, January 20, 1993, 1. "CBS Evening News," CBS, January 19, 1993.

2. Michael Kelly, "Ted Kennedy on the Rocks," *Esquire*, February, 1990, 200–200ff. *New York Times*, November 1, 1991, 10. *U.S. News & World Report*, November 25, 1991, 6. *Newsweek*, December 9, 1991, 25–26.

3. *New York Times*, March 29, 1994, B1. Anna Quindlen, "Trouble with Teddy," *New York Times*, October 19, 1991, 15. James Carroll, "The End of the Dream," *New Republic*, June 24, 1991, 22–25. Anthony Lee, "The Dead Kennedys," *Punch*, May 29, 1991, 26–29. *Newsweek*, December 9, 1991, 22–25. *Time*, April 29, 1991, 24–27. *New York Times*, October 19, 1991, 15. *New York Times*, October 26, 1991, 1. *USA Today*, October 29, 1991, 10A.

4. *Gallup Poll Monthly*, November 1990, 36. Haynes Johnson, "Why Camelot Lives," *Washington Post*, December 17, 1991, 21. "Who Killed JFK: The Final Chapter?" CBS, November 21, 1993.

5. Thomas Campbell, RTI, February 22, 1994.

6. *Newsweek*, March 30, 1992, 37. Herbert Barry III and Paul Elovitz, "Psychobiographical Explorations of Clinton and Perot," *Journal of Psychohistory* 20 (Fall 1992), 197–215. *U.S. News and World Report*, July 20, 1992, 29–36. Garry Wills, "Beginning of the Road," *Time*, July 20, 1992, 33–34, 55–59. Charles Allen and Jonathan Portis, *The Comeback Kid: The Life and Career of Bill Clinton* (New York, 1992). Jim Moore and Rick Ihde, *Clinton: Young Man in a Hurry* (Fort Worth, Tex., 1992).

7. William A. Degregorio, *The Complete Book of U.S. Presidents: From George Washington to Bill Clinton* (New York, 1993), 707. Allen, *Comeback*, 9. Moore and Ihde, *Clinton*, 23. *U.S. News and World Report*, March 30, 1992, 28.

8. Mauria Jackson Aspell, RPI, May 25, 1994. David Leopoulis, RPI, May 24, 1994.

9. Moore and Ihde, *Clinton*, 23, Aspell, RPI.

10. Democratic National Convention, C-SPAN, July 16, 1992. "48 Hours, Special Edition, An Interview with the President," CBS, March 24, 1993.

11. Aspell, RPI. Leopoulis, RPI. Joe Newman, RPI, May 24, 1994. *Newsweek*, July 20, 1992, 32–35. Moore and Ihde, *Clinton*, 25. William Jefferson Clinton, "What Today Means to Me," *Parade*, July 4, 1993, 4.

12. Allen and Portis, *Comeback*, 14. Leopoulis, RPI. Aspell, RPI.

13. John B. Jovich, ed., *Reflections on JFK's Assassination: 250 Famous Americans Remember November 22, 1963* (North Manchester, Ind., 1988), 113. *Newsweek*, November

8, 1993, 8. "November 22, 1963: Where Were You?" Turner Network Television, November 22, 1993. Leopoulis, RPI. Aspell, RPI.

14. Thomas Caplan, RTI, February 15, 1994.

15. Moore and Ihde, *Clinton*, 27. Ernest Dumas, ed., *The Clintons of Arkansas: An Introduction to Those Who Know Them Best* (Fayetteville, Ark., 1993), 47.

16. Campbell, RTI. Caplan, RTI.

17. Barry and Elovitz, *Journal of Psychohistory*, 206. *U.S. News & World Report*, July 20, 1992, 31. Degregorio, *Complete*, 712–713. Allen and Portis, *Comeback*, 46–52.

18. Stephen Smith, RPI, May 23, 1994.

19. Smith, RPI.

20. Moore and Ihde, *Clinton*, 65–68. Smith, RPI. Allen and Portis, *Comeback*, 123.

21. Degregorio, *Complete*, 714–715.

22. Allen and Pontis, *Comeback*, 127. Moore and Ihde, *Clinton*, 142–143.

23. *New York Times*, October 1, 1991, 1. *New York Times*, January 27, 1992, 8. *New York Times*, February 12, 1992, 10. *New York Times*, March 16, 1992, 25. *New York Times*, February 21, 1992, 10. *New York Times*, March 17, 1992, 10. *New York Times*, February 14, 1992, 10.

24. *New York Times*, April 3, 1992, 9. *Newsweek*, October 7, 1991, 38–39. CNN News, April 16, 1992. *New York Times*, March 16, 1992, 12; April 6, 1992, 8; April 25, 1992, 9; July 18, 1992, 8.

25. Aspell, RPI.

26. Smith, RPI. Leopoulis, RPI. Newman, RPI.

27. Joe Klein, "The Bill Clinton Show," *Newsweek*, October 26, 1992, 35.

28. *New York Times*, August 30, 1992, 15. Godfrey Sperling, "Clinton's Kennedyesque Image," *Christian Science Monitor*, March 24, 1992, 18. Jason Berry, "Clinton's Pursuit of the Kennedy Mystique," *Atlanta Journal*, March 22, 1992, 19. *Newsweek*, July 20, 1992, 32–35. David Streitfeld, "Bill Clinton, In Your Dreams," *Washington Post*, April 9, 1993, D1.

29. Caplan, RTI.

30. John Diamond, Associated Press, *Bowling Green Sentinel-Tribune*, July 16, 1992, 3.

31. Gennifer Flowers, "My 12-Year Affair with Bill Clinton," *Star*, February 4, 1992. *Newsweek*, January 27, 1992, 4. "Tonight Show," February 3, 1992. Mary Ann Barton and Paul C. Barton, eds., *Campaign: A Cartoon History of Bill Clinton's Race for the White House* (Fayetteville, Ark., 1993), 9.

32. Jack W. Germond and Jules Witcover, *Mad as Hell: Revolt at the Ballot Box*, 1992 (New York, 1993), 189. Barton and Barton, eds., *Campaign*, 21.

33. *Newsweek*, Special Election Issue, November/December 1992, 41. "Recalling 1960," *Christian Science Monitor*, March 19, 1992, 20.

34. *New York Times*, July 10, 1992, 1, 8, 9. Barton and Barton, eds., *Campaign*, 81.

35. *Newsweek*, July 27, 1992, 26. Democratic National Convention, C-SPAN, July 15, 1992.

36. Democratic National Convention, C-SPAN, July 15, 1992. Caplan, RTI.

37. Democratic National Convention, C-SPAN, July 16, 1992. Original film footage aired on "November 22, 1963: Where Were You?" TNT, November 22, 1993. *Newsweek* July 27, 1992, 26–27.

38. Peggy Noonan, "Behind Enemy Lines," *Newsweek*, July 27, 1992, 33. Eugene McCarthy, RTI, February 10, 1994.

39. Merrill D. Peterson, *Lincoln in American Memory* (New York, 1994), 165.

40. *Newsweek*, July 27, 1992, 32–33. Barton and Barton, eds., *Campaign*, 50. Moore and Ihde, *Clinton*, 14. George Will, "Whatever It Takes," *Newsweek*, March 23, 1992, 72.

41. For criticism of Clinton's use of the Kennedy image, see Maureen Dowd and Frank Rich, "Another Quest for Camelot," *New York Times*, July 17, 1992, 9; Ronald Steel, "The Bobby Gap." *New Republic*, May 25, 1992, 16–17; Mickey Kaus, "RFK Envy," *New Republic*, June 29, 1992, 13–14. *Newsweek*, October 7, 1991, 38–39. *New York Times*, March 16, 1992, 13. *Newsweek*, April 6, 1992, 26.

42. Jules Witcover, RTI, March 24, 1994. Howard Fineman, "The New Age President," *Newsweek*, January 25, 1993, 22–23.

43. Caplan, RTI.

44. Witcover, RTI.

45. *Newsweek*, October 26, 1992, 35. *Newsweek*, January 25, 1993, 22–23.

46. John Nichols, "A Handshake from JFK Fueled a Teenage Dream," *Toledo Blade*, November 4, 1992, 1. *New York Times*, August 4, 1992, 9. "Morning Edition," National Public Radio, September 11, 1992. *Newsweek*, September 21, 1992, 47–48. *New York Times*, July 30, 1992, 8. *Time*, November 16, 1992, 38. *Newsweek*, December 7, 1992, 29. Witcover, RTI.

47. Author's campaign buttons. *Toledo Blade*, November 4, 1992, 1. *Washington Post*, July 20, 1992, 6. *New York Times*, July 20, 1992, 10. *New York Times*, February 18, 1992, 1. *USA Today*, August 24, 1992, 5A. *Newsweek*, November 2, 1992, 58. *New York Times*, October 31, 1992, 10. "Morning Edition," National Public Radio, November 4, 1992.

48. *Newsweek*, August 3, 1992, 29. *Newsweek*, September 21, 1992, 50. Hugh Sidey, "Just Wild About Harry," *Time*, September 14, 1992, 40. *Newsweek*, Special Election Issue, November/December, 1992, 19.

49. *Time*, November 16, 1992, 28–29. Lance Morrow, "The Torch Is Passed," *Time*, January 4, 1993, 24. *Newsweek*, Special Election Issue, November/December, 1992, 5–6. "Today Show," NBC, November 5, 1992. *Newsweek*, November 16, 1992, 42. *Newsweek*, November 23, 1992, 64. *Time*, January 4, 1993, 37. *Newsweek*, February 1, 1993, 38.

50. "Morning Edition," National Public Radio, November 4, 1992. Degregorio, *Complete*, 719–723.

51. *Gallup Poll Monthly*, January 1993, 23. "Bill Clinton Interview," *Rolling Stone*, September 17, 1992, 55.

52. "Clinton: *Reencarnacion de J. F. Kennedy?*" *Casos Extraordinarios*, April 13, 1993, 3–5 (translated for the author by Javier Garza Ojeda). "JFK's Ghost Appears at Clinton's Inauguration," *Sun*, March 2, 1993, 17. "Clinton Meets with JFK," *Weekly World News*, July 20, 1993, 24–25.

53. *Newsweek*, March 1, 1993, 24–26. Joe Klein, "Bungee-Jumping," *Newsweek*, March 1, 1993, 29. *New York Times*, February 20, 1993, 1. Michael Elliott, "How Would Harry Handle This?" *Newsweek*, September 20, 1993, 26. "48 Hours, Special Edition: An Interview with the President," CBS, March 24, 1993. "Saturday Night Live," NBC, January 23, 1993. *New York Times*, February 15, 1993, III, 6. CNN News, February 22, 1993.

54. Michiko Kakutani, "Shifting Perceptions of a Presidency," *New York Times*, October 18, 1993, B2. Jonathan Alter, "Less Profile, More Courage," *Newsweek*, November 1, 1993, 33.

55. *New York Times*, March 2, 1993, 10. *New York Times*, May 5, 1993, B6. Bill Eppridge and Hays Gorey, *Robert Kennedy: The Last Campaign* (New York, 1993). *New York Times*, November 20, 1993, 8. CNN News, January 14, 1994. *New York Times*, January 15, 1994, 1, 6.

56. Joe Klein, "A Postmodern President," *Newsweek*, January 27, 1994, 19–21. Witcover, RTI.

57. Joe Klein, "A High Risk Presidency," *Newsweek*, May 3, 1993, 32–40. Joe Klein, "What's Wrong?" *Newsweek*, June 7, 1993, 16–19. *New York Times*, June 6, 1993, 10. *Atlanta Constitution*, June 7, 1993, 2. *Public Papers of the Presidents of the United States: William J. Clinton, 1993* (Washington, D.C., 1993) 1037–1039. See also, Tom Mathews, "The Lessons of Bobby," *Newsweek*, May 31, 1993, 26–28.

58. *New York Times*, August 25, 1993, 7. "CBS Evening News," CBS, August 24, 1993. Aspell, RPI.

59. Clinton was photographed with Vernon E. Jordan and singer James Taylor, *New York Times*, August 28, 1994, 1, 9. See also *New York Times*, September 1, 1994, 1, 13.

60. *Public Papers*, 1993, 2204–2208. *New York Times*, October 30, 1993, 5. "CBS Evening News," CBS, October 29, 1993.

61. *New York Times*, May 24, 1994, 10. *U.S. News & World Report*, May 30, 1994, 27.

62. *New York Times*, April 24, 1994, 12; April 25, 1; April 28, 10. Roger Stone, "Nixon on Clinton," *New York Times*, April 28, 1994, 15. Frank Rich, "I Am Not a Comedian," *New York Times*, April 28, 1994, 15.

63. *New York Times*, February 17, 1993, 12. Alan Brinkley, "At Last, Maybe, A Vision," *New York Times*, January 27, 1994, 15. *Newsweek*, March 21, 1994, 11.

64. Joel Achenbach, "Jack and Bill Went Up the Hill," *Washington Post*, July 20, 1994, B1. Richard Cohen, "Clinton II: The Sequel," *Washington Post*, August 2, 1994, 15. See also William Safire, "For the Haitian Legion," *New York Times*, May 9, 1994, 11; Joe Klein, "Hoping for Passion," *Newsweek*, February 1, 1993, 30. See also the political cartoon, "Ich Bin Ein Beginner," by Cammuso in *Newsweek*, July 25, 1994, and Joe Klein, "The Religious Left," *Newsweek*, July 25, 1994, 23.

65. President Bill Clinton to the author via the office of George Stephanopoulos, December 5, 1994.

66. Smith, RPI.

12. THE PRISON OF THE PAST

1. Lance Morrow, "JFK," *Time*, November 14, 1983, 67. See also Peter Goldman, "Kennedy Remembered," *Newsweek*, November 28, 1983, 61–64.

2. Anthony Lewis, *New York Times*, November 18, 1994, 15. See also *New York Times*, September 21, 1994, 12.

3. The entries were recorded by the author at "The Sixth Floor Museum: John F. Kennedy and the Memory of a Nation," on August 15, 1993.

4. *New York Times*, September 24, 1994, 8; September 29, 1994, 10. *Newsweek*, October 19, 1994, 30–31. "CBS Evening News," CBS, October 13, 1994.

5. *Gallup Poll Monthly*, November 1993, 4.

6. *Gallup Poll Monthly*, August 1993, 7; January 1994, 8; February 1994, 5; March 1994, 4. "If I Ruled the World: An Interview with Fran Lebowitz," *Mirabella*, November 1994, 111. *Newsweek*, November 7, 1994, 42.

7. *Newsweek*, November 7, 1994, 42.

8. *New York Times*, April 25, 1992, 9.

9. Jacqueline Kennedy Onassis Funeral Coverage, ABC News, May 23, 1994. *New York Times*, May 24, 1994, 10.

A Note on Sources

THIS STUDY WAS BASED extensively on primary evidence in the form of memoranda, letters, reports, speeches, oral histories, and logs available at seven research institutions: the John F. Kennedy Library in Boston, Massachusetts: the Lyndon Baines Johnson Library in Austin, Texas; the Richard Nixon Library and Birthplace in Yorba Linda, California; the Nixon Presidential Materials Project in Alexandria, Virginia; the National Archives, Pacific Southwest Branch, in Laguna Niguel, California; the Gerald R. Ford Library in Ann Arbor, Michigan; and the Jimmy Carter Library in Atlanta, Georgia. The endnotes will guide the reader through the specific collections used for this study. The Robert Finch Papers at the Richard Nixon Library and Birthplace were particularly helpful. Some relevant collections and files in the above libraries remain closed to researchers. These records include material related to Jimmy Carter's 1976 presidential campaign, Lyndon Johnson's recorded telephone conversations with Jacqueline Kennedy, and records related to the Nixon administration's covert investigation of Edward Kennedy's accident at Chappaquiddick. Although the Ronald Reagan Library is open to researchers, relevant materials pertaining to this study are still unprocessed. Nor are materials pertaining to the Bush presidency available to researchers.

Numerous political figures and their friends and advisers were interviewed. Recorded interviews with major political figures include Gerald R. Ford, George McGovern, Eugene McCarthy, Gary Hart, Michael Dukakis, and Geraldine Ferraro. Bill Clinton corresponded in writing. Recorded interviews with political advisers include Harry McPherson, adviser to Lyndon Johnson; Kathryn Bushkin, legislative assistant and press secretary to Gary Hart; Stephen Smith, political adviser to Governor Bill Clinton; and Hal Haddon, Gary Hart's campaign manager in 1984. Several boyhood friends of Bill Clinton were also interviewed, including Mauria Jackson Aspell, David Leopoulis, and Joe Newman. Thomas Caplan and Thomas Campbell, two of Clinton's college roommates at Georgetown University, were interviewed by telephone. And several reporters were interviewed, including Jules Witcover of the *Baltimore Sun*, and Denver journalists Fred Brown and Carl Hilliard. All these interviews helped to fill gaps in documented evidence. Several people declined to be interviewed, including Richard Nixon, Jimmy Carter, Ronald Reagan, Joseph Biden, and Dan Quayle.

Some secondary works require brief discussion. Newspaper and magazine articles about each president's and national contender's concern for the Kennedy image, or about their invocations of JFK, are detailed in the endnotes. Martin S. Fenton's and Robert U. Goehlert's *American Presidents: A Bibliography* (Washington, D.C., 1987) provides excellent bibliographies for each president. William A. Degregorio's *The Complete Book of U.S. Presidents: From George Washington to Bill Clinton* (New York, 1993) neatly summarizes each president's personal background, political career, presidential campaigns, and administrative accomplishments. A shrewd work that provides succinct and well-considered analyses of the last eight presidents is Robert Shogan's *The Riddle of Power: Presidential Leadership from Truman to Bush* (New York, 1991).

Several publications provide historiographical context for the chapter discussions. A superior study is Thomas Brown's *JFK: History of an Image* (Bloomington, Ind., 1988). It is well organized, succinct, and offers valuable endnotes and a bibliography. A dated but helpful work is Vincent L. Toscano's *Since Dallas: Images of John F. Kennedy in Popular and Scholarly Literature, 1963–1973* (San Francisco, 1978). In detailing Kennedy's evolving public image, however, neither Brown nor Toscano consider television docudramas produced regularly since 1974. Two early articles note the debilitating influence of docudramas on historical perceptions: Lance Morrow's "The History-Devouring Machine," *Horizon*, July 1978; and William Cohn's "History for the Masses: Television Portrays the Past," *Journal of Popular Culture* 10 (Winter 1976). Garry Wills's *The Kennedy Imprisonment: A Meditation of Power* (Boston, 1982) merits close reading. It addresses the disparity between JFK's public image and private self, and probes Edward Kennedy's inability to escape the myth of his martyred brothers. The book also offers a penetrating, though cursory, discussion of the haunting influence of JFK on his successors. See also Lance Morrow's "JFK," *Time*, November 14, 1983, and Peter Goldman's "Kennedy Remembered," *Newsweek*, November 28, 1983.

A detailed discussion of the materials relevant to the chapters on Lyndon Johnson can be found in the notes to my book *In His Steps: Lyndon Johnson and the Kennedy Mystique* (Chicago, 1991). For the purposes of this study I focused on material addressing Johnson's concern for John Kennedy's image and Robert Kennedy's efforts to deny LBJ access to the JFK legend. I augmented these discussions with information obtained from newly released materials, including memoranda from LBJ's bid to win the presidential nomination in 1960, his secretly recorded telephone conversations during the transition year, and recorded telephone conversations related to Jacqueline Kennedy's 1966–1967 lawsuit against William Manchester. The conference "Vietnam: The Early Decisions," sponsored by the Lyndon Johnson Library in October 1993, provided useful information on Johnson's decision-making process regarding U.S. military involvement in Southeast Asia. Interviews with Harry McPherson and Eugene McCarthy offer fresh insight into the influence of the Kennedy myth on presidential politics in 1968. Some particularly noteworthy discussions about this influence on Johnson can be found in Tom Wicker's "Lyndon Johnson vs. the Ghost of Jack Kennedy," *Esquire* (November 1965); Paul K. Conkin's chapter "In the Shadow of JFK," from *Big Daddy from the Pedernales: Lyndon Baines Johnson* (Boston, 1986); and Michael W. Schuyler's "Ghosts in the White House: LBJ, RFK, and the Assassination of JFK," *Presidential Studies Quarterly* 17 (Summer 1987).

Students of the Kennedy image should be familiar with numerous general works about Richard Nixon. Nixon's *Six Crises* (New York, 1962) presents a self-serving but revealing interpretation of the 1960 presidential campaign, particularly when viewed in conjunction with his memoranda to researchers written during the book's preparation. Theodore H. White's *The Making of the President 1960* (New York, 1961) and *The Making of the President 1968* (New York, 1969) refer to Nixon's infatuation with the Kennedy image. Also helpful are Jules Witcover's *The Resurrection of Richard Nixon* (New York, 1970), Joe McGinniss's *The Selling of the President 1968* (New York, 1969), and Timothy Crouse's *The Boys on the Bus* (New York, 1972). For a general understanding of Nixon's obsession with the Kennedy image during his administration, see William Safire's *Before the Fall: An Inside View of the Pre-Watergate White House* (New York, 1975); Herbert Klein's *Making It Perfectly Clear* (Garden City, N.Y., 1980); H. R. Haldeman's *The Haldeman Diaries: Inside the Nixon White House* (New York, 1994) and *The Ends of Power* (New York, 1978); Dan Rather's and Gary Paul Gate's *The Palace Guard* (New York, 1974); Stephen E. Ambrose's *Nixon: The Education of a Politician 1913–1962* (New York, 1987), and *Nixon: The Triumph of a Politician* (New York, 1989); Tom Wicker's *One of Us: Richard Nixon and the American Dream* (New York, 1991); Herbert S. Parmet's *Richard Nixon and His America* (Boston, 1990); and Garry Wills's *Nixon's Agonistes* (Boston, 1970). A probing essay comparing Nixon's and Kennedy's public image is David S. Kaufer's "The Ironist and Hypocrite as Presidential Symbols: A Nixon-Kennedy Analog," *Communications Quarterly* 27 (Fall 1979).

Some published works on Gerald Ford make brief reference to the Kennedy image, including John Casserly's *The Ford White House: Diary of a Speechwriter* (Boulder, Colo, 1977), Robert T. Hartmann's *Palace Politics: An Inside Account of the Ford Years* (New York, 1980), and Ron Nessen's *It Sure Looks Different from the Inside* (New York, 1978). Jimmy Carter's identity with the Kennedy image before and during the 1976 presidential campaign is mentioned in Betty Glad's *Jimmy Carter: In Search of the Great White House* (New York, 1980); Victor Lasky's *Jimmy Carter: The Man and the Myth* (New York, 1979); Jules Witcover's *Marathon: The Pursuit of the Presidency, 1972–1976* (New York, 1977); Elizabeth Drew's *American Journal:*

The Events of 1976 (New York, 1977); Martin Schram's *Running for President: A Journal of the Carter Campaign* (New York, 1976); and Kandy Stroud's *How Jimmy Won: The Victory Campaign from Plains to the White House* (New York, 1977). Particularly relevant articles include Blake Fleetwood's "The Resurrection of JFK," [*MORE*], March 1976; Robert S. McElvaine's "Franklin and Jack... and Jimmy?" *America*, October 23, 1976; and David Halberstam's "The Coming of Carter," *Newsweek*, July 19, 1976. Carter's struggle with the Kennedy image during the 1980 presidential campaign is mentioned in passing in Jack W. Germond's and Jules Witcover's *Blue Smoke and Mirrors: How Reagan Won and Why Carter Lost the Election of 1980* (New York, 1981), and Elizabeth Drew's *Portrait of an Election: The 1980 Presidential Campaign* (New York, 1981). Three articles that succinctly address Edward Kennedy's struggle with the Kennedy "mystique" in 1980 are L. Patrick Devlin, "An Analysis of Kennedy's Communication in the 1980 Campaign," *Quarterly Journal of Speech* 68 (November 1982); Steven V. Roberts, "Ted Kennedy: Haunted by the Past," *New York Times Magazine*, February 3, 1980; Stephen J. Wayne, "Public Perceptions About Ted Kennedy and the Presidency," *Presidential Studies Quarterly* 12 (Winter 1982). Stephen P. Depoe's "Requiem for Liberalism: The Therapeutic and Deliberative Functions of Nostalgic Appeals in Edward Kennedy's Address to the 1980 Democratic National Convention," *Southern Communication Journal* 55 (Winter 1990), effectively analyzes the paradox of Kennedy's triumphant appearance at the 1980 Democratic National Convention and the simultaneous rejection of his candidacy.

Several excellent works analyze Ronald Reagan's capacity to tap into national myths through rhetorical and theatrical devices. Books include Paul D. Erickson's *Reagan Speaks: The Making of an American Myth* (New York, 1985); Mary E. Stuckey's *Getting into the Game: The Pre-Presidential Rhetoric of Ronald Reagan* (New York, 1989) and *Playing the Game: The Presidential Rhetoric of Ronald Reagan* (New York, 1990); and Kurt Ritter's and David Henry's *Ronald Reagan: The Great Communicator* (New York, 1992). Effective articles about Reagan's rhetorical skills include William F. Lewis's "Telling America's Story: Narrative Form and the Reagan Presidency," *Quarterly Journal of Speech* 73 (August 1987); Walter R. Fisher's "Romantic Democracy, Ronald Reagan, and Presidential Heroes," *Western Journal of Speech Communication* 46 (Summer 1982); and Geoffrey S. Smith's "Memory and Aspiration in Recent Presidential Politics," *Queen's Quarterly* 95 (Winter 1988). A helpful essay devoted specifically to Reagan's invocations to JFK from 1981 through 1984 is Paul D. Erickson's "The Once and Future President: John F. Kennedy in the Rhetoric of Ronald Reagan," in *John F. Kennedy: The Promise Revisited* (New York, 1988). Peggy Noonan's *What I Saw in the Revolution: A Political Life in the Reagan Era* (New York, 1990) discusses JFK's influence on Reagan's speechwriter. Two cogent books on the celebrification of politics are Neil Postman's *Amusing Ourselves to Death:*

Public Discourse in the Age of Show Business (New York, 1986) and Richard Schickel, *Intimate Strangers: The Culture of Celebrity* (Garden City, N.Y., 1985).

Gary Hart's fondness for the Kennedys is expressed in his own written works, including *Right from the Start: A Chronicle of the McGovern Campaign* (New York, 1973) and *The Good Fight: The Education of an American Reformer* (New York, 1993). His published discussions of John and Robert Kennedy are more generous and forgiving than his assessment made during our 1992 interview. More noteworthy campaign books which address Hart's symbolic linkage with the Kennedy image include Susan Casey's *Hart and Soul: Gary Hart's New Hampshire Odyssey—And Beyond* (Concord, N.H., 1986); Elizabeth Drew's *Campaign Journal: The Political Events of 1983–1984* (New York, 1985); Peter Goldman's and Tony Fuller's *The Quest for the Presidency* (Toronto, 1985); Jack W. Germond's and Jules Witcover's *Wake Us When It's Over: Presidential Politics of 1984* (New York, 1985); and Sidney Blumenthal's *Our Long National Daydream: A Political Pageant of the Reagan Era* (New York, 1988).

The influence of the Kennedys on Michael Dukakis is given passing mention in Charles Kenney's and Robert L. Turner's *Dukakis: An American Odyssey* (Boston, 1988). A less helpful book is Richard Gaines's and Michael Segal's *Dukakis: The Man Who Would Be President* (New York, 1988). Several campaign accounts were particularly relevant to understanding Dukakis's use of the Kennedy image, including Jack W. Germond's and Jules Witcover's *Whose Broad Stripes and Bright Stars?: The Trivial Pursuit of the Presidency* (New York, 1989); Sidney Blumenthal's *Pledging Allegiance: The Last Campaign of the Cold War* (New York, 1990); and Christine M. Black's and Thomas Oliphant's *All by Myself: The Unmaking of a Presidential Campaign* (Chester, Conn., 1989). A superb work which lends insight into the personalities of the major presidential contenders is Richard Ben Cramer's *What It Takes: The Way to the White House* (New York, 1992).

Campaign biographies on Bill Clinton make occasional reference to the influence of JFK on his career. The best work is Charles Allen's and Jonathan Portis's *The Comeback Kid: The Life and Career of Bill Clinton* (New York, 1992). Also helpful is Jim Moore's *Clinton: Young Man in a Hurry* (Fort Worth, Tex., 1992). A useful but flattering account of Clinton's prepresidential career is *The Clintons of Arkansas: An Introduction to Those Who Know Them Best* (Fayetteville, Ark., 1993), edited by Arkansas journalist Ernest Dumas. Students of Clinton's early life will also find it useful to consider Virginia Kelley's *Leading with My Heart* (New York, 1994). Bob Woodward's *The Agenda: Inside the Clinton White House* (New York, 1994) offers no discussion about the influence of the Kennedy image on the Clinton presidency. Particularly useful articles regarding Clinton's invocations of John Kennedy in 1992 are Maureen Dowd's and Frank Rich's "Another Quest for Camelot," *New York Times*, July 17, 1992; Godfrey Sperling's

"Clinton's Kennedyesque Image," *Christian Science Monitor,* March 24, 1992; and Jason Berry's "Clinton's Pursuit of the Kennedy Mystique," *Atlanta Journal,* March 22, 1992. Postelection comparisons between Clinton and Kennedy are elaborated upon by Michiko Kakutani in "Shifting Perceptions of a Presidency," *New York Times,* October 18, 1993, and Jonathan Alter in "Less Profile, More Courage," *Newsweek,* November 1, 1993. An excellent summary of the 1992 presidential campaign is Jack W. Germond's and Jules Witcover's *Mad as Hell: Revolt at the Ballot Box,* 1992 (New York, 1993). See also Peter Goldman's *Quest for the Presidency* (College Station, Tex., 1994).

Index

A NOTE ON THE AUTHOR

Paul R. Henggeler is assistant professor of history at the University of Texas, Pan American. Born in Wantagh, New York, he grew up on Long Island, studied at the State University of New York at Cortland, and taught high school social studies before returning to graduate studies at Bowling Green State University in Ohio, where he received a Ph.D. in history. His first book, *In His Steps: Lyndon Johnson and the Kennedy Mystique,* was widely praised.